# Solar Flares

Liverpool Science Fiction Texts and Studies, 43

# Liverpool Science Fiction Texts and Studies

*Editor* David Seed, *University of Liverpool*

*Editorial Board*
Mark Bould, *University of the West of England*
Veronica Hollinger, *Trent University*
Rob Latham, *University of California*
Roger Luckhurst, *Birkbeck College, University of London*
Patrick Parrinder, *University of Reading*
Andy Sawyer, *University of Liverpool*

*Recent titles in the series*

21. Andy Sawyer and David Seed (eds) *Speaking Science Fiction: Dialogues and Interpretations*
22. Inez van der Spek *Alien Plots: Female Subjectivity and the Divine*
23. S. T. Joshi *Ramsey Campbell and Modern Horror Fiction*
24. Mike Ashley *The Time Machines: The Story of the Science-Fiction Pulp Magazines from the Beginning to 1950*
25. Warren G. Rochelle *Communities of the Heart: The Rhetoric of Myth in the Fiction of Ursula K. Le Guin*
26. S. T. Joshi *A Dreamer and a Visionary: H. P. Lovecraft in his Time*
27. Christopher Palmer *Philip K. Dick: Exhilaration and Terror of the Postmodern*
28. Charles E. Gannon *Rumors of War and Infernal Machines: Technomilitary Agenda-Setting in American and British Speculative Fiction*
29. Peter Wright *Attending Daedalus: Gene Wolfe, Artifice and the Reader*
30. Mike Ashley *Transformations: The Story of the Science-Fiction Magazine from 1950–1970*
31. Joanna Russ *The Country You Have Never Seen: Essays and Reviews*
32. Robert Philmus *Visions and Revisions: (Re)constructing Science Fiction*
33. Gene Wolfe (edited and introduced by Peter Wright) *Shadows of the New Sun: Wolfe on Writing/Writers on Wolfe*
34. Mike Ashley *Gateways to Forever: The Story of the Science-Fiction Magazine from 1970–1980*
35. Patricia Kerslake *Science Fiction and Empire*
36. Keith Williams *H. G. Wells, Modernity and the Movies*
37. Wendy Gay Pearson, Veronica Hollinger and Joan Gordon (eds.) *Queer Universes: Sexualities and Science Fiction*
38. John Wyndham (eds. David Ketterer and Andy Sawyer) *Plan for Chaos*
39. Sherryl Vint *Animal Alterity: Science Fiction and the Question of the Animal*
40. Paul Williams *Race, Ethnicity and Nuclear War: Representations of Nuclear Weapons and Post-Apocalyptic Worlds*
41. Sara Wasson and Emily Alder, *Gothic Science Fiction 1980–2010*
42. David Seed (ed.), *Future Wars: The Anticipations and the Fears*

# Solar Flares

*Science Fiction in the 1970s*

ANDREW M. BUTLER

LIVERPOOL UNIVERSITY PRESS

First published 2012 by
Liverpool University Press
4 Cambridge Street
Liverpool
L69 7ZU

This paperback version published 2014.

Copyright © 2012 Andrew M. Butler

The right of Andrew M. Butler to be identified as the author of this book
has been asserted by him in accordance with the
Copyright, Designs and Patents Act 1988.

All rights reserved. No part of this book may be reproduced, stored in a
retrieval system, or transmitted, in any form or by any means, electronic,
mechanical, photocopying, recording, or otherwise, without
the prior written permission of the publisher.

British Library Cataloguing-in-Publication data
A British Library CIP record is available

ISBN 978-1-84631-834-4 (cased)
978-1-78138-117-5 (limp)

Typeset by XL Publishing Services, Tiverton
Printed and bound by CPI Group (UK) Ltd, Croydon CR0 4YY

To Peter and Jennifer

# Contents

| | | |
|---|---|---|
| Acknowledgements | | ix |
| Prologue | | 1 |
| 1 | The Ends of First Sf: Pioneers as Veterans | 11 |
| 2 | After the New Wave: After Science Fiction? | 24 |
| 3 | Beyond Apollo: Space Fictions after the Moon Landing | 38 |
| 4 | Big Dumb Objects: Science Fiction as Self-Parody | 51 |
| 5 | The Rise of Fantasy: Swords and Planets | 65 |
| 6 | Home of the Extraterrestrial Brothers: Race and African American Science Fiction | 78 |
| 7 | Alien Invaders: Vietnam and the Counterculture | 92 |
| 8 | This Septic Isle: Post-Imperial Melancholy | 106 |
| 9 | Foul Contagion Spread: Ecology and Environmentalism | 120 |
| 10 | Female Counter-Literature: Feminism | 136 |
| 11 | Strange Bedfellows: Gay Liberation | 152 |
| 12 | Saving the Family? Children's Fiction | 168 |
| 13 | Eating the Audience: Blockbusters | 181 |
| 14 | Chariots of the Gods: Pseudoscience and Parental Fears | 192 |
| 15 | Towers of Babel: The Architecture of Sf | 206 |
| 16 | Ruptures: Metafiction and Postmodernism | 221 |
| Epilogue | | 236 |
| Bibliography | | 239 |
| Index | | 270 |

# Acknowledgements

I have been lucky, as always, with the people surrounding me, who have offered books, cakes, coffees, DVDs, downloads, food, photocopies, spare rooms and tea and sympathy. A partial list would include Adam Roberts, Andy Sawyer, Arthur Evans, Carol Ann Kerry-Green, Carol McGuirk, Catherine Butler, Colin Odell, Dave Roberts, Edward James, Elizabeth Billinger, Estelle Roberts, Farah Mendlesohn, I.Q. Hunter, Istvan Csicsery-Ronay Jr, James Kneale, Javier Martinez, Jennifer Woodward, Joan Gordon, Joshua 'Sha' LaBare, Mark Bould, Matt Hills, Matt Moore, Maureen Kincaid Speller, Mike Levy, Mitch Le Blanc, Neil Easterbrook, Pat Wheeler, Paul Billinger, Paul Kincaid, Peter Wright, Robert Edgar, Rob Latham, Roger Luckhurst, Sherryl Vint, Tim Long and Veronica Hollinger. My apologies to anyone I have omitted. Farah Mendlesohn and James Kneale both read chapters, but, as ever, any errors remain my own.

Thanks to the staff and librarians of the Special Collections, Sydney Jones Library, University of Liverpool, and extra thanks to those who helped me watch things I would not have otherwise seen. I am grateful to Canterbury Christ Church University for granting me teaching remission, without which this book would have taken even longer. And especial thanks to my editor at Liverpool University Press, Anthony Cond, who knows the meaning of patience.

To mine hosts and fellow patrons of the Two Doves – above all, Ben Parkinson, the executive editor, but also Craig Scannell, Dave Mahy, Dave Taylor, Ewan Martin, Gemma Rowe, Ian McNamara, Leo Grant, Lisa Claire and the Guinness crew – much thanks.

*A Note on Dates and References*
For print fiction I have tried where possible to give the dates of first magazine appearances as well as book form. Films are referenced by director and first year of release; in some cases international releases were delayed or have not occurred at all. For television programmes I have attempted to supply dates of original broadcasts; because of the regional nature of broadcasting, in some cases I have only given the year. I have abbreviated

*The Magazine of Fantasy and Science Fiction* to *F&SF* throughout. Page references are keyed to the edition I have used and listed in the bibliography; where this is not the first publication I have added this information.

# Prologue

There was a moment in October 1977 when I watched *Doctor Who* at my grandparents' flat. The particular episode was part of 'The Invisible Enemy' (1–22 October 1977), in which the alien-infected Doctor was cloned and then miniaturised in order to be injected into himself. I bring this up in part to demonstrate the pitfalls of historical accounts, but also because the notion of the invisible enemy is an almost perfect description of one recurring trope within this book. The same episode dates the events of Paul Magrs's extraordinary Young Adult novel, *Strange Boy* (2002); an appendix to that novel explains what *Doctor Who* (23 November 1963–) is, along with Spangles, *Battlestar Galactica* (17 September 1978–29 April 1979) and other aspects of late 1970s popular culture. Anyone who lived through the period may find it hard to avoid feeling nostalgic, but also to resist a sense of camp. After a period of being shunned, the 1970s has returned with added postmodern irony, as popular culture draws upon the period with varying degrees of love and ridicule. In tracing this era, I do not want to indulge in nostalgia, to find my own foundation myth in my own autobiography or to be overly guided by where sf ended up in subsequent years.

I have adopted the metaphor of the Invisible Enemy to describe the ideological battlegrounds of the 1970s. The 1960s had seen the emergence in the West of parallel movements for civil rights and women's and gay liberation, and some of the sf of the 1970s reflected these movements with varying degrees of subtlety, solidarity and anxiety. As Fredric Jameson notes, 'in the 60s, for a time, everything was possible [...] this period, in other words, was a moment of a universal liberation, a global unbinding of energies' (1984a: 207). Any advances occurred in spite of the opposition of specific individuals, as well as institutional racism, sexism and homophobia in forms such as white supremacy, patriarchy, heteronormativity, multinational capitalism and so on. Members of the dominant class of the period felt under attack, with the campaigns against the Vietnam War and the unfolding scandal of the Watergate break-in offering further evidence of the shifting balances of public opinion. On 17 June 1972, five men were arrested for breaking into the Democratic National Headquarters at the Watergate Complex, and an FBI investigation linked them to the campaign to re-elect Richard Nixon. Nixon had known about the break-in, and had secretly recorded conversations about it in the White House, and attempted a cover up. Before he could be impeached, Nixon resigned the presidency on 9 August 1974, being succeeded by vice-president Gerald Ford. The institute of the highest office was shaken.

Popular culture could offer a space for revolution, but equally might support the dominant ideology or facilitate a backlash. Robin Wood argues that the horror films of this period – many of which were set in a recognisable present day – attempt to make their audiences into 'monogamous heterosexual bourgeois patriarchal capitalists' (1986: 71), and mark a rearguard action against the liberalism of the 1960s. There was a generalised fear of the other, which could be seen in these films' representations of adultery, bisexuals, children, communists, gays, non-white ethnic identities, the proletariat, women, and so on. Horror and sf could work by metaphor, projecting the other onto aliens, robots and monsters, or into abstract entities such as forces of nature. This was not just limited to fantastical genres. Stephen Paul Miller argues that '[b]lockbuster bestsellers and films like *The Godfather*, *The Exorcist*, and *Jaws* posited hidden, unified, and seemingly uncontrollable forces that are met and defeated' (1999: 11). Miller's name-checking of Steven Spielberg points the direction in which popular culture moved. At the start of the decade, those forces were uncontrolled – see *Duel* (Steven Spielberg, 1971) or *THX 1138* (George Lucas, 1971) – whereas by the end of it, heroes had emerged who could triumph over such forces, notably in *Star Wars* (George Lucas, 1977), the projected fourth part – subtitled *A New Hope* – of the *Star Wars* sequence.

The standard narrative structure, described by critics from Aristotle to Tzvetan Todorov, depicts a social status quo being thrown into chaos when one or more characters suffer a peripeteia or reversal of fortune. The mechanism of the plot is then toward the restoration of the equilibrium or the establishment of a replacement status quo, most typically through a rite of passage such as a wedding or a funeral. J.R.R. Tolkien wrote of the grace of the happy ending, the eucatastophe, in which the world is redeemed, as well of the dyscatastrophe, where the protagonist's failure would enable a sense of catharsis (1964: 61). But the 1970s narratives were often amphicatastrophic – neither cheering nor cathartic. It might be that there is no second peripeteia, no restoration, or that the new equilibrium fails to satisfy. Such narratives offer neither escapism nor consolation, and sometimes berate their audiences for seeking either.

Many of the filmmakers of the 1970s had attended film school or served their apprenticeships as camera operators, editors and so forth in the 1960s, displaying largely liberal and sometimes pessimistic attitudes. As Hollywood began to process the 1975 withdrawal from Vietnam, the holding hostage of 444 Americans in Tehran between 4 November 1979 and 20 January 1981, and the Soviet Union's invasion of Afghanistan in December 1979, successful heroes were in short supply, but popular films began to depict them to console a depressed public. By 1981, when Ronald Reagan, a former Hollywood actor, entered the White House, a new optimism came to be reflected in dominant culture, and some of the minority groups who had made progress in the 1970s became scapegoats in the 1980s. The dominant culture's empire struck back against the liberation of oppressed groups.

Yet, for some commentators, the 1970s is a period in which nothing happened. It might either be constructed as the period in which the 1960s projects failed – with the early part of the decade co-opted into a 'long-1960s' – or blamed for the socio-economic conditions which shifted much of the Anglophone world to the right. In science fiction, the period marks time between the peak of the New Wave(s) in the 1960s and the emergence of the cyberpunks in the early 1980s. Cyberpunk writer and anthologist Bruce Sterling, in particular, elides the period from the history: 'SF has not been much fun of late. All forms of pop culture go through doldrums; they catch cold when society sneezes. If SF in the late Seventies was confused, self-involved, and stale, it was scarcely a cause for wonder' (1986: 9). For Fred Pfeil, it is the period when sf 'briefly becomes modernist' (1990: 83). Alexei Panshin, in a review column, opines that '[t]hese are desperately fragmented times. The Presidential campaign just past was notably lacking in leadership – the winning candidate won by being less visible than the losing candidate' (1973: 13). He argued that the era was one of factions and localised, specialist answers to problems. But he still saw possibilities for optimism; a year later he writes, with Cory Panshin: 'We are passing through a time of retrospection. An era is ending and we are looking again at our recent past as though it were a mirror in which we could see both what we have seen and what we are about to [see]' (1974: 63).

Brian W. Aldiss, in *Billion Year Spree* (1973), defines science fiction as *'the search for a definition of man and his status in the universe which will stand in our advanced but confused state of knowledge (science)'*, and notes that it is *'characteristically cast in the Gothic or post-Gothic mould'* (1973: 8), which offers both a function and a literary history for the genre. Writing too close to the 1970s to see where that search had reached, Aldiss resorts to a list of author names. The sf of the period turned to 'a more land locked and cerebral model, with problems posed rather than solved' (1973: 290). He does foresee a change: 'Academia and the middle class are moving in on sf and will create order out of chaos' (1973: 320). A dozen years later, when he revises the history as *Trillion Year Spree* with David Wingrove, there is a much more substantial account, focusing on Ursula Le Guin and Robert Silverberg. Aldiss and Wingrove explain that the period brought 'many ground swells into prominence: ecology, computerization, proliferation of nuclear power, psychoanalysis, sexual liberation and feminism, and an adverse reaction to drugs [... It was] a period of considerable maturation in the SF field' (1986: 322). The later part of the 1970s, they observe, become economically tougher for British writers.

In his chapter on the 1970s in Robert Holdstock's *Encyclopedia of Science Fiction* (1979), Malcolm Edwards notes how sf had changed since the New Wave: 'The change has been beneficial – indeed, necessary if sf is to claim serious attention as adult literature. Restrictions, largely the product of commercial magazine requirements [...] have been lifted' (1979: 176). Edwards also focuses in part on Ursula Le Guin and Robert Silverberg as the key figures of the period. Edwards is remarkably optimistic about the genre, although concerned that the commercial success of films will hold back the genre's bids for respectability, noting that it is painful to lump everything together 'like competing brands of washing powder in a supermarket' (1979: 188).

David Hartwell did not appear to share Aldiss's optimism about academics, despite publishing Samuel R. Delany's critical writing with his Dragon Press; academics were making raids on the field, paying more attention to sf writers who aspire to literature than to those who seek to entertain. Sf was a victim of its own success, diluted by commercialism, elitism, weight of numbers, fantasy, surrealism and 'fatigue and retrenchment' (1984: 192). He seems to swing from optimism to pessimism, arguing that '[t]here was much less that was new and colorful in science fiction in the 1970s and early 1980s [...] than in any previous decade [...] the field is showing signs of enthusiastic capitulation to a level of popular taste outside the boundaries of the genre audience' (1984: 182) – sf was going over to the dark side (Literature), with the shortlisting of novels such as *Gravity's Rainbow* (1973) and *Ragtime* (1975) for the Nebula Awards.

In his history of the genre, Edward James squeezes the 1970s into a chapter titled 'From New Wave to Cyberpunk and Beyond, 1960–1993'. James sees it as a period of fragmentation: 'feminism, fantasy, the consolidation of the advances made by the New Wave, the continuation of old themes under new guises, and the emergence of sf on the fringes of academia. [... Most significantly] sf for the first time invaded the entire cultural milieu of the Western world' (1994: 190). It is a period that clearly resists any label – indeed it is leaving the label of 'sf' behind. Brooks

Landon's historical account does not take a strictly chronological approach, but he gives prominence to the New Waves and cyberpunk in his fifth chapter; the seventies, as interregnum, were important for their fostering of feminist sf and part of the emergence of what he labels 'soft agenda SF' (1995: 175–79) from 'the New Wave and with the eco-feminist writing of the 1970s and 1980s' (1995: 176), in contrast with what John Clute calls Agenda sf or First sf. Adam Roberts's long history of science fiction also somewhat disappears the 1970s into the 1960s, as part of a chapter on 'The Impact of New Wave Science Fiction 1960s–1970s'. He focuses on a number of authors such as Aldiss and Philip K. Dick, as well as on feminist sf, but does not really isolate a defining theme of the period beyond noting that 'Golden Age optimism became harder and harder to maintain as the 1970s went on' (2005: 230), labelling one response to this 'New Wave', a force already active in the 1960s. A further chapter, 'Prose Science Fiction 1970s–1990s', is more about 1970s fandom than about fiction, before moving onto the 1980s and 1990s. Roberts suggests that in 1973 the sf community turns inwards, as Isaac Asimov is given the Hugo Award for *The Gods Themselves* (1972); that is, it becomes a constituency of fans rather than professional writers, the latter group being more outward looking in their Nebula Award shortlists. In their *Concise History*, Mark Bould and Sherryl Vint, having devoted separate chapters to definitions, pre-Hugo Gernsback sf and individual decades from the 1930s to the 1950s, glue the 1960s and 1970s together, but devote two chapters to the period – as they do with the 1980s and 1990s – with a final chapter on the first decade of the twenty-first century. Bould and Vint note a growing professionalism of the field, with a distancing from hard science and engineering, with sf becoming propagandist for different forms of change other than technological progress: 'Those seeking to enrol SF into projects such as feminism or environmental activism were less concerned with Campbellian extrapolation than with the capacity of SF images, ideas and techniques to articulate urgent political concerns' (2011: 145).

The three companions to science fiction periodise the genre in slightly differing ways – *Cambridge* running the 1960s and 1970s together, *Routledge* starting in 1964 (the year Moorcock started editing *New Worlds*) and ending in 1979, and *Blackwell* having separate chapters on the New Wave and Cyberpunk movements, but nothing explicitly on the intervening period – although it is obviously covered in chapters on feminism and British television. Rob Latham acknowledges the ending of the New Wave in the 1970s (2005: 214) and Bould alludes to punk, without specifically discussing the period, and notes cyberpunk's erasure of 1960s and, especially, 1970s forebears (2005: 223). Damien Broderick spends ten pages on the 1960s and half a dozen on the 1970s, the title of his chapter being suggestive: 'New Wave and backwash'. The 1970s 'can seem rather docile, even disappointing. It is widely regarded as an interval of integration and bruised armistice' (2003: 58). Some of the old guard learn from the New Wave, some of the upstarts settle down, but New Wave novels are not as startling as those published in the 1960s. Helen Merrick also begins her account with discussions of the New Waves, before moving to 'The stale 1970s' (2009: 107), a nod to Sterling – whom she contests with a long list of titles, many of which I will discuss in this volume – and 'The "feminine" invasion' (2009: 108) on the female writers of the period. While she does not dismiss the 1970s, and sees some of the output as being better than the 1960s fiction, it is the 1960s that dominate her account.

Roger Luckhurst reflects on the tensions in the accounts of a simultaneous boom and bust decade: 'the dying fall of a failed avant-garde or an era of marking time' (2005b: 169), suggesting that this is 'symptomatic of a wider set of confusions over what precisely took place in the decade' (2005b: 169). Luckhurst notes that Jameson's account of the 1960s colonises the historicity of the first part of the 1970s, with the 1970s as period shoehorned into 1973–79 (Jameson 1991: 296). The decade becomes dominated by Ford and Carter in the USA, industrial unrest in the UK, a sense of growing social crisis where the terms of the debate over rights were thrown into question by the recomplications of the very notions of sex, race and sexuality. Consciousnesses were being raised, but equally the powers that be – whether state or corporate – were being put on the defensive. Economic, social and ecological crises went hand in hand.

In this volume I have adopted a 'long 1970s' approach without going too far back into the New Waves: it begins somewhere after the 2 April 1968 premiere of *2001: A Space Odyssey* (Stanley Kubrick, 1968), the Apollo 11 moon landing (21 July 1969) and Richard Nixon's entry to office as president (20 January 1969). John F. Kennedy's dream of putting a man on the moon by the end of the 1960s marked a moment when the news echoed the imagination of several generations of visionaries – but such fantasies became harder to imagine. The moon had been visited, and was found wanting, as interesting as anyone's holiday snaps. Much sf shifted to rather more earthly concerns. Equally, the end point of the period is not as clear as the flipping over of a page of a calendar. The 4 May 1979 election of Margaret Thatcher, as the first female British prime minister, was the beginning of eighteen years of Conservative rule in Britain; the 4 November 1980 election of Ronald Reagan was the start of twelve years of Republican rule in the USA. Reagan's first two terms saw the space shuttle finally launched (12 April 1981) and the imagining of the Strategic

Defense Initiative, more commonly referred to as Star Wars. The second release in the *Star Wars* sequence, *The Empire Strikes Back* (Irvin Kershner, 1980), might be thought to book-end the period – although it would be odd to have no mention of *Return of the Jedi* (Richard Marquand, 1983). By then there was an association of sf with the blockbuster movie, and millions of dollars rode on the back of each release. *Blade Runner* (Ridley Scott, 1982) lies outside the period, as does *Neuromancer* (1984). It is difficult to write, however, without the sense of both works being on the horizon.

It is not my intention to tell the one and true history of science fiction in the 1970s – if only because prose fiction, film and television offer differing trajectories. To some extent there is the sense of the bifurcation of sf – on the one hand, a more intellectual, challenging and literary written form; on the other hand, a spectacle-driven eye-candy set of blockbuster movies – but such a division requires the use of selective evidence. The late 1970s sees some writers exiting the sf ghetto for the mainstream, as well as mainstream writers drawing on sf tropes, and the emergence of fantasy in the tradition of J.R.R. Tolkien (and Edgar Rice Burroughs), partly on the back of role-playing games. It was the best of times, it was the worst of times. I have attempted to identify various clusters of events, and a series of micronarratives.

This book offers readings of how the real-world politics of ethnicity, sex, gender, sexuality, class struggles, environmental and imperialism encourage certain narratives and downplay others, and shows the ways in which sf addresses the issues of these invisible enemies as litmus tests of the time. There is much sf of the period that is radical – and may have seemed more so at the time – but there is also a strain of conservatism and anxiety. 1970 saw sf largely sailing under the critical radar – while often offering a critique of mainstream culture and society from the margins – but by 1980 it was much more associated with synergistically organised multi-national corporations.

Since the early days of genre sf, there had been amateur publications, fanzines, and gatherings of fans. The first academic journal devoted to sf was *Extrapolation* (1959–). Some academics were teaching sf in various contexts. But it gained critical weight in the 1970s, with the establishment of the Science Fiction Research Association in 1970 in the USA and the Science Fiction Foundation Collection in 1970 in what was then North East London Polytechnic in Barking, Essex, UK. The former published the *SFRA Newsletter* (1971–93), the latter published *Foundation: The Review of Science Fiction* (1972–), a mixture of articles, reviews, interviews and occasionally poetry by academics, authors and fans. Meanwhile, in North

America, R.D. Mullen founded *Science-Fiction Studies* (1973–), featuring academic articles and reviews, with a slant in the latter towards non-fiction and critical editions rather than contemporary fiction. The three academic journals between them inevitably, but not necessarily deliberately, started a process of canon-formation, with Philip K. Dick, Ursula Le Guin and Stanisław Lem emerging as the key contemporary writers, and explored the variety of ways of theorising sf – especially Marxism and structuralism.

Some of the groundwork for this had been laid in the late 1960s. Delany began to argue that science fiction required a particular kind of reading protocol, which decoded the language in a particular way, word by word. He was to continue a rigorous and challenging intellectual exploration of the genre as his own novels became more experimental, producing a collection of essays, *The Jewel-Hinged Jaw* (1977), and a book-length semiotic analysis of Thomas M. Disch's 'Angouleme' (*New Worlds Quarterly* 1971), *The American Shore* (1978). Meanwhile, in Paris, Todorov published *Introduction à la Littérature Fantastique* (1970; translated into English as *The Fantastic* (1973)), which attempted a literary definition of the genre of the fantastic. Todorov identified two genres: the marvellous, in which amazing things are possible, 'the supernatural accepted' (1973: 42), ghosts, ghouls, vampires and so on; and the uncanny, 'the *supernatural explained*' (1973: 47), in which such phenomena are explained in terms of conspiracy, hallucination or even coincidence. The fantastic, for Todorov, is that class of text where the reader hesitates between the two genres: 'that hesitation experienced by a person who only knows the laws of nature, confronting an apparently supernatural event' (1973: 25). This hesitation, which usually collapses into either the marvellous or the uncanny, may be experienced by characters, the reader or both. A case could be made for science fiction to be a subset of the uncanny, because of the importance of the scientific method in the genre. However, Todorov locates it within the marvellous – specifically the instrumental marvellous – because '[the] narrative movement consists in obliging us to see how close these apparently marvelous elements [robots, extraterrestrials, alien locations etc.] are to us' (1973: 172). Because of this undecidability – which would map onto a tension noted by him between the real and the imaginary – sf might equally be designated as a branch of the fantastic. For Todorov, the generic boundaries are not rigid, and it seems likely that different works of sf would fit within each of the three categories or in the overlaps between them – the uncanny-fantastic, the marvellous-fantastic and the uncanny-marvellous.

The Canadian-based academic Darko Suvin also used the term translated as 'uncanny'; it derived from the Russian literary theorist Victor Sklovsky's *ostranenie*, literary devices which draw attention to themselves and make language seem unfamiliar. Drawing on his interest in the theatre and politics of German playwright Bertolt Brecht, and the Brechtian concept of *Verfremdungseffekt*, he labelled this process 'estrangement'. Estrangement makes the familiar unfamiliar and vice versa, and would lead people to perceive their world in a new way. Borrowing from Ernst Bloch, Suvin labelled the textual unit of novelty – robots, extraterrestrials, alien locations etc. – the 'novum'. The estrangement effect is navigated by a reader in terms of cognition – a rational, logical, extrapolative way of thinking, an idea Suvin developed from Brecht's description of the astronomer Galileo being able to work out universal laws of physics from observing the swinging of a chandelier. Events may seem impossible, but there is a logical rigour connecting them. For Suvin, '*SF is, then, a literary genre whose necessary and sufficient conditions are the presence and interaction of estrangement and cognition, and whose main formal device is an imaginative framework alternative to the author's empirical environment*' (1979: 7–8, italics in original), a position he advances in *Foundation* 2 (June 1972) and *College English* (December 1972). Proper sf represents estranging events, understandable through cognition – in a sense, application of the scientific method. Anything else is dismissed as fantasy.

The 1970s also saw a number of volumes announcing themselves as encyclopedias. Oddly, all of these were written by scholars from outside the United States, as if it were necessary to be at a distance from a genre dominated by New York publishers and Hollywood cinema and television. Donald Tuck updates his *Handbook of Science Fiction and Fantasy* (1954, 1959) as *The Encyclopedia of Science Fiction and Fantasy through 1968* (1974–82), Brian Ash edits *The Visual Encyclopedia of Science Fiction* (1977), a mixture of short articles and diagrams, with contributions from Brian W. Aldiss, Poul Anderson, Isaac Asimov, J.G. Ballard, John Brunner, Kenneth Bulmer, L. Sprague de Camp, Arthur C. Clarke, Edmund Cooper, Lester del Rey, Philip José Farmer, Harry Harrison, Damon Knight, Fritz Leiber, Larry Niven, Frederik Pohl, Keith Roberts, Josephine Saxton, Robert Sheckley, George Turner, A.E. van Vogt, James White and Jack Williamson, and a range of book covers as illustrations, and Robert Holdstock edits the *Encyclopedia of Science Fiction* (1978), essentially a series of themed articles, with contributions from Mike Ashley, Isaac Asimov, Malcolm Edwards, Alan Frank, David Hardy, Harry Harrison, Douglas Hill, Patrick Moore, Chris Morgan, Christopher Priest and Brian Stableford, again heavily illustrated with book covers. Finally, and most significantly, the Australian Peter Nicholls edits *The Encyclopedia of Science Fiction* (1979), using the Science Fiction Foundation collection – which he had administered from 1971 to 1977 – as a major resource, with the assistance of associate editors John Clute (born in Canada) and Brian Stableford (born in Britain). More than ever before, it was possible to perceive the history, scope and structure of the genre, and to take it seriously. Fanzines such as the British Science Fiction Association's *Vector* (1958–), Peter Weston's *Zenith* and *Speculation* (1963–73), Charles Brown's *Locus* (1968–, later a professional magazine) and Bruce Gillespie's *SF Commentary* (1969–) bring a new seriousness to their coverage of the field in the 1970s. Sf gained a respectability and profitability that it had never been able to claim before.

Since the field of sf is too big to cover in its entirety within a single volume, I have been forced to be selective, driven by the micronarratives. The early chapters of the volume deal with the attitudes of successive generations of sf writers – members of a generation publishing before the Second World War, the islands of the New Wave, and attitudes to sf after Apollo and the New Wave – as well as the rise of fantasy, and the resurgence of sword and planet fictions. The next chapters deal with a range of political issues: race; postcolonialism in Vietnam and England; environmentalism; feminism and gay rights. The final chapters trace sf out of the margins into other areas – children's fiction, blockbusters, pseudoscience and sf-horror, architecture and postmodern metafiction.

Inevitably there are omissions. My examples are primarily Anglophone, predominantly the products of the United States and the United Kingdom. What is striking, across the political spectrum, is how many people perceived a coming apocalypse created by invisible enemies. Many commentators welcome it, as 'the insistent denial of the traumatic events of our history has brought about the need for these repeated apocalyptic purgings, both real and imaginary, as if *this* time we will finally get right what was always right, and somehow never was right' (Berger 1999: 134). I begin with an older generation of sf writers, who in several cases were looking back on their own earlier careers, as well as looking back to a more certain world.

# 1
# The Ends of First Sf: Pioneers as Veterans

The stories of the early sf genre melded adventure with scientific marvels. Characters and themes were usually subservient to ideas. John Clute argues that '[the] result was an SF universe written in the shape of Man. Women and other aliens had visiting rights only' (1995: 130), and – to overgeneralise – this sf believed in the possibility of progress, whereby each new invention would work to liberate mankind (sic), and, even if engineering problems might occur, further technology would resolve them. The isolated genius could change the world and an individual hero could bring down a tyranny. This was the genre formulated by Hugo Gernsback in *Amazing Stories*, further refined by John W. Campbell at *Astounding*. The Gernsback-Campbell continuum was challenged within the genre by the editors of magazines such as *Galaxy*, *The Magazine of Fantasy and Science Fiction* and *If*, and writers such as Alfred Bester, Theodore Sturgeon, Philip K. Dick and Robert Sheckley, who had more literary sensibilities and often a radical agenda. Clute suggests that what he refers to as First or Agenda science fiction was further challenged by the launch of Sputnik in 1956, as Soviet technology trumped American. The New Waves of the 1960s then pushed the boundaries of the genre beyond recognition. After the death of Campbell on 11 July 1971 and as genre sf approached its fiftieth birthday in 1976 – which would coincide with the US bicentennial – some of the First sf generation writers were given large, much publicised advances. But some of them retrod old ground, albeit at novel length. This chapter will consider the works of Isaac Asimov, Robert A. Heinlein, Arthur C. Clarke, Clifford D. Simak, Ray Bradbury, Alfred Bester and Leigh Brackett, who had all started publishing by 1941.

Asimov remained known for his 1940s and 1950s work, the Foundation and the robot stories, and had not written an sf novel since *Fantastic Voyage* (1966), a novelisation of the Richard Fleischer film. The Hugo and Nebula Awards given to *The Gods Themselves* (1972) acknowledge his return;

it would be his only adult sf novel of the 1970s. A comment by Robert Silverberg about plutonium-186 inspired Asimov to write a short story for *New Dimensions*, edited by Silverberg, but it grew to novel length. He divided it into three sections, to be printed in magazines owned by UPD Publications – parts one and three in *Galaxy* (March and May 1972), part two in *Worlds of If Science Fiction* (March 1972) – before its appearance in a single volume. The scheduling of more or less simultaneous publication of the first two parts in separate venues with a conclusion in only one of them reflects the work's thematic tensions between unity, duality and trinity. Part of a quotation from Friedrich Schiller's play *Die Jungfrau von Orleans* (*The Maid of Orleans*, 1801), 'Against stupidity the gods themselves contend in vain', precedes each section. In the first, Peter Lamont becomes convinced that the newly discovered Electron Pump, which produces energy from an unstable isotope of plutonium being exchanged with a parallel universe for tungsten-186, is dangerous and will destroy both universes. The second part is set in the parallel world. Whereas part one had begun with chapter six, alternating with the first five chapters, then continued up to ten – drawing attention to the chronology of the story – this section is broken up as 1a, 1b, 1c, 2a and so on up to 6c, and then 7abc. This dramatises the idea that the aliens, Dua, Odeen and Tritt, form a triad as they are growing up, and will eventually merge into an adult, Estwald. The trio have been trying to communicate with Lamont their own fears of the Electron Pump, with no success. The final section moves back to the universe of the first section, but is set on the moon. A tourist shows a suspicious interest in the moon's power supply, and is revealed to be Denison, who had also had worries about the pump.

Although Asimov was part of First sf, James Gunn suggests that the patterning of section two 'is fully as stylist [sic] a device as any cast up by the New Wave' (1980: 208). The reader who encountered the novel in the separate magazines need not have read them in the novel's order, and might have moved from the alien to the more familiar, and old-fashioned, sf of 'Against Stupidity...' Asimov also imagined a tripartite rather than binary species identity; Golden Age sf had rarely speculated about the nature of sex and gender, but in the 1970s both explicitly feminist sf and the hard sf of Larry Niven's *Protector* (1973) and *Ringworld Engineers* (1980), Niven and Jerry Pournelle's *The Mote in God's Eye* (1974) and John Brunner's *Total Eclipse* (*Amazing* April and June 1974; 1974) questioned a male/female binary. Ina Rae Hark argues that the aliens Odeen, Dua and Tritt are 'obvious soundalikes for one-two-three. At different times they suggest id, ego, and superego; body, mind, and soul; and Father, Son, and Holy Ghost – without being a strict allegory for any of these' (1979: 283), and Gunn, also noting a Freudian parallel, relates them to characteristics of Parental, Emotional and Rational (1980: 204). A triad can also be found in part three: the intuitive Lunar tour guide, Selene, her sex partner Barron, and Denison. Rationality wins out over the other two elements – and thus over stupidity. Just as the 'female' Dua and Selene pair off as intuitive fearers of the pump, in part one the emotionalism of Lamont is ranged against the technology, the pump's discoverer Hallam is the father figure who is battled against, and Bronowski, a linguist brought in to translate the alien language (named for the author of *The Ascent of Man*, Jacob Bronowski), represents rationality.

Denison, at this part of the narrative, is presumably too emotional to hold sway, and he has to learn from his mistakes. Denison's solution to the danger involves exchange with a further para-universe, balancing the unleashed nuclear forces, but assumes there is no harm to that universe. This marks another move from dyad to triad. No attempt is made to imagine that universe – which may of course be merely the next in an endless chain – which is unfortunate, since Asimov's depiction of the alien is the best part of the book. Hark, having identified and then disentangled some of the complexity of the novel, admits that '[the] letdown the reader experiences when Estwald fails to reappear cannot be assuaged so easily' (1979: 285).

Robert A. Heinlein, one of the highest paid pulp writers, had begun to explore sex roles in *Stranger in a Strange Land* (1961), which had broken through to non-genre audiences. However, his embrace of sexual freedom and libertarianism was tempered by a privileging of the patriarchal and the military. *I Will Fear No Evil* (*Galaxy* July–December 1970; 1970) features Eunice Branca, the beautiful stenographer employed by Johann Sebastian Smith, the familiar post-*Stranger* archetype of the wise but cantankerous, self-certain, argumentative, superior and dirty old man. Smith's brain is transplanted into Branca's body, but some vestige of her identity remains, as the two engage in conversations throughout the rest of the book. Eunice teaches him to act like a woman, and cheers on his behaviour. Radically, femininity emerges as something that is performed rather than essential or innate, but the actual gender roles themselves are little challenged. Johann/Joan refuses to see anyone after his recovery until s/he has donned make-up and suitable clothes; s/he will be subservient to men, but as Joan Eunice Smith, she can manipulate the men around her through sexual appeal. Underscoring male paranoia about manipulative women and male fantasies about female desire, Joan and Eunice both allow men to think they are making free choices and dress (or undress) like exhibitionists. Joan also engages in much sexual activity – with her nurse, doctor, bodyguards,

Smith's lawyer, Eunice's widower and his new wife – and everyone appears to be sexually compatible despite the partners' memories of whom s/he used to be. Eunice desires men old enough to be her father, or even her grandfather. In a nod back to his solipsistic time-travel story '– All You Zombies –' (*F&SF* March 1959), in which the protagonist is both his/her parents, and in anticipation of the incest theme that was to appear in *Time Enough For Love* (1973), 'The Number of the Beast' (*Omni* October-November 1979; 1980) and *To Sail Beyond the Sunset* (1987), Joan is impregnated with his/her own sperm.

It is telling to compare the roles available in the novel to men and women – entrepreneur, lawyer, businessman, doctor, judge, bodyguard and artist vs. secretary, nurse, muse, whore and, finally, mother. As a woman, Joan never particularly suffers, aside from some legal frustrations that Johann's old boy network can largely overcome. Although, on a number of occasions, Joan claims she could remake her fortune from scratch, Johann's billions cushion his experiences and can pave his route through his new life. Heinlein stacks the odds in the character's favour – the Johann who insists there are some words that women should not use is displaced by a sexually predatory Joan and Eunice. Rather than being a radical text, it remains attuned to masculine pleasures.

*Time Enough For Love* resurrects Lazarus Long – who had first appeared in *Methuselah's Children* (*Astounding* July–September 1941; 1958) – in a narrative very different from those envisaged by Heinlein and Campbell in the Future History scheme they had drawn up in 1941. Long's many descendants need his twentieth-century wisdom to survive, and they are determined to save him or his knowledge. As Long comes to terms with his present, he recalls earlier experiences; his tone of voice is similar to Jubal Harshaw's from *Stranger* and Smith's. The final section emphasises the oddly taboo-breaking and conservative trajectory of the novel, as Long travels back in time and meets his mother and younger self, in a by-his-own-bootstraps moment of incestuous education. Peter Nicholls dismissed it as 'one of the worst science fiction novels of the decade' (1975b: 80), full of cop-out and wafer-thin sociology. Long's point of view is repeatedly asserted as correct – and the book digresses for two long sections of his maxims, which were also published separately in part in *Analog* (June 1974) and as *The Notebooks of Lazarus Long* (1978) – and almost any opposition is dismissed without serious consideration. In contrast to Nicholls, Russell Letson (1978) and Ivor A. Rogers (1978) see it as 'Heinlein's greatest work and a true SF masterpiece' (Mullen 1979: 211).

'The Number of the Beast' has a narration which shuffles between four characters named for characters from Edgar Rice Burroughs's Barsoom novels – Hilda Corners, her new husband Jacob Burroughs, his daughter Deety Burroughs Carter and her husband, Zebadiah Carter – with some attempt at differentiation of tone. Jacob invents a machine that can travel between different universes, which allows the characters to visit Barsoom or L. Frank Baum's Oz, as well as the locations of earlier Heinlein novels. As the central characters travel between universes, they bicker, argue, have sex in various permutations and talk endlessly about sexuality. For Clute, the book is a kind of inoculation against the old age Heinlein would have been facing, and the void beyond the universe: 'Every reality is someone else's fiction. God is the ultimate author. Robert A. Heinlein is God. He is not alone' (1981: 85). But this sense of solipsism is there in '– All You Zombies –' (F&SF March 1959), and in the sense that Heinlein provides his own answers to his own problems in his own imagined universes – he is his own authority.

Heinlein had been a commentator on the first moon landing for Walter Cronkite on CBS, alongside British writer Arthur C. Clarke. Clarke had been publishing sf professionally since 1946, having contributed to fanzines in the 1930s, and had reached a zenith of fame with his collaboration with Stanley Kubrick on the film *2001: A Space Odyssey* (1968). Despite the almost immediate decline of the US space programme, Clarke remained optimistic about the potential of technology – somewhat counter to the spirit of the time – and gained a huge advance for three novels: *Rendezvous with Rama* (1972), *Imperial Earth* (1975) and *The Fountains of Paradise* (1979). *Rendezvous* was a narrative centred on a Big Dumb Object narrative, set within a federal system of human civilisations within the solar system, to be discussed in Chapter Four. It retreats from the mysticism of *2001* to the laws of physics.

The same is true of *Imperial Earth*, published a year before the American bicentennial. It is 2276, the five hundredth anniversary of the 1776 American Declaration of Independence, and representatives of all nations, on Earth or beyond, are invited to the celebrations. The celebration of an American festival, in a context of a federation that is compared to the Commonwealth of Nations, shows Clarke building bridges between cultures. The nations which Titanian Duncan Makenzie considers welcoming – 'Albania, Austrand, Cyprus, Bohemia, France, Khmer, Palestine, Kalinga, Zimbabwe, Eire' (Clarke 1975: 101) – suggests that boundaries had been redrawn. A number of these regions were in the news in the first part of the 1970s with military actions and invasions – the Turkish occupation in 1974 of northern Cyprus, the Troubles in Northern Ireland, the Khmer coup in Cambodia, the ongoing Palestine–Israeli struggles – and Rhodesia had declared independence in 1965, renaming itself

Zimbabwe Rhodesia in 1979. Clarke seems to have his characters approve of the moves towards the unity of humanity, albeit with some sentiment at the loss of ethnic difference: 'It's getting more and more difficult to find a *genuine* black skin [...] it will be a pity when we're all the same shade of off-white' (1975: 125) – a statement in the immediate aftermath of a cameo of a professor pretending to be a Black servant. De Witt Douglas Kilgore notes Clarke's assumption that US racial problems can be solved by making 'difference and otherness [...] a thing of a primitive genetic past' (2003: 147–48).

Duncan Makenzie voyages from the supposed margins to the imperial centre and back again, to obtain a third-generation clone alongside his father/twin Colin and grandfather/twin Malcolm. There seems to be faith in genetic purity, which is apparently undercut by Duncan's experiences on Earth and his final choice of clone. Duncan is repeatedly suggested to be bisexual, although one sequence of him apparently making an assignation with Chief Engineer Makenzie is more about a space drive than a sex drive. Clarke focuses on the scientific travelogue of the moons of Saturn and realistic travel to Earth and space elevators rather than social progress. Duncan discovers that a childhood friend is involved in setting up a highly sensitive series of radio telescopes to detect alien life forms, which would shift Titan from the margins to the centre of the imperium, and indeed unsettle any such distinction in a human–alien relationship. But everything seems a little too easy, a little too nice – Clute sees the book as 'a kind of elated *prophecy* of a time to come beyond our time of troubles when population will be controlled, conflicts among nations stilled, sexual dimorphism soothed of those rough edges and coulisses we all skirt these days, and the world itself – the green Earth – will have been returned to its natural state' (1988: 113). Earth becomes a second Eden, as Makenzie comes of age.

Makenzie travels down to Earth via a space elevator, which had already been proposed by a number of scientists, based on the geosynchronous orbits that Clarke had suggested could be exploited for communications satellites. A wire could be stretched from a counterweight – an asteroid – to a ground station on the equator, and used to lift payloads and people into space with relative ease and much more cheaply (after start-up costs) than with conventional rocketry. Clarke reuses the concept in *The Fountains of Paradise*, his last novel of the 1970s. He sets much of the action in Sri Lanka, where he had lived since the 1950s, but moves and adjusts the island to provide the best jumping-off point for the elevator. Unfortunately this location, better than sites in Africa, the Americas or Oceania, is already occupied by a sacred Buddhist temple. Science battles against religion, just as earlier novels by Clarke played off the rational versus the sublime. The rest of the novel is a series of problems that require technological resolutions, with a climactic terrorist attack on the elevator. As with *Rama* and *Imperial Earth*, Clarke braids in an extraterrestrial civilisation, initially in the form of an alien probe, which passes through the solar system, and the aliens reach Earth in an epilogue. Clarke insists that this first contact changes everything, but states this as an article of faith, rather than something that he dramatises; it does not speed up or justify the building of the ring of elevators.

Still, the universe is a hostile, dangerous place and there is no second-guessing the universe's cold equations; Clarke is much more interested in these rules than in those of ideology. But his optimism, which seems escapist or naive in the 1970s context, suggests that human rationality can use those equations to keep sufficiently far ahead of the laws that would kill the ignorant. Even as the Apollo programme was being dismantled, Clarke imagines a future of federal territorial expansion, any problems solved by a slide rule. Relationships are rarely shown – Makenzie interacts with an old friend and those he was cloned from, but there is little sense of emotion, and in *Fountains* the elevator engineer gains a nephew for exposition purposes. The characters are game pieces – like the polyominoes of *Imperial Earth* – to be moved around the latest predictions of exotic planetary locations.

Other pulp writers beyond the big three were still writing. Clifford D. Simak had been active in the 1930s, and had balanced a career as a journalist with writing novels. Between 1970 and 1980, he published eleven, all with a sense of nostalgia for the rural and a distaste for the modern world. In *Out of their Minds* (1970), Horton Smith crashes his car into a dinosaur as he returns home to his own small town and spends a night in a house with people who he realises are cartoon strip characters – Snuffy and Loweezy Smith – created by Billy DeBeck in 1919. Fictional characters are interacting with the real world, from Arthurian knights to Mickey Mouse and Pluto, as a result of objections by the (human-created) Devil to clogged-up imaginations. Given that the delinquent, possibly werewolf, Ballard brothers have taken over Horton's old house, this may offer a critique of the British New Wave, which might be considered to be squatting in the place of First sf.

Several of the later Simak novels feature surreal quests – for example, *Destiny Doll* (*Worlds of Fantasy*, as *Reality Doll*, Spring 1971; 1971) strands its travellers on a largely desert planet which seems to be operating like a kind of Venus fly-trap. They tame hobby horses and dodge high velocity seeds fired at them by trees. 'A man can't take on a planet,' the mysterious pilgrim, Tuck, declares, 'He has to go along with it. He has to adapt. He can't bull his way through' (Simak 1973b: 96). Taking on a planet is what First sf characters did, but by the 1970s there was the sense that adaptation to the environment was necessary. In *Enchanted Pilgrimage* (1975) and *The Fellowship of the Talisman* (1978), significant historical manuscripts are the excuse for quest narratives involving eccentric collections of travellers. *A Choice of Gods* (1972) explicitly pits nature against technology, on an all but abandoned twenty-second-century Earth occupied by Native Americans and increasingly sophisticated robots. The human exiles wish to discover the secret of Native American teleportation, but there is a real fear that the returning population will upset Earth's recovering ecosystem. George Hay feels that the novel seems too familiar and comfortable and 'wishes that this writer for once would give us something that has one dimension more than what is, in effect, a mood piece' (1973: 74). The sentimental melancholy recurs in *Cemetery World* (*Analog* November 1972–January 1973; 1973); Earth is almost all given over to graves, and artist Fletcher Carson travels there to create a work of art.

The escape to the past, which features in most of Simak novels of the period, is eucatastrophic, somewhat at odds with the period. In two novels, the escape is foregrounded. In *Our Children's Children* (*Worlds of If* May–July 1973; 1974), millions of people start appearing from the future, on the run from unstoppable alien carnivores. The future humans plan to colonise the Miocene era – habitable, but sufficiently far back that they hope that there will be no time paradoxes. As the predators reach the present day, contemporary humanity also needs to flee. Clute was unimpressed, seeing Simak 'daydreaming through the afternoon of his career in one of the silliest and most absent-minded novels of recent years' (1974: 47). In *Mastodonia/Catface* (1978) archaeologist Asa Steele's dog travels back in time through a tunnel or portal created by an alien Steele comes to know as Catface. Steele goes into business with Rila Elliot, an old flame, who 'had come out of the past – at least twenty years out of the past – only the evening before' (Simak 1980a: 4), operating prehistoric safaris. The two of them retreat into the Sangamon interglacial period for legal and tax reasons, and attempt to create a settlement with minimal impact – evolution must not be diverted, nor must they leave any archaeological traces. The purity of the past must be preserved.

Simak's most sophisticated novel of the period is *The Visitors* (*Analog* October–December 1979; 1980), in which a number of black cuboids, apparently sentient and of extraterrestrial origin, land in Minnesota and begin to consume trees. The aliens may come in peace, but the unintended consequence is the likely destruction of the American economy, first through consumption of raw materials – forests and plantations – and then through gifting of advanced technology shaped like cars and houses. The end of scarcity will devastate the automobile and manufacturing economies, undercutting the American way of life. Two seemingly insignificant details are raised, but not developed. First, there is the importance of Indian or Native American lands and reservations, where a near-extinct civilisation maintains some vestiges of its rights (a theme that looks back to *A Choice of Gods*). A direct correlation is made between the sale in 1626 of the island of Manhattan by the Lenape to the Dutch. Simak twice invokes *The War of the Worlds* (1898), an invasion story in which the aliens are defeated by nature – specifically bacteria – but also one that makes explicit reference to the genocidal consequences of the process of colonialism. Just as European settlers wiped out the Tasmanians, so humanity faces the same fate. The narrative is left on a cliff-hanger, but it feels as if the processes of urbanisation and its impact on ecology are to be feared as much as the aliens themselves.

Theodore Sturgeon had acquired the reputation of being sf's stylist, although Harlan Ellison was to lament that he was 'writing things that are beneath [him]' (Fowler 1976: 14), while admitting that Sturgeon's works still demonstrated intelligence. The late 1960s marked a period of resurgence for Sturgeon, with a new collection, *Sturgeon is Alive and Well* (1971), whose title answered the rumour to the contrary. But Sturgeon only produced a couple of dozen stories in the 1970s, and struggled to complete a novel eventually published as *Godbody* (1986). Donald M. Hassler notes that Sturgeon's fiction explores the themes of 'loneliness and loves' (1979: 178), although Sturgeon claims he 'investigate[s love] by writing about it because […] I don't know what the hell I think until I tell somebody about it' (1977: 271). Brian Stableford suggests the stories are about 'the healing power of love and the power of love as stimulus in extreme situations' (1977c: 19); all too often for Sturgeon's characters love turns to loneliness, as it has remained unspoken.

In the Hugo and Nebula Awards-winning 'Slow Sculpture' (*Galaxy* February 1970), a misanthropic engineer cures a young woman of cancer by means of a potassium injection and a massive electric shock. He refuses to let her tell him her name, but by demonstrating her understanding of bonsai trees she seduces him into admitting his interest in her. Hassler notes that this encounter enables the engineer to finally 'make the meaningful human contact that will give coherence and significance to his inventions' (1979: 177). 'Case and the Dreamer' (*Galaxy* January 1973) in part turns out to be hallucination, as Case thinks himself the last survivor of a lost spaceship, revived centuries after the death of the next to last to die, Jan, by a strange blue being who calls himself the Doctor. Jan has loved Case, and vice versa, although neither of them has said anything to the other, and the Doctor has created a fantasy world in which Case had survived, hoping Jan might love it. In 'Blue Butter' (*F&SF* October 1974), a scientist, Stromberg, tries to tell the unnamed narrator why he has left his wife: his perception of the scale of the universe has meant that he feels he has not lived prior to marrying, and now is womanising to catch up for lost time. The vision of the world is pessimistic – 'We're going back now, all the way to methane and ammonia [...] It'll be clear back to before-the-beginning' (Sturgeon 2010a: 109-10) – and even Stromberg's search for pleasure leaves him isolated and pathetic, as well as using the remedy of blue butter to cure some kind of sexually transmitted disease.

Like Sturgeon, Ray Bradbury was predominantly a short-story writer, but he produced only one new collection in the 1970s, *Long After Midnight* (1976), with eleven stories originally published between 1946 and 1963, five from the 1970s and six that were new. In most of Bradbury's output, there is a sense of nostalgia – as Simak looks back to rural Wisconsin, so Bradbury looks back to Illinois – with the wonders of childhood contrasted to the disappointments of old age. Alongside the fantasy and horror, the only science-fictional story is 'The Messiah' (*Welcome Aboard* Spring 1971), in which a priest thinks he sees Christ in the church; this is him imposing his belief system upon one of the increasingly rare aboriginal Martians. It would fit into *The Martian Chronicles* (1946–50; 1950; also as *The Silver Locusts*; contents vary between editions) from a quarter of a century earlier; indeed it forms part of the narrative of the television adaptation *The Martian Chronicles* (Michael Anderson, 1980). This felt very staid and po-faced, its mini-series format allowing for the space of an extended narrative, but losing the nuances and rhythm of the original. The simulation of 1930s small-town America could be achieved, but the Martian civilisation never quite escapes the feel of camp – it is hard to take seriously. Bradbury also wrote theatrical and television adaptations of other earlier works. He almost always brought a sense of poetry to his fiction – his prose is poetic, while, ironically, his poetry is prosaic, albeit in the style of the muscular free verse of Walt Whitman. He published a juvenile fantasy, *The Halloween Tree* (1972), in which a number of children in fancy dress discover the meaning of the various costumes that they wear and learn that the various autumnal rituals recorded through history are attempts to ward off the fear of death, whether of individual humans, or of the sun as winter approaches. There is a sense that the old stories, as well as the old gods and spirits, which personify a whole series of human conceptions, are being forgotten, and need to be renewed.

Alfred Bester, whose first sf had appeared in *Thrilling Wonder Stories* in April 1939, returned to the genre in 1971 when the travel magazine, *Holiday*, for which he had written and which he had edited temporarily ceased publication. *The Computer Connection* (as *The Indian Giver* in *Analog* November 1974–January 1975; 1975, variant title *Extro*) is a typically manic Bester novel, featuring a group of time-travelling immortals named for significant historical figures in a post-apocalyptic world. Hilary Bailey suggests that the protagonist, Edward Curzon, is a wish-fulfilment figure for Bester, and hard to identify with, and enumerates the book's flaws as showing 'the author's lack of feeling for his hero [...] indifference in the guise of cool, and general staggering around the stage bumping into the scenery' (1976: 89). It was nominated for the Nebula Award in 1975 and the Hugo in 1976, but, as with Asimov, this was perhaps a nostalgic nod to a veteran writer. *Golem*$^{100}$ (1980) focuses upon a coven of rich women who attempt to raise a supernatural beast. Stableford suggests that 'Bester deliberately unfetters his imagination and abandons all semblance of control to let his fancy run riot' (1981: 98), whereas Algis Budrys complains that the novel 'repudiate[s] everything he has ever shown us about storytelling' (1981: 40). Bester's earlier novels had been pyrotechnical displays, including typographical tricks, but his use of diagrams, pictures, Rorschach tests and collages to represent the experiences of his characters invited the charge of self-indulgence. His fast-paced, haunted, technologically advanced narratives pointed towards the possibilities to be explored in cyberpunk, but are in themselves failures.

Also returning to the genre was Leigh Brackett. She had begun her publishing career with 'Martian Quest' (*Astounding* February 1940). Much of her early work was planetary romance, drawing upon the same Barsoom stories of Edgar Rice Burroughs that were to inspire *'The Number of the Beast'*. Some were loosely linked, but a more concentrated attempt to form a series character came with her creation of Eric John Stark in 'Queen of the Martian Catacombs' (*Planet Stories* Summer 1949), 'Enchantress of Venus' (*Planet Stories* Fall 1949) and 'Black Amazon of Mars' (*Planet Stories* March 1951), a Mercury-born human orphan adopted by the local species and named by them N'Chaka, man-without-a-tribe. Stark's new family is killed, and he is imprisoned, but Simon Ashton eventually liberates him and becomes a mentor. Brackett returned to her hero in the story 'Stark and the Star Kings', written with her husband Edmond Hamilton for the delayed Harlan Ellison anthology *The Last Dangerous Visions* (the story eventually appeared in a joint posthumous collection, *Stark and the Star Kings* (2003)), and a trilogy, The Book of Skaith, comprising *The Ginger Star*

(*Worlds of If* January–April 1974; 1974), *The Hounds of Skaith* (1974) and *The Reavers of Skaith* (1976).

Astronomical advances had rendered Brackett's depictions of Mercury, Venus or Mars obsolete, the sort of locations that would now feel like pastiche. The action is thus relocated to Skaith, a planet in another solar system, where Simon Ashton has been captured and Stark, owing his mentor a debt, goes in search of him. In the sequel, Stark is at the head of a pack of genetically engineered telepathic dogs, the northounds, bending local tribes to his will to unsettle the rule of the feudal Wandsmen lords with the threat of the dogs, but always at risk of being torn apart by the pack himself. In the final volume, the sense of the planet as part of a wider system is foregrounded, with Stark being hated because of the hope for escape from Skaith that he inspires: an evacuation would cause chaos because it could not take place quickly, and power vacuums could open up as peoples were displaced and the authority of the Wandsmen undercut. There is more of a sense of the inhabitants of Skaith being genetically engineered, but having forgotten the technology, than in the earlier volumes. Stark does not develop as a character and speedily recovers from injuries, being driven only by a sense of restorative justice against those who had captured Ashton. Throughout, he has to repress or use his own sense of savagery, even as he seeks to exert his civilising influence. The trilogy resurrected a Burroughsian archetype of the superior human intervening in the events of a richly cultured alien planet, but not being able to draw upon much of their own superior human technology. Whereas the Barsoom and early Stark stories had been written in the pre-Cold War context of American colonialism, the late Stark trilogy comes as American soldiers were being withdrawn from Vietnam, in a more cynical, disappointed age. The forces of progress stand against those of stability, but that instability is equally fearful. Diane Newell and Victoria Lamont note that 'the earliest Stark tales depicted the Earth-led galactic empire as exploitative of the worlds in its path, [but the trilogy cast] the Galactic Union as liberators' (2009: 39). These were narratives that C.J. Cherryh would exploit in her novels, with a greater awareness of the complex political ramifications.

Parallel to Brackett's career in the sf and fantasy pulps, she had also written crime thrillers and, from *The Big Sleep* (Howard Hawks, 1946), with William Faulkner, she worked in Hollywood, eventually being commissioned to write the script for *The Empire Strikes Back* (Irvin Kershner, 1980). After her death, Ray Bradbury, Harlan Ellison and Michael Moorcock all phoned George Lucas, offering to polish the script without being credited (Arbur 1982: 6), but the then unproduced scriptwriter Lawrence Kasdan was brought in. Brackett's version has remained largely unread, available only in manuscript at Eastern New Mexico University and the Lucasfilms archives. The script follows the same general shape as the finished version, but does not contain the significant revelation that Vader is Luke Skywalker's father.

With the obvious exception of Brackett, these writers carried on into the 1980s in much the same vein as they had entered the 1970s. Asimov, Heinlein and Clarke all turned to sequels; in the case of the first two there was an attempt to braid their oeuvres into a single narrative. Perhaps the only real difference in their careers was a turn towards the book market from the magazine one, a change outside their control and one that was also to be forced on some of the New Wave writers.

# 2
# After the New Wave: After Science Fiction?

The sf writers who started publishing in the 1950s and 1960s pushed at the boundaries of subject matter and style within the genre, at a time when taboos were being loosened. In Britain, Michael Moorcock, who took over the editing of *New Worlds* in 1964, encouraged his contributors to experiment with both content and form. But falling sales saw it move from magazine to paperback format – after issue 200 (April 1970) and a subscribers-only issue (March 1971), both edited by Charles Platt, *New Worlds* became *New Worlds Quarterly*. Only six issues were produced by Moorcock between 1971 and 1973, with Platt co-editor of *New Worlds 6* (1973). Hilary Bailey and Platt edited *New Worlds 7* (1974) and Bailey *New Worlds 8* (1975), *New Worlds 9* (1975) and *New Worlds 10* (1976). Three issues appeared in 1978, with two more in 1979. The title was then dormant until David S. Garnett resurrected it in 1991.

But it would be as misleading to centre the New Wave on *New Worlds* alone as it would be to spread the term out to cover everything other than hard science fiction or First sf. In the US, Harlan Ellison edited *Dangerous Visions* (1967) and *Again, Dangerous Visions* (1972), which offered more liberal attitudes to sex, religion and narrative experimentation than most of the magazines. A third volume, *The Last Dangerous Visions*, was announced, which was to have included stories by almost all the other active sf authors from the period, but this has yet to appear. Ellison admitted, 'It was just my luck that I was the guy in America and Mike Moorcock was the guy over here [...] I like stirring things up' (Fowler 1976: 17). Others were also at work: Frederik Pohl's magazine *Worlds of If*, which he edited from 1961 to 1969, was also open to more adult fare, as was *The Magazine of Fantasy and Science Fiction* (1949–). There were also various original anthologies: *New Writings in SF* (1964–77) edited by John Carnell to 1972 and thereafter by Kenneth Bulmer; *Orbit* (1966–80) edited by Damon Knight; *Quark* (1970–71) edited by Samuel R. Delany and Marilyn Hacker; *Universe* (1971–87) edited by Terry Carr; and *New Dimensions* (1971–80) edited by Robert Silverberg. In general, the paperback rather than the

AFTER THE NEW WAVE: AFTER SCIENCE FICTION?   25

magazine was becoming the place of first publication, and paperbacks were more liberal than the sf pulps. Ellison suggests a historical inevitability to the New Wave – it might have been that Bailey, Carnell, Carr, Delany, Hacker, Platt and Pohl would have been able to change things without *New Worlds* or *Dangerous Visions*. Indeed, Carnell had published an editorial by J.G. Ballard in 1962 that offered a credo for the New Wave. Sf changed – Delany's *Dhalgren* (1975) was not only publishable but also became a best-seller. This chapter will consider the works of Moorcock, Ballard, M. John Harrison, Brian W. Aldiss, John Brunner, Ellison, Thomas M. Disch, John Sladek and Barry N. Malzberg as the New Wave moved from short form in periodicals to novels.

Moorcock was a prolific writer, partly in order to fund *New Worlds* – Elric novels and collections (including *The Sleeping Sorceress* (1971) and *The Dreaming City* (aka *Elric of Melniboné*, 1972)), the Swords of Corum trilogy (*The Knight of the Swords* (1971), *The Queen of the Swords* (1971) and *The King of the Swords* (1971)) and the Chronicles of Corum trilogy (*The Bull and the Spear* (1973), *The Oak and the Ram* (1973) and *The Sword and the Stallion* (1974)). His central protagonists, along with Dorian Hawkmoon from the History of the Runestaff Trilogy (1967–69), formed aspects of a heroic archetype, the Eternal Champion, which Moorcock explored within different fantasy universes. A contemporary version of the character, Jerry Cornelius, appeared in the Cornelius Tetralogy (1969–77) and various short stories, and a far-future, decadent avatar, Jherek Carnelian, was central to *The Dancers at the End of Time* (*An Alien Heat* (1972), *The Hollow Lands* (1974) and *The End of All Songs* (1976)). The Oswald Bastable trilogy (1971–81) offers a very different vision of the anti-hero, in three distinct alternative universes, although minor characters link it to the meta-series. Moorcock could appeal to his various sf and fantasy readerships as a loyal audience, but he can also be accused of the same sort of solipsism that was to be engaged in with the late novels of Isaac Asimov and, especially, Robert A. Heinlein.

In addition to his entertainments, Moorcock also wrote more serious works. *Breakfast in the Ruins: An Novel of Inhumanity* (1972) reuses a character name from 'Behold the Man' (*New Worlds* 1966; exp. 1969), Karl Glogauer, there a time traveller from the 1970s crucified in place of Christ, here a man in 1971 who meets a Nigerian photographer who wants to have sex with him. Glogauer might be an aspect of the Eternal Champion; certainly there are many versions of him, as the sex scenes are intercut with a variety of life stories for Glogauer between 1871 and the present day. This is the sort of shattered hero figure that had been typical of the New Wave. The repetitive format – a section in italics, a narrative and a series of questions – is also part of the New Wave experiment with the form of the novel, a variant on Ballard's condensed novels of *The Atrocity Exhibition* (1969), and indeed on the structures of the Cornelius novels. Glogauer's transformation into a black man places the Nigerian as his alter ego, as well as offering a Jungian allegory of the psyche confronting the shadow side of the self.

*Gloriana, or The Unfulfill'd Queen: A Romance* (1978) emerges the year after the Silver Jubilee, twenty-five years after the start of the period hailed with post-war optimism as the New Elizabethan Age. Moorcock revisits Edmund Spenser's incomplete allegorical epic, *The Faerie Queene* (1596). Elizabeth I becomes Gloriana, daughter of Hern and queen of Albion, and her chief advisor, Lord Montfallcon, is an amalgam of William Cecil and the Earl of Leicester. Moorcock's own use of the occultist John Dee, via his Hermetic speculations, enables him to connect his multiverse into what would otherwise be quasi-fantasy as alternative history – Gloriana's favourite, Una, nods towards the recurring character Una Persson, particularly associated with Jerry Cornelius, Pyat echoes Colonel Pyat – central to the Pyat tetralogy (1981–2006) – and Korzeniowski recalls a character in the Oswald Bastable trilogy, named for Joseph Conrad's birth name, Józef Korzeniowski. The book's dedication, to the memory of Mervyn Peake, points us toward the Gormenghast books: *Titus Groan* (1946), *Gormenghast* (1950) and *Titus Alone* (1959; rev. 1968, edited by Langdon Jones). The first two of these feature the life of Titus, the 77th Earl of Gormenghast, as he grows to adulthood and faces up to his power and responsibilities, and also the rise of the Machiavellian Steerpike, from kitchen boy to master of ritual; Montfallcon's agent, Captain Quire, an adventurer, spy and assassin, is a version of Steerpike, able to use his knowledge of the secret geographies of the palace and the interweaving networks of invisible conspiracies for his own ends. On the surface the court appears calm and stable, but only because anything that challenges it has been eradicated or exiled into the inner spaces of the walls. As Bailey observes, 'the palace must stand for the individual brain [...] where in light and airy halls and corridors music plays and events takes place according to an ordered patter while, scuffling about in darkness, suppressed facts, disorderly memories and unadmitted disgusting feelings go their way undetected' (1979: 87). By means of murder, framing and seduction, and ultimately the rape of Gloriana, Quire re-represents himself as Prince Arthur – a name pointing to King Arthur, as well as to Henry VIII's elder brother – and, as represented in the future tense, Albion goes from glory to glory. The rape is an expression of repressed desire and correspondences of geography and anatomy – as in the Fisher King myth which links ruler and land, so Gloriana *is* Albion. Gloriana, unfulfilled according to the novel's subtitle, achieves orgasm, in an event that, according to her, redeems her. History is, however, written by the winning side, and this may be more of Quire's propaganda.

Moorcock's works inspired guitarist Dave Brock to form Hawkwind in Notting Hill and Ladbroke Grove in 1969, a band whose 'space rock bridged progressive and psychedelic punk' (Albiez 2003: 358), suffused with sf imagery in their lyrics and on their record packaging, with guitars and synthesisers trying to recreate trip-like experiences. After their debut album, *Hawkwind* (1970), a largely instrumental work, they were fronted by Robert Calvert, who wrote an sf narrative for a twenty-four-page booklet, *The Hawkwind Log*, contained within the sleeve of *X In Search of Space* (1971). *Doremi Fasol Latido* (1972) developed the imagery, alluding to the notion of the music of the spheres. The fourth album, *Hall of the Mountain Grill* (1973), minus Calvert, had David Hardy and Barney Bubbles artwork, clearly sf in tone, and the fifth, *Warrior on the Edge of Time* (1975), had lyrics written by Moorcock and related to the Eternal Champion. *Astounding Sounds, Amazing Music* (1976), marking a move from United Artists to Charisma Records, saw the return of Calvert. The title alludes to the two sf pulp magazines, with each track representing an sf story. *Quark, Strangeness and Charm* (1977) continued the sf theme, with tracks inspired by Roger Zelazny and Norman Spinrad. The band split from their management on an American tour, Calvert, Brock and drummer Simon King releasing an album, *Hawklords* (1978). This title draws from Michael Butterworth's novels *The Time of the Hawklords* (1976) and *Queens of Deliria* (1977), co-credited to Moorcock, and featuring the band members as characters in pulp sf narratives. Having regained legal rights to the band's name, they released *PRX5* (1979), including the tracks 'Jack of Sparrows', based on a Zelazny novel of the same name (*F&SF* 1971; 1971) and 'Robot', which alludes to Asimov's Three Laws of Robotics. They closed the decade with their tenth studio album, *Levitation* (1980), again minus Calvert, with an instrumental inspired by a Philip José Farmer series of novels, *World of Tiers* (1965–93).

Ballard, whose *High-Rise* (1975) had inspired a track on *PRX5*, had moved away from his weather-based disasters and condensed novels of the 1960s, writing a technological disaster trilogy more or less set in the present, with *Crash* (1973), *Concrete Island* (1974) and *High-Rise*. Some of his short stories critiqued the technologised media landscape: 'The Greatest Television Show on Earth' (*Ambit* Winter 1972) depicts the rise and fall of time-travelling documentary crews, wiped out in the parting of the Red Sea, with a strong suggestion that God has prevented further broadcasts, and 'The Life and Death of God' (1976) dramatises the unintended consequences of scientific proof of God, including church-led atheism. The Second World War casts a shadow over Ballard's work, as he headed towards writing his fictionalised autobiography, *Empire of the Sun* (1984). An adulterous love triangle intersects with an apparent holdout from the war in 'One Afternoon at Utah Beach' (1978) – although it turns out to be the cuckolded husband who is the soldier holding out against invasion – and echoes of the air force campaigns underlie 'My Dream of Flying to Wake Island' (*Ambit* Autumn 1974), with its disinterred crash aircraft and unfulfilled desire to reach a former military base, target of a Japanese raid the day after Pearl Harbor. Runways are seen as starting points rather than endings – the aircraft in Ballard's stories are more likely to crash than to touch down, and his pilots, like his astronauts, fly inwards as well as out. *The Unlimited Dream Company* (1979) enfolds an airman, Blake, in Shepperton, a town west of London on the Thames and split by the M3, where Ballard lived for most of his adult life. The protagonist's name is an allusion to William Blake, the Romantic poet, whose prophetic work *Milton: A Poem* (1804–10) offers various visions of a hallucinatory London and an apocalyptic world. Ballard's twentieth-century Blake steals a plane from Heathrow and crashes into Shepperton, where he becomes a totemic figure. He anoints the people with his semen, and eventually turns them into birds. John Clute notes scenes in the novel and on its original dust-wrapper that allude to British painter Stanley Spencer, who had depicted biblical scenes of 'apocalyptic prelapsarian paradise' (1980a: 85). The novel's surrealism was to mark a temporary narrative goodbye to England, even as Ballard invoked a transcendent pantheism in his own backyard. Increasingly he became a social commentator and reviewer who had transcended the pulps. He was to serve as inspiration for the 1980s generation of writers, as well as to write for a new British sf magazine, *InterZone*, one of whose editors, David Pringle, tirelessly documented Ballard's work.

Brian Aldiss engaged with existing science fiction by writing two parasitic novels, *Frankenstein Unbound* (*Fantastic* March and May 1973; 1973) and *Moreau's Other Island* (1980), as well as writing a history of sf, *Billion Year Spree: The History of Science Fiction* (1973). *The Eighty-Minute Hour: A Space Opera* (1974) offered a parody of the subgenre, with a sunken post-holocaust Britain, huge dams, concentration camps on Mars, cyborgs and manic invention. David I. Masson, while enjoying the creativity, argues that 'the book has no obvious bite' (1975: 201), only play. Similarly, Pringle describes *The Malacia Tapestry* (1976) as 'an ahistorical utopia' (1977: 96), too removed from significant commentary on the real world. The novel blurs and questions generic boundaries: it is not quite fantasy, because of its deployment of technology – Otto Bengston has invented a crude ancestor of cinema, which the narrator Perian de Chirolo uses to seduce the high-born Armida. It is set in a kind of alternative renaissance, an Italianate city-state – with shades of 'Babylon, Byzantium and Shakespeare's London' (Pringle 1977: 95). *Enemies of the System* (*F&SF* June 1978; 1978) is more straightforwardly dystopian, and a much greyer novel as a result, as tourists from Earth are stranded on Lysenka II; Brian Stableford calls it 'essentially hollow' (1979: 97), and fears that Aldiss is becoming lazy and self-indulgent. But Aldiss had two bigger projects on the horizon, a Yugoslavia-based satire, *Life in the West* (1980), part one of a tetralogy, and the Helliconia trilogy (1982–85), set on an alien planet with an extremely long year.

M. John Harrison had been taken up with the British New Wave and, as a regular reviewer for *New Worlds*, offered frequently searing critiques of the genre. His own novels and short stories comment on sf and fantasy: 'During the seventies he tackled a series of major "speculative" forms – the archetypically British post-apocalyptic novel in *The Committed Men* (1971), the heroic fantasy in *The Pastel City* (1971) and the space opera in *The Centauri Device* (1974) – and tried to rebuild them' (Davidson 2005: 265). Aldiss characterised the 'cosy catastrophe' by its solidly middle-class heroes having a good time: 'a girl, free suites at the Savoy, automobiles for the taking' (1973: 294), and Christopher Priest defined it by the representation of inconvenience to such classes with delays to the milk, post, evening newspaper and commuter train (1979: 194). Harrison saw *The Committed Men* as drawing attention to 'the illusions central to the genre. The clearest illusions we have are to do with "meaning" and "choice", with self-determination, problem-solving' (1989: 5). Harrison's apocalyptic England, poisoned by the invisible killer radiation, offers neither cosiness nor consolation to its readers. Nor do *The Pastel City* and its sequel *A Storm of Wings* (1980) and attendant short stories, collected in *Viriconium Nights* (1985), offer the pleasures of fantasy within their dying earth or Burroughsian sword-and-planet milieu. Harrison subverts the genre's illusions in order to reveal the readers' latent anxieties: 'stories of immortality reveal death at the heart of themselves, stories of communication inarticulacy, stories of vast space and interstellar flight, oppression and earthboundness, and so on' (1989: 5). Sublime images of ancient civilisations and cultures are raised – much as Tolkien allows a fetishisation of the mythic past behind *The Lord of the Rings* (1949–50) – only for the narrating voice to deny their importance. Harrison is closer in spirit to Peake, but Colin Greenland notes that 'Gormenghast was never like this, nor Malacia, nor Gloriana's Albion' (1981: 102), suggesting that Harrison is responding against both the doxa of the genre and its critics. Greenland observes that *Storm* offers 'No heroes. [...] No elves' (1981: 102), and Nick Freeman argues that Harrison rejects the post-Tolkien fantasy's 'clear-cut moral polarities and narrative schemes that are both linear and punctuated by would-be spectacular set pieces' (2005: 275). We are not given reassurance through catharsis; this is amphicatastrophe. In Harrison's rewiring of American First sf, his space opera *The Centauri Device*, the can-do, morally certain hero of that subgenre is replaced with John Truck, the last of the Centaurans, a species who lost out against humanity. Rjurik Davidson describes the Truck in the first part of the novel as passive rather than active, the victim of events rather than their master, pursued by the Union of Arab Socialist Republics and Israeli World Government – the geopolitics clearly a reaction to the Middle Eastern conflict which had flared up between Israel and its neighbours in the Six-Day War of June 1967 and the Yom Kippur War of October 1973, the latter feeding into the ongoing Cold War stand-off between the USA and the USSR. In the second half of the book, Truck becomes active, having been faced with a continual demand that he take sides, just as in the real Cold War superpowers divide their world into allies and enemies. Davidson argues that the novel is caught between the thirst for revolution and renovation of the 1960s and 'a seventies disillusionment with politics and ideology' (2005: 270). Science fiction and fantasy seemed to offer Harrison resistible choices of destroy or be destroyed, as he pushed against the boundaries of what the form could do.

John Brunner continued a prolific rate of sf publication until *The Shockwave Rider* (1975), which ended a thematic tetralogy begun with *Stand On Zanzibar* (1968), *The Jagged Orbit* (1969) and *The Sheep Look Up* (1972). Ironically, this slowing of output coincided with his growing critical reputation – a number of articles explicated his work in *Science Fiction Studies* and Joe de Bolt edited a collection, *The Happening Worlds of John Brunner: Critical Exploration in Science Fiction* (1975). The tetralogy portrays the coming apocalypse of overpopulation, starvation, pollution, drugs and arms deals and racial strife, noting that resources are finite and running down, and often using modernist techniques borrowed from John Dos Passos's *U.S.A.* trilogy (1930–36). Those novels have short chapters forming intertwining strands of narrative and incorporate newspaper clippings and other documents; Moorcock had used a similar technique in the Cornelius tetralogy. *The Shockwave Rider* takes its title from Alvin Toffler's bestseller *Future Shock* (1970), which argues that the world's population is finding it increasingly difficult to adapt to overwhelming technological change. Brunner's novel imagines an overloaded future, and centres on Nick Haflinger, who repeatedly reinvents his identity in order to avoid capture by a government agency. Eventually Haflinger develops a worm – an early example of a computer virus – to outwit the surveillance of the powers-that-be. *Total Eclipse* (*Amazing* April and June 1974; 1974) is more traditional in form, but rejects the optimism that its place of publication had stood for. An ethnically diverse group of thirty scientists investigate an extinct alien species that evolved from Stone Age to advanced technology in a short period of time. Parallel to this is the disintegration of Earth and its culture – '*The Kenya-Uganda War, the Indonesian famine, the Argente plague, that terrible tsunami*' (Brunner 1974: 25) – so the scientists are marooned as they uncover the secret of the lost civilisation. Brunner brings an increasingly dark tone to the usually upbeat subgenre of hard science fiction. Fredric Jameson notes the book's doubling of its twin themes, of whether humans will become extinct as the aliens did, and 'the question of how we can possibly understand radical difference' (2005: 102), whether that is alien or human difference.

Like that of Brunner, Disch's work can be characterised by pessimism and dark humour. An American short story writer and novelist, his career flourished when he moved to London in the 1960s. His early sf is mostly dystopian, refusing to allow his characters the consolations of the happy ending. *334* (1967–72; 1972), a collection of linked stories set at 334 East 11th Street, depicts a housing project in an overcrowded future New York. One of them, 'Angouleme' (*New Worlds Quarterly* 1971), became the subject of a book-length semiotic analysis in Delany's *The American Shore* (1978). Tom Shippey notes that 'Disch uses much of the "hardware" of Brunner or Pohl or Asimov – the host mothers, the genetic regulations, the mechanical cartoons, the institutionalisation of historical research' (1975: 85) but that he does not share those authors' optimism 'that something can be done' (1975: 85). A sense of failing and entropy suffuses everything in these stories. But by the 1970s, Disch was moving away from sf, with a historical novel, *Clara Reeve* (as Leonie Hargrave, 1975), poetry – collected in, for example, *Highway Sandwiches* (with Platt and Hacker, 1970), *The Right Way to Figure Plumbing* (1972), *ABCDEFG HIJKLM NPOQRST UVWXYZ* (1979), *Burn This* (1982) and *Orders of the Retina* (1982) – and a series of anthologies – including the dystopian *The Ruins of Earth* (1971) and *Bad Moon Rising* (1973) and the utopian *The New Improved Sun* (1975). With composer Greg Sandow, he wrote two operas, *The Fall of the House of Usher* (1975), based on the Poe tale, and *Frankenstein* (1979). He returns to sf with *On Wings of Song* (1979), discussed in Chapter Eleven, and *The Brave Little Toaster* (*F&SF* August 1980; 1986), a children's fiction in the mode of Sheila Burnford's *The Incredible Journey* (1961), although here it is household appliances rather than animals who set off across country.

Like Disch, his occasional collaborator, John Sladek moved to London in the mid-1960s and was a regular contributor to *New Worlds*. His short fiction divides up into several types: experimental stories about bureaucracy, sometimes in the shape of forms, Kafka-esque stories of individuals caught up in a loss of identity (such as 'Name (Please Print):' (*New Worlds Quarterly 5* (1973)) and parodies of other sf writers, such as Isaac Asimov ('Broot Force' (*F&SF* September 1972)) and Philip K. Dick ('Solar Shoe Salesman' (1973)). His second sf novel, *The Müller-Fokker Effect* (1970), is a mixture of high-level conspiracy theories and lunatic xenophobia, with anti-communist groups, right-wing racists, unlikely Native Americans and evangelists, and a flight of fancy discovering a secret code in the number pi. Sladek brings an absurd logic to his satire, which, like the best comedy, seems all too plausible. Sladek was not to return to novel-length science fiction until *Roderick, or The Education of a Young Machine* (1980), the first book of a diptych in the UK, with *Roderick at Random* (1983); in the US it was planned to be published as a trilogy, but only part of the first novel appeared as Timescape ceased business. The eponymous protagonist is an experimental robot, attempting to become human in a society that is becoming increasingly mechanised and buried under bureaucracy. The novel engages with the history of robots in sf, especially the Three Laws of Robotics advanced by Asimov, and is part of the New Wave critique of First and other earlier sfs. Sladek also worked outside sf, creating an American private detective, Thackeray Phinn – 'By an Unknown Hand' (1972) won *The Times* Detective Story Competition, and was followed by the novels *Black Aura* (1974) and *Invisible Green* (1977) – and writing a non-fiction work on pseudoscience and crank beliefs, *The New Apocrypha* (1973).

Platt reversed the trajectories of Disch and Sladek by moving to the USA in 1970, where he became sf editor for Avon Books. However, *The Gas* (1970) was first published in Paris by an imprint of erotic publisher Olympia Press, followed by *The Image Job* (1971) and *The Power and the Pain* (1972). *The Gas* is a perverse variant on the cosy catastrophe – Istvan Csicsery-Ronay dubs it a '*petite apocalypse* [...] a bourgeois male hero [...] is separated from his family and surroundings by a monstrous intrusion into the familiar' (2009: 448) – which anticipates Ballard's *Crash* in its combination of technology and sexuality, as a yellow gas erodes sexual inhibitions as it spreads across England. The protagonist has repeated sexual encounters with women and men (including a priest), as he heads for safety in Scotland, and the erotic escapades and violence grow as the novel progresses. There is no escape, though: the novel ends with incest being taken as normal. Platt revised it for Savoy Books in 1980, the Manchester-based imprint, which had also published Delany's *The Tides of Lust* (1973; 1980), but unfortunately ongoing legal problems and police raids on the publisher limited distribution.

A society also falls apart in *The City Dwellers* (1970; revised as *Twilight of the City* 1977), through an odd combination of overcrowding and low birth rate. Each of the four sections is a distinct vignette and, as the second section is set in the countryside, not even the city itself becomes a continuous character throughout the novel. The opening is a near-future depiction of a rock music culture, with groupies and new sexual mores, which forms a contrast with the monogamy later enforced in the city. In order to increase economic efficiency, the population is herded into cities, but the consequent fall of quality of life is a contributing factor in a collapse in the birth rate, made worse by men outnumbering women by a factor of three to one. Raids then have to be organised to steal women from the small, scattered groups of individuals who have opted to live outside the civic centres. With no clear technological solution to the birth rate problem – and in the first section Jamieson is researching why some generations produce large families and some small, to no effect – the crash is inevitable and it seems will only accelerate.

In America, Harlan Ellison risked becoming better known for his editing than for his writing. He also worked in television, notably in the Canadian-filmed *The Starlost* (22 September 1973–5 January 1974), set on a generation starship, which was so altered in production that Ellison had his credit changed to Cordwainer Bird; his pilot episode was novelised with Edward Bryant as *Phoenix Without Ashes* (1975). 'A Boy and His Dog' (*New Words* April 1969) was adapted into a film by L.Q. Jones in 1975, adding a layer of misogyny not present in the original. Meanwhile, Ellison kept up a steady stream of short stories, and new collections brought works from the 1950s and 1960s back into print. He noted that his books were becoming 'less and less identifiable as anything like science fiction' (Fowler 1976: 17), admitting to elements of what he saw as fantasy. He aimed to write the stories he wanted to, and notes that many writers with literary aspirations – Disch, Moorcock, Spinrad, Kate Wilhelm, Barry Malzberg, George Alec Effinger and Ian Watson – were leaving sf for the mainstream, while Robert Silverberg was abandoning writing altogether. Meanwhile, he sees his own work as becoming more autobiographical in intent if not subject matter: 'my stories reflect my search for an understanding of myself, an examination of various elements of my persona' (Fowler 1976: 12). This produced many stories that seemed radical and some that seemed more conservative, both as angry reactions to the contemporary world. Ian Watson wrote that 'Ellison, staunch enemy of narrow-minded bigotry, WASPism, Moral Majorityism et cetera, is – let us whisper it – a Calvinistic moralist, or Jehovist moralist' (1982: 89). The eponymous protagonist of 'Knox' (*Crawdaddy* March 1974) has a name that points to the Scottish Calvinist, although here the first name is Charlie rather than John, and the character is someone who is struggling against his conditioning to kill those perceived as enemies of the state – whether by ethnicity or politics. Knox is one of the damned, rather than one of the Elect, and commits suicide; his wife Brenda, whom he had resisted killing, seems equally programmed in her own way. It is not clear that human nature can escape damnation. 'Shatterday' (*Gallery* September 1975) features Peter Jay Novins's encounter with his own alter ego, and his attempts to undermine him; the alter ego meanwhile claims he is the real and better Novins. Ellison notes that the story came from his own realisation that he wished his own mother would die, and how the parent–child relationship for him had reversed: 'I am, in effect, my own father' (Fowler 1976: 12). 'Jeffty Is Five' (*F&SF* July 1977) won both the Hugo and Nebula Awards, and focuses on a boy who remains at the age of five and is immersed in the culture of his childhood, while the narrator ages and notes the changing of the world. There is a sense of the greater authenticity of the past when compared to the present, a more innocent world than the present that is too easily dismissed as outdated; the story still risks having the nostalgia of a Ray Bradbury. This is undercut by the chronological complexities of the periodisation of Jeffty's and the narrator Donny's memories, which are articulated from a point in the 1970s. Ellen R. Weil argues that 'Donny is permitted to have Ellison's memories – and Ellison is permitted to speak with the voice of Donny' (1988: 32).

Barry N. Malzberg was very prolific as a novelist during the first half of the 1970s, but he announced his retirement from science fiction. He felt that he was 'was *invisible* outside of the confines of the market itself' (1976a: 106), but had not been able to break through into a non-genre medium. He felt rejection from both camps: 'Denied as a literary writer, loathed and largely isolated within s-f' (1976a: 107). According to Brian Stableford, 'a career in science fiction makes demands upon a writer which are, as far as he is concerned, intolerable' (1977a: 135). Malzberg had worked for the Scott Meredith Literary Agency from 1965 and had been an editor for both *Amazing Stories* (November 1968 and January 1969) and *Fantastic* (December 1968 and February 1969). Malzberg admits that science fiction 'allowed us to go as far as we wanted artistically for a while' (1976a: 108), but there were limits. Science fiction, he notes, is a series of narratives about technology and technological change, and too often the narratives offer a kind of consolation against future shock; Malzberg's novels are amphicatastrophic – he 'explores anxiety' (Stableford 1977a: 136).

Whereas typical sf narratives appeared to be psychological explorations that pose as technical problem-solving, Malzberg seems to suggest in his novels that these actions form an avoidance of real problems. The competent hero, who had been pioneered by Heinlein within the First sf tradition, has no place in Malzberg's work; in fact, his protagonists are 'usually unable to handle the problems that face them; [...] even the most basic problems of day-to-day living' (Layton 1991: 71), and these problems are often internalised problems, which remain unresolved. Malzberg's novels take up New Wave forms of fragmentation, offering 'fractured forms to represent fractured consciousness' (Layton 1991: 77). His novels shift in shape, in viewpoint, in tense, in certainty – his narrators are frequently unreliable, and rarely have the full picture of event. Typically downbeat is *Guernica Night* (1975) – named for Pablo Picasso's anti-war painting *Guernica* (1937), inspired by the horrors of the aerial bombing of Guernica during the Spanish Civil War – in which suicide is seen as the only sane option in a tightly ruled society. The young people who take up this option see suicide as the final trip, a term uncomfortably close to the 'Final Solution'; murder and suicide are uncomfortably close to each other in this scenario, with suicide in effect being murder by society.

The captain in *Beyond Apollo* (1972) – who may be called Joseph Jackson or Jack Josephson – might have committed suicide, or might have been murdered by the novel's narrator, Harold Evans. As Layton notes, Jack Josephson is a name which points to John F. Kennedy, the assassinated son of Joseph Kennedy, whose tragic death Malzberg repeatedly returns to as a New Wave-style iconic moment of what has gone wrong with America. In *The Destruction of the Temple* (1974), a director re-enacts the assassination for entertainment purposes. The novel's title invokes the Jewish temples in Jerusalem, the first destroyed in 586 BCE when the Jews were exiled, and the second, built on the same site, destroyed by the Romans in 70 CE. Abraham Zapruder, who filmed the Kennedy motorcade, is a saint in *The Sodom and Gomorrah Business* (1974), as an unnamed narrator and his friend Lawson go into a decaying New York city in search of women, having rejected the compulsory homosexuality of student life, only for the narrator to rape a woman. A New York gang captures the two, with Lawson being killed and the narrator recruited to the gang's aims by being forced into heterosexual intercourse in their harem. In *Scop* (1976), the eponymous protagonist is convinced that his world of 2040 is the result of the assassinations of John Kennedy, Robert F. Kennedy and Martin Luther King, and keeps time-travelling to witness and, perhaps, prevent their violent deaths. At the same time, the novel appears to suggest that Scop has actually been the assassin – as one Lee Harvey Os*bourn*, the shift of name suggesting either an alternative reality or more unreliability on the part of a narrator. That Scop is castigated for what he has been trained to do suggests how society is rigged: 'the individual is punished for acting as the society earlier has conditioned him' (Tidmarsh 1977: 152). *The Last Transaction* (1977) is the purported autobiography of an American president, sandwiched between a *Who's Who*-style biography and a posthumous summation; the president has ended up in the role by accident, because no one else wanted to face the curse of presidents elected on a twenty-year cycle: William Henry Harrison (died in office 1841), Abraham Lincoln (assassinated 1865), James A. Garfield (assassinated 1881), William McKinley (assassinated 1901), Warren G. Harding (died in office 1923), Franklin D. Roosevelt (died in office 1945) and Kennedy (assassinated 1963). Malzberg is not the only writer of the 1970s to invoke 22 November 1963; Wilson Tucker's time travellers consider visiting that day (as well as that of the crucifixion) in *The Year of the Quiet Sun* (1970), and it is a branching point for events between two alternative universes in Gregory Benford's *Timescape* (1980).

Games as rigged activities are central to a number of Malzberg's novels – Tidmarsh argues that 'Malzberg stacks the odds against success' (1977: 153), but we tend to forget the role of author as puppeteer and locate the cheating in the hands of enemy aliens or faceless human bureaucracies. In *Overlay* (1972), an alien is engaged upon a plot to destroy the Earth by driving four losers to despair, which seems to be something that there is no way of countermanding – as Stableford notes, 'The odds, as every punter knows, are loaded' (1977a: 141). An overlay is a price offered on a given result that would pay more than the true odds, which is likely to be a manipulation of the fair results. In *The Day of the Burning* (1974), a welfare bureaucrat, George Mercer, who has been forced to ask impossible questions of his clients, has been given the task of persuading the Galactic Overlords that Earth is worthy of joining the Galactic Federation – if he fails the planet faces destruction. In *Tactics of Conquest* (1974), the future of Earth is played out in a game of chess of which we know the result, and it is not at all clear which result is the one which will benefit Earth. The consequences of winning or losing are never entirely clear, nor is it certain that these are in fact the only possible outcomes. The narrative continues through an alphabetical glossary of chess terms, beyond the apparently final checkmate.

The New Wave writers express a pessimism about the world that is very different from the feel of First sf; some problems are not surmountable, irrespective of technological development. As Aldiss characterises it, 'the New Wave was anti-technological and anti-power orientated, with a resulting powerful release of libido. Significantly, while the New Waves paid due tribute to their more illustrious hard sf predecessors, the technocrats could find no good in what was new: it had dirty words, guys did dirty things to girls, people went to bed instead of to Mars. The technocrats felt themselves threatened' (1978b: 10). The death of the young president Kennedy in 1963 – a president associated with Camelot, and later to be suspected of various affairs – showed how optimism could crash, and he was the one who, on 25 May 1961, had promised to put a man on the moon by the end of the 1960s. New technology was not liberating, was not solving problems, but instead alienated the individual and led to a new sense of estrangement: future shock. In 1976, Malzberg suggested that there was '[no] future. Perhaps no future for writing in our time' (1976a: 107). It is unsurprising that some of the writers left the genre, or ended up writing about the present day. There was a real sense that there were invisible forces at work, that the game of life was rigged – and that entropy, chaos and disaster would always win. The Apollo moon landings should have been the coming of age of sf – and in many ways they were, as the optimism about the capabilities of humanity proved to be well-founded. But the motives for going to the moon were not pure, and there could only be one first time. The New Wave, especially in the work of Ballard, offers journeys into inner rather than outer space, and Malzberg, among others, sees little difference between the two. By the end of the 1970s, however, space opera would return and become more popular than ever before. The pessimism about heroes would be reversed.

# 3
# Beyond Apollo:
# Space Fictions after the Moon Landing

Millions of viewers had watched the footage of Neil Armstrong stepping onto the moon on 20 July 1969, an event that marked the climax of the space race. The physicist Gerard K. O'Neill notes: 'Apollo was begun at a time when the mood of the nation was vastly different from now [1976]: then we had confidence in our abilities, we saw our living standards increasing rapidly, our money was sound and we did not yet see limits to our continued growth' (1978: 128). John F. Kennedy's assassination on 22 November 1963 meant Apollo lost its champion – his successor, Lyndon Baines Johnson, had to continue the programme in homage to his predecessor. Richard Nixon, elected in 1968 and in office in 1969, had no such burden, and was overseeing what had become an expensive land war in Vietnam in addition to other financial problems. O'Neill argues: 'The late 1960s and 1970s [became] a time of disillusion, of slow economic growth coupled with inflation, and of living standards improving only slowly. [… We] passed through a distrust of anything technological' (1978: 128). The moon landing was undeniably an American triumph, but repetition dulled the spectacle. *Apollo 12* reached the moon on 19 November, but *Apollo 13* in April 1970 was nearly a disaster as equipment failed. The days of the programme were numbered. Joe Haldeman recalls: 'After the first couple of moon shots, Americans were pretty blasé; NBC were showered with complaints when it dared interrupt the Super Bowl to show two clowns walking around on the Moon' (1993: 156–57). *Apollo 17* was the last manned trip in November 1972. Having won a propaganda battle against the Soviets, there was no economic benefit to space travel. A staffed, orbiting satellite, *Skylab*, was launched on 14 May 1973, but abandoned less than a year later; it was allowed to fall back into Earth's atmosphere in July 1979. The wasteful, expensive Saturn V launchers, which propelled the Apollo lunar landing modules, needed to be replaced by a more economic vehicle, but the first space shuttle mission did not take place until

12 April 1981, and the mixture of scientific and military demands compromised its design. Haldeman blames Nixon's hostility to Kennedy's legacy: 'The deficiencies of the shuttle are largely the result of Nixonian parsimony' (1993: 153).

If the public had tired of space travel in the early 1970s, sf had been increasingly sceptical since the days of *Sputnik*. Clute argued that 'the beginning of the Space Age [w]as a turning point, a point beyond which the quasi-organic conversation of American sf – for the moment let me call it First SF – began to ramble, and to lose the thread of the story' (1995: 9). In narrative terms, the success of Apollo and various planetary probes closed down possibilities for fiction. The solar system was revealed to be a hostile environment, largely inimical to life, and it was no longer feasible to recount the building of a backyard spaceship or the corporate or governmental struggles to set up a space mission. Simply putting a human on the moon was no longer enough to sustain a science-fiction novel. This chapter will discuss several of Barry Malzberg's novels, but tellingly the focus is on television and film – the dangers of space and space missions in *Solaris* (Andrei Tarkovsky, 1971), *Moonbase 3* (9 September–14 October 1973), *Dark Star* (John Carpenter, 1974), *The Incredible Melting Man* (William Sachs, 1977), scepticism about the space programme in *Alternative 3* (20 June 1977) and *Capricorn One* (Peter Hyams, 1978), adventure narratives *UFO* (1970–73), *Space: 1999* (4 September 1975–7 May 1978) and *Star Trek: The Motion Picture* (Robert Wise, 1979), a dark space opera, *Blake's 7* (2 January 1978–21 December 1981) and the rather less sombre *Battlestar Galactica* (17 September 1978–29 April 1979), *Galactica 1980* (27 January 1980–4 May 1980), *Buck Rogers* (20 September 1979–16 April 1981) and *Scontri Stellari Oltre la Terza Dimensione* (*Starcrash* (Lewis Coates, 1979)). The estrangements of space give way to a flexible series of exotic locations for drama.

Barry Malzberg's works explore astronauts' psyches, depicting them fighting as much for their mental as for their physical health, alienated by their training and the technology – as in many works of Robert Sheckley, alien environments have an estranging impact on humans. *The Falling Astronauts* (1971) centres on Richard Martin, whose panic attacks have led to his suspension from flying duties. When a new mission starts to go wrong, he wants to tell everyone the truth about what is going on, but the public is no longer interested in space flight. *Revelations* (1972) features a television chat show whose host, Marvin Martin, attempts to assassinate the reputations of his guests, including Walter Monaghan, who supposedly walked on the moon. Monaghan wants to confess that the Apollo missions were faked. Malzberg clearly saw astronauts as little better than cargo, whose heroism facilitated the space programme's attempt to distract the public from the Vietnam War; the winding down of the war in the 1970s meant that the missions were surplus to requirements. *Beyond Apollo* (1972) completes a thematic trilogy, as astronaut Harold Evans is debriefed – interrogated, in fact – about the possible murder of the captain of a Venus mission. While one explanation for the murder is homosexual panic, this is one of several excuses; it might be that the captain committed suicide. But 'all that happens is tentative at the story level and may not have happened' (Layton 1991: 75), and so even the need for an explanation is to be questioned. The novel's undecidability annoyed some readers, including Bob Shaw, who said it was 'the epitome of everything that has gone wrong with science fiction in the last ten years or so' (1975b: 67). The novel's anti-space theme makes it ironic that it won the John W. Campbell Memorial Award. Shaw suggests that it peddles the New Wave lie that 'venturing into space induces insanity' (1975b: 69). On the other hand, Joanna Russ hailed it as 'a passionate, fine, completely realized work' (1973a: 30).

Similar themes feature in other Malzberg novels about space travel. In *The Day of the Burning* (1974), there is the suspicion that the Venus mission wastes money that could be better spent on improving conditions on Earth. *On a Planet Alien* (1974) satirises the narratives of planetary societies joining federations – a theme shared with *The Day of the Burning*. Hans Folsom captains a mission to an alien planet, named Folsom's Planet in an act of imperialistic appropriation, and his aim is to bring knowledge to the natives. Folsom becomes doubtful about his actions, and whether his crew is carrying out his instructions; by the end of the novel he even considers that they have somehow gone back in time to help human evolution. In this novel it is not clear whether space has driven him mad – the space agency training has clearly been inadequate on a metaphysical level – or whether some alien defence mechanism is at work on his consciousness.

*Solaris*, a loose adaptation of Stanisław Lem's novel (1961), is a grimy vision of the future, in which psychologist Kris Kelvin (Donatos Banionis) is assigned to the spaceship orbiting the mysterious ocean world of Solaris. As Stacey Abbott observes, Kelvin 'finds a lived-in environment, not overly laden with technology and scientific apparatus but rather cluttered with debris and rubbish, reflecting the disoriented psychological state of the cosmonauts. The *mise en scène* is more concerned with inner psychology than an imagined future' (2009: 464). These humans are not in their proper places and are accompanied by supposedly dead people. Solaris seems to be generating solid incarnations of loved ones from people's minds – in Kelvin's case Hari (Natalya Bondarchuk), his former wife. His response is to kill her, but she reappears. If this is a telepathic construction of Hari, then she must be his idealised vision of her, one coloured by other emotions around his perceptions of her, rather than the genuine article. Many of Tarkovsky's films are concerned with memories of loved ones and family members, the past haunting the present as a preferable period: 'Each [film] sets a quotidian world, grey, monological, and violent, against an anti-world which is dynamic, malleable, and full of colour, the dominion of possibility and of choice' (Salvestroni 1987: 294). The boundaries between the worlds are porous, however, giving something of a dream quality. Kelvin returns to Earth, to the dacha once owned by his now-dead father, where he kneels at the feet of someone we take to be his father, in a re-enactment of Rembrandt's painting *The Return of the Prodigal Son* (1669). The vision is an oddly conservative looking back and commemoration of patriarchy and home – very much at odds with the Western fetish of youth of the era, but then Kelvin is a distinctly middle-aged cosmonaut. The camera pulls back, to reveal that the dacha is on an island in the mists of Solaris. The reality of what we have seen is questionable within the context of the film, indeed we cannot be certain that any of the scenes set on Earth are to be taken as real. Tarkovsky offers no answers, preferring simply to use the estrangements of space as another way of exploring the estrangements of time; this is a moment of Todorovian fantastic.

Between seasons ten and eleven of *Doctor Who* (23 November 1963–), as the long-running series emerged from several years of largely Earth-bound adventures, producer Barry Letts and script editor Terrance Dicks created and produced a distinctly realist series – *Moonbase 3* – even if a central British role in a European venture seemed unlikely. The UK's Act of Accession to Europe was dated 22 January 1972, marked by Brian Hayles's script for *Doctor Who*, 'The Curse of Peladon' (29 January–19 February 1972), which depicted a planet's ambivalence about joining a federation (although Nicholas Whyte has suggested there are as many resonances with the political situation in Northern Ireland (Whyte 2006)). The BBC science correspondent, James Burke, acted as an advisor for the *Moonbase 3* series, giving it a veneer of scientific realism, and the central characters were new director David Caulder (Donald Houston), security officer Michel LeBrun (Ralph Bates), chief engineer Tom Hill (Barry Lowe) and psychologist – and token female – Dr Helen Smith (Fiona Gaunt). Each week the characters faced a problem which required a technological or psychological solution, in the context of the mission's limited budget. Caulder had no illusions about the dangers they all faced: 'Out there is a remorseless, implacable enemy; the most hostile environment Man has ever met. Now we must fight it together.' The laws of physics, the nature of a vacuum, the shift in gravity and the scarcity of oxygen, water and other resources make the moonscape itself an antagonist, without the need for human saboteurs, let alone hostile aliens. While there were moments of genuine tension – in one episode it seems likely that ace astronaut Hill will die in a space capsule – the pace was a little slow and, despite some good special effects, the series felt a little studio-bound and mundane. The series' aesthetic prevented the introduction of monsters and other aliens, and the location was limiting. There was no second series.

Space was also threatening, and spaceships dirty, in *Dark Star*, expanded from John Carpenter's student project filmed at the University of Southern California and co-written with Dan O'Bannon – who went on to work on *Alien* (Ridley Scott, 1979), which maintained the world-weary attitudes of astronauts. Carpenter admired the small, close-knit groups of men he saw in many of the films of Howard Hawks, but the lazy, bickering, untidy slobs of campus living in *Dark Star* are very different in tone. Doolittle (Brian Narelle), Talby (Andrejiah Pahich) and Boiler (Carl Kuniholm) are jaded and bored, they have heard each other's stories and jokes too many times, whereas their captain, Powell (Joe Sanders), is in suspended animation after an accident. Their lives are made even less bearable by the presence of an alien, basically a beach ball with hands and feet, which causes chaos when it escapes. Whereas the computer HAL in *2001* and the android Ash in *Alien* are a threat to the astronauts because of their programming, here a problem is posed by the existential musings of an artificially intelligent bomb, which jams in the *Dark Star*'s bomb bay and insists on exploding.

The low-budget film *The Incredible Melting Man* shows the impact of a space mission on its astronauts. A ship in orbit around Saturn is struck by solar flares, which kills one astronaut and leaves the other, Steve West (Alex Rebar), hospitalised with extreme burns. His face is continually melting and he has been driven mad by his experiences. West escapes from his hospital bed and kills anyone who crosses his path. The film rapidly mutates into a hybrid of the *Frankenstein* (1818) narrative, in which a scientific creation, mistreated and abandoned by its creator, seeks revenge, and the slasher sub-genre, soon to be formalised by *Halloween* (John Carpenter, 1978), in which the past victim of a community's crime seeks increasingly bloody revenge upon that society. West kills both innocent bystanders and friends and relatives, before the climactic fight at an industrial refinery; this generic element stands in for the military-industrial complex that is held to be responsible for the perversion of good science into bad. No one has learned from the disaster, with the truth of West's death being lied about, and another mission to Saturn is launched, suggesting that history may be repeated. In the aftermath of the Watergate cover-up, it was easy to believe in government conspiracies, and that the public were not being told the truth. Journalism had fed the public's scepticism; Bob Woodward and Carl Bernstein had pursued Richard Nixon for the *Washington Post*, as seen in *All the President's Men* (Alan J. Pakula, 1976). This does, however, need to be balanced by a new version of *The Front Page* (Billy Wilder, 1974), which had shown the pressures on truth thanks to the need for a scoop, and *Network* (Sidney Lumet, 1976), which had dramatised media manipulation, taking a pot-shot at the cynicism of television.

Rumours about the Apollo missions being faked had been circulating since the late 1960s, part of an ongoing suspicion of the American administration. There was some disbelief at the speed with which the US had moved from satellites to human missions. The quality of the footage, the state of the flag planted on the moon, the absence of stars from photographs, the odd shadows and horizon and the length of delays in earth–lunar communications were all taken as evidence that the landings were faked, presumably to aid a propaganda war against the Soviets. Such conspiracies explain a scene in *Diamonds Are Forever* (Guy Hamilton, 1971), where James Bond (Sean Connery) runs through a Hollywood set for a moon landing and steals a moon buggy; this might be where the landings were allegedly staged. Bill Kaysing's *We Never Went to the Moon* (1974) implied that the Apollo programme was about ensuring a constant flow of money to NASA and other agencies and corporations. Don Wilson's *Our Mysterious Spaceship Moon* (1975), a title which echoes the Spaceship Earth of speeches by the US Ambassador to the United Nations, Adlai Stevenson, and engineer Buckminster Fuller in 9 July 1965 and 16 October 1967 respectively, suggested that the regularity of the satellite's orbit, of a size and distance to offer perfect eclipses, was part of the evidence that the moon was in fact artificial, a huge spaceship left in a parking orbit. George H. Leonard's *Someone Else is on Our Moon* (1977) supposedly analysed moon photographs featuring odd crash patterns on craters and marks which looked like tyre tracks, suggesting that this was evidence for alien life. Such conspiracies were exploited and added to by *Alternative 3*, an Anglian regional production for ITV in Britain, which purported to be a documentary about a brain drain of scientists – these apparently were becoming part of a Russo-American attempt to ensure the survival of humanity after the coming ecological crisis. The apparent solution was a Mars base, supposedly established in the early 1960s. The original planned broadcast date of 1 April 1977 would have revealed it as a spoof, but this did not stop some people from claiming the programme to be true, with subsequent denials only adding to their beliefs. The lack of any repeat of the programme, as well as its failure to be picked up by American broadcasters, just offered more positive evidence.

*Capricorn One* is a conspiracy thriller based upon the premise that NASA would be more willing to fake a mission to Mars than risk the public failure of such a project. However, the fact that the audience is aware of the confidence trick from the start limits the sense of paranoia. The narrative divides between three astronauts – Charles Brubaker (James Brolin), Peter Willis (Sam Waterson) and John Walker (O.J. Simpson) and a journalist, Robert Caulfield (Elliott Gould). The conspiracy widens as each person Caulfield talks to vanishes, and his own life is destroyed. The astronauts, meanwhile, have been blackmailed into going along with the charade for fear that their families will be harmed; soon they realise that they cannot be allowed to return to their everyday lives and are likely to die in the faked return to Earth. The communications between ship and Earth seem particularly poorly handled, with insufficient time delay – either by the fictional version of NASA or by Hyams – and seem enough to reveal the hoax. In the end, such conspiracies depend upon the notion that the tendrils of the secret services and other agencies are sufficient to trace all the conspirators and preventing any information from leaking out, but that they cannot put a human on the moon. In *Revelations* and his other anti-space novels, Malzberg anticipated that such deceit would depend on astronauts behaving like machines, going along with the publicity ethos. One moment they had to appear as clinical engineers, the next they had to be poetic heroes.

Space stations and moonbases were battlegrounds in the twenty-six episodes of ITV drama *UFO* (1970–73), described by Baird Searles as 'competent and non-inane' (1973: 103). Co-creator Gerry Anderson, his then wife Sylvia Anderson and producer Reg Hill had spent much of the 1960s making children's sf with marionettes, such as *Thunderbirds* (1964–65) and *Captain Scarlet and the Mysterons* (1967–68), for Lew Grade's ITC, associated with the ATV franchise of the ITV network. After a live action film, *Doppelgänger* (aka *Journey to the Far Side of the Sun* (Robert Parrish) 1969), Anderson filmed *UFO* at the MGM studios in Borehamwood. It features an international, quasi-military organisation – SHADO (Strategic Hidden Alien Defence Organisation) – with ground vehicles, a submarine that could launch planes, an armed moonbase, an early-warning satellite and a secret base under a fully functioning film studio (Borehamwood), defending Earth against a mysterious species of aliens who are apparently kidnapping humans to harvest their organs. While the series draws on elements of Anderson's children's programmes, its characters smoke in offices, submarines, space bases and hospitals, take drugs, commit adultery, and do not always succeed. Commander Ed Straker (Ed Bishop) was the one constant figure, as instigator and leader of SHADO. Captain Paul Foster (Michael Billington) is a second action figure, initially investigating his own close encounter with an alien craft and often viewed with suspicion by the authorities. Straker's right-hand man, Colonel Alec Freeman (George Sewell), is stolid and dependable, although in early episodes is seen eyeing female security officers and secretaries. The aliens themselves are kept low-key – Foster befriends one in 'Survival' – with episodes devoted as much to the cover-up of aliens as to defending Earth from them; in 'The Square Triangle' an alien is mistaken for a cuckolded husband and murdered by an adulterous couple, and the husband is eventually killed as well. In one rather postmodern episode, 'The Mindbombs', Straker finds himself as an actor in an sf series being filmed at the studio. There were nods towards sexual equality – a minor female character, Colonel Virginia Lake (Wanda Ventham), is promoted to replace Freeman after the actor left in a filming hiatus, although many of the women were in effect receptionists. Straker's insistence on the lack of racial discrimination is not matched in hiring policies for crew. The tough decisions Straker has to make anticipate the growing lack of public trust in authority, and the tone was sufficiently dark that a second series was not commissioned.

Instead, ITC wanted to make the moonbase and space sequences more central to the series. A new format, *Space: 1999* emerged, in which a nuclear explosion on the moon propels the satellite, and Moonbase Alpha, into deep space, away from the Earth. For the second series, Fred Freiberger, one of the producers of *Star Trek* (8 September 1966–3 June 1969), was brought in to try to increase the programme's appeal to the American audience. Some of the more philosophical aspects were dropped, and the amount of action increased. The ensemble of actors resembles the *Star Trek* crew, although there are a few more women in the regular cast than had been the case with the American show. The central roles for Martin Landau (Commander John Koenig), Barbara Bain (Dr Helena Russell) and Barry Morse (Professor Victor Bergman) were also designed by executive Lew Grade to sell the series to a USA network. This attempt failed, although individual stations did show episodes. Alan Frank argues that 'the scripts were banal [… and] the leading characters were dull and uninteresting, falling back on stock stereotypes and emotional clichés so that they never became alive in any sense or were able to transcend their material' (1978: 85). M. Keith Booker suggests that the format left the characters 'without any real mission and left the series without any real point' (2004: 80). A third series was planned, but budgetary cuts and falling ratings doomed a concept aesthetically stranded in mid-Atlantic.

*Star Trek* itself had been cancelled in 1969, but had continued in syndication. The production of a film was mooted when creator Gene Roddenberry suggested it at the 1968 Worldcon, initially as a prequel to the television series. A continuation, *Star Trek: The Animated Series* (8 September 1973–12 October 1974), was made by Filmation, with most of the original regular cast voicing their roles. Chris Bryant and Allan Scott, who had co-written *Don't Look Now* (Nicolas Roeg, 1973), wrote a film treatment 'Planet of the Titans' in 1975, but in 1977 the heavily revised script was abandoned in favour of going back to *Star Trek: Phase II*, for which Alan Dean Foster wrote a two-hour pilot, 'In Thy Image', about a starship returning to Earth in search of its creator, and Theodore Sturgeon, Norman Spinrad and Richard Bach were commissioned to write episodes. The project was stalled by the cancellation of Paramount's plans for a television network that was to have broadcast it. Eventually, spurred by the success of *Star Wars* and *Close Encounters of the Third Kind* (Steven Spielberg, 1977), the first of a number of films, *Star Trek: The Motion Picture*, was produced, with a plot based upon the return of V'ger, one of the Voyager probes, sent by NASA to explore the solar system in a grand tour in the 1970s – two had been launched in 1977, and the *Voyager 1* fly-by of Jupiter was in early 1979. Retrofitted and enhanced, the probe thinks that humans are an infestation of the Earth's environment and believes they deserve to be destroyed.

The narrative has to be expanded to fill a cinema screen, for example in a long, slow sequence of Admiral Kirk (William Shatner) being taken across to the refitted *Enterprise* by Scotty (James Doohan). This establishes the sheer scale of the ship, with the duration of the journey fetishising the white metal tubes and curves of a feminised spaceship. The narrative is broken-backed, the first half concerned with getting the old crew back together again, with Spock (Leonard Nimoy) the last to join, having returned to Vulcan. The second half of the film starts with the restoration of the warp engines, announced by the original series' signature tune by Alexander Courage, rather than the new Jerry Goldsmith theme. Kirk winks, ostensibly at Chekov (Walter Koenig) but actually breaking the fourth wall and acknowledging the audience.

An Oedipal triangle is established on the *Enterprise* – Kirk battles for supremacy with the new captain, Willard Decker (Stephen Collins), gaining mutual respect as they trade wisecracks, and the Deltan crewmember Lt Ilya (Persis Khambatta), coded simultaneously as celibate and sensual, becomes a point of rivalry between them. V'ger, with its surrounding cloud, its matrix of virtual civilisations and its series of irised entry points, is coded as feminine and childlike, needing to be penetrated by masculinist military might. Christine Cornea links this to the sex roles debates of the period: 'the crew [...] successfully re-territorialise or take back their space. [... The imagery is] strongly encoded as feminine and the narrative crises that these images are associated with seems to suggest that it was a feminine force that caused not only the aesthetic and narrative shifts within the genre itself but also the destabilising events of recent history' (2007: 96). Aside from Ilya, it is the men that act – Uhura (Nichelle Nicholls) remains little more than receptionist, and Dr Christine Chapel (Majel Barrett) has a traditional nurturing role, despite her promotion from nurse. In the end, emotion – love and sacrifice – triumphs over logic, even for V'ger, and the probe vanishes into space. The original crew gather together on the bridge and head out into space, in imitation of the original five-year mission.

In Britain, the BBC1 adventure space opera *Blake's 7* inverted *Star Trek*'s Federation: *Blake's 7*'s Federation was a totalitarian power structure, making slaves of various planetary societies and designating any dissidents as criminal. Sue Jenkins argues that *Star Trek*'s Federation is 'voluntary, benevolent, egalitarian, and in principle pacific, [whereas] *Blake's Seven* [*sic*] exists against a background of corrupt totalitarianism, militaristic, imperialistic and oppressive' (1982: 43). If *Star Trek* was *Wagon Train* to the stars, then this was *The Dirty Dozen* (Robert Aldrich, 1967). The initial protagonist, Roj Blake (Gareth Thomas), who gives his name to the series, wishes to expose and bring down the corruption of the administration, and is then arrested on trumped-up charges of treason. While in transit, Blake escapes with fellow prisoners, Kerr Avon (Paul Darrow) and Vila Restal (Michael Keating), acquiring an alien spaceship that they call the *Liberator*. As Jenkins notes, the difference in sentiment between *Enterprise* and *Liberator* is striking. One is a vessel for a group of people who see themselves as benign agents of a colonial power; the other contains a loose band of individuals who are fighting against the genocidal agents of a colonial power. The tensions of the narratives then grow from Blake's desire to attack the Federation and find resources that will help their mission, and his associates' wish to preserve and enrich themselves. Vila's repeated cowardice is a problem, as is Avon's resentment of Blake's assumption of authority. Meanwhile, they are pursued and repeatedly trapped by Travis (in series one played by Steven Greif, in series two by Brian Croucher), who is obsessively tracking them on behalf of Federation president Servalan (Jacqueline Pearce). The characters can achieve no more than minor victories because of the need to sustain the ongoing Federation story arc; in some episodes the characters are lucky to escape with their lives. Brian Aldiss, discussing British sf in general, notes that

[it] is American sf which confronts us with the alien personalised. There are probably historical reasons for this – white and black Americans being themselves aliens in a red land – but whatever the reasons, the effect is generally to make us (the Earthmen) goodies and the intruders baddies. Much drama is to be had from confrontations but it is surely more sophisticated as well as better theology to recognise evil within ourselves rather than as an external phenomenon. Pretending otherwise leads to the limp pastoral of *Startrek* [sic], where half a dozen sexless saints go forth and impose American diplomacy on a naughty galaxy. (1978b: 11)

In *Star Trek* the only heroic deaths tended to be those of newly introduced security officers; in *Blake's 7* no character was safe. Strongman Olag Gan (David Jackson) was first to be written out, and at the end of the second series Blake was separated from the rest of the characters in the chaos of 'Star One' (3 April 1979), only to reappear at the climax of the fourth series, 'Blake' (21 December 1981). Characters were venial, self-serving, petty and selfish, very far from the mutually supportive crew of the Enterprise. Everyone had their price.

Avon seemed to develop a love/hate relationship with Servalan, possibly playing both sides of the struggle, possibly furthering the revolution. Jenkins suggests that he is a more extreme version of *Star Trek*'s Spock, with Blake's Kirk being replaced in narrative function by Del Tarrant (Steven Pacey): 'equally brilliant, efficient, logical and, incidentally, physically courageous' (1982: 44). But Avon is avaricious and cruel, in a way that Spock never was. Jenkins notes the extreme distinction in mood between a series conceived at the start of the utopian 1960s and one playing out at the end of the dystopian 1970s: 'events in the real world have slid rapidly in entirely the opposite direction to that envisaged by Roddenberry' (1982: 45). In 1966, contemporary social and sexual mores limited female characters to little more than receptionists; a decade later a woman could portray a Thatcher-like, cold-hearted villain. In some ways it was not a particularly impressive advance, but it made a change from passive characters.

The series was developed and its first season was written by Terry Nation, creator of the Daleks for *Doctor Who* and the post-viral apocalypse drama, *Survivors* (16 April 1975–8 June 1977). However, his influence waned, and only six episodes were to follow with his by-line. Chris Boucher was script editor for the whole series and scripted the final episode, 'Blake', apparently killing almost all of the surviving characters in a shoot-out. He had also worked on *Doctor Who*, writing 'The Face of Evil' (1–22 January

1977), which introduced the character of Leela (Louise Jameson), the following serial, 'The Robots of Death' (29 January–19 February 1977), whose featuring of violent strangulation was controversial in a series for a family audience, and 'Image of the Fendahl' (29 October–19 November 1977), which also contains violence from Leela and more brutal attacks on the Doctor. David Maloney, producer of the first three series, had directed some of *Doctor Who*, and directed three *Blake's 7* episodes. The final series was produced by Vere Lorrimer; in a prolific career, he had directed sixty episodes of *Dixon of Dock Green* (9 July 1955–1 May 1976), one of *Doomwatch* (9 February 1970–14 August 1972), as well as a dozen episodes of *Blake's 7*.

*Blake's 7* overlapped with three further American space operas: *Battlestar Galactica*, *Buck Rogers* and *Galactica 1980*, all developed by Glen A. Larson. In *Battlestar*, first released as a theatrical film outside the USA in July 1978, then shown on ABC, the twelve colony worlds of humanity have been in a lengthy war with the robotic Cylons. The survivors come together in a convoy that goes in search of Earth. Individual episodes then document this quest and the ongoing Cylon attacks. M. Keith Booker notes that it 'quickly grows repetitive' (2004: 88), and indeed parts of the footage are used repeatedly. Central to the series are the wise Commander Adama (Lorne Greene), his character name suggesting Adam, the first man, and his son Captain Apollo (Richard Hatch), suggesting the sun-god, who becomes a foster-father to the child Boxey (Noah Hathaway). Apollo's best friend is the womanising and apparently parentless Lieutenant Starbuck (Dirk Benedict), whose name echoes that of the mate of the *Pequod* in Herman Melville's *Moby-Dick* (1851), but may also have been inspired by a space pirate, Elon Cody Starbuck, in comic book writer Howard Chaykin's *Star*Reach* (1974). John Dykstra, who had worked on *Star Wars*, designed some of the special effects and there was a strong sense that the series was rather too close to that film. 20th Century Fox sued Universal for plagiarism on behalf of Lucas, but Universal noted that *Star Wars* had drawn on a number of sources, including the Buck Rogers serial and comics. Colin Greenland describes *Battlestar Galactica* as 'sf twice removed, so thin you can see through it' (1980a: 36). He objects to the clarity of the stakes, the heroes and villains, the suspicion of peace and creation of a fictional alien other. In particular, he worries at 'the ease with which this particular mean and hostile [patriotic] myth can be remobilised after fifteen years' rust[, …] put in a cheap and shoddy vehicle and sent trundling through the stars' (1980a: 37). The series was cancelled, following declining ratings, although it was briefly rebooted as *Galactica 1980*, in which Adama tries to lead the Cylons away from the rediscovered Earth.

The success of *Star Wars* inspired NBC to develop a pilot of *Buck Rogers in the 25th Century* (Daniel Haller, 1979), which, edited, became the first part of a television series of the same name. The character had first appeared as Anthony Rogers, a war veteran who wanders into a cloud of radioactive gas and wakes up over four hundred years later, in Philip Francis Nowlan's 'Armageddon – 2419 AD' (*Amazing* August 1928), and was featured in further magazine adventures, plus newspaper cartoons, syndicated from 7 January 1929 as *Buck Rogers in the 25th Century A.D.*, a radio series (1932–47), a twelve-part movie serial, *Buck Rogers* (Ford Beebe and Saul A. Goodkind, 1939), starring Buster Crabbe, and an ABC television serial (15 April 1950–30 January 1951). Perhaps unsurprisingly, the character had clearly interested George Lucas, who used a clip from the serial as a prologue to *THX 1138* (1971). In the 1970s television series, Buck Rogers (Gil Gerard) is an American shuttle astronaut who returns to a post-nuclear holocaust Earth, several hundred years after being accidentally frozen. Alongside Colonel Wilma Deering (Erin Gray), and under the command of Dr Elias Hauer (Tim O'Connor), Rogers attempts to protect Earth from various external threats. Rogers succeeds where the regular space force fails, because he has a natural talent rather than being dependent upon computerised strategy. He also displays an unreconstructed masculinity that is alternately found annoying and refreshing by the twenty-fifth century. The series featured Mel Blanc – who had voiced Daffy Duck and Bugs Bunny for Warner Bros. – voicing 'the comic chattering robot, Twiki' (Booker 2004: 90), the comic relief robot having become obligatory in America space opera (although *Doctor Who* had K9).

Larson was not the only person to try to ape the Star Wars saga – in Italy the abysmal *Scontri Stellari Oltre la Terza Dimensione* (*Starcrash* (Lewis Coates, 1979)) mixed *Star Wars* with Ray Harryhausen-style stop motion animation and visual styles from *Barbarella* (Roger Vadim, 1968), as smugglers Stella Star (Caroline Monro) and Akton (Marjoe Gortner) are inexplicably drawn into an attempt by the Emperor (Christopher Plummer) to find his lost son Simon (David Hasselhoff) and defeat the evil Count Zarth Arn (Joe Spinell). The blockbusters with budgets that followed *Star Wars* were all too serious, and lack most of the doubts of the characters in the works discussed in this chapter. But above all – and *Scontri* followed in a line which included *Star Wars* and *Alien* – the opening shot of a seemingly endless, rumbling spaceship became a staple of the genre. But it was the look that these blockbusters took from Agenda sf: space was simply a setting for action adventure, rather than the venue for extrapolation. The psychological investigations of New Wave sf were largely ignored in film.

# 4
# Big Dumb Objects:
# Science Fiction as Self-Parody

At one point the characters in Michael Coney's *Charisma* (1975) compare their situation to earlier sf: 'Straight out of H.G. Wells, eh? You ever read Wells, Alan?' Alan has, and admits, 'The man had quite an imagination, in his day. [...] It was good stuff, once. Reads a bit slow, now' (1975: 13). In this chapter, I will examine sf that engages with precursors to the Gernsback–Campbell continuum: Mary Shelley (Brian Aldiss and a number of films), H. G. Wells (Aldiss, again, film adaptations and sequels or rewritings by Manley Wade Wellman and Wade Wellman, George H. Smith, K. W. Jeter and Christopher Priest) and Jules Verne (Michael Moorcock). The nineteenth-century writers had been active during the period of European imperialism, with the scramble for Africa and an exploitation of South East Asia and Oceania. European privilege had assumed that the rest of the world offered them exploitable resources and the slave trade redistributed populations with implications to this day. European colonialism was in decline during the 1970s, while American neo-colonialism was in evidence. Some of these writers addressed the political assumptions of imperialism. One means of doing so was through the imagining of a colossal novum, a recurrent trope that has been labelled the Big Dumb Object (Kaveney 1981: 25) – especially in novels by Larry Niven, Arthur C. Clarke, Bob Shaw, Christopher Priest, Frederik Pohl, Philip José Farmer, Douglas Adams and Terry Pratchett – whose vast scale ensures that sf teeters on the edge of self-parody. This produces sf that is in part about sf.

Many candidates have been suggested for the first sf narrative, at one extreme classical myths and works by Plato, Homer, Ovid or Lucian of Samosata for a long history of a mode, at the other the pulp magazines of editors such as Gernsback for a generic history. Aldiss's *Billion Year Spree* (1973) offered a *literary* account in which sf's ur-text was Mary Shelley's *Frankenstein* (1818) – 'the first real science fiction novel' (Aldiss 1973: 26; cf. 29). Aldiss dramatised his thesis in *Frankenstein Unbound* (1973), in which an American politician, Joe Bodenland, notes that '*Frankenstein* was regarded by the twenty-first century as the first novel of the Scientific Revolution and, incidentally, as the first novel of science-fiction' (1982: 47). Bodenland slips back in time to the start of the nineteenth century, where he encounters Mary Shelley, Percy Shelley, Lord Byron, Victor Frankenstein and Frankenstein's Creature. *Frankenstein* is here inspired by real-life events. The novel's form – messages addressed to Bodenland's wife and recorded diaries – echoes Shelley's use of the epistolary form, although she nests a series of narrators within each other so that the Creature's words are sometimes recounted by Frankenstein and sometimes recorded in letters sent by an Arctic voyager, Robert Walton, to his sister. However, the means by which Bodenland's diary reaches us is not explained. There is a knowing reference to the Oedipus myth (as well as to that of Faust) in which Bodenland, 'a vicarious wish-fulfillment for Aldiss' (McLeod 1980: 162), has sex with the 'mother' of science fiction, and thus inserts himself into this generic history.

The Frankenstein narrative had inspired plays and satirical cartoons, and in time was filmed by Universal Studios and Hammer. James Whale's 1931 adaptation, for Universal, removed the framing narrative of Arctic exploration, and eclipsed the original novel in impact. Exploitation remakes, such as *Dracula vs Frankenstein* (Jesús Franco, 1971), *The Erotic Rites of Frankenstein* (Jesús Franco, 1972) and the Andy Warhol-produced *Flesh for Frankenstein* (Paul Morrissey, 1973) added sexual content, while *Blackenstein* (William A Levey, 1973) was a blaxploitation version. A television movie, *Frankenstein: The True Story* (Jack Smight, 1973), inspired as much by earlier films as by the book, added Byron's doctor, Polidori (James Mason), to the narrative. *Young Frankenstein* (Mel Brooks, 1974) was a loving parody of the 1930s Universal films, Gene Wilder bringing a distinct mania to the role and highlighting the clichés of the popular imagination of the story. *The Rocky Horror Picture Show* (Jim Sharman, 1975) blends such nostalgia – Sharman reused sets and locations from Hammer horror films and had intended to shoot the opening in black and white – with sex comedy.

Bodenland, like Coney's characters, also invokes Wells – 'the old nursery classic [...] *The Time Machine*' (Aldiss 1982: 23). Aldiss argues in *Billion Year Spree* that '[a]mong science fiction writers past and present, Wells [...] is one indisputable giant [... He] has an abundance of imagination as well as inventiveness' (1973: 117). Wells pioneered many of the major themes of sf – time travel, vivisection, alien invasion, invisibility, travel to the moon, environmentalism and utopia – and used them as a springboard for philosophical and political enquiries. Aldiss had already engaged with Wells in 'The Saliva Tree' (*F&SF* September 1965), marking Wells's centenary. He delayed publication of *Moreau's Other Island* (1980), a sequel to *The Island of Doctor Moreau* (1896), for a number of years (Collings 1986: 7), so the writing of the novel would have been closer to the US involvement in Vietnam, rather than the politics of the Soviet invasion of Afghanistan in December 1979. Calvin Roberts crashes near an island on his way back from a diplomatic mission to the moon, and discovers that this was the location for the experiments of the real Moreau (McMoreau) – Wells had fictionalised real events. Roberts learns that '[a]fter McMoreau's death, an assistant not mentioned in Wells's novel carried on his work for several years. Then he passed on as well, and the inhabitants of the island were then left on their own to survive as best they could' (Aldiss 1980b: 40). Mortimer Dart, a man disfigured by side effects of thalidomide and who has a mechanical suit to replace his vestigial limbs, continues the experiments. This Moreau is not causing suffering in the name of a misguided science; he is a victim of science taking revenge or seeking self-empowerment through science. Roberts threatens to expose Dart to the American government, only to discover that they are funding his experiments. The novel makes a political shift from a potential for a critique of British colonialism from within to a critique of American colonialism from outside.

A number of Wells's novels were filmed in the 1970s, often unfaithfully. *The Island of Dr Moreau* (Don Taylor, 1977) is an uneasy mix of prestige literary adaptation and horror film, which owes much to *The Island of Lost Souls* (Erle C. Kenton, 1933). The film is set in 1911, although Moreau (Burt Lancaster) demonstrates a knowledge of genetics much closer to the 1970s, when scientists began genetic engineering with the manipulation of E. coli and mice genes. The ending, in which the experimented-upon hero Andrew Braddock (Michael York) wakes up cured, is somewhat unconvincing and unsatisfactory, and Baird Searles complains that 'the socko ending that they were obviously leading up to – that the girl [Mari (Barbara Carrera) ...] is really only of Moreau's creations – is inexplicably and totally cut out' (Searles 1977c: 54). Wells's *When the Sleeper Wakes* (1899) contributes the basic idea for *Sleeper* (Woody Allen, 1973), in which a New Yorker is cryonically frozen for two centuries, and 'The Empire of the Ants' (*The Strand* December 1905) gives a title to *Empire of the Ants* (Bert I. Gordon, 1977), in which property developers face giant ants which have been mutated by contact with nuclear waste. *H.G. Wells' The Shape of Things to Come* (George McCowan, 1979) unashamedly uses the writer's name for a cash-in on *Star Wars* (George Lucas, 1977): human survivors of a war with robots now live in domed cities on the moon. Wells appears as a character in *Time After Time* (Nicholas Meyer, 1979) – an adaptation of Karl Alexander's novel written at the same time – in which Wells (Malcolm McDowell) pursues Jack the Ripper (David Warner) through time to 1979 San Francisco, where the time machine is on display.

Wells's fiction is mixed with Arthur Conan Doyle's in *Sherlock Holmes's The War of the Worlds* (1975), assembled by Manley Wade Wellman and Wade Wellman from various stories they had published in *F&SF*. Set in 1901, six years after the publication of Wells's novel in the real world, Holmes learns of an impending alien invasion by looking at a crystal egg that is a Martian artefact, and works with Professor Challenger – from *The Lost World* (1912) and four sequels. The Wellmans take liberties with Wells's original plot and make no attempt to reproduce Conan Doyle's prose. George H. Smith's *The Second War of the Worlds* (1976), the fourth book of five in the author's Anwwr series, is set on an alternative Earth, and features Mr H and Dr W battling off the aliens – they are never quite identified as Holmes and Watson, possibly for copyright reasons. K. W. Jeter's *Morlock Night* (1979) is a sequel to *The Time Machine*, in which the Morlocks invade Victorian London, having stolen the murdered Time Traveller's vehicle. Edwin Hocker, who had heard the Traveller's tale, defends London, in a narrative that quickly invokes Arthurian legend and the Fisher King, with a dying King Arthur and multiple versions of the sword Excalibur needed to defeat a cosmic battle between Merlin and his enemy Merdette.

Christopher Priest's *The Space Machine: A Scientific Romance* (1976) reworks both *The Time Machine* and *The War of the Worlds* (1898), as the travelling salesman Edward Turnbull meets Amelia Fitzgibbon and, by accident, uses the time travel machine to journey through space to Mars. Fitzgibbon and Turnbull foment revolt before returning home to prevent a Martian invasion. Brian Stableford dismissed it as '[the] ultimate in sophisticated in-jokes' (1977b: 54) and accused it of being 'a nostalgic salute to frivolous reading' and 'a veiled insult' (1977: 55). Much of Priest's output offers an ongoing critique of the orthodoxies of sf and he describes Wells as a 'primitive' (Kincaid 1999: 7). But Wells does situate *The War of the Worlds* in terms of colonialism and racism; Priest, reusing the fictional events at the end of the period of British imperialism, has Fitzgibbon and Turnbull observe a colonising power in action. Fitzgibbon's role as consciousness-raising activist was imagined in the context of white anti-Apartheid campaigners such as Helen Suzman, Helen Joseph and Ruth First, and she is not limited by Victorian mores – if anything it is Turnbull who needs liberating.

Rather than Wells, Moorcock draws on Jules Verne in the Oswald

Bastable trilogy, although Bastable is the name of a character invented by E. Nesbit in *The Story of the Treasure Seekers* (1899) and several sequels. Moorcock offers a commentary on the imperialism and racism inherent in many of the scientific romances and adventure narratives published between about 1870 and the outbreak of the First World War, congruent with the height and beginning of decline of the British Empire, and to reflect upon the same issues in the 1970s. Brian Baker argues that 'Moorcock insists that colonial discourse not be simply seen as a historical artefact' (2005: 47), as the impacts of French, British and American imperialism had led to the Vietnam War and the resurgence of the Troubles in Northern Ireland and mainland Britain. In *The Warlord of the Air* (1971), a story supposedly related by the opium-addicted Bastable to Moorcock's grandfather, he travels from 1903 to an alternative 1973, where the First World War never happened. In *The Land Leviathan: A New Scientific Romance* (1974), a manuscript given by Una Persson (who had appeared in the Cornelius Quartet and other works) to Moorcock senior, America and Europe have returned to barbarism due to a global technological war. Bastable had been in an airship in the first volume, but here joins a submarine crew, whose captain is a version of Joseph Conrad rather than Verne's Captain Nemo. *The Steel Tsar* (1981), supposedly given to the present-day Moorcock by Persson, features a German–British alliance menaced by the Japanese empire and the building of a literal man of steel, and was written in the context of the Soviet invasion of Afghanistan in December 1979 – a country in which Britain had fought a number of wars in the nineteenth century.

The pleasures of these fictions are the intertextual recognition of the sources, but there was a more generalised pleasure from the fictional encounter with a novum – the Big Dumb Object. Such objects – things that cannot exist, that defy the laws of gravity, engineering or economics, described as if they were indeed the case – evoke a sense of estrangement in characters and readers/audiences. They pose an enigma for the characters to unwrap, a puzzled shared with the audience. The protagonists need to be resourceful and intelligent enough to survive and penetrate the mystery with their cognitive abilities, being cast into the role of hero in what seems to be a fantastical landscape. As consumers of such texts, we wish the answers to be withheld for as long as possible, and sometimes the author – standing in as the alien intelligence behind the wondrous construction – refuses to divulge the answer to the questions we have. This often leaves a further, critical question – is there a deeper sense of purpose to the work, or is it merely a piece of pastiche, toying with our imaginations?

Larry Niven's *Ringworld* (1970) is a key example of this trend; perhaps hinting at earlier pulp imaginings, Roz Kaveney notes that 'he brought back into fashion – naively but effectively – the resonances and charms of the Big Dumb Objects' (Kaveney 1981: 25). The Ringworld is a cylindrical planet with a sun at its centre. The protagonists crash-land on the planet, leaving them to explore an often hostile environment many times the size of Earth while also investigating how to return home again. Christopher Palmer seems uncertain how seriously we are to take the artefact, which is not being explored by normal humans but, rather, by the virtually immortal (wealthy playboy Louis Wu), the incredibly lucky (Teela Brown), the unreasonably aggressive (Speaker-to-Animals) and a member of a different, superior species (Nessus): 'everything that has happened to them has happened because of the extraordinary power of Teela's luck, whether amazing escape, or, contrariwise, the crash which has marooned them on this Ringworld' (2006: 101). This allows Niven massive narrative sleight of hand, whether getting his characters into dangerous situations to add to the drama, or to justify illogical moments in the plot. *Ringworld Engineers* (1980) returns to the artefact to correct the engineering mistakes he had made in imagining the Ringworld's construction; the Ringworld apparently requires many devices to make everything work.

Any exploration of a landscape can be read as an interior journey of self-discovery, so the Big Dumb Object can be used to reveal the attitudes and presuppositions of its (usually) human discoverers. In practice, the Big Dumb Object performs a number of roles: it draws attention to the work of science-fiction authorship, it marks a conceptual breakthrough for the characters and readers, and it invokes the sublime. Dating back at least as far as Longinus' 'On the Sublime' in the first century CE, this term is used to label writing which creates a feeling of lift and exaltation, stirring the soul. In eighteenth-century thought, the sublime refers to the powerful feelings that can be experienced from the observation of nature – most noticeably the landscapes witnessed by travellers on the Grand Tour, such as mountains, volcanoes and icescapes, as described by Mary Shelley. Artists such as J. M. W. Turner, John Martin, Joseph Wright of Derby and Frederic Edwin Church depicted the sublime in paintings.

The conceptual breakthrough is a dramatic moment of revelation in sf, when the protagonist's worldview is opened up to new possibilities. The character undergoes a paradigm shift – and this eureka moment is shared by the viewer or reader, evoking a sense of wonder. The conceptual breakthroughs occasioned by Big Dumb Objects often require a move from local to global or even universal thinking, as everyday life stands revealed as being part of a much bigger and more complex system. Readers or viewers may then be moved to consider their own positioning in the universe, and to speculate on the systems of which they are unaware. Underlying many of these Big Dumb Objects is the sense of humanity needing a helping hand in development, as in Erich von Däniken's *Erinnerungen an die Zukunft: Ungelöste Rätsel der Vergangenheit* (*Chariots of the Gods?: Unsolved Mysteries of the Past* (1968)), and its sequels, as well as a number of imitators.

The Big Dumb Objects offer a substitute for the anti-climax of the Apollo programme: sf had to raise its imaginative game after lunar excursions went from pipe dream to has-been, without quite returning to the space opera excesses of the 1920s and 1930s. De Witt Douglas Kilgore suggests that Arthur C. Clarke's *Rendezvous with Rama* (1972) still reflects the ethics of its period, despite being set in the future: 'the notion that the conquest of space will be an extension of a human imperium; use of the recent past as a template for the social and political institutions of the future; the projection into the future of a sociomilitary enterprise with a clearly defined hierarchy of responsibilities and skills; an ethic of the genius of science as represented by specific individuals; and confidence that even the most frightening and insoluble problems can be overcome by scientific advancement' (2003: 127–28). This is true of a number of the works discussed within the rest of this chapter.

*Rendezvous*, the first of two books by Clarke in the 1970s to win both the Hugo and Nebula Awards for best novel, begins with a cylindrical spaceship being misidentified as an asteroid on a trajectory dangerously close to the inhabited portions of the solar system. Alerted by Spearhead, an early warning system for meteors, the United Planets organisation scrambles a mission. Commander Norton's party dock with and enter the cylinder, and begin a partial exploration of it in the twenty-one days they calculate that they have before the object leaves the system. As it heads towards the Sun, the interior defrosts and comes to life, or at least an ecosystem begins working, but there is no sign of sentient life on board, nor is there much evidence of those who made the artefact. Just as in *Ringworld* (and the Clarke co-scripted *2001: A Space Odyssey* (Stanley Kubrick, 1968)), the reader is left guessing as to the object's true purpose and the novel's ending leaves room for sequels – Ramans do everything in threes – to such an extent that Nicholas Ruddick suspected that there would be none (1985: 48). In fact, four years later Clarke co-wrote *Rama II* (1989) with Gentry Lee, followed by *The Garden of Rama* (1991) and *Rama Revealed* (1993).

*Rama* shows dedicated professionals at work, cautiously exploring the unknown, and always aware that behind them are any number of committees and bureaucracies. This has led to accusations of boringness, but it is part of the realism effect of the depiction of fantastical events. Ruddick notes that '*Rama* fails to offer, it seems, a vision of human transcendence coming as a result of the alien encounter' (1985: 42). Knowledge of the existence of aliens means that humanity is potentially changed forever. Clarke in *Childhood's End* (1951) and *2001* had envisaged aliens that would guide humanity's evolution, but these aliens have no knowledge of the existence of humanity, let alone a wish to uplift. A rendezvous suggests an arranged, romantic meeting – this is not such an encounter.

Clarke depicts a process of colonisation; the choice of the name *Endeavour* for the ship captained by Norton explicitly points back to the voyages of Captain James Cook. Cook's party imported terminology from Europe for the flora, fauna and geography found in New Zealand and Australia; the Raman explorers name city-like constructions New York, London, Paris, London, Moscow and so on. The name 'Rama' is an appropriation of a Hindu deity, astronomical mapping having exhausted Greek and Roman mythology. The society of which Norton is part is ostensibly multicultural, but the fabric of the novel hardly represents this: 'white women and people of color are an integral part of the central team of "spacemen," and national or cultural "others" are integrated into sameness by anglophonic names' (Kilgore 2003: 128). While Cook might have perceived himself as superior to the civilisations he encountered, Norton is forced to respect the superior technology his mission discovers. The novel ends with the alien craft presumably refreezing, just as Norton's frozen sperm is used to impregnate one of his indistinguishable wives to whom he has been sending identical messages throughout the novel.

Whereas the thrust of *Ringworld* and *Rama* is a brief exploratory mission, the issue of new real estate and colonisation is explored in Bob Shaw's *Orbitsville* (*Galaxy* June–August 1974; 1975), and in two belated sequels, *Orbitsville Departure* (1983) and *Orbitsville Judgement* (1990). A space transportation and exploration corporation, run from Iceland like a sea-faring empire, dominates Earth in Orbitsville. When Captain Garamond witnesses the accidental death of oligarch Elizabeth Lindstrom's son, he panics and sets off into space. He discovers a Dyson Sphere about two astronomical units in diameter (this is the size of a sphere that would be defined by Earth's orbit). This new territory questions Lindstrom's power – she can no longer maintain a monopoly on emigration from an overcrowded Earth and Garamond is too significant and visible to have assassinated. Lindstrom still wants to profit, through transportation, although Garamond argues that it is 'intolerable that there should be any kind of economic brake on the natural and instinctive flow toward the new land' (Shaw 1975a: 78). The size of the territory is such that it could easily absorb the entire human race, undercutting land values. He suspects that Lindstrom's corporation has been maintaining the upward pressure on Earth's population to aid the value of the emigration market, even to the extent of interfering with contraceptive technology.

A comparison is made between Orbitsville and the style of colonisation of the American west – there is a limit to what technology will work on Orbitsville, which would make progress from the planet's one entry point slow and labour-intensive. It is possible to make comparisons with Westerns as to the likely rearrangement of law and order. With the distance of each society from a centralising power, there are ongoing squabbles over the ownership of particular plots: metallurgy is likely to be an issue, although the object seems relatively poor in such resources. The existence of, if not indigenous people, then earlier species of settlers, suggests parallels with the First Nations. The novel critiques human mistreatment of these civilisations – this was also the era of the revisionist Westerns such as *Little Big Man* (Arthur Penn, 1970) and *The Outlaw Josey Wales* (Clint Eastwood, 1976). But if Shaw is sensitive to issues of race, the novel is less open-minded about gender: Lindstrom is the evil snow queen, a manipulative monster, Aileen Garamond is stupidly slow to spot any threat to her family's well-being, and most of the other women are defined only in terms of their reproductivity.

Priest praised Shaw's novel at the expense of Clarke's and Niven's. He argues that 'the test of good science fiction is, or should be, an examination of the idea rather than the notion' (Priest and Watson 1976: 56). The idea must come with the extrapolation from the novum at the heart of an sf narrative, which can be represented well or poorly, but it also has a moral tone and seems to be identifiable with a worldview, political in the widest sense of the word. For Priest, *Ringworld* 'is a startling notion. However a brilliant notion does not by itself create a novel, nor even an science fiction idea' (Priest and Watson 1976: 58). He summarises the novel as suggesting that 'man's spirit of curiosity and adventure is irrepressible' (Priest and Watson 1976: 58), while admitting that '[what] *is* said is hardly worth saying at all' (Priest and Watson 1976: 58). Nor does he like *Rendezvous*, which he dismisses as unimaginative and plotless, noting that 'the level of characterization is that of a boy's adventure magazine' (1974b: 93). In contrast, Priest claims: 'In Niven's book the protagonist is the artefact itself [...] In Shaw's book the protagonist is a man' (1979: 200). The protagonist of *Orbitsville* is Garamond, but his antagonist is the conjunction of the Dyson Sphere and Lindstrom, with the artefact being something that he has to come to terms with before he can resolve his conflict with Lindstrom. While *Orbitsville* involves curiosity and adventure, the novel is much more about the containment of the outward urge and the shift from the economics of exchange to the economics of the hearth: the artefact 'acts as a sort of cosmic sponge to soak up and dispose the outward drives of super-technological civilisations' (Priest and Watson 1976: 59). The politics surrounding the Ringworld are trivial, and the political crisis of Rama is easily defused; *Orbitsville* confronts colonialism head-on.

Priest effectively reverses the Big Dumb Object paradigm in his novel which 'comes closest to most people's idea of "trad" science fiction' (1990a: 96), *Inverted World*. The protagonist, Helward Mann – whose appellation places him in a tradition of significant character names such as Billy Pilgrim – is an apprentice in a small, self-contained city. This city moves northwards, a couple of miles at a time, on rails, with the rails from the south being taken up and reused on the next leg. Helward is in training to join the Future guild, a group of men who survey the terrain in front of the city, but first he has to work in the other guilds, and endure a gruelling and bewildering trek to the south. Helward penetrates the secrets of the city, as the other teams begin to discover the ways that their strange objects work. On observing the Sun – which is shaped like two hyperboloid cones – he comes to the conclusion that the planet is the same shape, and that travelling north and south will have a time-distorting effect relative to the city, which is called Earth. Whereas at the start of the novel, Helward feels trapped by the rules of the city, and the ways of the guilds with their secretive oaths, by three quarters of the way through the book he is alienated from it by his shift in age from the people he has grown up with, and by his wife's rejection both of their marriage and of the city's progress. Helward has lost father, wife and child and, since his mother was one of those brought into the city to provide daughters – preserving genetic diversity, although this is never stated – and has left without her son, he has been rejected at birth.

Peter Nicholls describes *Inverted World* as 'pure hard-core science fiction' (1975a: 186), while noting a coolness in characterisation. If there is a flattening of affect in the novel, it could be explained as the product of Helward's upbringing outside a family, but equally it could be an imitation of what Priest may have perceived as a flatness in Clarke's characterisation. The novel begins in the first person, told by Helward, with the estranging statement of an age in miles, then changes to the third person focalised on Helward, before returning to first-person narration. The final section is in the third person, focalised on Kate, a woman from outside the city. The shifts in point of view prevent us from identifying too closely with the narrator; a final switch is necessary to see his perceptions from another angle. The city has reached a river too wide to bridge. Kate insists that it is not a river – and Priest obliquely reveals that this is the Atlantic Ocean. The planet turns out to be Earth – the sort of conceptual breakthrough twist ending used by *Planet of the Apes* (Franklin J. Schaffner, 1968) and spoofed at the end of the first radio series of *The Hitch-Hiker's Guide to the Galaxy* (8 March–12 April 1978) – and the city was the creation of a particle physicist who invented a translateration generator. Unfortunately, this device has a perceptual and genetic impact on its inhabitants, caught within the field, leading to the misconstruals of the novel. At the end, only Helward is the prisoner of his mindset, and he dives off the end of the bridge, in a movement into the abyss reminiscent of Ballard's early protagonists. Nick Hubble notes that this move north – in fact west – is into the future, and may have enabled Helward to reach the optimum where time stands still: he is 'distanced from the "reality" of the city, without switching to the alternative "reality" of twenty-second century Earth, which would entail an irrevocable separation' (2005: 42). Helward's coming of age suggests a rejection of the conceptual breakthrough; Priest's novels often feature a choice between two binary alternatives and the protagonist chooses a third option.

Frederik Pohl's *Gateway* (1977), which won the Hugo, Nebula, Locus and John W. Campbell Memorial Awards for Best Novel, features a vast, hollowed-out asteroid full of alien spaceships built by an mysterious alien race, the Heechee. A whole economy is built upon entrepreneurs who, singly or in groups of various sizes, risk taking a ride in one of these ships in search of exploitable resources. The story of Robinette Stetley Broadhead is told in two parallel narratives, his journey to a black hole and the psychoanalysis of his survivor guilt; Pohl also intersperses other documents through the narrative. Humanity learns to use the mysterious alien artefacts, but not to fully understand them, with the final revelation of the novel being Broadhead's infantile repressed homosexuality rather than face-to-face first contact. The first sequel, *Beyond the Blue Event Horizon* (1980), nominated for Hugo and Nebula Awards, depicts Broadhead as incredibly wealthy and a major figure on Earth, survivor of several missions. Now he bankrolls an attempt to find a food bank in outer space that will counteract famine on Earth, although the explorers reckon without the makers of the artefact, who might resent being stolen from. Again, there is a critique of the colonial impulse, on which America was built. While the tendency had been for Big Dumb Object sequels to attempt to explain the mysteries of the first novel, here the solution is again deferred.

Philip José Farmer's Hugo Award-winning *To Your Scattered Bodies Go* ('The Day of the Great Shout' January 1965, 'The Suicide Express' March 1966 *Worlds of Tomorrow*; 1971) is also a Big Dumb Object narrative. The

Victorian explorer Richard Burton awakens after his death on the shore of a river, and realises that he is surrounded by all of humanity between Neolithic times and 2008, fixed at the age of 25, infertile, virginal, and circumcised if male. Everyone has been provided with a cylinder, or grail, which produces food and tobacco to prevent starvation. Society is understandably anarchistic, but Burton forms together a small band of people, including Peter Jairus Frigate, a stand-in for Farmer, and Alice Hargreaves, Lewis Carroll's inspiration for Alice. Together, they head up-river, in search of both the river's source and an explanation of why they have all been brought together. Their progress is halted when they are captured by a society run by Tullius Hostilius, third king of Rome, and Hermann Göring, a senior Nazi, and Burton is killed again, awakening downstream. Since he is repeatedly reunited with Göring rather than randomly resurrected, the two suspect a conspiracy. The nature of the planet is that it must be artificial – a single river zigzags south from the north pole, and north again across the other hemisphere, and the axis is so stable that there are no seasons. It is unlikely that resurrection would be a natural process – the title of the novel alludes to John Donne's 'Holy Sonnet VII', in which the poet calls for the last judgement, only to realise that he is still marked with sin and must repent. One explanation given is that the planet is a means of allowing people to reach a higher ethical or moral state; another is that it is a huge experiment to watch humanity.

The potential sublimity of the length of the river and the size of humanity is rather eclipsed by Farmer's penchant for introducing real historical personages, and it feels as though the protagonists encounter more known, real people than is statistically likely. As if fearful of this, Farmer notes that 'Burton had met three Jesus Christs, two Abrahams, four Richard the Lion-Hearteds, six Attilas', and so forth (1974: 174). While Farmer has the space to explore metaphysics and issues surrounding racism (anti-Semitism is a recurrent theme), the spotting of cameos is the dominant reading pleasure. Franz Rottensteiner suggests that the resurrection of humanity 'on such a gigantic scale would have offered a chance of a unique meeting of minds; but all Mr. Farmer presents us is the old trite quarrel of survival and petty warfare' (1973: 97). Farmer is playing with the historical personages, and collapsing together time and space, but for Rottensteiner it never gets beyond games, a cynical format in the mass-market age. Russell Letson suggests that this grand-scale environment allows Farmer to explore 'the limitations and contradiction of heroism as well as the distance between the herd and hero' (1977: 37). Burton, with his language skills, his experience of exploration, and his ability to integrate within various differing cultures, appears as the resourceful hero in the Heinleinian mode, but the repeated questioning and justification of his racism undercut this to some extent.

The first series of *The Hitch-Hiker's Guide to the Galaxy*, scripted by Douglas Adams, parodied sf in general, among wider satiric targets, and was influenced by Kurt Vonnegut and Robert Sheckley, among other writers. Adams's radio series began with the demolition of the house belonging to Arthur Dent (Simon Jones) to make way for a bypass, following this with the destruction of the Earth to make way for a hyperspace bypass. He is rescued by his alien friend Ford Prefect (Geoffrey McGivern) and travels to the fabled Magrathea, home of a corporation of planet-builders. Earth is thus itself a big dumb object, a manufactured, planet-sized computer designed to discover the Ultimate Question, to which it is known that the answer is 42. The first series ends with Arthur and Ford stranded on Earth in the prehistoric past, in an example of comic circularity. A Christmas episode was commissioned and broadcast at the end of 1978. A second series (21–25 January 1980) features the characters visiting the president of the galaxy, an old man in a shack, while Dent finds a giant statue of himself. The series constantly builds up the trivial and knocks down the colossal. Adams balanced writing the series with scripting the *Doctor Who* serial 'The Pirate Planet' (30 September–21 October 1978), in which a hollowed-out planet is used as a pirate ship, and acted as script editor for season seventeen of *Doctor Who*, including his scripts for 'City of Death' (with David Fisher and Graham Williams, as by David Agnew, 29 September–20 October 1979) and 'Shada' (cancelled mid-filming due to an industrial dispute). The first four episodes of the radio series were rerecorded and released as LPs as *The Hitch-Hiker's Guide to the Galaxy* (1979), with episodes five and six, originally co-written with John Lloyd, heavily revised as *The Restaurant at the End of the Universe* (1980). Novelisations were released under the same titles in 1979 and 1980 – the latter folding much altered versions of the Christmas episode and the second series into its adaptation of episodes five and six. The material was also performed on stage and on television (5 January–9 February 1981). Adams in time moved from cult success to bestseller.

Another British parodist destined to become a bestseller was Terry Pratchett, whose second novel *The Dark Side of the Sun* (1976) lampooned targets such as *Ringworld* and its genetics for good luck, Isaac Asimov's Laws of Robotics and Psychohistory and the Norstrilia stories of Cordwainer Smith, and had a title which alluded to Pink Floyd's concept album *The Dark Side of the Moon* (1973). The Wu-like protagonist, wealthy heir Dominickdaniel Sabalos, goes in search of the lost species of Jokers, who left many Big Dumb Objects behind them when they vanished. Pratchett's third novel, *Strata* (1981), was sf and partly set on a flat planet, a technological version of what was to evolve into the Discworld in *The Colour of Magic* (1983). But by then a fantasy boom was well under way.

# 5
# The Rise of Fantasy: Swords and Planets

Technology, with its potential to be misused, had long been distrusted – the threat of the Bomb and the war machine in Vietnam being merely the latest sources of anxiety. In his survey of the representation of technology in popular film, Steven L. Goldman notes that the films' 'messages, deliberately crafted to appeal to what were believed to be widely prevalent attitudes, values, and fears, have remained pretty much the same' (1989: 289), which is to say, broadly anti-technological. Even highly technologised films, such as the Star Wars trilogy, 'opposed technology to virtue' (Goldman 1989: 288) and pitted the purity of Jedi hearts and spirits against the technology of the evil Empire. But, equally, some distrusted the escapism of pure fantasy. Arthur C. Clarke's dictum about the indistinguishability of advanced technology and magic might be dramatised in a novel by the discovery of sophisticated machinery as evidence for forgotten knowledge – as Pratchett shows in *The Dark Side of the Sun* (1976) and *Strata* (1981). Besides, the discovery would allow for a kind of conceptual breakthrough that might justify fantasy in terms of 'cognitive estrangement' (Suvin 1979: 7), although Suvin was to dismiss fantasy for another two decades (2000). The possible scientific explanation for magic puts such texts into the genre outlined by Tzvetan Todorov in *The Fantastic* (1970; translated into English 1973), hesitating between the marvellous and the uncanny. The 1970s featured the publication of much science fantasy and, especially in the second half of the decade, a boom in fantasy.

Just as some of the sf of the period looked back to Shelley, Wells and Verne, sword and planet fiction recalled Robert E. Howard's Conan stories and Edgar Rice Burroughs's Barsoom books, which could be located on the fantasy side of science fiction. This chapter will begin with an examination of such science fantasy, including films inspired by Edgar Rice Burroughs's novels and *Zardoz* (John Boorman, 1973), before going on to consider the Tolkienesque tradition and the response to it, as well as bestselling works by Anne McCaffrey, Piers Anthony and Robert Silverberg. It will end with an examination of fantasy in music and role-playing games.

Amicus Productions made three films based on Burroughs's novels, with some cooperation from the author's estate. The first was *The Land That Time Forgot* (Kevin Connor, 1975), based on the Burroughs story (*Blue Book Magazine* September 1918), heavily rewritten by the producers from a script by Michael Moorcock and James Cawthorne. During the First World War, a mix of American mariners and German submariners reach Caprona, a barely accessible island in the south Atlantic, last charted in the early eighteenth century. Like Arthur Conan Doyle's *The Lost World* (1912), the area contains prehistoric fauna, as well as various tribes of primitive humans. One group of sailors work at extracting oil for fuel for the ship, and another, including Bowen Tyler (Doug McLure) and Lisa Claydon (Susan Penhaligon), go north to investigate the island. Claydon is a strong, usually self-reliant, character, who looks shocked when she shoots someone dead, but does not stand by entirely helplessly when the men fight each other. As someone with scientific knowledge and training, she comes to the conclusion that evolution here occurs on a linear, individual basis: microbes evolve into reptiles into mammals into various versions of humanity, in a sort of single-lived transmigration of souls and metamorphosis. At one end of a river is basic life, at the other the triumph of civilisation, which here seems to take the form of skinny-dipping. Claydon argues that life can only go one way.

The box office success of *Land* led Connor in 1976 to direct McLure with Hammer stalwart Peter Cushing in a version of Burroughs's *At the Earth's Core* (*All-Story Weekly*, April 1914; 1922). David Innes (McClure) has financed a drilling machine to descend far into the Earth. On its inaugural expedition in the Welsh valleys with its designer, Dr Abner Perry (Cushing), they discover a subterranean lost world where telepathic reptile-birds, Mahars, and their humanoid overseers rule English-speaking stone-aged humans. Whereas *Land* had used puppets, *Core* employs men in rubber suits; the back projection is also unconvincing. Cushing, in a performance that harks back to his two film outings as Doctor Who, seems to be mostly playing the doddery professor for laughs. The film dramatises a series of captures and escapes, and some attempt at spectacle.

Connor returned to Burroughs's Caprona trilogy with *The People that Time Forgot* (Kevin Connor, 1977), based on the story from *Blue Book Magazine* (October 1918). Tyler's friend, Ben McBride (Patrick Wayne), and a photographer, Charly Cunningham (Sarah Douglas), are part of a search and rescue mission, but crash-land their biplane after a pterodactyl attack. The team encounters a variety of dinosaurs and primitive humans, but the ideas from the first film about evolution are not developed, and Cunningham's feminism is balanced by the semi-nakedness of the primitive Ajor (Dana Gillespie). Bigger volcanic explosions than in the first film accompany Tyler's rescue, but he dies as the others escape. By now Edgar Rice Burroughs Inc were not involved, and the third part, *Out of Time's Abyss* (*Blue Book Magazine*, November 1918), was not produced; Amicus only made one more film, the horror portmanteau *The Monster Club* (Roy Ward Baker, 1980).

These particular Burroughs narratives looked to lost civilisations elsewhere on or in Earth, where his Barsoom stories had been set on Mars, with further novels set on Venus. Other writers imitated his narratives of human adventuring on a low-technology planet; any machinery stays in the hands of a secretive and hierarchical elite, the vestiges of an earlier civilisation. Often the society is part of an old colony or a planet about to join an empire. Much of this was series work – for example, Lin Carter published eight novels in the Callisto sequence (1972–78) and five in the Green Star sequence (1972–76), in homage to Burroughs, plus five novels, three published between 1973 and 1977, inspired by Leigh Brackett's 1940s and 1950s version of Mars. From 1972 to 1980, Kenneth Bulmer published the first twenty-four novels of the Drey Prescott series, under the pseudonym Alan Burt Akers, set on Kregen in the Antares system of Scorpio. Robert Holdstock wrote the Berserker series under the penname Chris Carlsen – *Shadow of the Wolf* (1977), *The Bull Chief* (1977) and *The Horned Warrior* (1979) – and contributed several novels to the Raven series as Richard Kirk – *Swordsmistress of Chaos* (with Angus Wells, 1978), *A Time of Ghosts* (with Wells, 1978), and *Lords of the Shadows* (1979). The third volume, *The Frozen God* (1978), and fifth, *A Time of Dying* (1979), were written by Wells alone. The first six Horseclans novels, by Robert Adams – *The Coming of the Horseclans* (1975), *Swords of the Horseclans* (1976), *Revenge of the Horseclans* (1977), *A Cat of Silvery Hue* (1979), *The Savage Mountains* (1979) and *The Patrimony* (1980) – featured ongoing battles between post-apocalyptic tribes, able to communicate with both horses and genetically engineered sabre-toothed tigers; they also included some uncomfortable sequences of paedophilia. Much of C.J. Cherryh's early work fits into this subgenre, as do Marion Zimmer Bradley's Darkover novels – begun with *The Planet Savers* (1958), and added to in the 1970s with *The Winds of Darkover* (1970), *The World Wreckers* (1971), *Darkover Landfall* (1972), *The Spell Sword* (1974), *The Heritage of Hastur* (1975), *The Shattered Chain* (1976), *The Forbidden Tower* (1977), *Stormqueen!* (1978), *Two to Conquer* (1980) and a 1979 revision of *The Bloody Sun* (1964). Samuel R. Delany explored the politics of sexuality and power, especially bondage within a racial context, in his Return to Nevèryon series (1976–87), beginning with 'The Tale of Gorgik' (*Asimov's* Summer 1979), and provided an introduction to Joanna

Russ's *Alyx* (1976), collecting her feminist sword and planet stories first published between 1967 and 1970.

A less nuanced image of gender, bondage and sadomasochism was presented by John Norman, the pseudonym of John Lange, a professor of philosophy, in his Gor novels that began with *Tarnsman of Gor* (1966). Norman published one every year in the 1970s aside from 1973: *Assassin of Gor* (1970), *Raiders of Gor* (1971), *Captive of Gor* (1972), *Hunters of Gor* (1974), *Marauders of Gor* (1975), *Tribesmen of Gor* (1976), *Slave Girl of Gor* (1977), *Beasts of Gor* (1978), *Explorers of Gor* (1979) and *Fighting Slave of Gor* (1980). The books depicted a Nietzschean theme of male dominance, with females as increasingly willing subservient slaves; he explored this concept in a non-fiction book, *Imaginative Sex* (1974), with an examination of bondage and sadomasochism, complete with suggestions of sexual scenarios for married couples to use. Mary Gentle calls the novels 'rape and revenge fantasies' (Gentle 1987: 10). L.J. Hurst, alluding to a work by the Marquis de Sade, suggests that 'Philosophy in the Bedroom has become a ranting in the prison camp' (Hurst 1985: 54), and suggests that the books are typical of the American New Right.

The film *Zardoz* is sf masquerading as fantasy, beginning with Exterminators worshipping the flying stone head of their god, Zardoz, and being rewarded with guns to control the number of Brutals. One of these Brutals, Zed (Sean Connery), discovers that this is all part of a confidence trick in a post-apocalyptic society, while a group of quasi-immortal Eternals live in comfort. The name Zardoz is derived from *The Wonderful Wizard of Oz* (1900), a novel in which a small-time conjuror passes as a mighty ruler. The film sets up an opposition between technology and nature, although technology such as guns is used in the destruction of the dictatorial technology in the form of a computer, the Tabernacle, and Zed, representative of the pure masculine animal nature the Eternals lack, is the product of a eugenics programme. Baird Searles suggests that '[both] the story and the style show enormous sophistication' (1974a: 82), whereas Vivian Sobchack notes that the film is a big budget sf film which has 'an awkward and self-conscious desire to use the didactic possibilities of science fiction combined with a misguided compulsion [...] to make the visually or intellectually obvious perfectly clear' (1987: 158). John Brosnan concurs, dismissing it as a '[c]ontender for the position of "Most Pretentious and Self-Indulgent SF Film Ever Made"' (1978: 222), although he is impressed by the special effects and Geoffrey Unsworth's photography – Unsworth, having been a camera operator for Michael Powell and Emeric Pressberger, worked on *2001: A Space Odyssey* (Stanley Kubrick, 1968), and was to work on the first two *Superman* films (Richard Donner, 1978, Richard Lester,

## THE RISE OF FANTASY: SWORDS AND PLANETS 69

1980). Like Nicolas Roeg, Boorman here eschews a linear narrative, intercutting flashbacks and current events, and ending with the future ageing of Zed from middle-aged man to skeleton, although the anachrony had been more effective in *Point Blank* (John Boorman, 1967) in introducing an ambiguity as to the reality of events. Boorman had also had ambitions to film *The Lord of the Rings* (1954–55), but failed to raise the finances.

J.R.R. Tolkien's novel was to have the biggest impact upon the fantasy of the 1970s, although his death in 1973 deprived the world of any authentic sequel. He had been working on his mythos since about 1915, in part as a way of exploring his invented languages, and this gave a richness and depth to his adventure tales. His son, Christopher Tolkien, along with Guy Gavriel Kay, began the work of assembling the available manuscripts into a publishable form. *The Silmarillion* (1977) presents both an origin story for Middle-earth and an account of the history of that world up to the end of *The Lord of the Rings*, with Sauron emerging as the former servant of the evil Melkor. They attempted to work with the latest versions of Tolkien's manuscripts they had access to, but on occasions had to invent linking materials. Tolkien had struggled to find a framing device for his narratives, and the direct depiction of the quasi-historical events risked being of lesser dramatic interest than as enriching details underlying a narrative such as that of *The Lord of the Rings*. In 1980, Christopher Tolkien edited *Unfinished Tales*, a collection of manuscripts and drafts, demonstrating some of the world-building his father had engaged in, but this time made no attempt to impose consistency or finality. The critical apparatus offered the kind of textual exegesis usually reserved for a William Shakespeare or a John Milton, and paved the way for a subsequent twelve-volume edition of *The History of Middle-earth* (1983–96).

In 1978, the animated feature *J.R.R. Tolkien's The Lord of the Rings* was released, directed by Ralph Bakshi, whose debut animated feature was *Fritz the Cat* (1972), an x-rated adaptation of Robert Crumb's adult comic strip. Unable to secure funding from United Artists for three films, Bakshi agreed to split the narrative in half, although in the event only the first part was completed. The narrative adapts *The Fellowship of the Ring* and much of *The Two Towers*, although the script eliminates whole sequences and crosscuts between story arcs. While the film maintains Tolkien's rhythm of shifting from set-piece tension to celebratory feasting, the tone is largely serious and dark, with limited comic relief from the hobbits. Bakshi speeded up the animation process by making extensive use of rotoscoping, in which footage is shot and then animation is superimposed; this allows for a very three-dimensional effect, with fluid, realistic movements. The backgrounds vary in style, sometimes a stylised if flat realism, sometimes more expressionistic. Whatever the faults of the compressions and omissions of the adaptation, it is clear that Bakshi took his source seriously and offered an adult rather than juvenile version of the trilogy.

However, not all critics felt that it deserved to be treated as serious fiction; Moorcock was dismissive of Tolkien and much fantasy in his 1978 essay 'Epic Pooh'. For him, Tolkien, in *The Lord of the Rings*, betrays a romantic (as opposed to romanticised) tradition, both of narrative and landscape, in his celebration of the bourgeois hobbits with their utopian way of life standing against the faceless, unexamined hordes of Mordor. Moorcock sees the Shire as 'a suburban garden, Sauron and henchmen are that old bourgeois bugaboo, the Mob' (1987: 125). As Tolkien was born in what is now South Africa, and emigrated to the English Midlands at an early age, it might not be such a surprise to see this attitude, especially when this already threatened idyll is contrasted with the battlefields of western Europe he would have witnessed in the First World War. This is one explanation as to why he retreated into a world of invented languages and why he might wish for the consolations of simpler notions of morality. Moorcock ridiculed such cosiness as anti-urban and anti-technology, and suggested that *The Lord of the Rings* represented a romanticised, conservative rural past that consoled and comforted its readers. The cosiness draws upon A.A. Milne's Edwardian parlour fantasies for children: 'Writers like Tolkien take you to the edge of the Abyss and point out the excellent tea-garden at the bottom, showing you the steps carved into the cliffs and reminding you to be careful because the hand-rails are a trifle shaky' (Moorcock 1987: 127).

Moorcock argues that the British 'middle-classes turn increasingly to the fantasy of rural life and talking animals, the safety of the woods that are the pattern of the paper on the nursery room wall' (1987: 137). Such fictions fulfil a desire for retreat from the everyday world, especially in this case of the early 1970s, which can be seen either as proposing a retirement from the political – but is in effect a move to the right – or as a search for oppositional strategies at a period when the traditional political processes were ineffectual. Moorcock does not reject escapism altogether, but in the process escapist fiction still needs to ask questions: 'it should provide a release from anxiety but give us some insight into the causes of anxiety' (1987: 138). The retreat from the city as iconic of modern ills is also reflected in the growth of interest in ecology and environmentalism, and was also part of mainstream culture. The BBC sitcom *The Good Life* (4 April 1975–10 June 1978) explored one childless couple's attempts at self-sufficiency without leaving suburbia, whereas David Nobbs's *The Death of Reginald Perrin* (1975), adapted into *The Fall and Rise of Reginald Perrin* (8

September 1976–24 January 1979), featured a series of failed attempts by a middle-aged marketing manager to escape contemporary reality – daydreams, a faked suicide, a shop selling useless objects and a health commune. In the absurdist world of the sitcom, where the watchwords are paralysis and entrapment, escapism can never succeed; in fantasy it may, although Moorcock and M. John Harrison argue it should not.

Another target of Moorcock's scorn, Richard Adams, drew upon his own Second World War experiences in relating to his daughters the tales which formed *Watership Down* (1972), with later sections of the novel seemingly offering a representation of totalitarian societies in the form of General Woundwort's Efrafa, with echoes of concentration camps and Nazism. Thirteen publishers had rejected the novel before Rex Collins Ltd agreed to release it, and it became a bestseller. Adams's story takes a colony of rabbits from a warren that faces destruction to a new location on Watership Down, and gives the rabbits a whole mythology and belief system of their own. The portrayal of talking animals suggested that Adams was offering a spiritual allegory or fable, even if the details of that allegory were not rigorously thought through, nor free from the risk of being dismissed as whimsy. The novel was adapted into a British animated film in 1978, initially directed by John Hubley, who had worked on *Bambi* (David Hand, 1942) and who was used to realistic rural backdrops. The animators worked from illustrations to the book as well as from real-world locations; the animals, however, were anthropomorphised, in order to aid audience identification with the characters. Hubley died of a heart attack in 1977, so the producer, Martin Rosen, completed the film.

For better or worse, the works of Tolkien had set the aesthetic and ideological template by which future fantasy would be measured. Stephen Donaldson's trilogy, The First Chronicles of Thomas Covenant, Unbeliever, which consisted of *Lord Foul's Bane* (1977), *The Illearth War* (1978) and *The Power that Preserves* (1979), bore a cover quote comparing them to 'Tolkien at his best' and was swiftly followed by a second trilogy, beginning with *The Wounded Land* (1980). This was a much darker story than Tolkien's, with a morally ambiguous and dislikeable character at its heart. Covenant, a bestselling author who has been diagnosed with leprosy, wakes up in the Land after being run down by a police car. Covenant is told that it is prophesied that the Land will be destroyed, before he returns temporarily to Earth and loses two fingers. This allows him to be identified as the reincarnation of an ancient hero on his return to the Land; on a third visit, he finds that his potency has been restored, and he rapes Lena, who had previously healed his leprosy. Driven by remorse for his own actions and self-hatred – the state of the Land mirrors his psychology – he spends the first trilogy attempting to save a realm he does not entirely believe in, and Donaldson maintains a Todorovian sense of the fantastic. While the name 'Thomas' signals doubt, 'Covenant' perhaps points towards the biblical agreements between God and humanity: the covenant of law and of grace. Covenant has come to doubt both; whereas '[in] marrying and buying a house, he has accepted the social, moral, and economic laws of his community' (Slethaug 1993: 50), post-leprosy he doubts all laws, is suspicious of power and seems unwilling to accept salvation. In the third volume, he chooses possible death over unreality. His actions – and scepticism – have destroyed the Staff of Law, leaving the Land still at risk, as he discovers at the start of the second trilogy. Covenant again has to save the Land, at the risk of destroying it, and is repeatedly faced with the negative consequences of his actions.

Novels would be long, part of a trilogy or longer series, with a map at the front and based on a quest bringing together a group of disparate characters. Most of the imitators took only the appearance of *The Lord of the Rings*, without the copious etymological underpinnings that had driven Tolkien. The genre fell easily into self-parody and cliché. But nevertheless there was a huge market for this material. Brian Stableford notes that prior to about 1970 most fantasy was published on the side of sf lists, as something sf writers wrote – as opposed to other, more clearly delineated genres such as horror. In fact, Stableford argues, sf was something that fantasy writers did: 'most of the people writing and reading science fiction were "really" fantasy writers and readers who were making do' (1998: 23). Readers wanted 'wild, colourful and flagrantly impossible adventures' (1998: 23), and sf sufficed, in the absence of fantasy. Stableford notes that DAW Books editor and writer Lin Carter dismissed Terry Brooks's *The Sword of Shannara* (1977) as the worst book ever written (Stableford 1998: 23), but that did not stop huge sales. Algis Budrys noted that 'Random House and Ballantine have gone to extraordinary lengths to make the product attractive to booksellers, and to tell them that the product is attractive to customers' (1977: 105). The novel, written over a decade, has been described as 'a scaled-down model of *The Lord of the Rings*' (Mendlesohn and James 2009: 110), and its events and characters repeatedly ape Tolkien's. A series of sequels and prequels were to follow, from *The Elfstones of Shannara* (1983) to the present day.

The Pern sequence of novels by Anne McCaffrey had begun with 'Weyr Search' (*Analog* October 1967) and 'Dragonrider' (*Analog* December 1967–January 1968), edited into the novel *Dragonflight* (1968), and common sense would suggest that these are fantasy tales since they feature flying dragons – 'one of the most familiar icons of high fantasy' (James 1994:

# THE RISE OF FANTASY: SWORDS AND PLANETS 73

182). But Pern is a human colony, albeit one that has been reduced to a low level of technology by the Thread that rains down from the sky unless harvested by dragons and their riders, who have a telepathic bond. Brian Attebery suggests, however, that the 'Dragon books are [...] not extrapolative: nothing in our world would lead us to anticipate the planet of Pern' (1992: 106), meaning that many critics would not class them as sf. It is tempting to dismiss the novels as escapist or romance, and Chris Morgan, for example, notes that *The White Dragon* (1978) is 'deliberately written [...] to appeal to a relatively unsophisticated mass audience – for children of all ages, if you like' (1979: 13). At the same time, the series' intergeneric nature makes for interesting tensions between the rules and reading strategies of each genre, as this is fantasy masquerading as sf. McCaffrey also comments on gender politics – some of the characters resist the restricted roles offered to women, and Mendlesohn and James point out the subtle invocation of homosexuality in the habits of the mating rituals between dragons and between riders (2009: 106).

Another best-selling author was Piers Anthony, British-born but long resident in Florida, whose Battle Circle trilogy (*Sos the Rope* (1968), *Var the Stick* (1972) and *Neq the Sword* (1975)) centres on combat, on an post-apocalyptic Earth, using basic weapons such as swords, sticks and daggers. After a number of sf novels, he started the ongoing fantasy series set in Xanth – whose name plays on the pronunciation of his own name and which, in the map at the front of the first volume, *A Spell for Chameleon* (1977), looks like Florida. In the first novel, Bink is threatened with exile to Mundania, because he has no magical talent. In the second, *The Source of Magic* (1979), Bink and his friends go in search of the source of Xanth's magic, and in the third, *Castle Roogna* (1979), Bink's son Dor is sent eight hundred years into the past to solve a mystery and learn the skills needed to rule Xanth. Increasingly, Anthony uses his plots as a means to depict exotic flora and fauna based on punning names, and posing logical puzzles for his characters to solve.

Robert Silverberg began a sequence of fantasy novels and novellas with *Lord Valentine's Castle* (*F&SF* November 1979–February 1980; 1980), although the quest narrative obscures some science-fictional window dressing – a number of aliens and, at the climax, weather machines. Majipoor is presented as a backwater planet, large in size but lacking in the metals necessary for a technology-based civilisation. It is ruled on a day-to-day basis by a coronal, the representative of a largely unseen pontifex, and devotion to the rulers seems universal. A threat to this hereditary system comes when the rightful Lord Valentine is usurped, and abandoned without memories on the other side of the planet. Spurred by seeing the fake lord's tour of his domain, he has a sense of some memory loss and joins a travelling troupe of jugglers. Soon his knowledge of his true identity returns, and he goes in search of the Lady of the Isle of Sleep, gathering support as he travels. As Ian Watson noted in his review, 'the political rationale here is, incredibly, that of the Divine Right of Kings' (1981: 76), with the problem being that it is the wrong monarch on the throne, not that a usurper is ruling. While late in the novel it is revealed that the fake Valentine is greedy – behaving like real-world medieval kings in his expectation of hospitality – the thrust of the narrative is towards stability of rule, with none of the unsettling ambiguities of the characterisation of Silverberg's earlier sf from the 1970s.

Fantasy narratives were not confined to words and images; they were also expressed through music and play. The former was not a new phenomenon, with operas, operettas and classical music all drawing from time to time on fairy and fantastical tales. In fandom, genre materials inspired the writing of new songs or the setting of new lyrics to existing tunes in the form of what they called 'filk'. Leonard Nimoy's song 'The Ballad of Bilbo Baggins' (1968) had bridged the gap between sf and fantasy in having *Star Trek*'s Spock singing a tribute to *The Hobbit*, whereas Swedish instrumentalist Bo Hansson recorded *Sagan Om Ringen* (*Music Inspired by Lord of the Rings*) (1970), as well as *El'Ahrairah* (*Music Inspired by Watership Down*) (1977); the intervening two albums *Ur Trollkaren's Hatt* (*Magician's Hat*, 1972) and *Mellanväsen* (*Attic Thoughts*, 1976) were similar in style, but did not have a built-in cult audience of the same size.

The emerging genre of symphonic rock – a mixture of psychedelic rock with electric guitars, primitive keyboards, and occasionally flutes, yodelling and full orchestras and choirs, with songs extending far beyond the three-minute pop number tied to an overarching narrative – was much inspired by fantasy and science fiction. Canadian rock band Rush released a track called 'Rivendell' on their album *Fly By Night* (1975). Yes's double album *Tales from Topographic Oceans* (1973) was suffused with mystical imagery, although vocalist Jon Anderson's tendency to treat the voice as just another instrument suggests that no sustained, coherent message was intended. Songs such as 'Starship Troopers', on *The Yes Album* (1971), would appear to be science-fictional at first glance, but it is the music that transports the listener, and the track does not allude to the Robert A. Heinlein novel. The cover of Yes's fourth album, *Fragile* (1971), depicted a wooden spaceship above a disintegrating planet and subsequent releases featured more paintings by Roger Dean. *Going for the One* (1977) and *Tormato* (1978) featured artwork by Hipgnosis, who had designed many of Pink Floyd's albums; the former had a picture of Century Plaza Towers,

## THE RISE OF FANTASY: SWORDS AND PLANETS 75

Los Angeles (Minoru Yamasaki, 1975) and the latter a man drumming in front of a landscape, with a smashed tomato on it. *Tormato* featured more science-fictional and fantastical imagery – 'Future Times/Rejoice', 'Arriving U.F.O.' and 'Circus of Heaven' – as well as the ecological plea 'Don't Kill the Whale'. Meanwhile, Rick Wakeman, who had played keyboards with the Strawbs (1969–71) and Yes (1971–75, 1976–80 and intermittently since 1989) had created large-scale concept albums: *The Six Wives of Henry VIII* (1973), *Journey to the Centre of the Earth* (1974) and *The Myths and Legends of King Arthur and the Knights of the Round Table* (1976), the latter two being performed live with large orchestras.

On a similar scale were the orchestral compositions of David Bedford, who had been a keyboard player for Kevin Ayers and the Whole Earth Bands, alongside bass player Mike Oldfield, who subsequently became known for the hit *Tubular Bells* (1973). Bedford conducted an orchestral version of the album (1975), one of several collaborations with Oldfield which included the orchestrations for Oldfield's second solo album, *Hergest Ridge* (1974), also broadcast in an orchestral arrangement. Bernard Benolie is sceptical about Bedford's tone poem *Star's End* (1974), suggesting that it sticks together 'Messiaen-like bird calls, echoes of [Maurice Ravel's] *Daphnis and Chloe*, bits of Vaughan Williams modality, very simplified Bartók' (1977: 19), but praises the first part's 'orgasmic climax for guitars (improvised) and orchestra' (1977: 29), noting Oldfield's contribution. Benolie suggests that it 'conjures up a latter-day Erich Wolfgang Korngold composing a Science-fiction love scene, say for [Roger Vadim's 1969 film] *Barbarella*' (1977: 29). Other works by Bedford with Oldfield were inspired by epic poems, *The Rime of the Ancient Mariner* (1975), declared 'grimly bad' (Benolie 1977: 28), and *The Odyssey* (1976), 'a sonic trip of great fun' (Benolie 1977: 28). A later release, *Instructions for Angels*, featured Oldfield and Mike Ratledge, formerly of Soft Machine, a band formed by Ayers, Robert Wyatt and Daevid Allen in 1966. Bedford's inspiration from astronomy and sf is further demonstrated by a fourteen-and-a-half-minute *avant garde* piece, *Jack of Shadows* (1973), 'for solo viola, four flutes, two horns, trombone, tuba, two cellos, and two double basses' (Cleman 1980: 421), inspired by Roger Zelazny's novel (*F&SF* 1971; 1971).

Allen had discovered works by writers of the Beat Generation in a bookshop in Melbourne and travelled to Paris in 1960, staying at the Beat Hotel in the Latin Quarter, frequented by poet Allen Ginsberg, and visiting jazz clubs. Travelling to Dover the next year, he wanted to be part of a band, and, inspired by the mythology of jazz musician Sun Ra, formed a trio with Wyatt, performing at William Burroughs's happenings in London, before he helped found Soft Machine. Refused re-entry to Britain after a European tour, Allen settled with his partner, academic Gilli Smyth – who performed as Shakti Yoni – in Paris; in the lead up to the May 1968 student protests, they formed the band Gong. Their albums – including *Camembert Electrique* (1971) and the trilogy *Flying Teapot* (1973), *Angel's Egg* (1973) and *You* (1974) – offered an expansive fusion of psychedelia, quasi-Eastern mysticism, concept albums and fantasy, with overt drug references. The band continued through many incarnations, changes of personnel and different names over the next forty-plus years. The Radio Gnome trilogy drew upon Allen's own mystical experiences, especially at Deià, Majorca; Zero the hero has a vision in the Charing Cross Road and goes through a process of seven initiations, enabling him to leave his body for the Planet Gong. Having gained an audience with the Octave Doctors (which appear in the form of a giant eye inside a cone inside an egg-shaped aura), he is charged with bringing the vision to the rest of the world via a music festival, but fails. Allen's cosmology of pot-head pixies, flying saucers, flying teacups and flying teapots, the Planet Gong, the pirate radio-like Radio Gnome and the recurring characters such as Mista T. Being, Herbert Herbert Esq, Fred the Fish, Selene the Moon Goddess, the Good Witch Yoni and the Submarine Captain offer a kind of mind-expanding science fiction.

Ken McLeod notes that '[the] impressive banks of keyboards, the complex myriad of knobs and dials associated with the analogue synthesizers of 1970s progressive rock (not to mention the considerable programming skill needed to effectively control such machines), and the increasingly advanced and variegated number of electronic guitar effects, were roughly analogous to the advanced technology being developed and exploited in the real space programme' (2003: 346), noting how technologised British progressive rock became. The 'authentic' experiences occasioned by drugs could be replicated or guided by technological means of mixing (in stereo or quadraphonic sound) and elaborate lighting and stage shows, with lengthy improvised instrumentals. Sometimes the sound was as much the product of the engineers and producers as the musicians. For example, Alan Parsons, an engineer at Abbey Road who had worked on Pink Floyd's *The Dark Side of the Moon* (1973), formed the Alan Parsons Project in 1975 with Eric Woolfson, a songwriter and manager. Studio-based for most of their career, their first record was *Tales of Mystery and Imagination* (1976), a concept album inspired by the stories ('The Tell-Tale Heart', 'The Cask of Amontillado', 'The System of Doctor Tarr and Professor Fether' and 'The Fall of the House of Usher') and poems ('A Dream Within A Dream', 'The Raven' and 'To One in Paradise') of Edgar Allan Poe. This hit album was followed by LPs which seem to rework or remix the musical ideas, especially the bass lines; first *I Robot* (1976), initially intended as homage to Isaac Asimov, although the adaptation rights were unavailable, and the lyrics seem to deal mainly with paranoia and keeping going in adversity rather than with the Three Laws of Robotics, then *Pyramid* (1978), which contained references to pyramids and pyramid lore, especially on 'Pyramania'. Seven more studio albums and two compilations followed, before Parsons and Woolfson split in the 1980s.

Fantasy did not just offer a soundtrack to life; it offered the chance for play. Role-playing games frequently drew on fantasy – the breakthrough game being *Dungeons & Dragons* (1974) by Gary Gygax and Dave Arneson, revised in 1977 and several times since. Players would create characters with a variety of skills, strengths and weaknesses established by the throwing of various dice, and then perform as them with other players in an imagined adventure organised and refereed by someone acting as the Dungeon Master, who either worked from a professional published scenario or had created his or her own. Many competitors followed, with their own rules, including *Tunnels & Trolls* (1975), *Traveller* (1977), *RuneQuest* (1978) and one based on *Star Trek* (1978). In *Quag Keep* (1978), Andre Norton wrote a novel explicitly based on and featuring a role-playing game. The novel oscillates between power fantasies of wish-fulfilment and warnings of over-involvement in fantasy, where gamers are controlled in the fantasy world by dice-like wristbands.

There is no doubt that role-playing games vastly expanded the market for fantasy, creating a network of potential readers, producing new writers and providing existing writers with a market for which to sell rights. If gamers were stereotyped as male nerds with poor social skills, this was no more than had been claimed about sf fans in general, and probably about as true. What was clear, although it would take another three decades to be fully acknowledged, was that there was a large and developing market for fantasy across the media, even if it was a genre that seemed often to be looking backwards rather than forwards.

# 6
# Home of the Extraterrestrial Brothers: Race and African American Science Fiction

The sf community frequently sees itself as a ghetto, a term which has racial connotations, especially in respect to Jewish people. There has been a significant contribution to the field by Jewish-American writers – Jack Dann's anthology *Wandering Stars* (1974), with contributions by Isaac Asimov, Carol Carr, Avram Davidson, George Alec Effinger, Harlan Ellison, Horace L. Gold, Bernard Malamud, Pamela Sargent, Robert Sheckley, Robert Silverberg, Isaac Bashevis Singer and William Tenn, demonstrates their diversity – but their ethnic or racial identity is not necessarily identifiable within the presumed socio-economic location of most sf readers, editors and writers. Nor have critics sufficiently examined the notions of whiteness as an ethnic identity and white privilege that underpin the assumption that the majority of science fiction's audience is Caucasian. One group perceived to be largely absent from American sf is African Americans, a demographic of immigrants who were brought to America against their will. Mark Dery suggests that 'African Americans […] are the descendants of alien abductees; they inhabit a sci-fi nightmare in which unseen but no less impassable force fields of intolerance frustrate their movements' (1994: 180). It might be that if their everyday experience is science-fictional, African Americans have comparatively little need to write sf. More likely is that the cultural productions of African Americans are not recognised as being sf by the readers and critics of the field. Some of the novels by the two most significant African American sf writers from the 1970s, Samuel R. Delany and Octavia E. Butler, will be discussed in this chapter, as will some of the African American sf music and film of the period. But first I will explore sf's attempt to map race relations through metaphor or indirectly in novels by Robert Silverberg, Gardner Dozois and Philip K. Dick, and in the Planet of the Apes movies.

Complex notions of race arose from the fifteenth century onwards, at about the time that European exploration came into contact with the

Americas. Race had come to define a lineage, often expressed in terms of blood, tracing individual ancestry back to the children of Noah or Adam. During the eighteenth-century Enlightenment, Carl Linnaeus had classified living things into kingdoms, orders, classes, genera and species, but the physical and geographic differences within, for example, finches, led to further subdivision by biologists into distinct races or bifurcating species. To label someone as being part of a separate race is thus to question their membership of the human species, and this reinforces Western power structures and white privilege (Smedley 2007: 196). The spectra of skin colour, physiques, facial features and hair type can be used to divide humanity into an arbitrary number of races (Gossett 1997: 82). Nancy Jesser suggests that 'race is the sign and symbol, culturally and socially constructed to stand for bloodlines and genetic links' (2002: 58). Race has an ideological existence, even if materially it may be disputed; racism has very material consequences. The invisible forces of ideas are given power by a series of laws, especially those that grant rights and privileges to a dominant population.

The economic powerhouses of the southern United States were the cotton, sugar and tobacco plantations, worked by slave labour, that dated back to the period of British and French colonial rule. There were laws (and social pressures) against the intermarriage of white plantation owners and black slaves in Virginia and Maryland (Smedley 2007: 148–49); such laws were extended to all black people. Miscegenation was viewed as diluting the (white) blood, with a risk of degeneration reversing the 'advances' of evolution; racism motivated a whole series of fears about disease, pollution, seduction and corruption derived from the notions that boundaries between states were being crossed (Smedley 2007: 249–50). Laws varied from state to state: in some places it was legally possible for a person with less than an eighth, or sometimes a quarter, of African ancestry to be considered white, but in other areas any African ancestry would define an individual as black, and thus subject to draconian laws (Hickman 1997).

Science fiction prefers to deal with race by means of metaphor, rather than with an exploration of existing material conditions. The physical differences that are used to demarcate human races become insignificant in the encounter with the alien; as the European encounter with the other defined race in one set of terms, so the human encounter with the other will define it in another. Robert Scholes and Eric Rabkin argue that '[the] presence of unhuman races, aliens, and robots, certainly makes the differences between human races seem appropriately trivial' (1977: 188). Humans are no more enlightened in their dealings with aliens than whites were in their encounters with Africans and African Americans; Edward James ponders whether 'the latent xenophobia [...] has not been transferred from the human to the alien' (1990: 28). Both Silverberg and Dozois have written novels set within postcolonial contexts, where (white) human beings have had to acknowledge their misinterpretation of alien cultures.

Silverberg's *Downward to the Earth* (*Galaxy* November 1969–March 1970; 1970) depicts Gundersen returning to Holman's World, now restored to its aboriginal name, Belzagor. At first, he is happy to play up to stereotypes of colonisers to amuse the tourists, but it is clear that he has a much more subtle understanding of the indigenous species, the elephant-like nildoror. He wants to investigate the ritual of rebirth he learned of on his previous time on the planet, and gains permission to go up country where he becomes part of the ritual. Physically transformed, he realises that he has completely misunderstood the relationship between the nildoror and another species on the planet, the sulidor. The novel alludes to Joseph Conrad's *Heart of Darkness* (*Blackwood's Magazine* 1899; 1902), where Marlow, like Gunderson, travels through a jungle landscape. Whereas Marlow is repelled by Africa and is exposed to a vision of genocide, Gunderson transcends his earlier state through ritual: 'a union of minds and immortality' (Kam 1975: 27). Gunderson becomes a messianic figure, determined to bring change to his fellow humans and purged of his earlier sins.

In Dozois's *Strangers* (*New Dimensions IV* (1974); expanded 1978), Joseph Farber falls in love with Liraun, a Cian, which is against the mores of the society; the Cian are referred to as 'niggers' (1978: 39) and he is told 'You can fuck niggers if you want, but don't you think about marrying them! We don't marry our niggers back home' (1978: 71). Farber persists, and is modified to become a Cian, and marries Liraun. This sets off a chain of cultural rites that will end with the birth of a child and the death of Liraun. Farber might not be racist, but he does not understand their culture. Such allegories risk reinforcing difference in a negative way by suggesting that non-whites are indeed aliens. Gregory E. Rutledge argues that 'Black Americans are akin to *aliens* in North America in that they are not indigenous, just like other North American *alien* cultures (e.g., Asians)' (2000: 130). But, equally, the white population is not indigenous, so an ideology of naturalisation is operating within this mindset.

It is an understatement to assert that, a century after the end of the American Civil War, civil rights was still a live issue in the United States, and indeed remains so to this day. Disputes over the election of Abraham Lincoln in 1860 had led seven southern states to declare that they had seceded from the union to form the Confederate States of America. This was regarded as rebellion and led to years of civil war to save the union (Brogan 1986: 324–55). The northern states' victory in 1865 was marked by the Thirteenth Amendment, abolishing and prohibiting slavery. The Fourteenth Amendment (1868) allowed Blacks to be considered citizens of the USA and the Fifteenth (1870) extended voting rights to all men irrespective of race (women did not get the vote until 1920). Despite theoretical equality, in practice housing, education, leisure, transport and other aspects of life were rigidly segregated, either as separate institutions, or divided into 'whites-only' and 'blacks-only' areas, under the so-called Jim Crow laws. Racism was very visible through the first two-thirds of the twentieth century.

A new phase of campaigning began in the mid-1950s. On 1 December 1955, in Montgomery, Alabama, activist Rosa Parks refused to give up her seat in a bus and move to the black section. This sparked a bus boycott, and a series of protests and marches, with Dr Martin Luther King as the most prominent figure. Malcolm X, seeking African American separation and supremacy rather than integration, formed the Organization of Afro-American Unity in 1963, and Huey Newton and Bobby Seale established the Black Panther Party in Oakland in 1966 with a Marxist agenda. The forces of oppression responded with violence – ongoing lynchings, attacks on churches, the assassinations of X and King, the bombing of the Cleveland Black Panthers' headquarters and attempts to discredit the movements.

Philip K. Dick's *Flow My Tears, the Policeman Said* (1974), largely completed by the end of 1970, was one of the few sf novels to engage with such politics, extrapolating an oppressive police state in which, alongside forced labour camps and besieged university campuses, African Americans are under attack following a second civil war. The Tidman Act has limited African Americans to one child per couple, thus halving the population every generation; a comparison is made with numbers of whooping crane, which were down to a couple of hundred birds in the wild. Just as African Americans were over-represented in the frontline fighting of the Vietnam War (Brogan 1986: 677), relative to the general population, so the labour camps are disproportionately non-white. The existence of such ethnic cleansing is revealed only once the protagonist, talk show host Jason Taverner, has been drawn into the hallucination of Alys Buckman, but his lack of surprise suggests that it is true in his real world as well. However, once Alys has died and reality reasserts itself, her grieving brother and lover, Police General Felix Buckman, encounters an African American, Montgomery L. Hopkins, who has three children. Unless Dick has forgotten his details – he frequently wrote speedily and clumsily – this would seem to suggest that the reality at the end of the novel is not the same as that at the start. While Felix feels catharsis at this encounter with Hopkins, it risks being racist in its simplification of black patriarchs bringing a sense of recuperation to white heroes through the 'authenticity' of their noble suffering. Equally, there has been a long history within American literature of nomadic white heroes travelling with a non-white male outside civilisation (Fiedler 1960).

When white culture attempted to represent African Americans, it tended to choose from a limited range of stereotyped roles. Shulamith Firestone notes that, within the context of white capitalism, the African American male 'can give in to the white man on the white man's terms, and be paid off by the white man (Uncle Tomism) (2) He can refuse such an identification altogether, at which he often surrenders to homosexuality. [To prove that] at least he is not a woman [he may treat] "the bitches" with open contempt [... Or] (3) He may attempt to overthrow the Father's power' (1979: 108–109). There is thus a sexualised battle between the phallic power and potency of the white patriarch and the dangerous, potentially explosive, young black 'buck'. The first and third of these African American stereotypes are equivalent to the female stereotypes of the mammy, a domesticated figure – a housekeeper, a nurse, kindly and wise – and the Jezebel – sexually liberal, aiming to seduce, and usually punished within the narratives. A third female figure is the tragic mulatto, a figure of mixed racial ancestry, often trapped between two cultures and rejected by both, showing the supposed dangers of intercultural relations. A fourth is the sapphire, a belligerent, angry woman, named for Sapphire Stevens in the sitcom *Amos'n'Andy* (radio 1928–55; television 1951–53).

The Planet of the Apes movies, television series and novelisations problematically explored the American interracial tensions of the period. Based on Pierre Boulle's *La Planète des Singes* (1963; translated as *Monkey Planet*), *Planet of the Apes* (Franklin J. Schaffner, 1968) features a three-man space mission which crashes on a distant future Earth ruled by a coalition of chimpanzees, orang-utans and gorillas, with humans as slaves. It is only in the final reel that Taylor (Charlton Heston) realises that this is a post-nuclear Earth, by finding the half-buried Statue of Liberty. Viewed in the context of the ongoing struggle for civil rights, the film attempts to reverse the hierarchy of white privilege and puts (mostly white) humans in an oppressed position. The white audience is likely to identify with the human slaves, and cheer on Taylor to overthrow the ruling elite. The racist association of Africans and African Americans with monkeys further encourages us to map the ethnic dynamics of late 1960s America onto a future where African Americans have revolted against white power and have ended up reversing the old power structures. As the films progress through a sequel, *Beneath the Planet of the Apes* (Ted Post, 1970) – which ends with the nuclear destruction of the Earth – and three prequels – *Escape from the Planet of the Apes* (Don Taylor, 1971), *Conquest of the Planet of the Apes* (J. Lee Thompson, 1972) and *Battle for the Planet of the Apes* (J. Lee Thompson, 1973) – the series traces a history from animal experimentation on apes, to apes as servants and slaves, to insurrection. Lest the allegory be missed, in *Conquest* the one decent human, MacDonald (Hari Rhodes), who rescues the chimpanzee Caesar (Roddy McDowell) from execution, is black, and his ethnic identity is repeatedly used to stress his sympathy with the apes. There seems to be a historical inevitability to the failure of integration – the human space crews of *Planet* and *Beneath* are captured and enslaved, and in turn the ape space crew, who travel from the future to Taylor's time in *Escape*, also find themselves prisoners. Taylor can only find peace by leaving the ape civilisation – as Christine Cornea argues, 'conflict is not resolved through peaceful understanding, and a conclusion is only brought about upon the geographical separation of ape and man' (2007: 182). The films offer a negative view of the potential failure of multiculturalism, as they retell escaped slave narratives and show the potential of one section of society to become parasitic upon the other. Brief alliances may be established between apes and humans, but there is too much distrust and bad history on both sides for this to endure. *Battle* ends with a battle between apes and a cult of mutant humans from a radioactive city, which points back to the cult of *Beneath* who worship the bomb which will finally wipe out all life, before returning to a framing narrative of the Great Lawgiver (John Huston) talking to ape and human children. Here is the suggestion that history has been changed, that peaceful coexistence is possible, and it is explained that there are many possible futures. The television series (13 September–20 December 1974) repeatedly focused on human potential for violence, compared to civilised if oppressive apes, and an animated version *Return to the Planet of the Apes* (6 September 1975–11 September 1976) featured yet another human crew thrust into the ape society, fighting for their freedom.

While the films are an exploration of white racism and interracial relations, the use of apes as a metaphor for another ethnicity is problematic. The apes are an uneasy coalition of species, and the narratives do not treat the three equally; chimpanzees tend to show empathy, gorillas aggression and orang-utans wisdom. Eric Greene suggests that Rod Serling – who wrote early drafts of the first film – drew on his own feelings of exclusion as a Jew from white society (1996: 25) and that the chimpanzees are meant to represent Jewishness – 'intelligent, virtuous, and admirable' (1996: 150). The gorillas are meant to represent racist stereotypes of African Americans – 'inherently stupid, physically powerful and belligerent' (1996: 150). It is not clear what the orang-utans are meant to stand in for – possibly for whiteness, but Greene offers no explicit parallel. Susan Bridget McHugh notes an early English slippage in usage in 'orang-utan' also being applied to chimpanzees, and suggests that '[in] spite of their similar ape-identity, the elision of divisions of labor and species fundamentally separates orang-utans from chimpanzees, and both from gorillas' (2000: 55), suggesting a class or other ideological differential which trumps ethnic identity. But the Apes sequence both examines the dynamics of racism and can be used to express white fears about the Civil Rights movement. It is a moot point whether this is an attempt to appeal to multiple audiences or an inevitable consequence of a metaphor played out in texts by different directors and screenwriters. There were several *Planet of the Apes* novelisations, of the movies (*Beneath*: Michael Avallone, 1970, *Escape*: Jerry Pournelle, 1973, *Conquest*: John Jakes, 1974, *Battle*: David Gerrold, 1973), live-action television series (four books by George Alec Effinger, 1974) and animated series (as by William Arrow; the first, *Visions from Nowhere* (1976), and third, *Man, the Hunted Animal* (1976), were by William Rotsler, the second, *Escape from Terror Lagoon* (1976) by Donald J. Pfeil).

Futures imagined by African American sf writers were rare before the 1970s – with exceptions such as George Schuyler in the 1930s and the early works of Samuel R. Delany. Gregory Rutledge argues: 'Because of the nature of race relations in the 1960s, the publishing industry was unprepared for a Black futurist-fiction author who forced readers to address the lingering legacy of racism' (2000: 130). The tactics of the Civil Rights movements had inspired the feminist movements – Shulamith Firestone argues that *'racism is sexism extended'* (1979: 105) and that the mechanics of capitalism primarily discriminated against women, and only secondarily against African Americans. There was a grouping of utopian feminist writers in the 1970s, but no African American counterpart. Hoda M. Zaki suggests: 'In their depictions of all-Anglo utopias, feminist SF writers neither criticize racial discrimination nor anticipate a future which would correct the wrongs of a fundamental social, political, and economic injustice' (1990: 247). Exceptions, such as the Hispanic protagonist of Marge Piercy's *Woman on the Edge of Time* (1976), were rare. The only female African American sf writer to emerge in the 1970s was Octavia E. Butler – arguably the most significant omission from the first edition of the *Encyclopedia of Science Fiction* (1979).

Delany's earlier 1960s novels had mostly been quests, especially artistic ones, and if *Dhalgren* (1974) continues that trend, then entry into a landscape or location is a psychological journey into the self. Rutledge, following the work of William L. Van Deburg (1992), suggests that '[d]eveloping [...] knowledge of one's *Black* – as opposed to *Negro* – self was viewed as an incremental process essential to Black Power/Arts movements' (Rutledge 2000: 133), and although he was analysing Delany's *The Einstein Intersection* (1967) and *Nova* (1968), his comment would seem to apply to *Dhalgren* as well. Before he began it, Delany turned to experimenting with writing pornography, with *Hogg* (written 1968–73; published 1995) and *The Tides of Lust* (1973). The latter features the sexual adventures of an African American sea captain and two children, Gunner and Kirsten, as well as sexual encounters with and among the inhabitants of an unnamed American port. Maxim Jakubowski describes it as 'Delany's most powerful book, in effect an over-powering tale of Satanism, sex, magic, evil, and excess with pronounced homosexual traits' (1978: 63). It draws upon various versions of the Faust myth in its examination of the unintended consequences of a search for secret knowledge and alludes to *The Strange Case of Dr Jekyll and Mr Hyde* (1886) in its depiction of the id. While the novel might invoke 'the American stereotype of the black male's sexual potency' (Renault 1983: 118), all of the characters are remarkable for their sexual prowess; as Robert Elliot Fox argues, 'there is no sense of racial inferiority' (1996a: 53). The more damaging issue surrounds the representation of African American women; Renault says 'there are no black *women* in the novel' (1983: 118), although Fox disagrees, saying there is no 'foregrounded black woman' (1996a: 54). He suggests that Delany's original title for the novel, *Equinox*, dramatises the narrative's symbolism as it offers a 'balance of light and dark' (1996a: 55).

*Dhalgren* became a bestseller both inside and outside the sf genre. Drawing on his experiences of countercultural, communal life during the late 1960s (as later detailed in his memoir, *Heavenly Breakfast* (1979)), Delany begins the novel with an unnamed young male protagonist approaching the semi-abandoned city of Bellona – a variant of New York, after some kind of unspecified apocalypse. The protagonist gains a series of names – the kid, Kidd, William Kidd, possibly even William Dhalgren – and renown as a poet. Kidd is on the borderlines of identities: 'half-Indian, half-white, half-mad, half-named, bisexual, one-shoed, ambidextrous, willful, labile, poet, and hero' (Gawron 1996: 83). He joins both a *ménage à trois* with an older woman and a younger man, and a gang, the Scorpions. Fox suggests that the name of the gang points to a section heading in *Heavenly Breakfast*, as well as to *Scorpio Rising* (Kenneth Anger, 1961), 'a homoerotic motorpsycho nightmare' (1996a: 99, 100) which features several leather-clad bikers. It also echoes 'The Scorpion Garden' (1975), Delany's introduction to *Hogg*. Kidd can be seen as a modernist version of Orpheus, the chief poet within Greek mythology, a worshipper of Apollo and, in Ovid's account, a lover of youths after the death of his wife Eurydice; here the underworld is Bellona.

The issue of ethnicity in the novel has divided critics; Barbour argues that 'the Black community is simply there [in Bellona], and despite the ineradicable social alienation of its racial heritage it is not of cultural importance' (1979: 100). This might be understandable, as Delany might not have wanted to be pigeonholed as an author who focuses on racial issues – as Littlefield puts it, 'a writer concerned only with racial identity, revenge motifs, and expressing the frustrations of the oppressed' (1982: 238). Fox argues, 'Race and racism are not tangential; they are near the novel's centre, especially when they overlap with the psychosexual, with patterns of desire' (1996b: 104). One of the central events of the novel is the alleged rape of the white teenager June Richard by black folk hero George Harrison – a name which invokes but does not refer to the Beatles' guitarist – and she is now fixated on him. The truth of the incident is in doubt, but it is a reference to the fear of black male potency – the young buck – and black males' supposed fixation on white female purity and allure. Kid has a divided racial heritage – he is part Cherokee, thus a member of an indigenous population – and thus he is estranged from himself. He gains power over the largely black Scorpions. As Jean M. Gawron notes, 'the high percentage of blacks left in Bellona has given them majority rule. Nevertheless, because Bellona *does* still live in the real world, blacks as a group in Bellona continue to act like blacks, a people severed by history from the lines of power' (1996: 77). The African Americans have gained majority, but not power, because of white flight – the wealthier whites have moved to the suburbs and abandoned the city to them, as happened in many northern American cities, in part because of the Brown vs. Board of Education Supreme Court Decision (1954) which had been designed to desegregate schools. As populations fall, so does tax revenue, and thus local government infrastructure crumbles, encouraging those who can move to depart. Bellona is left as a city with a small population, and a finite amount of resources that may be liberated for survival.

Octavia E. Butler also divided some of her critics. Jenny Wolmark argues that she wrote books that undercut the 'dualities between male and female, black and white, human and animal, that form the framework for repression' (1993: 45), and Jim Miller suggests that 'her largely dystopian fictions challenge not only patriarchal myths, but also capitalist myths, racist myths, and feminist utopia myths' (1998: 336). But there are those who wish that she had pushed her ideas further: Nancy Jesser argues that Butler's representations of the demands of the body are 'remarkably conservative in relation to women's behavior and heterosexuality' (Jesser 2002: 45), suggesting that women are altruistic and self-sacrificial whereas men are violent and potentially rapists.

Her fiction of this period is dominated by the Patternist series (1976–84), the novel-length exception being her singleton *Kindred* (1979). The first Patternist novel, *Patternmaster* (1976), is set latest, and the subsequent four volumes (ending with *Clay's Ark* (1984)) were not published in chronological order. *Patternmaster* features a largely male power struggle between telepaths – Coransee and Teray, sons of the dying patternmaster, Rayal – and their relationships with the non-telepathic, slave-like mutes and the hostile, mutant Clayarks. The follow-up, *Mind of My Mind* (1977), features a power struggle between a body-hopping telepath, Doro, who has been working to breed individuals with psychic powers, and Mary, who is able to gather and awaken psychic talents. The events cover a period of decades, in order to allow characters to grow up, and seem to be set more or less in the present and presumably near future. *Survivor* (1978) seems set to one side from the series; Alanna is adopted by missionaries and gets caught up in the politics of a hostile alien planet, mediating between different species. Cherry Wilder notes that '[the] book is packed with ideas but they are of unequal worth and an air of compression and plain bad editing hangs over the story' (1979: 91); another problematic element is the convenience with which characters of different species can apparently reproduce. Finally, *Wild Seed* (1980) returns to Doro's breeding programme, covering a period from sixteenth-century Africa to nineteenth-century America, and pits him against Anyanwu, a shape-shifter, able to turn into any animals she has eaten. While we know that Doro must survive, the fate of Anyanwu is less certain, and, in a twist ending, she turns out to be Emma, the long-lived female who acts as mentor to Mary, among others, in *Mind*.

Through these four novels, Butler explores the use and abuse of power, although a distinction needs to be made between a racial hierarchy (drawing on the history of slavery and immigration) and a sexual one (open to a critique on feminist grounds). For Jesser, Butler 'undermines racial essentialism as corrupt and unscientific, [but] retains a commitment to a qualified essentialist stance toward the biologically sexed body' (2002: 39). In *Wild Seed*, where Doro's body-hopping and Anyanwu's shape-changing mean that their sexual dynamic can be reversed and they can have same-sex encounters. Doro's sense of *droit de seigneur* over his descendants is never really limited. The altruism of the female characters leads them to points where they have had enough – a sort of self-willed suicide.

The fluidity of bodies means that Doro and Anyanwu are part of a specific culture unconnected to skin colour or racial identity. For Butler, race 'is a historical category written onto the body' (Jesser 2002: 40), and it can just as easily be rewritten. The unwitting participants of Doro's genetic experiment are transported to America like slaves, and they are in effect his property. This power abuse continues irrespective of his ethnicity. In turn, the paranormal abilities of Mary's pattern can control the behaviour of those around them, and, by the time of *Patternmaster*, the mutes, the non-telepaths, are slaves and can be physically abused. Alanna, in *Survivor*, is of mixed race – 'She's Afro-Asian from what she says of her parents. Black father, Asian mother' (Butler 1978: 31) – and moves the sequence beyond a white/black paradigm; at the time Butler was writing, Vietnamese and Cambodian refugees were struggling alongside African Americans for housing, educational and economic equality. Alanna is well placed to negotiate between the different groupings of the novel but again, as with Doro and to some extent Coransee, it is the female who must assimilate. Butler's pragmatism seems at odds with her feminism.

The bicentennial year of 1976 sparked much retrospection on the origins of the USA and, coupled with the Civil Rights movement and the 1960s anniversary of the American Civil War, the age of slavery was up for re-examination. The most direct handling of the materials – sf's version of Alex Haley's *Roots: The Saga of an American Family* (1976; televised 23 January 1977–30 January 1977) – was Butler's *Kindred*. Its protagonist, Dana, is a would-be writer, struggling to make ends meet as an independent if married African American in 1976. Against her will, she finds herself drawn back to 1815 Baltimore, where she saves the son of a plantation owner from drowning. Quickly she realises that young Rufus Weylin is her ancestor, and that she will not come into existence if he dies. Further slips through time allow her to meet Rufus at various points in his life, and she attempts to teach him more liberal ways to improve the lot of their slaves; her husband is caught up and stranded for five years in the past, during which time he attempts to free slaves. Dana oscillates between hatred for and protectiveness towards Rufus, until her ancestor is born. The historical sections are harrowing, with regular beating and whipping of major characters. Any African American is white property: children are bought and sold like commodities and individuals are dispensed with once their utility is over. While the slaves are perceived as work animals, a few of the women are chosen as concubines for powerful white males. At best mixed-race children might have slightly better conditions – Dana teaches Rufus's children to read, for example. She is repeatedly cast in a maternal role – as protector of her genetic heritage, rather than of future generations.

The African American impulse to imagine the future went into film (to some extent) and music, forerunners of what Mark Dery was to call Afrofuturism – '[s]peculative fiction that treats African-American themes and addresses African-American concerns in the context of twentieth-century technoculture' (1994: 180) – imagining an increasingly cyborgian future from Motortown. Theirs is a future white men do not see – indeed, Dery asks, 'Can a community whose past has been rubbed out [...] imagine possible futures?' (1994: 180), largely excluded from many accounts of science fiction. The musician Sun Ra claimed that he had had a mystical experience in the 1930s, being teleported to Saturn and tasked with communicating with the world through music. The change from his birth name of Herman Poole Blount was an attempt to find an authentic, non-slave identity; the teleported kidnapping inverted slavery's kidnaps. Kodwo Eshun argues that black subjectivity is impacted upon by the history of captivity and relocation: 'The idea of slavery as an alien abduction means that we've all been living in an alien-nation since the eighteenth century. The mutation of African male and female slaves in the eighteenth century into what became negro, and into an entire series of humans that were designed in America. That whole process, the key behind it all is that in America none of these humans were designated human' (1998: 192–93). The alienation is heightened by the centrality of slavery – in one form or another – to industrial capitalism, and Chris Cutler argues that black culture, largely a folk culture, 'had been able in a unique way to come to terms with the alienation at the heart of the capitalist production and commodity exchange' (1993: 51). Even Sun Ra's choice of instrumentation relates to the need for liberation; the practice and imitation of earlier styles and tunes on, for example, guitars puts the player into a subsidiary role until such time as the instrument is mastered, but with a Moog or other new synthesisers there is the chance 'not merely to play with or become the slave of such an instrument' (Cutler 1993: 70). In the 1970s, Sun Ra released at least twenty-five albums, with titles such as *Solar Myth Approach* (1971), *Outer Space Employment Agency* (1973) and *On Jupiter* (1978). The film *Space is the Place* (Jim Newman, 1974) documented the story and the music.

George Clinton, who had been active in music since the 1950s, fronted two overlapping bands, Parliament and Funkadelic, signed to distinct record labels, Revilot Records/Invictus Records and Westbound Records/Casablanca Records respectively. Ken McLeod describes Parliament's albums as 'an empowering mixture of glib science fiction fantasy, street slang and ancient black history' (2003: 343), in which Clinton takes on the persona of Starchild, bringing funk from the aliens to the people of Earth. *Mothership Connection* (1975) established Parliament's musical style, and was followed by *The Clones of Dr. Funkenstein* (1976) and *Funkentelechy Vs. The Placebo Syndrome* (1977). Parliament drew upon a history of ancient Egyptian dynasties, suggesting that the escape into music (whether cosmic jazz or p-funk) was a return to an earlier reality, prior to the European enslavement, as well as being an escape from the 'existential vacuum induced by commodity alienation' (Cutler 1993: 53).

In the late 1960s, Hollywood began use low-budget films to target an urban black audience: 'black narratives, [which] featured black casts playing out various action-adventures in the ghetto' (Guerrero 1993: 69). An exploitation of the anger of the Civil Rights movement, and offering a visible representation of African American characters, the films can be criticised for the degree to which they embrace and exploit existing stereotypes, especially in their portrayal of women – but the characters are not noble or suffering in the ways in which they were in liberal Hollywood films such as *In the Heat of the Night* (Norman Jewison, 1967) and its sequels, and *Guess Who's Coming to Dinner* (Stanley Kramer, 1967). There were private eye films (*Shaft* (Gordon Parks, 1971) and its sequels), horror films (*Blacula* (William Crain, 1972)), gangster films (*Black Caesar* (Larry Cohen, 1973)), tough kick-ass heroine films (*Cleopatra Jones* (Jack Starrett, 1973) and *Foxy Brown* (Jack Hill, 1974)). *Blacula* was sufficiently successful to warrant a sequel, *Scream Blacula Scream* (Bob Kelljan, 1973) and further horror films followed: *Blackenstein* (William A. Levey, 1973); *The Thing with Two Heads* (Lee Frost, 1972); *Sugar Hill* (Paul Maslansky, 1974); *Abby* (William Girdler, 1974); *House on Skull Mountain* (Ron Honthaner, 1974); *J.D.'s Revenge* (Arthur Marks, 1976) and *Dr. Black, Mr. Hyde* (William Crain, 1976).

Whereas many blaxploitation films were escapist entertainment exploiting a particular racial demographic, *Blackenstein*'s revisioning of the *Frankenstein* (1818) narrative could hardly help having a political edge. A soldier, Eddie Turner (John Du Sue), treads on a landmine in Vietnam and returns to America a quadriplegic; his fiancée, Dr Winifred Walker (Ivory Stone), is convinced that the efforts of Nobel Prize-winning Dr Frank N. Stein (John Hart) can aid his full recovery. Harry M. Benshoff argues that '*Blackenstein* makes it explicit that its black Vietnam veteran lost his limbs in a white war; he is still preyed upon by white mad science when he is turned into a monster' (2000: 37). He is in hospital because of white politics, he is being treated by white medicine and is being bullied by white orderlies; it is hardly surprising that he is turned into a murderous monster after such treatment. The monster becomes recuperated in many of the

1970s blaxploitation films, which turn 'vampires, Frankenstein monsters, and transformation monsters into agents of black pride and black power. "Normality," represented by black heterosexual couples and black (and white) authority figures, also appears in these films, but unlike most Hollywood horror films of previous eras, audience sympathy is often redirected away from those figures and toward the figure of the monster, a specifically black *avenger* who justifiably fights against the dominant order – which is often explicitly coded as racist' (Benshoff 2000: 37). Ed Guerrero notes that with the flood of forty films trying to cash in on the success of *Super Fly* (Gordon Parks, Jr, 1972), '[p]rototype quickly stumbled into stereotype and stale formula, and critical blowback from black activists, intellectuals, and political organizations was intense' (2009: 91). The racist monstrosity can easily overpower the appropriation: 'in *Blackenstein* the monster has hairy hands, while his Afro-natural hair is moulded into a square, box-like head reminiscent of Boris Karloff's Frankenstein monster. Blaxploitation horror films may have attempted to reappropriate the genre for racial advancement, but the genre's deeply embedded structure still worked to reinscribe racist tropes' (Benshoff 2000: 42–43).

As monster, Turner cannot triumph, he cannot kill the ones really responsible for his plight, and he is torn apart at the film's climax. African Americans were overrepresented in the forces which went to Vietnam: 'The army was largely composed of black enlisted men, who had joined up to escape poverty and prejudice, and now felt, with some justice, that their white officers gave them most of the nastiest and most dangerous work to do' (Brogan 1986: 677). If some African Americans felt as though they were seen by some white people as otherwise than human, Vietnam was a whole new world again and the processes of colonialism were contributing to more violent deaths.

# 7
# Alien Invaders:
# Vietnam and the Counterculture

Grand claims have been made for the centrality of the Vietnam War to American science fiction; H. Bruce Franklin argues that 'America's war in Indochina cannot be dissociated from American SF, which shaped and was reshaped by the nation's encounter with Vietnam' (1990: 341). America was attempting to make the world safe for its own interests, but this just seemed to raise more doubts, both at home and abroad. Invisible enemies who supposedly threatened the American Dream on an ideological level were also to be confronted, in a series of proxy wars against communism. Vietnam was the site for one such campaign, and it was necessary to introduce a draft to supply the US armed forces. However, the supposedly technologically superior force was unable to achieve victory. In 1975, after years of street protests in America and outside American embassies, the troops made a humiliating withdrawal from the territory. Susan Sontag suggests that the media's coverage of the war did much to turn public opinion against it – not so much the television news as the newspaper photography, especially Nick Ut's famous photograph of Kim Phúc, 'a naked South Vietnamese child just sprayed by American napalm, running down a highway toward the camera, her arms open, screaming in pain' (1977: 18).

Alasdair Spark asserts that 'SF certainly did not split into overt camps' (1990: 114) over Vietnam, but perhaps the division lines had been drawn already, broadly speaking between New Waves and old guards. Kate Wilhelm and Judith Merril had been drawing up a petition against American involvement in 1968, and this sparked Poul Anderson to collect names for a petition supporting the war. Both lists were published as adverts, first in *The Magazine of Fantasy and Science Fiction* (March 1968) and then on facing pages in *Galaxy* (June 1968) (Franklin 1990: 341, 354). Of the hawks, only three of them published in *Dangerous Visions* (1967), Harlan Ellison's groundbreaking anthology, whereas sixteen of the doves did (Spark 1990: 115), and there was an old guard/new wave division. The examples which will be discussed in this chapter, however, all take a negative view of the conflict: a film, *The Happiness Cage* (aka *The Mind Snatchers*, Bernard Girard, 1972), and works by Harlan Ellison, Ursula Le Guin, Harry Harrison, Gene Wolfe and Joe Haldeman, as well as the Star Wars trilogy, while a wider countercultural response was depicted in novels by Philip K. Dick, and in the film *A Clockwork Orange* (Stanley Kubrick, 1971).

Vietnam had become part of French Indochina by 1885, although the events of the Second World War led to an attempted Thai takeover in 1940–41, followed by Japanese occupation until their surrender in 1945. In the years that followed, there was a scramble for control, with Chinese and Kuomintang troops in the north and British and French troops fighting from the south. The north repeatedly claimed an independent democratic republic, backed first by the Chinese and then by the Soviets; France was forced to relinquish its colonial claims in 1954. The communist support for the Democratic Republic of Vietnam in the north meant that America felt compelled to give military support to the (Southern) Republic of Vietnam, with the south also under threat from forces within. America feared a domino effect of Southeast Asian countries turning to communism one by one, so, when battleships were attacked in August 1964, air assaults and invasions by ground forces were authorised. Meanwhile, opposition had been growing in America, targeted at the Democratic Party whose presidency had escalated the war; Richard Nixon, elected president in 1968, planned withdrawal, but, in an attempt to contain the People's Army of Vietnam, secret American bombing raids were launched on Laos and Cambodia. This drove the forces into Cambodia, where they came into contact with Pol Pot and his Khmer Rouge army. It was not until the end of April 1975 that the final American evacuation came, with Cambodia soon in control of Pol Pot. The defeat revealed that 'the most cherished institutions of American legality were, it seemed, riddled with corruption' (Britton 1980/1981: 4). There were doubts over whether US intelligence had been truthful and Nixon's strategy for Cambodia had circumvented Congress. In the meantime, the revelations that Nixon had been part of a conspiracy to bug the Democrats' headquarters at the Watergate Hotel and Office Building, in the run-up to the 1972 election, led to the president's resignation in August 1974 and the installation of vice-president Gerald Ford in his place.

There was an initial reluctance to represent the Vietnam War on film. The only significant dramatisation during the conflict was the pro-military *The Green Berets* (John Wayne and Ray Kellogg, 1968); it was another decade before the release of *Coming Home* (Hal Ashby, 1978), *The Deer Hunter* (Michael Cimino, 1978), *Go Tell the Spartans* (Ted Post, 1978) and

*Apocalypse Now* (Francis Ford Coppola, 1979). Even these films sidelined Vietnam, focusing instead on the home front, veterans returning home or border conflicts in or near Cambodia; *Spartans* was an exception. Several more years went by before *Platoon* (Oliver Stone, 1986), *Full Metal Jacket* (Stanley Kubrick, 1987) and *Casualties of War* (Brian De Palma, 1989) confronted Vietnam more directly, and *Aliens* (James Cameron, 1986) offered a science-fiction version. The half-mad, avenging Vietnam veteran had already become a film staple, whether Travis Bickle (Robert De Niro), the eponymous *Taxi Driver* (Martin Scorsese, 1975), or Charles Rane (William Devane) in *Rolling Thunder* (John Flynn, 1977), which has Vietnam 'on hand to provide the mad mess with its psychological rationale, and the symptom of 'social breakdown'' (Britton 1980/1981: 9), or the experimental subjects of *Blackenstein* (William A. Levey, 1973) and *The Happiness Cage*. Vietnam becomes an excuse or alibi for the state of the nation, and in the search for reconstruction and reconciliation of the American way there is reason for a shift to the right from the social radicalism associated with those who had opposed the war. The war in Vietnam dramatises attacks from 'external forces which are radically beyond control, seemingly absurd or irresistible' (Britton 1980/1981: 5), although they were also perceived to be enemies within.

*The Happiness Cage* is a film adaptation of a play by Dennis Reardon. A military-funded research institute in West Germany houses three patients, two of who have been to Vietnam (and possibly the third, Reese (Christopher Walken), has been there too, but he is so often punished for misbehaviour that he may not have made it out of Europe). One has already undergone electric shock therapy to stop him from feeling pain, in an attempt to subdue him, but the process kills him. Reece and Miles (Ronny Cox) are both diagnosed as schizophrenic, hate silence and seem to like to pick fights with others. Miles, having raped a nurse, is next to undergo treatment, and becomes addicted to the stimulus, which clearly arouses him. Finally, Reese is forced into having the operation, but it will require repeated treatments. Soldiers are required to be violent, but the distinction between appropriate and inappropriate violence is ideological.

A Frankenstein's monster resembling Boris Karloff (from *Frankenstein* (James Whale, 1931)) is invoked in Ellison's 'Basilisk' (*F&SF* August 1972), when American soldier Vernon Lustig seems to become a scapegoat, pursued by angry townsfolk. Alasdair Spark links the violence of the story to films of the period – *Bonnie and Clyde* (Arthur Penn, 1967), *The Wild Bunch* (Sam Peckinpah, 1969) and *Soldier Blue* (Ralph Nelson, 1970) – although those 'slow-motion fountains of blood' (1990: 125) are all set in a historic past. The story does not mention Vietnam, but as Lustig is Medevac'ed to Saigon, it seems reasonable to assume the story is set in Indochina. Lustig has been captured and interrogated by the enemy, in what amounts to torture by Viet Cong, but fights back in a fit of fury and kills all but one of his captors. Back in the US, having been tried for treason, he tries to pick up the pieces of his life – his family have moved away in shame, his girlfriend has married someone else – but violence follows and the local people chase the creature that they have turned into a monster. Otherwise, the story departs from realism with Lustig's possession by a basilisk, a legendary serpent able to kill with as single glance, and here representative of a distinctly demonic Mars, god of war. Violence begets violence, in an unjustifiable cycle.

Ursula Le Guin had been campaigning against the war, but in 1968 she was in London, and as 'a guest and a foreigner, I had no such outlet' (1989: 127) for non-violent demonstrations. Instead, she wrote *The Little Green Men*, which was published as 'The Word for World is Forest' in *Again, Dangerous Visions* (1972), edited by Ellison. Part of the Hainish sequence, it features a forested world, Athshe, which is being partly colonised by Terrans as New Tahiti, in search of timber for an ecologically barren planet. Trouble with the otherwise peaceful natives comes after Major Davidson rapes one of the planet's denizens, who are *de facto* slaves. The Athshean's husband, Selver, attacks Davidson, and there is a massacre of one of the human encampments. The Hainish authorities agree that Athshe is to be left alone, and the surviving colonists have to withdraw. The 'alien invaders of a foreign land' (Franklin 1990: 350) who are defeated by a supposedly inferior military force in a forest (or jungle) environment parallels Vietnam. There is a risk in romanticising the Athsheans, as anthropologist Lyubov does, and he ends up both misunderstanding their culture and causing trouble as a result. Athsheans are perceived as being at one with nature, seeing no world beyond the forest and operating within a sort of dreamtime. Alasdair Spark notes that '[l]iberation [of this planet] as a restoration of a primeval stasis had little to do with the changes demanded by Vietnamese Marxism' (1990: 123). However, we have only been given a partial view of their culture, and, given that Selver knows about violence as a tactic, their society may never be the same again.

While Vietnam is part of Southeast Asia, it can also be perceived as being west of the United States, and it is also possible to read this attempted colonisation as part of 'the myth of the American frontier, westward expansion, the Indian Captivity Narrative, the cautionary tale of going native and of succumbing to sin and corruption' (Hantke 2001: 270). European Americans have not learnt from their genocidal encounters with the First Nations peoples, and are repeating the rape of paradise. Carol P. Hovanec notes the characters' 'reactions to New Tahiti mirror the American ecological experience which has ranged from rapture to fear to coexistence' (1989: 85): Davidson is the puritan, afraid of the land and people, now a warrior and merchant, whereas Lyubov, the poet and scholar, sees the people as noble savages. New Tahiti becomes America and Vietnam, as Vietnam becomes America. Norman Mailer had asked *Why Are We in Vietnam?* (1967) in a novel about a father and son on an Alaskan hunting trip; the answer is perhaps that Vietnam is just treated as an extension of America. Just as in *The Deer Hunter*, which is deemed a Vietnam War film despite only a few minutes of it being set in the country – little more than the Russian roulette sequence – so such a reading 'erases Vietnam itself from the narrative' (Hantke 2001: 270). Vietnam is one more vehicle for imperialism, and Le Guin was perhaps more interested in the ecological impact on her fictional planet than the historical specifics of Indochina: 'The victory of the ethic of exploitation, in all societies, seemed as inevitable as it was disastrous' (1989: 127). The lives of thousands of people are sacrificed in an attempt to protect the American way of life and its economy.

Harry Harrison's satiric 'Commando Raid' (*Prime Number* 1970) addresses economic conflicts, mentioning Vietnam, although it is set in a different jungle war. An Aid Corps unit tries to take a village peacefully, but Private Truscoe nearly kills its headman when he misunderstands their mission. This time the army have been invited in to the country, unlike the all-out aggressive, but ultimately failed, Vietnamese operation, which earned the Americans 'the undying hatred of everyone there, both north and south, and the loathing of the civilised world' (Harrison 1977: 122). But this invading army's reconstruction will benefit the country, bring it clean water, clear the deadly insects and improve medicine and farming. It is clear that the motives for this are not entirely altruistic – Harrison has a notion of how the world interconnects, with events in the developing world having an impact on the developed, and vice versa, but all the same it perhaps has too rosy a view of American investment. It is tantamount to economic imperialism, certainly cultural imperialism, placing Western values above those of the rest of the world.

Gene Wolfe's 'The HORARS of War' (*Nova 1* 1970) recounts the story of a Vietnam-like conflict from the point of view of an embedded undercover journalist, known only as 2190, who has had his bones replaced with metal to be able to pose as a robot or HORARS. HORARS is clearly a homophone for horrors, but it rather unwieldily stands for *H*omolog *OR*ganisms (*A*rmy *R*eplacement *S*imulation). The campaign is a jungle one, with guerrilla fighting, and the humans are on the losing side; the benefit of robot warriors is, as Spark notes, the fact they 'have no relatives to protest at their death' (1991: 122). It is not clear whether 2190 is a human posing as a robot, or whether he has been programmed to think so – he cannot tell for certain, and we cannot trust the media that he is part of. The story is a metaphor for the dehumanising impact of war and the necessary programming of military training.

Wolfe had been a soldier in Korea. Very few sf writers served in Vietnam: Charles L. Grant, Howard Waldrop, David Drake and Joe Haldeman were all drafted. Haldeman had tried to register as a conscientious objector, and then tried to join the Peace Corps, but he was still called up. He failed to get work at a nuclear power plant, and then as an assistant medic. Describing his arrival in Vietnam, Haldeman wrote: 'we were about an hour from landing when I first had the sense of entering an alien world [...] I couldn't recognize any of the stars' (1993: 139). Being under fire and having people dying around him also felt like an alien world, and he felt that he had become an accessory to murder. He was wounded, and hospitalised for five months, 'which introduced me to another alien world, the mundane one of drug dependence' (1993: 146). The whole experience was one of estrangement: 'Through all this succession of alien worlds I was aware of being a stranger in a strange land, moving through physical, emotional, moral, and existential *terra incognita*. What I wasn't prepared for was returning home and finding yet another alien world' (1993: 146). After a mainstream novel inspired by his experiences, *War Year* (1972), he turned to sf, and wrote *The Forever War* (*Analog* June 1972–January 1975; 1974), the story of William Mandella, lover of Marygay Potter, who is conscripted into a war against the alien Taureans. On returning to Earth, subjectively only a short time later, they find that Earth culture has changed too much for them to feel comfortable and they sign up for another mission. After more tours of duty, that see the two separated, Mandella is the oldest surviving veteran at the end of the war.

The novel is both a translated autobiography – William is Haldeman's middle name, Mandella a near anagram of his surname, Mary Gay Potter was his wife's maiden name – inspired by his time in Vietnam, in hospital and return home, and a dialogue with Robert A. Heinlein's rather more gung-ho *Starship Troopers* ('Starship Soldier' *F&SF* October–November 1959; 1959), where the soldiers are volunteers and become citizens through becoming veterans (Gordon 1980: 33–4, Spark 1990, Spark 1991). Haldeman called his novel 'an extended metaphor on Vietnam, mainly about the alienation of soldiers and veterans from the culture they risked their lives to protect – and also about the tendency of powerful weapons to bite their owners' (1993: 146–47). Spark sees the climax of the novel as 'the paradigm of Vietnam combat fiction: a base is set up to bait the enemy;

it is attacked, overrun, and hand-to-hand fighting ensues' (1991: 157). Roz Kaveney, in her survey of the 1970s in sf, argues that the novel looks increasingly like a glamorized moan about the experience of combat, concentrating as it does on the angst involved in being shot at and the dislocation of coming home to a changed society' (1981: 15), and prefers Le Guin's take on the political aspects of conflict. Joan Gordon notes that '[the] soldiers are ordered to kill innocents, not women and children as in Vietnam, but teddy bear aliens, because they *might* be dangerous, though no effort is made to communicate and find out whether there is actual danger beyond the assumption' (1980: 32).

This detail helps a reading of *Star Wars: Episode VI – Return of the Jedi* (Richard Marquand, 1983) as being in dialogue with the Vietnam campaign – the Ewoks are versions of teddy bear aliens. Jim Hoagland asserts that 'implicit [in the Star Wars saga] is an entire commentary on the American involvement in Viet Nam' (cited in Pielke 1983: 155), but Robert G. Pielke insists that '[we] are supposed to have a good time with the film without being troubled, upset, or otherwise provoked to deep thought' (1983: 145), although Lucas had worked on the script of *Apocalypse Now*. Steven Paul Miller argues that there was 'an ideological need for such a fantastic war to repair Vietnam's rip in enabling Cold War perceptions. *Star Wars* helps renew Cold War commitments to a binary opposition between good and evil' (1999: 98). A return to moral absolutes was required. By *Return of the Jedi*, a more direct engagement was permissible, with the forested moon of Endor standing in for the jungle warfare of Vietnam, but if the guerrilla warfare tactics of the Ewoks (who seem to have several thousand tree trunks lying around waiting for endless ambushes) are meant to evoke the Viet Cong's defeat of a militarily superior foe, then the United States is oddly associated with the Empire; to have the West allegorised as a band of plucky freedom fighters and rebels can only be understood as an ideological assertion. The context that Lucas was to provide for *Star Wars: Episode IV – A New Hope* (George Lucas, 1977) locates it in Cold War practices: 'The plot of *Star Wars* is essentially an espionage race, between getting the plan of the Empire's monstrous Death Star into rebel hands so that they can destroy it, and Lord Darth Vader's and [...] the Empire's efforts to discover the location of the rebel base on the dark side of a distant planet's moon' (Miller 1999: 99). But the reading is there to be made – possibly as part of the blockbusters' multivalent desire to reach as wide an audience as possible, including those who had been part of the counterculture.

The proxy battles of the Cold War had long been analysed by Philip K. Dick in his science fiction. War, whether a constant spectacle around which a society is structured or a brief event that changes everything, is an assumed backdrop to most of his fiction. Dick had signed the petition against the war, had been assumed to be left of centre and seemed to be on the edge of the counterculture that opposed America's involvement in Vietnam. Dick's involvement with the counterculture, specifically with drug users and dealers, led him to a series of personal crises, which would both change his life utterly and give a new autobiographical edge to his work. At this point, Dick's cultural capital began an ascension that still seems not to have peaked. The signs had not been good – *Our Friends from Frolix 8* (1970) had been a rerun of *Solar Lottery* (1955) and *The Three Stigmata of Palmer Eldritch* (1964), with a stratified society structured by a corrupt system, and *We Can Build You* ('A. Lincoln, Simulacrum', *Amazing* November 1969–January 1970; 1972) was a manuscript that dated back to 1962. Dick's fourth marriage, to Nancy Hackett, broke down in September 1970, and he was left alone in a house that was supposedly open to drug users and dealers. In November 1971 his house was broken into, and the police were unhelpful in solving the case. In subsequent years Dick evolved a number of theories as to who was responsible for the break-in: the secret services, members of the Episcopalian church which his late friend James Pike, Bishop of California, had been part of, Black Panthers, drug users – or possibly he had done it himself. Dick took up an invitation to go to Canada, and checked in at a clinic for heroin addicts, having tried to kill himself. The relationship he had wanted to have in Canada did not work out, however, and when Dr Willis McNelly negotiated for Dick to donate his manuscripts to California State University at Fullerton in 1972, he moved back to the United States and settled in Fullerton. There he was to meet the aspiring writers James Blaylock, K.W. Jeter and Tim Powers, and his future wife, Tessa. He returned to completing *Flow My Tears, the Policeman Said* (1974) and began writing *A Scanner Darkly* (1977).

Three of the four novels that he wrote in the 1970s centre on relationships between the individual and the state, mediated by police forces and other representatives of law and order. The police state feared by many of those in the counterculture at the end of the 1960s, after the National Guard had fired on protestors, came to the fore in differing ways in the novels. In his earlier works, security guards and policemen are generally not to be distrusted, but in *Flow*, Police General Felix Buckman, while not an entirely sympathetic figure – none of the four main characters is –has been working within the system to close down prison camps in order to spare people's lives, and has resisted any offer of promotion, so that he can remain at a level where he can have an impact upon the camps; he is perhaps more admirable than the ostensible main character, Jason

Taverner. In an era defined by so much violence and disorder, love – for older people, parents, pets, siblings, spouses, strangers, younger people, and even objects of art – can still be felt and is depicted by Dick. Much of *Flow*, however, depicts the opposite of love – informing on others, which risks their arrest and incarceration in the forced labour camps, drawing as much on contemporary Western propaganda about Soviet Russia as on Nazi-era Germany concentration camps. Dick had researched the latter while preparing to write *The Man in the High Castle* (1962). While this was certainly not the first time he had imagined a totalitarian United States, *Flow* is its most detailed depiction, where friendship is to be bought and sold, and loyalty to the state might mean self-betrayal. Meanwhile, the student campuses, source of much revolutionary fervour through the 1960s, are ringed by the police and the National Guard, and are besieged enclaves. The society is also one of surveillance, with huge files held on everyone.

Nixon was to offer inspiration for Ferris F. Fremont in Dick's *Valisystem A*, but in *Flow* appears inscribed in a carpet as 'God's Second Only Begotten Son' (1974: 117). The events of the Watergate break-ins and Nixon's bugging of his own conversations in the White House were still unfolding as Dick completed the revisions. Nixon, born in Yorba Linda in 1913, was a member of the House of Representatives for southern California (1947–50), gaining fame for his role in the 1949 Alger Hiss perjury trial – Hiss had denied being a communist agent – and his anti-communism. In 1950 he won a senate seat for California in an ill-tempered campaign that smeared the reputation of his Democratic rival, Helen Gehagan Douglas, leading her to coin the nickname 'Tricky Dick' for him. Having served as Vice President to Dwight D. Eisenhower from 1953, he stood in the 1960 presidential elections, narrowly losing to John F. Kennedy, before finally winning in 1968 and being re-elected in 1972. Philip José Farmer, in a letter to an Australia fanzine, blamed the middle classes and trade unions for getting him re-elected, declaring: 'Nixon is anti-education, anti-poor, anti-black, anti-science, *und so weiter*. He is, most of all, pro-Nixon, pro-rich, pro-military, pro-Nixon, pro-repression, pro-Nixon' (Farmer 1973b: 141). Nixon's closer relations with China – which he visited in February 1972 – and Russia were in fact symptomatic for Farmer of the president's tyranny. As Nixon's reputation fell, the loss of Kennedy was felt ever more keenly.

It is tempting to read Dick's own anxieties into *Flow* – the collapse of his marriage, his flight to Canada and a new life, and checking into a rehabilitation centre – were it not for the suspicion that the manuscript largely pre-dates these events and that Dick is living out Taverner's fall. Both Dick and Taverner were born on 16 December – the author at home in 1928, the character at Memorial Hospital in 1946 – both had had agents for nineteen years and both are in their early forties. But Buckman has a twin sister, Alys, and Dick also had one, Jane, who had died shortly after birth. Dick had settled in Berkeley, California, with his mother, in 1938 and attended the University of California at Berkeley for a term, probably in autumn 1949; Buckman studied there: '"I got my master's at Berkeley"' (Dick 1974: 107). Berkeley been a centre for student unrest for a century and, in autumn 1949, there was a period of a controversy over patriotism: 'Berkeley was the only major institution to sustain a major faculty revolt against restrictive anti-Communist personnel policies in the form of the loyalty oath controversy of 1949–50' (Lipset 1972: 137); the academics had refused to pledge their allegiance to the state. In *Flow*, Dick was to spare Berkeley the oppressive treatment meted out to other university campuses, which were ringed by security cordons, although it is hard to be certain whether Dick's sympathy for Felix causes his alma mater to be spared, or whether some residual distaste for the institution causes him to see it as collaborationist. The Berkeley resistance may have strengthened its ideological enemies: 'The Berkeley disturbances were credited with having played an important role in electing Ronald Reagan in California in 1966. The Chicago demonstrators helped elect Nixon in 1968' (Lipset 1972: 250). The protestors against the Vietnam War at the 1968 Democratic Convention in Chicago gave Republicans control of the US for eight years; Reagan's period as governor was to pave the way for his successful election to the White House in 1980, keeping the Democrats in opposition for twelve years. The result of left-of-centre protest was a move to the right.

If Taverner/Buckman form a composite self-portrait in *Flow*, then this is repeated in *A Scanner Darkly*, where drugs enforcement agent Special Agent Fred is called upon to monitor a group of drugs users of which he himself, as Bob Arctor, is part. However, Dick insisted in an afterword that 'I am not a character in this novel; I am the novel. So, though, was our entire nation at this time' (1977: 254). Dick's own drug use had mainly been amphetamine-based, starting in the early 1950s, but he had spent time around users and dealers. He included himself among the list of victims of drugs – individuals punished for playing, as he saw it – in the afterword. *The Anderson Tapes* (Sidney Lumet, 1971) had been a mainstream representation of covert surveillance, with the tapes, wiretaps, bugs and photographs destroyed as embarrassments to the surveillance communities, rather than used as evidence to convict Sean Connery's protagonist. The state apparatus is not reassuring in its operations, and Watergate might have been in Dick's mind as he planned his book. *Scanner* continues the theme of self-betrayal raised in *Flow*; Nixon had spied on himself. Arctor and his friends are suspicious – paranoid is not an appropriate word – that undercover agents may have infiltrated their circle, and believe that undercover narcs would probably have longer hair than real hippies. Ruling culture mimics counterculture in order to undermine it; in the end – as was to be seen in *Radio Free Albemuth* (1985) – it destroys counterculture through capitalising and marketing it. Dick's novel here shows the downside of the 1960s counterculture.

Dick drew upon then-current research in split-brain theory to describe the mental breakdown which Arctor/Fred undergoes. The right hemisphere of the brain is concerned with imagination and spatial awareness and the left with logic and linguistics: right-brain Arctor as the free-associating junkie, left-brain Fred as the rational law enforcement agent. Occasionally one of them hears a short passage of words – Beethoven's *Fidelio* or Goethe's *Faust* (1806) in the original German, discussions about split-brain theory – as if something is leaking from the other half of the brain. This division is the result of taking Substance D, a drug which Dick invents for the novel, and to which Fred has become addicted in his attempt to spy on the junkies. Eventually Arctor/Fred buckles under the pressure and has a breakdown, and is sent to New-Path, a rehabilitation centre that he is unlikely ever to leave. His girlfriend, Donna, turns out to be another agent, who has used him to get to New-Path, and there are agents even among the recovering addicts, posing as patients. In the fields around the buildings, *Mors ontologica* is grown in the form of blue flowers; this is the organic basis of Substance D., and it seems as if some branch of the state is experimenting with addicting its citizens.

It was while researching split-brain theory in spring 1974, and shortly after the publication of *Flow*, that two events happened which were to mark the rest of Dick's life: an experiment with mega-doses of vitamins and a delivery of painkillers after a dental operation. In *Psychology Today*, Dick read about how water-soluble vitamins were being used to resynchronise left and right brain hemispheres of schizophrenics (Ross 1974). Pondering what would happen to a normal brain, Dick tried the article's recipe, with remarkable results as he mistook the dosages. Writing to Peter Fitting, he recalled: 'I found myself flooded with colored graphics which resembled the nonobjective paintings of Kandinsky and Klee, thousands of them one after the other, so fast as to resemble "flashcut" use in movie work' (1991: 142). These provided him with the inspiration for the scramble suit worn by Special Agents. Meanwhile, Dick needed medication after treatment for an impacted wisdom tooth, and became fascinated by the light given off from the fish – which is to say Christian – symbol worn by the woman who delivered his medication. Dick claimed: 'I suddenly experienced what I later learned is called anamnesis – a Greek word meaning literally, "loss of forgetfulness". I remembered who I was and where I was. […] The girl was a secret Christian and so was I. We lived in fear of detection by the Romans' (1995a: 23). He heard voices speaking to him – one on the radio that swore at him, another that told him his baby son had a hernia – and he became convinced that he could see bits of ancient Rome in contemporary California. As the months went on, Dick began to keep a journal investigating his experiences and trying to establish their meaning for the status of the universe and in relation to his own work – theorising that it might have been God talking to him, but he was equally open to it being the prophet Elijah, an incarnation of Sophia (holy wisdom), alien contact, telepathy from scientists in Leningrad, Bishop Pike, his dead sister Jane or a result of drug use. At the same time, Dick never quite lost the sense that this could have been burnout after the traumas of the previous ten years, and that he might be losing his mind. One recurring idea was that the date was really 70 CE, the temple had fallen at Jerusalem, and the intervening two millennia were a delusion created by some kind of counter-god. The theology was hardly new – *The Cosmic Puppets* ('A Glass of Darkness' *Satellite* December 1956; expanded 1957) had two opposed gods, and a Gnostic sense of creator vs form-destroyer runs through the milieu. What is new is that Dick put himself at the centre of the narrative.

Except that, to some extent, he didn't. In *Valisystem A*, the novel he wrote first and sent to a new editor at Bantam, Mark Hurst, Phil Dick appears as a sceptical science-fiction writer, in a quasi-contemporary setting where the Nixon-like president, Ferris F. Fremont, is pushing a McCarthyite pro-American agenda and setting up detention camps for dissidents. Phil's friend, Nicholas Brady, is the one who has the visions, and they appear to be part of a campaign to overthrow Fremont. Brady attempts to persuade Dick to publish secret messages in his novels – *Flow* includes the two-word cipher 'King Felix' (1974: 222) between two paragraphs, which is apparently part of this – and subliminal messages are to be included in songs, in a reference to *The Man Who Fell To Earth* (Nicolas Roeg, 1976), where Newton (David Bowie) tried to communicate with his alien family via records. Dick is invited to betray his friend – just as the author was apparently writing letters to the FBI about critics Fredric Jameson and Peter Fitting and Polish author Stanisław Lem, denouncing them as potential enemy agents – and is eventually arrested, with a government hack brought in to ghost-write his novels as a kind of acceptable manifestation of dissent. More secret messages appear – Brady was not the only recipient of instructions from the alien force. Dick again splits his protagonist into the logical and the intuitive, with himself as logical.

When Dick sent the novel to Hurst in late 1976, the latter expressed a few reservations (Hurst 1986: 7). Rather than making the minor revisions that were probably needed, Dick – who had planned to write *Valisystem A* for DAW Books simply for the money (1992: 326) – completely rewrote the novel. Dick remained as first-person narrator, but this time the theophany was experienced by his friend Horselover Fat – whose name is a translation of Philip (Greek: lover of horses) Dick (German: fat). Again, there is the rational/intuitive split, which provides Dick with an alibi for his sanity: it is not he who has seen God/aliens/whatever, but his friend. Two further friends, Kevin and David, are versions of Jeter and Powers – as characters sceptical and devout respectively – but it is notable that the initials of Phil, Kevin and David are PKD. Here the action is even more tied to a realistic 1970s, with the possibly fantastic intervention of some kind of higher being. Dick increases the amount of philosophical speculation – but this is a decade in which Erich von Däniken's *Erinnerungen an die Zukunft: Ungelöste Rätsel der Vergangenheit (Chariots of the Gods? Unsolved Mysteries of the Past* (1968)) became a bestseller, so a narrative about alien intervention would make economic sense. No one accused Kurt Vonnegut of insanity for including himself as a character in *Breakfast of Champions, or Goodbye Blue Monday* (1973), although it might be seen as self-indulgent. But when *VALIS* (1981) finally appeared, some feared for its author's sanity. To some extent, this had already come into question, through the delivery of such speeches as 'If You Find This World Bad, You Should See Some of the Others' (September 1977) at the second Festival International de la Science-Fiction de Metz, France, where Dick's philosophically grounded accounts of reality were taking on an autobiographical hue; the Metz speech would have been confusing enough, given that it needed to be simultaneously translated, but a miscommunication meant that Dick and his translator cut different passages in their attempt to shorten the script. Letters to critics, fans and other authors added to a general sense that Dick was not necessarily in the same world as anyone else.

Through his novels of the 1970s, Dick represented the ruling class's revenge upon the counterculture and, while individuals were acting of their own free will, Dick had a sense that they were punished far too much for their actions. Stanley Kubrick's 1971 adaptation of Anthony Burgess's *A Clockwork Orange* (1962) showed society's vengeance upon its violent youths. Burgess's story of the rehabilitation of the ultraviolent Alex (Malcolm McDowell) was written in a futuristic slang, Nadsat, which Kubrick tried to maintain with a voiceover, and had a final chapter with a contented Alex, which was omitted from the American version of the novel which Kubrick, despite being a British resident, had read. Alex's sexual and violent encounters are choreographed to classical music and 'Singin' in the Rain', and it is music which is then used as part of the aversion therapy to resocialise Alex. Alex's actions are shocking, and rightly so, but the authorities' actions are also reprehensible; as in *The Happiness Cage*, the cure may not be much better than the condition, a mark of the moral uncertainty of the age. Kubrick's brilliant marshalling of production design, along with careful use of location shooting, creates a visually impressive environment which swings between utopia and dystopia. Kubrick had already shown his distaste for war in *Dr Strangelove*, and was to turn to the subject of Vietnam in *Full Metal Jacket*; the corrupting and dehumanising impact of violence is clear in all three films.

Vietnam marked the intersection of three conflicts: between colonial powers and the formerly colonised, between two ideological superpowers, and between ruling culture and counterculture. It was neither the first nor the last proxy war between the USA and USSR, but in the humiliation of a technological superpower there it left perhaps the largest psychological scar. The protest movement – along with those mobilised for African American civil rights – was to fight for ecology, feminism and gay liberation from the late 1960s, in an effort to make a better world away from the bourgeois, patriarchal, capitalist norms. Meanwhile, one of America's staunchest allies, Great Britain, was divesting itself of an empire and reconsidering its role on the world stage.

# 8
# This Septic Isle: Post-Imperial Melancholy

Gray Watson writes of *Jubilee* (Derek Jarman, 1978) that '[if] England, this sceptred isle, has fallen into chaos and disarray, and needs to be redeemed, this is the manifestation at a national, political and historical level of an archetypal pattern of fall and redemption which embraces each individual psyche as well as the whole cosmos' (1996: 44). Just as William Blake's poetic vision of Albion had embraced personal, nationalistic and cosmic mythologies, and had tried to steal them back from the usurping church and state, so Jarman wished to reclaim patriotism from those who had sullied it. In the late 1960s it had seemed that Swinging London was the cultural capital of the world, with Carnaby Street, the Beatles and the Rolling Stones, and Judith Merril had titled an anthology *England Swings SF* (1968). But it was a struggle to publish *New Worlds* – which moved from a monthly schedule to a supposed quarterly to an occasional paperback – and the British film industry went into one of its periodic retreats.

Harold Wilson had been the Labour Prime Minister since 16 October 1964, but was unexpectedly defeated by the Conservative Edward Heath on 18 June 1970, as inflation began to grow and unemployment increased. The union of Great Britain and Northern Ireland was in danger of breaking up – there was a bombing campaign in Ireland and England by the IRA, and on 8 March 1973 a referendum over Northern Ireland joining the Republic of Ireland, which was defeated. The British economy shrank under Heath, as industrial unrest led to three-day weeks and frequent power cuts to conserve coal stocks for the first three months of 1974. Heath called a general election for 28 February 1974, under the slogan 'Who Governs Britain?', failing to gain a working majority even after negotiations with the Liberal Party. After Heath resigned on 4 March, Wilson formed a minority government, holding a further election on 10 October that returned a majority of three seats for Labour. The government began a programme of social reform and Britain voted to stay in the European Economic Community with a 5 June 1975 referendum. But unemployment was still rising when Wilson resigned on 16 March 1976, with James

Callaghan voted in by the party to replace him from 5 April. Callaghan entered into a pact with the Liberal Party in 1977 to maintain his majority, but was being forced to make cuts in public spending in an attempt to reduce inflation. The 1977 Silver Jubilee was an insistence, against all odds, on the greatness of a Britain that was being divested of its last elements of empire: Cyprus, independent since 1960, was divided by a Greek coup d'état and then a partial invasion by Turkey in 1974; Rhodesia, having declared unilateral independence in 1965, became a republic in 1980; the New Hebrides, jointly ruled by Britain and France, became independent Vanuatu in 1980; and the remote Falkland Islands were occupied by Argentina in 1982. Referenda for the establishment of a Welsh Assembly and a Scottish Assembly were held on 1 March 1979 – the former was defeated, the latter passed, but without a big enough majority. Callaghan lost a confidence motion on 28 March, with a general election called for 3 May. Margaret Thatcher, leader of the Conservative Party, defeated him, becoming Britain's first female prime minister.

Roger Luckhurst suggests that this period was characterised by 'post-imperial melancholy', citing Paul Gilroy's suggestion that there are 'interminable and increasingly desperate speculations about the content and character of the shrinking culture that makes England distinctive' (Gilroy 1999: 16, cited in Luckhurst 2005a: 79). This Englishness seeks solace in the special uniqueness of the landscape – which needs to be distinguished from the alienating landscapes of the (former) colonies – and the legal definition of Britishness, as regulated by the Immigration Act (1971) and the Race Relations Act (1976), culminating in the British Nationality Act (1981). The various reactions to this – on a spectrum between an England-for-the-English racism to the embracing of multiculturalism – result in a range of cultural responses. Luckhurst notes 'the rise of extreme right-wing nationalism and race riots in the 1970s […] and the mourning of an English civilisation' (2005a: 79). Some writers fight a kind of rearguard action, asserting England's continued significance; others produce obituaries for Englishness or dance upon its grave. Brian Aldiss declares that '[ours] is, on the whole, a technophobe culture' (1978b: 10), and Luckhurst suggests the English countryside is seen as redeeming melancholy, placing English sf in a pastoral tradition and perhaps presupposing the ambivalence towards technology and the city as previously expressed by Blake, Wordsworth and their contemporaries. This chapter will discuss English sf written by D.G. Compton, Keith Roberts, Christopher Priest, Robert Holdstock, Garry Kilworth and Michael Moorcock, the James Bond films and television series *Doctor Who* (23 November 1963–) and *1990* (18 September 1977–10 April 1978), and the film *O Lucky Man!* (Lindsay

Anderson, 1973), ending with further examination of *Jubilee*.

Compton portrays a fallen vision of England in his novels; he had been a crime writer, but shifted to sf with the marketing of *The Quality of Mercy* (1965) by Hodder and Stoughton. They paid him a salary to write more novels, and meanwhile his books appeared from Ace in America. He published *The Steel Crocodile* (aka *The Electric Crocodile*, 1970), set in a near-future, quasi-totalitarian England full of surveillance and monitoring. Dr Matthew Oliver is persuaded to work at a secret scientific establishment in Colindale, where it is rumoured that something is being developed which will assure conformity from everyone to the rule of law. Counter to the dubious progress of science represented here there is the religious faith of Oliver's wife, remaining resolute that God would not test people beyond breaking point even as she is led away to a prison camp. Another research base is at the centre of *Chronocules* (aka *Chronicules* and *Hot Wireless Sets, Aspirin Tablets, the Sandpaper Sides of Used Matchboxes, and Something that Might have been Castor Oil*, 1970), where scientists employ questionable ethics in their choice of research subject, roping in a local man with learning difficulties to experiment on. *The Missionaries* (1972) marked a departure from the last few novels by representing an alien invasion – with the aliens coming in the form of biker boys and their girlfriends, posing as missionaries, depicting youth culture as usurping threat, although perhaps a decade behind the times (with shades of *The Quatermass Conclusion* (Piers Haggard, 1979), actually written in the early 1970s).

Compton's sales were poor, and Ace and Hodder dropped him, so Gollancz's purchase of *The Continuous Katherine Mortenhoe* (aka *The Unsleeping Eye*, 1974) ought to have marked his comeback; however, they did not publish him again until *Ascendancies* (1980). Later filmed as *La Mort en Direct* (*Death Watch*, Bertrand Tavernier, 1980), *Mortenhoe* remains his best novel. In a world marked by increased longevity, Mortonhoe is told that she has a fatal disease and is offered money to take part in a documentary about her upcoming death. Her narrative is intercut with that of Rod, a man who has cameras planted in his eyes, who surreptitiously films her, and that of Vincent Ferriman, an unscrupulous producer: 'What we don't have in the novel is simply a person laid out before us as a continuous whole' (Butler 2005: 70). She is edited, in a novel presumably written at the time of the broadcast of *An American Family* (11 January 1973–29 March 1973) and published at the time of *The Family* (3 April–26 June 1974), early fly-on-the-wall documentaries which may be naively taken as unmediated access to reality but were anything but. She is also unaware that she is actually healthy. Neil Barron was unconvinced that the novel was sf (1979: 2368), and Tom Hosty felt the same about the near-future window dressing of the lesser-known sequel, *Windows* (1979): 'escalating street-violence and terrorism, motoring a thing of the past, [...] a straggle of bandit-baronies, marriage a renewable five-year contract' (1980: 74). The self-blinded Rod searches for redemption and attempts to rescue his marriage.

Compton's next novel – after Gregg Press reprints in 1976 of *The Electric Crocodile* and in 1977 of *Synthajoy* (1968) – was to come out from small press Borgo, with supporting materials by academics George Edgar Slusser, Robert Scholes and Eric Rabkin. *A Usual Lunacy* (1978) is set in another near-future anarchy, where it has been discovered that sexual attraction is a kind of contagious virus – Colin Greenland notes that the book has '*lots* of dirty bits' (1980b: 91), and it is a notion worthy of a William S. Burroughs or a David Cronenberg – but Compton is perhaps too literary to confront the decadence with sufficient relish. *Ascendancies* is another narrative of infidelity, between a widow, Caroline Trenchard, and an insurance agent, Richard Wallingford, after the former falsely claims for the death of her husband, who is most likely one of the many disappeared. Such vanishings are accompanied by a smell of roses; equally mysterious are a kind of heavenly singing and the manna-like drift of food falling from the sky. All these elements are connected, but the novel does not explain how. It portrays a booming Britain on a three-day week; this ironically echoes Heath's 1974 measure to conserve limited coal stocks.

Keith Roberts, who had begun publishing sf and illustrations in the 1960s, was especially associated with English locations in his work; Paul Kincaid considers that all but nine of his over 120 short stories and ten novels were set in English places or analogues for them, and in particular 'a very distinct area of southern England, around Purbeck and Corfe Castle' (2005: 59). Roberts's most significant work of the 1970s was the story-cycle *The Chalk Giants* (1974), parts of which had been published between 1970 and 1973 in *New Worlds*. The title refers to 'the great prehistoric carvings on the chalk uplands of Britain, and particularly to the ithyphallic giant, armed with a club, that looms above the Dorset village of Cerne Abbas' (Ruddick 1989b: 15–16), which makes a contrast with the landscape itself, viewed as female within the novel. Both Ruddick (1989b: 19) and Kincaid (2005: 61) note the significance of Paul Nash for the novel (Nash's mentee, Eric Ravilious, produced a woodcut, *May*, and a watercolour, *The Wilmington Giant*, of another chalk figure, in Sussex rather than Dorset), but Roberts' work continues a neo-romantic tradition which can be traced back to Samuel Palmer, Thomas Bewick and Blake. The British edition of *The Chalk Giants* features a linking narrative about a character trying to escape a nuclear explosion and situates the stories almost as dreams. In a Fisher King-like impulse, the 'king must marry his land' (Kincaid 2005: 61) in order to save it, but this in fact does not happen, as Atha (a cognate of King Arthur) replaces him, along with a new religion, and 'we are doomed to repeat the same mistakes' (Kincaid 2005: 61). Luckhurst notes that 'the future is a repetition of the primitive past' (2005a: 83), with its sense of an English landscape being both future and past, the cycle noted by Watson.

Richard Cowper's Kinship trilogy also has a cyclical vision of history. Born John Middleton Murry Jr, he began publishing sf as Cowper in the 1960s. His novels tended to be set in present-day or near-future England – D. West describes Cowper as 'resolutely English' (cited in Cowper 1980: 51) in a review of the satire *Profundis* (1979) – and often feature social unrest and rioting. *Kuldesak* (1972) was a rare foray into a distant future, a Wells-inspired narrative of distinct species of humans living underground, controlled by a computer. His most important work was *The Road to Corlay* (1978), the first book of a trilogy continued with *A Dream of Kinship* (1981) and *A Tapestry of Time* (1982), expanded in later editions with 'Piper at the Gates of Dawn' (1976), a title which recalls both the 1967 debut album of the Pink Floyd – and thus English musical surrealism – and chapter seven of Kenneth Grahame's *The Wind in the Willows* (1908), in which Rat and Mole journey in search of a lost otter cub across the landscape, and have an encounter with Pan, the pagan spirit of the English countryside. Maureen Kincaid Speller suggests 'there are distinct resonances, which suggest that Cowper may have had Grahame's nature philosophy in mind, as a model for the Creed of Kinship' (2005: 95). More significant for Speller are the references to the poetry and mysticism of Yeats – falcons, gyres, spinners – which might be somewhat ironic given Yeats's Irish nationalism. Yeats's cyclic vision dovetails the birth of Christ and (more or less) Yeats's present in a two-thousand-year span, with Cowper's imagined 3000 AD being halfway through the next cycle. For Cowper, Speller suggests, '[to] reach a point where redemption is achieved is not to reach a goal, or even a new beginning [...] but rather to begin another cycle in which the balance of power will pass from the individual to the system and back again, like the movement of a pendulum' (2005: 89). The British Isles is a flooded archipelago and has returned to a medieval level of technology, ruled over by a repressive Church. Opposition to this comes from the heresy of the White Bird of Kinship, which liberates the oppressed English survivors, with a boy piper as its prophet. Ashley Rock dismisses the 'idyllic rusticity' (1979: 79) of this future by comparison to W.H. Hudson's *A Shepherd's Life: Impressions of the South Wiltshire Downs* (1910), and this is a romanticised image of Albion. The real world's class struggle of peasants and landowners – partly via gamekeepers – is displaced onto religious persecutions, and the battle between individual revelation and orthodox doctrine. Murry may have borrowed his pseudonym from William Cowper, a nature poet and writer of hymns, who contrasted God's countryside with man's towns (see, for example, *The Task* (1785) – 'The Sofa' (Book I, line 749)), and was a significant forerunner to the Romantics.

Priest's *Fugue for a Darkening Island* (1972) fits into the disaster novel tradition, comparable to J.G. Ballard's 1960s novels, but deconstructs the British cosy catastrophe, in which the apocalypse disrupts the old life, delaying trains and the daily delivery of post and newspapers until a small band of survivors rebuild society (Priest 1979: 194). While trains are delayed – the protagonist Alan Whitman at one point tries to catch one to London – and bourgeois life is inconvenienced, there is no sense of a coming reconstruction. Written in the wake of British fears about immigration and Enoch Powell's 'Rivers of Blood' speech of 20 April 1968, but before the expulsion of Asians from Uganda by Idi Amin in 1972, some of whom came to Britain as refugees, the novel examines the impact of a mass exodus from Africa, both on a liberal college lecturer, Whitman (whose name is a letter away from 'whiteman') and the British Isles (the eponymous darkening isle) as a whole. Britain collapses under both a civil war and ongoing clashes with the African immigrants (the Afrims). Whitman's first-person narration is told out of strict chronological sequence, although it details his life up to the time of the arrival of the Afrim refugee, his life as a refugee with his wife and daughter and his time on his own once the three have been split up. The juxtaposition of the subtly different first two paragraphs – amongst other things, in the first he has white-coloured skin, in the second he has black – show the transformation of Whitman, but the breakdown of chronology echoes both the fracturing of his life and wider society. Priest's narrators tend to be partial or otherwise unreliable, and sometimes it is difficult to square Whitman's ability to be at key events with the lack of transport, the rarity of petrol and the number of checkpoints.

Priest appears to suspend moral positioning: is the novel itself racist, or are its characters racist? The word 'nigger' is used, but in a context in which this may be condemned as paranoia about invasion; the more frequent use of 'negro' is also potentially offensive, although less so in the early 1970s. The Afrims murder and rape people and behave in brutal ways, but then so does the indigenous population. Luckhurst invokes *Heart of Darkness* (*Blackwood's Magazine* 1899; 1902), calling the arrival of an invading boat crashing into London Bridge – still under construction when the novel was written – 'a kind of reversal of the opening pages' (2005a: 81), although

Conrad's novel recalls the invasion of savage Britain by the civilised Romans. The British population is not homogeneously white, although Whitman's narration underplays the diversity of Africa.

Priest begins *A Dream of Wessex* (1977) with 'The Tartan Army had planted a bomb at Heathrow' (1977: 1), and, just as the previous novel's British government had passed aggressive and repressive laws to 'protect' the Afrim, so 'the Scottish Assembly had been surrounded by British troops – to protect the elected representatives, according to Westminster' (1977: 95). By 1985, this Britain has withdrawn from Northern Ireland, and now faces a mainland bombing campaign by Scottish separatists with IRA expertise; Priest wrote in the context of IRA car bombs in London in March 1973, various bombs in August 1973, the M62 coach bombing of 4 February 1974, the Guildford and Birmingham pub bombings in 1974, and many other incidents in the period. Here Priest's model is the ontological games of Philip K. Dick, continuing a process of subverting familiar sf styles: 'I'm saying that you mustn't take this stuff too seriously […] don't believe in these dreams' (Kincaid 1999: 5).

A private scientific establishment develops a neurhypnological projector, which enables a group of people to dream a society into existence – apparently 2135, a world racked by geological and political upheavals. A series of seismic upheavals has split the west country off from the rest of England, Scotland and Wales, creating a quasi-autonomous unit; meanwhile the Soviet Union has taken over mainland England, and America is now Islamic, after a serious disruption in the world market for oil. It is the description of a Wessex mosque that is a final estranging indicator that the world described after the third chapter is different from the 'real' world and this fictional 1985. In using 'Wessex', and in explicitly referring to 'Hardy country' (1977: 7), Priest invokes the fictional milieu of Thomas Hardy, a novelist and poet best known for his books describing everyday life in a vanishing feudal agricultural world – with perhaps a nod to Roberts's version of Dorset in *The Chalk Giants*. Two crises loom: not everyone returns from this dream world, and Wessex changes as a new member, Paul Mason, joins the group of dreamers. Indeed, as they assemble in the future world, it becomes less and less clear that 1985 is real – even within the context of the novel. The project is accused of being 'pleasantly comforting' and 'an escape from reality' (1977: 67), by Mason, the very person who darkens it with his participation. The dream stands as the practice of writing sf – accused of fantasy, wish-fulfilment, escapism and so forth, although Priest's novels are not cosy.

Priest co-edited an anthology of British writing, *Stars of Albion* (1979), with another novelist, Robert Holdstock. Holdstock's early novels – interspersed with pseudonymous sword and planet novels and novelisations – have a sense of the fluidity of time and space. *Eye Among the Blind* (1976) is set on Ree'hdworld, a human colony for several hundred years, with the Ree'hd and the Rundii people still living on the planet, peaceful until the time of the book. Robert Zeitman has arrived on Ree'hdworld, both to warn of the plague killing and displacing humanity through the galaxy, and to attempt reconciliation with his former wife, who is studying the Ree'hd. This coincides with the reappearance of Maguire, a blind man who had died seven hundred years previously, who begins to perceive what is going on. The indigenous people are changing, and it is clear that time is not entirely linear on the planet. In *Earthwind* (1977) – prefaced by a quotation from Yes's *Tales from Topographic Oceans* (1973) – time oscillates on the planet Aeran, so that the future appears to be fixed and predictable. It is a colony world – its inhabitants having recreated Neolithic behaviour from their unconscious. This world is explored by Elspeth Mueller, an amateur anthropologist who wishes to keep the Aerani isolated from humans, Peter Ashkar, a user of the *I Ching*, and Gorstein, a spaceship captain, who are bringing monitors to Aeran to record what is going on there. Mueller is slowly drawn into the Aerani culture, as Ashkar finds his oracle can only cope with probability, not certainty, and Gorstein reverts to savagery. Holdstock had visited Ireland while writing the novel, to research megalith builders, but his writing only took flight when he connected Celtic myth to family melodrama in Albion in 'Mythago Wood' (*F&SF* September 1981). Kincaid argues that *Earthwind* is 'not the origins of Holdstock's obsession with the birth of Celtic and pre-Celtic culture, but we are surely seeing the first inklings that this is his subject, his root matter' (1993: 8).

Garry Kilworth's third published novel, *Split Second* (1979), shares Holdstock's interest in earlier stages of civilisation, but pushes it back to Cro-Magnon times. Divorced archaeologist Paul Levan finds ancient remains in a dig on Cyprus, and his son, Richard, who accidentally damages part of his father's equipment, finds himself in the skull of a prehistoric boy. Greenland complained that the novel lacked 'symmetrical organization' (1980d: 95) in its structuring of past and present elements. Time travel had been part of Kilworth's paradox story, 'Let's Go to Golgotha' (1975), which won a Gollancz/*Sunday Times* science-fiction story competition. All of the witnesses to Christ's crucifixion are time-travelling tourists who were told to vote for Barabbas being freed. Kilworth had travelled widely as he was growing up and looks far beyond English landscapes in his early work. *In Solitary* (1977) features a long since colonised Earth, with a lonely human, Cave, digging into the mudflats to discover human history. *The Night of Kadar* (1978) shows what appears to be the start of the colonisation process, with a quasi-Islamic Earth mission arriving at an alien planet with thousands of settlers in embryo – but the planet already has an indigenous species. Anthony Wolk suggests that 'the central concern of the novel is the [indigenous] tribe's evolution of a culture of their own choice' (1979: 90); his first two novels explore processes of colonisation and their impact on self-determination, a live debate in an era of British decolonisation.

Moorcock also addresses issues of colonialism in his work, repeatedly using satiric forms. His international Jerry Cornelius 'thrillers' – *The Final Programme* (1968), *A Cure for Cancer* (*New Worlds* March–July 1968; 1971), *The English Assassin* (1972) and *The Condition of Muzak* (1977) – along with various short stories, some collected in *The Lives and Times of Jerry Cornelius* (1976) and *My Experiences in the Third World War* (1980), feature a countercultural version of the British spy James Bond. In *The Final Programme*, Jerry attempts to defeat his brother Frank's plan to build a computer that will control the world, and raids his dead father's house in search of Frank and their sister Catherine. In the second novel, Cornelius returns, but is an African Caribbean with white hair, in a Europe occupied by America in an expansion of the Vietnam War. He works with and against Bishop Beesley, and his sexuality and ethnicity are fluid. In *The English Assassin*, Cornelius spends much of the time in a coma, while Europe disintegrates. The final volume has resurrected him, in another enactment of the redemption of England and the individual, but there is the strong suggestion that Cornelius is a teenager who has fantasised these adventures, undercutting all that has gone before. The novels eschew linearity, breaking down into vignettes of encounters between characters, and interspersed with news clippings reporting the disintegration of the present-day world. The film version of *The Final Programme* (aka *The Last Days of Man on Earth*, Robert Fuest, 1973) offers a tidier narrative than the novels, with Cornelius (Jon Finch), Miss Brunner (Jenny Runacre) and a group of scientists breaking into his father's house in search of a microfilm and to kill Frank (Derrick O'Connor). Miss Brunner, who has an ability to absorb people, wishes to combine with Cornelius to produce the perfect, hermaphrodite human messiah, but instead produces a wisecracking caveman who sounds like Bogart. The fashionable suits, the helicopters, planes and fast cars, international locations, the secret base complete with submarine and laboratory and the climactic fights with Cornelius elevate the feel of Bond, but Cornelius lacks the necessary competence and charm.

The actual James Bond films were increasingly divorced from the geopolitics of the Cold War which Moorcock had satirised, choosing instead to focus on wealthy individuals holding the world to ransom from their secret base, only to be defeated by a wise-cracking Bond and his various gadgets. Sean Connery returned to the role in *Diamonds are Forever* (Guy Hamilton, 1971), in which recurring villain Blofeld (Charles Grey) attempts to build a space-based laser gun. Connery was replaced by Roger Moore, who played Simon Templar in the television series *The Saint* (4 October 1962–9 February 1969) and Lord Brett Sinclair in *The Persuaders!* (17 September 1971–25 February 1972), and who had supposedly been considered for Bond in *Dr No* (Terence Young, 1962). This version of the character, unveiled in *Live and Let Die* (Guy Hamilton, 1973), was more obviously a playboy than Connery's, often dressed in lounge suits, speaking in witty one-liners and indulging the sense of self-parody, even 'a superficial air of postmodernism' (Shail 2008: 156), as if the films were admitting how preposterous they were. Like *Diamonds are Forever*, *Live and Let Die* makes much of American settings, especially New Orleans and (in homage to blaxploitation) parts of New York. It is also set in a former British colony, Jamaica, with the plot involving a rather more credible attempt to flood the American market with illegal drugs. A black Bond girl, Rosie Carver (Gloria Hendry), who cannot be trusted and is shot in the back by a villain, is typical of the film's conflicted attitudes to race. *The Man with the Golden Gun* (Guy Hamilton, 1974) acknowledges the energy crisis of the 1970s, with Bond sent after a vital part of solar power technology. The reclusive assassin Francisco Scaramanga (Christopher Lee) has stolen the device and can auction this technology to either side of the Cold War, or to an OPEC country that may well suppress it. Scaramanga, as individualist millionaire, contrasts himself with Bond: 'You work for peanuts, a hearty well done from her Majesty the Queen and a pittance of a pension', whereas Scaramanga can afford a secret base inside an island in communist Chinese territory. *The Spy Who Loved Me* (Lewis Gilbert, 1977) demonstrates a certain degree of Cold War entente, as Bond and a Russian agent, Anya Amasova (Barbara Bach), join forces in search of two stolen submarines, one British, one Russian. Karl Stromberg (Curt Jürgens), a reclusive millionaire, wishes to hold the world to ransom by firing nuclear missiles at the superpowers. *Moonraker* (Lewis Gilbert, 1979) is an attempt to take the series into the outer space adventures of *Star Wars* (George Lucas, 1977), but the first half of the film is an international cat and mouse thriller closer to *Live and Let Die*, with Jaws (Richard Kiel) returning from *The Spy Who Loved Me*. There is a nod to *Close Encounters of the Third Kind* (Steven Spielberg, 1977) as the key code to a secret laboratory is that film's five-note musical sequence used to communicate with UFOs. The millionaire villain, Drax (Michael Ironside), threatens the world with killer germs from a space station, but draws attention by stealing a space shuttle.

At one point in the BBC television series, *Doctor Who*, companion Jo Grant (Katy Manning) compares the Doctor (Jon Pertwee) to Bond and finds him lacking. This is part of a plot to deceive the Master (Roger Delgado), the villain in the Malcolm Hulke scripted 'Frontier in Space' (24 February–31 March 1973). This does nod to the change in the format in the early 1970s – the central character had previously been established in the series as a mysterious exile from his own people rather than a state employee, unwilling to use guns but happy to use gadgets. When Patrick Troughton departed the role and was replaced by Pertwee – which coincided with the shift from black and white to colour – the character was stranded on Earth by his own species, the Time Lords, as punishment for his interference in the concerns of other civilisations. The Doctor took employment with UNIT (the United Nations Intelligence Taskforce), which had been established as an international body dedicated to defeating alien invasions and first appeared on screen in Derrick Sherwin's 'The Invasion' (2 November–21 December 1968). The use of military hardware increased realism in the series, but the downside was that there were fewer available plots: essentially variations on first contact, alien invasion, disaster and terrorism. An alien invasion features in Holmes's 'Spearhead from Space' (3–24 January 1970), followed by the discovery of a lost reptilian species in Hulke's 'Doctor Who and the Silurians' (31 January–14 March 1970), then astronauts discover something nasty in David Whitaker's 'The Ambassadors of Death' (21 March–2 May 1970) and the seventh season concludes with a parallel universe in Don Houghton's 'Inferno' (9 May–20 June 1970). The eighth season introduces an evil Time Lord and recurring villain, the Master, an equivalent to Bond's Blofeld, who appears until the actor's tragic fatal car crash. But Earth-bound adventures proved too limiting, so the producer, Barry Letts, and script editor, Terrance Dicks, introduced stories in which the Doctor was sent on missions by the Time Lords and then freed him with the tenth anniversary story, Bob Baker and Dave Martin's 'The Three Doctors' (30 December 1972–20 January 1973). The UNIT years put England at the heart of alien invasion – other locations are hardly mentioned – and, while there might be a temptation to read them in relation to immigration anxieties, this was before the wave of Asian refugees.

The military background to the Pertwee era exposes tensions in the format: for a character that dislikes weapons, he causes a lot of people to die. The Doctor tries to resist the Brigadier's urge to blow things up, for example in the case of the (misnamed) Silurians, and the Sea Devils in the serial of the same name (26 February–1 April 1972). It is notable that in the case of the Silurians, Sea Devils and Draconians ('Frontier in Space'), all written by the left-leaning Hulke, are reptilian species that wrongly garner suspicion, and in Hulke's stories it is the military that is to be feared. In 'The Curse of Peladon', the Doctor wrongly suspects the Ice Warriors. But any invading force that will not coexist with an indigenous species has to be destroyed, as in Baker and Martin's 'The Claws of Axos' (13 March–3 April 1971). At a point when Britain had a relatively low military profile – and before the resurgence of the Troubles in Northern Ireland – the UNIT narratives provide Britain with a role in world affairs without anyone having to go overseas (although occasionally they get to leave the planet). The moral complexities are faced in Nation's 'Genesis of the Daleks' (8 March–12 April 1975), where the Doctor (by then played by Tom Baker) hesitates in his attempt to wipe out the Daleks, wondering whether the existence of such evil does not create a greater good. The setback rather than annihilation which then seems to occur – indeed, which might have been what was going to happen all along – offers a sense of fair play rather than aggression.

The series' equivalent of the 'Bond girls' was a number of young, female companions who had platonic relationships with the often rather patriarchal and patronising Doctor. The status of the companion is an index of the tension between narrative need (someone to explain the plot to and be rescued) and the impact of feminism (someone who is intelligent and can rescue herself and the Doctor). Pertwee's first companion, Liz Shaw (Caroline John), is a scientist who thus needs fewer explanations, but was replaced after one season by Grant. She is given to holding hands with male characters and leaves at the end of series ten in Robert Sloman's 'The Green Death' (19 May–23 June 1973), married off to one of the serial's characters. By the mid-1970s it was difficult to ignore feminism, so the new companion, professional journalist Sarah Jane Smith (Elisabeth Sladen), stows away in the TARDIS at the start of Robert Holmes's 'The Time Warrior' (15 December 1973–5 January 1974). At times she is represented as strident, with her determination to be independent getting her into dangers that then require a male rescuer. A male companion was added for the twelfth season, Harry Sullivan (Ian Marter), who had to show heroism but not overshadow the Doctor. Smith's successor, Leela (Louise Jameson), introduced in Chris Boucher's 'The Face of Evil' (1–22 January 1977), is good with weapons, especially throwing knives, suggesting the most feminist companion yet, but at the same time her skimpy costumes encourage heterosexual male objectification of her body. Her character is married off at the end of David Agnew's (Graham Williams and Anthony Read) 'The Invasion of Time' (4 February–11 March 1978), and at the start of the sixteenth season (28 October 1978–24 February 1979) the Doctor is paired with a supposed equal, the Time Lady Romana (Mary Tamm). However, the narrative template requires a maiden-in-peril, so the character slowly loses her agency; Tamm left the series, with the character Romana then 'regenerated' so that she could be played by Lalla Ward, from the start of Nation's 'Destiny of the Daleks' (1–22 September 1979). Whereas the Doctor's regenerations had been in response to traumatic events, or imposed by the Time Lords, this was presented almost as a female character's whim within the series. The characters are allowed more banter than with the first version of Romana, and they are more equal than the earlier relationships.

Unresolved sexual tension also occurs in the first season of the BBC series *1990*, which is set in a British surveillance state with curtailed civil liberties. Given mentions of three-day weeks, the need for a union card, attacks on second jobs and moonlighting, this dystopia is extrapolated from the power of the trade unions and the travails of the British governments of the era. While the upper echelons of society have access to luxuries, imported goods and spirits, as well as the right to have a large family and a good education, the working class have limited rations and may even be sterilised. Dissidents are sent for electroshock brainwashing, or deprived of citizenship and cast out as nobodies. Jim Kyle (Edward Woodward), a journalist for the one remaining private newspaper, tries to expose the injustices and secretly works to help some individuals illegally emigrate, always in danger of being implicated himself. In the first series he tries to establish a working relationship with Delly Lomas (Barbara Kellerman), the deputy controller of the APC, the very visible secret police, in an attempt to ease conditions, with the possibility of something more romantic developing. Lomas and her rival deputy controller, Henry Tasker (Clifton Jones), along with the incompetent comic relief home secretary Dan Mellor (John Savident), were replaced in the second series by Lynn Blake (Lisa Harrow) and home secretary Kate Smith (Yvonne Mitchell), the latter sounding increasingly like the then leader of the opposition and future prime minister, Margaret Thatcher. Kyle struggles to avoid sinking to the level of his opponents, rejecting violence and, in the final episode, kangaroo courts; he also refuses money from emigrants and only deals with the spiv-like black marketeers as a last resort. Creator Wilfred Greatorex had also worked as script editor on *Danger Man* (11 September 1960–12 January 1968) and was creator of *Secret Army* (7 September 1977– 15 December 1979) and *Airline* (3 January 1982–28 February 1982), and directors of individual episodes included Alan Gibson and Peter Sasdy, who had worked on Hammer horror films. The series is some of the darkest sf in television history.

British politics are central to *O Lucky Man!* (Lindsay Anderson, 1973), featuring Mick Travis (Malcolm McDowell) as a travelling salesman driving through a landscape that seems to be on the brink of war. Wanting to better himself, he becomes an assistant to the politician Sir James Burgess (Ralph Richardson) who is selling chemicals to corrupt African dictators. Travis is jailed for government corruption, and on being freed he auditions for a film for Lindsay Anderson. Britain in the 1970s is clearly rotten; however, casting a blacked-up Arthur Lowe as Dr Munda from the African state of Zingara appears racist, unless it is interpreted as a commentary on Britain's exporting of racist attitudes. But the film is a carnival, with songs performed by the Animals marking transitions between sequences and commenting on the narrative, before a celebratory party with the actors, crew and the band at the end of the film.

If the use of the Animals allows Anderson to update the estrangement effect of the chorus of a Greek play, the casting of Adam Ant, Siouxsie and the Banshees, Toyah Willcox, Little Nell, Hermine Demoriane, Jordan (Pamela Rooke), Lindsay Kemp, Jack Birkett and Richard O'Brien in *Jubilee* (Derek Jarman, 1978) fosters a punk ethos of 'anarchists, sex-fiends, sadomachochists, pyromaniacs and "no-future" philosophy' (O'Pray 1996: 68). Their characters alternate bored games with acts of murderous violence, a commentary upon the state of Britain at the time of Queen Elizabeth II's silver jubilee. *Jubilee* is 'structured in a way calculated to frustrate spectators expecting complete or uninterrupted footage of its featured performances' (Monk 2008: 83). The set piece is the performance of 'Jerusalem' (1804) by 'Amyl Nitrite' (Jordan), a version very different from Sir Hubert Parry's 1916 patriotic appropriation of Blake's words. Jarman's script is dedicated to Blake (Wymer 2005: 61), attempting to reclaim Blake's sentiments. However, many of Jarman's characters sell out to media mogul Borgia Ginz (Birkett), who has turned Buckingham Palace into a recording studio. The near-future satire, filmed mostly in the remaining bombsites and soon to be redeveloped warehouses on the Thames, is framed with Elizabeth I (Jenny Runacre) and John Dee (O'Brien), linking the first Elizabethan age to the second by alchemy, but the promised golden age has not come: 'the sexual liberation of the 1960s had failed to liberate anything else and had created Pornotopia, rather than the New Jerusalem envisaged by Blake' (Wymer 2005: 63). Jarman's microbudgeted, artistic and highly personal films reflect upon the Matter of Britain, perhaps more precisely the Matter of England, but his post-imperial melancholia sees little escape from the debased and corrupting forms of patriotism and 'heritage' under Thatcher.

# 9
# Foul Contagion Spread: Ecology and Environmentalism

Science fiction often depicts the interaction between the environment and its inhabitants. There are correlations between individuals, their physical setting and the surrounding flora and fauna; an ecosystem of greater or lesser consistency is depicted. The environment itself may become a character in the narrative, especially as an antagonist to the hero, an often unstoppable and sometimes invisible set of forces. The continued rise of consumerism and the post-industrialised West in the 1970s, as represented in an increasingly global and globalised media, put a growing strain on raw materials, fuel and labour. Earth was imagined as a single unit, for example as the Spaceship Earth of a speech by Adlai Stevenson in 1965, in Kenneth E. Boulding's 'The Economics of the Coming Spaceship Earth' (1966), which contrasted open and closed systems, and in Buckminster Fuller's *Operating Manual for Spaceship Earth* (1968). Harry Harrison adopted the phrase to refer to the moral he perceived behind *Soylent Green* (Richard Fleischer, 1973), a loose adaptation of his *Make Room! Make Room!* (*SF Impulse* August–October 1966; 1966): it 'shows what the world will be like if we continue in our insane manner to pollute and overpopulate Spaceship Earth' (1984: 146), an idea he had already advanced in his short story 'Commando Raid' (1970): 'The richest countries better help the poorest ones, because it's all the same spaceship' (1977: 122). Barry Commoner argued that there was only one ecosystem, and that everything came from somewhere and went somewhere, with resources likely to be turned from useful to useless. Natural systems kept resources generally renewable. James Lovelock's Gaia hypothesis suggested that the systems of the Earth maintained the balance of the environment through homeostasis, but human action pushed this beyond natural limits. Earth Day was first marked in 1970, raising awareness of the threats to biodiversity, and the following year Greenpeace started campaigning, as the back-to-nature imperatives of 1960s counterculture spread. Denis Cosgrove notes how two photographs from space in particular, *Earthrise* (December 1968) and AS17-148-22727 (7 December 1972), one taken of the Earth from space, the other from the moon, captured the popular imagination, the latter in particular gaining a 'quasi-mantric status [...] among *Whole-earth* enthusiasts' (1994: 276). The Earth, isolated in the blackness of space, becomes an entire, contained system.

Sf, meanwhile, could show alternatives to the Earth's current environment – as exemplars, two novels by Hal Clement and Frederik Pohl will be looked at – and the impact of the environment in general on characters is visible in Michael Coney's novels. The meltdown of society through consequences of humanity's impact on the environment is shown in *No Blade of Grass* (Cornel Wilde, 1970), *Doomwatch* (9 February 1970–14 August 1972), *The Omega Man* (Boris Sagal, 1971) *Soylent Green*, John Brunner's *The Sheep Look Up* (1975), *Survivors* (16 April 1975–8 June 1977), Gore Vidal's *Kalki* (1978) and Gregory Benford's *Timescape* (1980). Meanwhile, a raft of films depicted nature's revenge on humanity, with *Phase IV* (Saul Bass, 1974) as a stand-out example. Threats from outer space which might doom Earth's environment included comets and meteors, as in Benford's *In the Ocean of Night* (1976), Larry Niven and Jerry Pournelle's *Lucifer's Hammer* (1977), John Baxter's *The Hermes Fall* (1978), *Meteor* (Ronald Neame, 1979) and Benford and William Rotsler's *Shiva Descending* (1980). There was also the threat of alien invasion, witting or otherwise – *The Andromeda Strain* (Robert Wise, 1971), Boris and Arkady Strugatsky's *Roadside Picnic* (1972, trans. 1978), *Stalker* (Andrei Tarkovsky, 1979) and *The Invasion of the Body Snatchers* (Philip Kaufman, 1978). Some writers tried to imagine ways of surviving the anticipated disasters – going off-planet in *Silent Running* (Douglas Trumbull, 1972), cloning in Pamela Sargent's *Cloned Lives* (1976) and Kate Wilhelm's *Where Late the Sweet Birds Sang* (1976). Humanity goes back to nature in Ernest Callenbach's *Ecotopia* (1975), Wilhelm's *Juniper Time* (1979) and Sally Miller Gearhart's *The Wanderground: Stories of the Hill People* (1979), in various forms of separatist society.

Clement and Pohl both offer classic sf representations of alien environments. Clement's *Star Light* (*Analog* June–September 1970; 1971), a sequel to *Mission of Gravity* (*Astounding* April–July 1953; 1954), centres on a Human-Mesklinite mission to supergiant planet Drawnh, jeopardised by the species' distrust of each other and their invisible agendas. They also work on faulty scientific assumptions – the weather forecasts provided to the Mesklinites are based on Earth-style water environments, whereas Drawnh has a water-ammonia mix that performs differently according to temperature. Pohl's *Jem: The Making of a Utopia* (*Galaxy* November 1978–July 1980; 1979) foregrounds the environmental pressures that Gerard K.

O'Neill suggests were facing an Earth-bound humanity in the 1970s: 'energy, food, living space and population' (1978: 18). It depicts 'a racial, political and economic conflict, imposed upon an alien and rather fragile ecology' (Greenland 1980c: 61), as an old Cold War binary of capitalist vs communist has given way to a tripartite system of oil producers (OPEC and Britain), food producers (the USA, Canada, parts of the Soviet Bloc) and people producers (the Third World, China, Pakistan, India), locked in a more complex set of struggles. Having destroyed the Earth's ecosystem, the search for living space finds the same structures in Jem's dominant species, effectively air, ground and underground; here though there is cooperation rather than competition, which the humans eventually discover among themselves.

Michael Coney produced four interlinked novels – *Mirror Image* (1972), *Syzygy* (1973), *Charisma* (1975) and *Brontomek!* (1976) – that explore environmental systems. Three feature alien colony worlds, and *Charisma* has a series of parallel worlds. All of them have individualist anti-heroes who find themselves bound into an awkward relationship with Machiavellian bosses of large corporations. In *Mirror Image*, the Hetherington Organisation works its colonists hard. One indigenous species can metamorphose into the person that the observer most desires, literally making love not war. However, Hetherington turns these 'amorphs' into slaves that will make more economic workers and attempts to create a superman from combining an amorph with six supposed genii. Meanwhile, humanity's attempt to fix the sand in the area where a refinery is being built has disrupted the natural cycle of the soil, causing native vegetation to fail.

*Syzygy* is set on Arcadia, a planet with six moons that line up every fifty-two years, triggering devastating tides and a strange wave of violence throughout the animal and human population of the planet. The gravitational forces have an impact upon the plankton, transforming it into a series of telepathic minds that, in self-defence, boost people's feelings of hatred and fear. In extreme circumstances it can work people like puppets. An elderly member of the community observes 'The Minds are bitchy […] They've had so much trouble with us that they've got vindictive. […] Can you blame them? We're the intruders after all. They've been here for thousands of years' (Coney 1973: 148). This is the mirror image of *Mirror Image*; whereas the aliens of Marilyn produce humanity's ideal, here it is the darkest parts that get emphasised.

While the events are continued in *Brontomek!*, which is also a follow-up to *Mirror Image*, the former only makes sense in the context of the characters and narrative of *Charisma*. Reflecting Coney's experiences as hotelier, the novel is set in a small coastal town and research station in

Cornwall, where John Maine is caught up in two conspiracies – one the business interests of the wealthy Mellors, the other an experiment to send people between parallel universes. Maine falls in love with Susanna, a woman who comes from those parallel universes, and goes in search of her. But he can only go to universes where he has already died, and suspects that he will die too. Coney confessed that 'the plot was getting a little complex; from time to time I'd lose myself as to which world I was supposed to be in' (Wingrove 1989: 41). This marked a contrast with *Brontomek!*, which 'wrote itself' (Wingrove 1977: 10) and where the character of Susanna reappears, as one of the amorphs.

The solution to the disaster of *Syzygy* provides the problem of *Brontomek!*: the disaffected youths have discovered that chewing a kind of root both gives them a euphoric feeling and makes them immune to the control of the Minds. The Hetherington Organisation uses its financial muscle to buy up the planet for its drug, but it has reckoned without the natural cycle of the plant, which loses potency as the moons move out of alignment. Without its commodity, the organisation withdraws. Notions of work permeate the sequence: the need for the various colonies to work together, like ants or bees, is clear, with those who break out on their own held up to criticism. The protagonist is in a complex, contradictory position: often trying to hold together a community, while being a individualist working for an egoist, and in fear of the masses in the shape of the Minds or the amorphs. The collective is only safe if harnessed in the right direction, but which direction that might be is not always clear. The corporation is both a society and an environment, perpetuating itself through the reproduction of capital and exploitation of resources. The Minds work in a similar manner, unifying the many in the one, symbiotically coexisting with their environment and going through a cycle of boom and bust. Equal numbers of men and women colonise each planet, with an assumption of heteronormativity, that one man will be faithful to each woman and that men will be more productive if their surplus labour is directed to building their own domestic space. This is undercut by the death, natural or criminal, of some of the major female characters, and the tendency of the protagonists to fall in love with the wrong woman.

Sf often provided a warning function over humanity's impact on its environment, especially about pollution, the dangers to the ozone layer and global warming. The destructive impact of pollution on wheat and grass plants was portrayed in *No Blade of Grass*, loosely based on John Christopher's *The Death of Grass* (1956). John Custance (Nigel Davenport) takes his family north to Scotland from London, in hopes of escaping the collapse of civilisation. John Brosnan dismisses the film as 'crude and rather disjointed' (1978: 197), in part because the distributors cut several scenes, but admits that it does have some good set pieces. There is the sense that the film's political aims got in the way of its craft – Anderson argues that, as *Soylent Green* and *The Omega Man* were to show, '[i]mportant statements about issues confronting the citizens and society of the 70's would be lost in the mire of polemics and poor filmmaking [...] *No Blade of Grass* succumbs to the lure of taking the easy way out' (1985: 22–23). The tension between action adventure and message is not resolved.

Kit Pedler and Gerry Davis, who had created the cybermen for *Doctor Who* (23 November 1963–), co-created *Doomwatch* for the BBC, with Terence Dudley as its producer. The series centred on a government watchdog, Doomwatch, officially known as the Department for the Observation and the Measurement of Scientific Work. Dr Spencer Quist (John Paul), the leader, had worked on the h-bomb, and is aided by Dr John Ridge (Simon Oates), a dandy figure, and Toby Wren (Robert Powell), a researcher, in investigating the dangers of pollution, radiation and genetic engineering. Three adaptations of episodes appeared in the book *Doomwatch: The World in Danger* (1975) – 'The Plastic Eaters' (9 February 1970), 'The Red Sky' (6 April 1970) and 'Survival Code' (11 May 1970) as 'A Bomb is Missing' – with *Mutant 59 The Plastic Eater* (1971) using the plot of the pilot episode, although not the characters, and *Brainrack* (1974) and *The Dynostar Menace* (1975) exploring similar themes. A 1972 feature film, directed by Peter Sasdy, added Ian Bannen (as Dr Del Shaw) and Judy Geeson (as Victoria Brown) above the billing for the series's regular cast, and features an island contaminated by dumped chemicals, and the consequences for those who eat the locally caught fish. Pedler and Davis left the programme as they felt that Dudley had neglected the ecological themes in favour of thriller elements, and Oates left as well. Pedler maintained an interest in ecology, writing *The Quest for Gaia* (1979) in support of Lovelock's hypothesis, with advice for practical developments and adapting lifestyles.

*The Omega Man*, a loose adaptation of Richard Matheson's *I Am Legend* (1954), sees a human-created plague released in a war between the People's Republic of China and the Soviet Union, wiping out almost all of humanity. Infected survivors behave like zombies or vampires, and travel around in gangs; the only immunised survivor, Robert Neville (Charlton Heston), is hunting for their nests. Neville is trying to make more of the serum, but the Luddite gangs see such technology as a heresy of the old days. In a curious piece of radicalism, prepared for by the incongruous scenes of his watching and apparently enjoying *Woodstock* (Michael Wadleigh, 1970), he gets to bed the African American Lisa (Rosalind Cash)

– a rare example of interracial desire in a Hollywood movie. When Lisa is infected, she has to white up, making the contrast of healthiness and infection even greater. When Neville is finally killed, in a Christ-like pose, he is saving others, including Lisa and a number of children. The white patriarch offers a beneficent sacrifice for the others.

*Soylent Green* begins with the representation of a transition of New York from its early industrial days to an overcrowded near future, where living space is at a premium, and real food is rare, most people subsisting on soylent red and soylent blue, products of the Soylent Corporation – a name which suggests soya beans and lentils, protein-rich legumes associated with vegetarian lifestyles. The passing of another patriarch in an act of self-sacrifice in an official government suicide booth is clearly meant to be a moment of pathos, with the loss of his knowledge – just as the Librarian (Ralph Richardson) announces that they have lost the entire thirteenth century in *Rollerball* (Norman Jewison, 1975), although there his character does seem to have a hint of ironic anarchistic glee about him which suggests a wilful act of sabotage. The middle-aged hero, Thorn (Charlton Heston), discovers that the corporation has come up with a variation on the solution to overcrowding and malnutrition that had been proposed with satiric intent by Jonathan Swift's *A Modest Proposal* (1729): recycle human bodies as food, the new soylent green. Harry Harrison suggests that the twist 'will have been twigged by the audience early on' (1984: 145), rather than this being a final climactic revelation. As Brosnan notes, the 'cinema audiences are left to decide for themselves whether [Thorn] will be believed by anyone, so the ending is ambiguous' (1978: 204), and perhaps nothing would be done.

*The Sheep Look Up*, the third part of a cautionary tetralogy written by John Brunner, takes its title from John Milton's pastoral elegy, *Lycidas* (1637): 'The hungry sheep look up, and are not fed, / But swoll'n with wind, and the rank mist they draw, / Rot inwardly, and foul contagion spread'. The novel interweaves pollution, contamination, the side-effects of combining chemicals, agricultural failure, landslides caused by sonic booms and escalating civil unrest. Meanwhile, diseases are rife, not only because they are mutating naturally, but because the antibiotics in food are making them less effective at combating disease. Brunner intercuts sections with newspaper clippings and fictional documentation. The nearest the novel has to a hero is Austin Train, an ecologist treated as a terrorist by the powers that be. But he is fighting a losing battle, the pendulum of pollution has swung too far, and balance can only be restored by a massive act of genocidal depopulation. Stephen H. Goldman suggests the novel represents humanity 'penned in by a world completely hostile to [its] continued existence' (1978: 266), but the novel also makes it clear that humanity bears the responsibility for this.

Various restarts of society are attempted in *Survivors*, a BBC television series created by Terry Nation, first transmitted four days after the final episode of his *Doctor Who* script 'Genesis of the Daleks' (8 March–12 April 1975). A Chinese scientist accidentally infects himself in a laboratory and then, having travelled abroad, causes the deaths of 95 per cent of the world's population. The first series depicts a number of British survivors coming together in a small community. However, there is a tension between the wish to reintroduce technology, exemplified by Greg Preston (Ian McCulloch) and his exploration of hydroelectric generation, and the initial Luddism of Charles Vaughan (Denis Lill), who nevertheless wants the women to become pregnant in order to repopulate the world. This tension replicates a tension in the production team, between Nation, who wished the characters to be nomadic, and presumably scavengers, and producer Terence Dudley and author Jack Ronder, who were more interested in developing fictional self-sustaining communities. A year after the Conservative party had campaigned (in the context of strikes and the three-day week, and a referendum on staying in the then EEC on the horizon) on the slogan, 'Who runs Britain?', the series offered a number of models for new societies, from the benign *de facto* dictatorship of Abby Grant (Carolyn Seymour) and Preston and then Preston and Vaughan, to more Machiavellian divisions of labour and ownership, which include slavery, eugenics and executions. The final resurrection of an electricity generator in Scotland foregrounds the power tensions between Scotland and England, where the economic exploitation of North Sea oil had caused problems; in the future of *Survivors*, England may end up subject to Scotland. The potential neo-industrial revolution is questioned by the series – as a new working class would need to be created. The central characters of the programme are largely middle-class – engineers, architects, academics – and white, with the women mainly in the role of mothers, nurses, cooks and carers. This too is questioned, in the episode 'Over the Hills' (16 June 1976), where a number of the women reject pregnancy, and a group of characters coded as working-class are shown as more interested in partying than in working. The new world order has merely seen exchanges of power between branches of the bourgeoisie and the aristocracy, evidenced by the repeated sequestration of ancestral piles, castles, rectories and other major buildings.

A social experiment is at the heart of Gore Vidal's *Kalki* (1978), in which an American Vietnam veteran, James J. Kelly, having discovered that the government is developing a new neutron bomb, declares himself to be

Kalki, the tenth avatar of Vishnu, and plans the end of the world. Having wiped out the world's population with E. coli, he plans to restart the human race with his wife and the help of six sterile assistants, who will help teach the children. The narrator, a bisexual aviator called Teddy Hecht Ottinger, is meant to be a media pundit, having written (with the aid of a ghost-writer) an autobiography which has had something of the impact of Germaine Greer's *The Female Eunuch* (1970), and now becomes part of Kelly's organisation as a journalist and unwitting co-conspirator. Vidal sets up a world that is already most of the way to destruction – Richard Delap describes it as a 'feeble parody of American bad taste' (1979: 35) – and the coming apocalypse is embraced by America. That Kelly has miscalculated the plan is hardly a surprise. The technical problem is how Ottinger can both ventriloquise Vidal's own opinions and join the rest of the dead: her ending is written by Kelly/Kalki.

Benford's *Timescape* fuses ecological warning with extrapolations about quantum physics, and won the Nebula, BSFA and John W. Campbell Memorial Awards. The events narrated in the novel oscillate between a point then eighteen years in the future – an ecologically doomed, violent 1998 – and a point eighteen years previously, a pre-John F. Kennedy assassination 1962. The scientists in 1998 realise that they are past the tipping point that means that disaster is almost certain, but discover that with the use of tachyons they can communicate with the past and try to avert the oncoming disaster. Rather than leading to paradox, the novel takes up the many-worlds interpretation of quantum physics and allows at least one universe to branch off safely while the 1998 scientists Benford depicts are still doomed. The Jonbar Point, at which one alternative universe diverges from another, is a high school student visiting the Dallas School Book Depository in 1963 in search of a publication by one of the historical scientists, averting Oswald's assassination of Kennedy.

While the environment becomes an antagonist in these narratives thanks to human action, a wide variety of films featured animals as aggressively seeking revenge on humanity – for example *Frogs* (George McCowan, 1972), *Kingdom of the Spiders* (John Carlos, 1976), *The Swarm* (Irwin Allen, 1978) and *Piranha* (Joe Dante, 1979). In *Phase IV*, ants start behaving aggressively, and wipe out their natural predators. Scientist Ernest Hubbs (Nigel Davenport) gets government funding to set up a research station in the Arizona desert to find a way of stopping them, employing games theorist and translator James Lesko (Michael Murphy) to try to find a way of communicating with a hive mind intelligence. The design, as might be expected from Bass – better known for posters and title sequences for directors such as Alfred Hitchcock, Otto Preminger and

Martin Scorsese – is striking, if at times a little reminiscent of *2001: A Space Odyssey* (Stanley Kubrick, 1968): the opening shots of a strange eclipse, the monolith-like anthills (which echo Easter Island statues in their profile), the ant point of view and the final transcendent shift as Lesko and orphan Kendra (Lynne Frederick) enter the ant world. Searles hails its 'extremely handsome photography' (1974c: 79) but admits that 'most of the film is more or less a shambles' (1974c: 81). The finale was originally longer, but was trimmed back by a nervous distributor: 'Bass originally filmed a spectacular, surreal sequence lasting four minutes, showing what life would be like on the "new" Earth' (Brosnan 1978: 228). This survives in Barry N. Malzberg's novelisation, *Phase IV* (1973), which is based on Mayo Simon's script rather than the re-edited film, and situates this as 'Phase Five' (Malzberg 1973c: 127), imagining that a space battle in another galaxy caused the magnetic storm that triggered the change in the ants' behaviour. The repeated descriptions and depictions in both film and novelisation of the ants as lacking individualism, being committed to a common goal and being part of a strictly regimented society could have been read as an allegory of a communist totalitarian society in an earlier age. But there is a repeated insistence that the humans are like ants: the joint project of the research, their own disposability, the rules and regulations of bureaucracy all undercut individual agency. Lesko writes in his diary, '*We were turning into ants ourselves*' (Malzberg 1973c: 81). The abandoned plots of land in the ironically named Paradise City form squares like those plotted in the attempted conversation between Lesko and the ants. There is a shift of perspective during the film, where the phases are first presented as part of Hubbs's project, but in fact represent the ant evolution. While the scientists assumed they were studying ants, it is they who are the rats in the maze. Lesko's diary provides the suggestion that humanity will fall before the ants, but the film presents it as some kind of progression or apotheosis, rather than necessarily a cataclysm.

Humanity's downfall may not be from a natural threat on Earth or its own actions; it might also face extraterrestrial dangers from meteors and comets that might collide with or pass close to the Earth. While physicist Luis Alvarez and his son, geologist Walter Alvarez, did not advance the theory that the dinosaurs had been wiped out by a massive meteor impact until 1980, sf writers were already thinking of the possibilities of extinction events. Humanity needed an early warning system and Arthur C. Clarke, always the space advocate, showed one in *Rendezvous with Rama* (1972); it detects the alien spaceship that is central to the novel. In *In the Ocean of Night*, first of his Galactic Central series, Benford describes a large meteor, Icarus, which is on a collision course with India. In the process of planting bombs on the rock in order to destroy it, astronaut Nigel Walmsley discovers evidence for extraterrestrial life, but has to annihilate it. A few years later, another anomaly is discovered in the solar system, which turns out to be an alien spacecraft, and Walmsley is able to get involved in what is the first of a series of alien encounters. Benford envisages technological solutions to problems, but still shows a deteriorating Earth. The novel also includes a degree of social extrapolation – Walmsley is in a group marriage with two women, although the groundbreaking nature of this obscures the fact that pretty well all the other characters are male.

The Hugo Award-nominated *Lucifer's Hammer* is more optimistic in its pleasures of destroying the world and the triumph of technology. There is a long countdown to disaster, followed by the consequences of the collision, and rebuilding society afterwards. The knowledge of the forthcoming disaster allows some people to start the selection of what contemporary cultural artefacts need to be preserved – and with special pleading sf novels are among these. In the closing pages there is a battle for the control of a power station – just as the hydroelectric generating station becomes vital in *Survivors* – between those who have a technological future in mind, and those who are new Luddites. Society will not start from a clean slate, but with chosen artefacts of the old ways, and with the consequent risk of repeating the same mistakes.

Baxter's *The Hermes Fall* features an asteroid that imperils humanity. It aspires to Michael Crichton's sense of verisimilitude, mixing real organisations with invented ones. The suspense comes from wondering whether the unstoppable force can in fact be stopped – a nuclear warhead is aborted, and a hurriedly scrambled space mission is scuppered by an act of sabotage by an evangelical astronaut who believes the asteroid is God's work. While the other astronaut survives very much against the odds, the impact of the asteroid in the Atlantic rather than on the mainland USA means that the last third of the book can describe the effects of the consequent floods, tsunami and storms. The waters devastate the Americas and Western Europe, and what was once fertile land is now salinated.

The film *Meteor* (Ronald Neame, 1979) turns a similar premise into an all-star movie with Sean Connery, Natalie Wood, Trevor Howard, Martin Landau and Henry Fonda. The comet Orpheus's collision splits the meteor Hermes into fragments, one of which destroys an observing space mission, the others providing a series of minor disasters in the build-up to the destruction of the Eastern seaboard of the United States. Ranged against these are the United States's Hercules nuclear missiles – contrary to the 1967 Treaty on Principles Governing the Activities of States in the Exploration and Use of Outer Space – and the Soviet equivalent, Peter the Great, which might be able to deflect the meteor off course. Connery, playing a former NASA scientist, has to persuade the two nations to cooperate, and is himself caught up in the cataclysm with the burial of their secret base under the AT&T Building.

Benford cowrote another meteor collision novel, *Shiva Descending* with William Rotsler, where various attempts are made to prevent the inevitable collision, with chapters counting down to the impact. A side effect of the attempts to destroy the asteroid is that the remainder goes into an Earth orbit, thus giving any state with a space programme a new source of iron to exploit; apocalypse is transformed into rights grab. Clute sees a 'fin-de-siècle melancholy to the book' (1980c: 42).

*The Andromeda Strain* (Robert Wise, 1971) displays some of the ambiguities of Michael Crichton's 1969 source novel. Science provides both a problem and its solution: Project Scope has brought materials back to Earth from space, and has led to the transmission of a killer extraterrestrial virus into the environment. A group of scientists are brought together to find an antidote, and to cure the two survivors from an afflicted small American town. Technology is thus the antagonist of the film, and the means by which a solution is found to the problem. Director Wise had displayed a social conscience in his *The Day the Earth Stood Still* (1951), and here maintains, albeit downplayed, the military intent of the retrieval of viruses from the novel. He also agreed to scriptwriter Nelson Gidding's change of sex of one of the scientists – Dr Peter Leavitt becomes Dr Ruth Leavitt (Kate Reid). The choice of actress allows them, as Searles notes, to avoid 'all the stereotyped inanities (not even a beautiful female biologist)' (1971: 240). The muted emotions of the characters – although Leavitt objects to their treatment – and the lack of a romantic subplot, along with a repetitive set (the different levels of the laboratory are the same scenery, painted different colours), perhaps leaves the film feeling a little austere. The characters are ranged against 'the implacable immensity and perversity of nature' (Anderson 1985: 30), and there are invisible forces at work – physical, gravitational, biological and environmental, but also political, ideological and social – that are greater than individual characters and which cannot be overcome. The careful pacing of what Searles describes as 'probably the best s-f film to come along since 2001' (1971: 62) is sacrificed toward the end, when Dr Mark Hall (James Olson) has to deactivate the laboratory's self-destruct mechanism.

In the Strugatsky brothers' *Roadside Picnic*, nominated for the John W. Campbell Memorial Award in 1978, human beings suffer from pollution left by alien tourists. There are six locations where advanced technologies have been found or strange physical properties observed. These Zones are now being explored by scientists, with the aid of local guides or Stalkers, a word used to refer to those who lead hunters to their big game prey. Humans can barely comprehend what they have found.

The Strugatsky brothers adapted this novella very loosely as *Stalker* for Tarkovsky, leading to a film as beautiful as it is baffling, much rewritten during a troubled period of production. After some kind of unclear, presumably nuclear, disaster, the Stalker (Alexander Kaidanovsky) leads two people, a writer (Anatoli Solonitski) and a professor (Nikolai Grinko) – he refuses to learn their names, or give his own – into the Zone, in which everyone is at risk and where they will make some kind of wish, in a kind of post-apocalyptic *Wizard of Oz*, a feeling intensified by the film's shift from black and white at its opening to colour in the Zone. Despite the frequent, repeated warnings, no crisis occurs, and the film seems to come full circle, with the characters where they started, with no certainty to whether they ever entered the Zone – or, alternatively, if everywhere is in fact the Zone. Salvestroni observes: 'it cannot be concluded from *Stalker* that something actually can happen in the Zone – i.e., that the protagonist does not imagine everything' (1987: 301). The film can be seen as a good example of Todorov's notion of a fantastic text. The reality of the filming, however, was stark, as the locations where the Zone was filmed, a hydroelectric station near Tallinn, were being heavily polluted by a chemical plant upstream, and it is believed that this hastened the director's death in 1986; the accident at the Chernobyl power station on 26 April 1986 led to the area around it being referred to as the Zone, and its local inhabitants as Stalkers.

Kaufman's remake of *The Invasion of the Body Snatchers* (Don Siegel, 1956) acknowledges its antecedent by giving Siegel and the original's star, Kevin McCarthy, cameos, but is very different in tone from the earlier film's ambiguous Cold War sensitivities, concerned instead with therapy culture and the sense of alienation people were feeling in the 1970s. Whereas the original begins with the sense of normality in a small town slowly being undermined, in this version we already know where the plot will go. The film opens on an alien planet, with jellyfish-like aliens who then travel across space and fall on San Francisco. The camera angles sometimes divert from the horizontal axis, so that buildings appear to loom. Bennell (Donald Sutherland), here a health inspector rather than a doctor, has already witnessed violence in response to his work. A priest lurks incongruously on the park swings, a schoolgirl disappears into the bushes, and too many people are running in the streets. As the paranoia grows, the strange thing is that the boyfriend Geoffrey Howell (Art Lindle) of Bennell's colleague Elizabeth Driscoll (Brook Adams) is attentive and kind to her, but is also apparently meeting up with random strangers. The psychiatrist and best-selling self-help guru Dr David Kibner (Leonard Nimoy) is dismissive of Elizabeth's fears, as he is of another woman's suspicions about her husband. At first this is perhaps just a man being dismissive of a woman's feelings, but it soon emerges that Kibner is one of the pod people, and is persuasive about the relief which the transformation offers: an escape from emotions. He explains, 'We came here from a dying world. We drift through the universe, from planet to planet, pushed on by the solar winds. We adapt and we survive. The function of life is survival'. Here their rise seems unstoppable: the police and military are involved, and while Bennell burns down one hatching factory, the pods are already exported to the rest of the world. In the original, Bennell escapes; the remake is more sinister.

Some writers tried to imagine technological means that would allow survival through the coming ecological apocalypse. One solution might be to go off-planet; *Jem* dramatises the ambiguities of this. O'Neill suggests that humanity should build a series of space stations, and exploit minerals in the low-gravity environments of the moon and asteroids, as well as harvesting solar energy which could be transmitted down to Earth. Using a term coined by Isaac Asimov, O'Neill argues that it is 'planetary chauvinism' to discount space stations as potential living environments, and he describes possible designs: rotating spheres or toroids of a mile in diameter and two rotating cylinders about five miles in diameter. His ideas were first developed in teaching a physics course at Princeton University in 1969, in the context of widespread student protests and cuts, and were eventually published in an article in *Physics Today* (April 1974), 'The Colonization of Space', before being developed at book length as *The High Frontier: Human Colonies in Space* (1976). While NASA showed some interest in his ideas, and O'Neill testified before Congress in hope of unlocking funding, the set-up costs were felt to be too prohibitive; the project would have required scores of shuttle launches, each of which would cost millions of dollars.

*Silent Running* (Douglas Trumbull, 1972) depicts arks in space that have been used to protect flora and fauna while the damaged Earth ecosystem is repaired. Now, however, the spaceships are needed for commercial use and the habitats must be destroyed. While most of the crews obey the orders from Earth, Freeman Lowell (Bruce Dern) resists, and is willing to kill his companions to save the environments. Vivian Sobchack observes that the space freighter 'literally becomes a coffin for its crew […] the visuals emphasize the vastness of solitary confinement, the deadness of a hermetically sealed existence which is silent and unyielding in its evocation of eternal loneliness' (1987: 71). Freeman, clearly a symbolic name, is accompanied in his actions by three squat robots, dubbed Huey, Louie and Dewey after Donald Duck's nephews, whose fates we end up caring about more than the humans'. Searles criticises their appearance in his review, suggesting that '"comic relief" in serious films went out a long time ago' (1972: 31), but, as Brosnan observes, they are the 'direct ancestors of cute little Artoo Deetoo in *Star Wars*' (1978: 215), not to mention Muffit in *Battlestar Galactica* (17 September 1978–29 April 1979, which uses footage from *Silent Running*), Twiki in *Buck Rogers in the Twenty-Fifth Century* (20 September 1979–16 April 1981) and the robots in *The Black Hole* (Gary Nelson, 1979). The film is heavy-handedly ecological in its message, complete with Joan Baez singing folk songs about nature, although there is a tension between the need to preserve environments and the rather stale, human-free ecosystem that survives isolated from the rest of the universe: the environment can be preserved for its own sake, or as a resource for humans.

Sargent's *Cloned Lives* uses the idea of cloning as part of the solution to Earth's problems. Drawing on three earlier works – 'A Sense of Difference' (Roger Elwood (ed.) *And Walk Now Gently Through the Fire* (Philadelphia: Chilton, 1972)), 'Clone Sister' (Joseph Elder (ed.), *Eros in Orbit: A Collection of All New Science Fiction Stories About Sex* (New York: Trident, 1973)) and 'Father' (*Amazing* February 1974) – she depicts the lives of a number of clones derived from the genes of the widowed Paul Swenson, Edward, James, Michael, Kira and Albert. A second female clone has been created, but dies during the pregnancy. This sexual imbalance is perhaps telling – there was perhaps a sense that authors could only perceive a limited number of narratives as open to female characters (Russ 1972). The clones take different routes in their careers and the ways that they deal with the catastrophe. Sargent claimed that she was 'trying to write a reasonably realistic near future novel, a "hard science" book, so to speak, but with fully realised characters' (Elliot 1982: 63).

Clones are also bred as a survival tactic during an environmental crisis in Wilhelm's *Where Late the Sweet Birds Sang*, which drew in part upon an earlier story of the same name published in *Orbit 15* (1974) and won the 1977 Hugo Award for best novel. As an isolated family become infertile, they decide to breed by cloning, hoping that a few generations down the line the children will be able to breed naturally again. There is a loss of individuality among the group, as the clones elect to continue scientifically rather than naturally, and a consequent loss of creativity. Individuality seems linked to fertility, and Paul Kucera notes the sense that the natural catastrophe is a symbol of failed connectedness with both the Earth and the individual (2007: 366). Survival lies in a return to a less technological (and thus alienating) state – a kind of 'back to nature' of which Clifford D.

Simak might approve.

This attitude needs to be separated from the rest of fallen humanity, before the whole world can be saved. Callenbach's *Ecotopia* was a green bestseller; published just before the American bicentennial, it present an 'ecological, steady-state, decentralized, cooperative, democratic, peaceful, and relatively egalitarian' (Cummings 1989: 69) area of the north-western United States that had seceded from the Union. Curiously old-fashioned, owing more to late nineteenth-century utopian writings than contemporary sf, the novel is presented as a series of newspaper columns and diary entries by a sceptical American journalist, Will Weston, visiting this utopia. Bülent Somay notes that '[the] central principle of Ecotopia is that humankind should live in balance with the fellow creatures of nature rather than dominate them' (1984: 26); the citizens work twenty-hour weeks, have access to free medicine, birth control and abortion, waste less and recycle more and use public magnetic trains and bicycles to get around. The internal combustion engines, and the need for roads, are more or less unknown. The society is less competitive, and more feminine, with more women in politics and a female president (at a time when almost all real-world leaders were men). Many of the old city centres have been razed, to make way for agriculture of various kinds. Such as seceded state is given credibility by references to the real-world Biafran campaign in Nigeria in 1969 and Bangladesh's independence from Pakistan in 1971; reference is also made to Quebec's independence and a Scandinavian unification. Somay, however, objects to the balance of this pocket society, which, paradoxically, he sees as limiting the scope for utopia, as stability should be an end in itself. In ecological terms, though, a stable system is one that will survive.

In Wilhelm's *Juniper Time* (1979), nominated for the 1979 Nebula Award for best novel, environmental disaster in the western USA leads to an eastward migration, but Jean Brighton moves west to join up with and learn from Native Americans: 'she learns to achieve a difficult balance, how to adapt the environment to meet her needs and how to adapt herself to survive on what is available' (Collier 1980: 79). Again there is a return to an earlier sort of society, although the apparent evidence that emerges for alien life makes things more complex.

Finally, in Sally Miller Gearhart's *The Wanderground: Stories of the Hill People* (1979) women live in rural communities, attempting to avoid the technology of the surviving male cities and maintaining a community through telepathy and an oral, poetic culture. Occasionally women may enter the cities, but men are not allowed out of the cities, because of the sense that they are always potentially rapists, whether of women or of natural resources. There were thus connections between the concerns of those who critiqued the impact of man (as opposed to humanity) upon the Earth and the concerns of feminists; Françoise d'Eaubonne coined the term 'ecofeminism' in 1974 to describe the overlap. Ecofeminists argue that the patriarchal ownership of land has led to the over-exploitation of natural resources, with women and subject races being either displaced to less productive territory or used as slave populations. As Joanna Russ notes: 'if men are kept out of these societies, it is because men are dangerous. They also hog the good things of the world' (1995: 140). There has been an association between campaigners for women's rights and for the environment since the nineteenth century, with opposition to vivisection and the appropriation of birds for their feathers for fashion. *The Wanderground* is at the radical end of feminism: rather than engaging in an attempt to reform the existing sexist society, the novel imagines that women move elsewhere. There is a danger here of falling into the essentialism that situates woman as nature (in opposition to man as culture), but the resulting separatist narrative cannot help but offer role models for female behaviour and expression.

# 10
# Female Counter-Literature: Feminism

*The Wanderground: Stories of the Hill People* (1979) situates itself as part of '[a] female counter-literature without letters […] literacy that denounces writing through writing' (Klarer 1990: 328). But then, in her book *The Dialectic of Sex* (1970), Shulamith Firestone insists that 'feminists have to question, not just all of *Western* culture, but the organisation of culture itself, and further, even the very organisation of nature' (1979: 12). As the structures of patriarchy run deep, feminists need both to understand the existing mechanics of the world and to imagine how it could be otherwise. Firestone argues that the capitalist system is arranged in such a way as to perpetuate itself, and yoking women to childrearing is part of this. In the 1970s, science fiction offered both dystopias and utopias built around gendered structures. This chapter will examine the ways in which female authors engaged with gender, usually using those genres, with a discussion of the writings of Sue Payer, Ursula Le Guin, Kate Wilhelm, Vonda N. McIntyre, C.J. Cherryh, Joanna Russ, Suzette Haden Elgin, Marge Piercy, Suzy McKee Charnas and Kit Reed, before a brief examination of the symposium on women and sf in the fanzine *Khatru* and the short stories of James Tiptree Jr.

The kind of feminism prominent in the 1970s had emerged in the 1960s – although feminism dates back much longer – and was crystallised in the USA by the formation of the National Organization of Women in June 1966. Books such as Betty Friedan's *The Feminine Mystique* (1963), Mary Ellman's *Thinking About Women* (1968) and Kate Millett's *Sexual Politics* (1970) examine the ways in which, in the post-Second World War West, women were being encouraged to become housewives and mothers, and how culture furthered such an ideology. NOW campaigned for equal rights and pay for women through the 1970s. In some cases, there were attempts to extend access to contraception and abortion so that reproduction became a woman's choice rather than something imposed upon her by men; this remains controversial. Millett's *Sexual Politics* and Sandra Gilbert and Susan Gubar's *The Madwoman in the Attic* (1979) marked the emergence of a feminist literary criticism, which argued that patriarchal discrimination was a political act, and that this manifested itself within literature, in the workplace and in the bedroom. In addition to raising consciousnesses, feminist literary criticism rediscovered women who had been omitted from the masculinist canon – see Ellen Moers's *Literary Women* (1976) and Elaine Showalter's *A Literature of their Own* (1977) – and a number of companies were set up which specialised in publishing new works and reprinting classics by women, such as the Feminist Press (1970), Virago (1973) and Onlywomen Press (1974). Feminists began to explore female psychology, role models and structures.

Sf allows speculation about the future of sex roles for both men and women, as well as opportunities for the examination of possible feminist futures, or the consequences if inequalities are allowed to continue, but its women were often invisible or outnumbered by men. Harlan Ellison's anthology *Dangerous Visions* (1968) had included only three female writers out of thirty-two; his follow-up, *Again, Dangerous Visions* (1972) featured Joan Bernott, Lee Hoffman, Judith Ann Lawrence, Le Guin, Evelyn Lief, Russ, Josephine Saxton and Wilhelm, plus Tiptree, as part of its forty-two or forty-three contributors (Barry Malzberg also appeared as K.M. O'Donnell). Despite women-only anthologies in the 1970s – such as *Women of Wonder* (1975), *More Women of Wonder* (1976) and *The New Women of Wonder* (1978), all edited by Pamela Sargent, and *Millennial Women* (1978), edited by Virginia Kidd – all-male or token women contents were the norm. For example, aside from one story by Naomi Mitchison, none of Peter Weston's three *Andromeda* anthologies contains any women writers and Christopher Priest's *Anticipations* (1978) admits to its lack of women.

The literary construction of female identities can be seen in Payer's *Second Body* (1979). Wendy Anderson suffers catastrophic complications while giving birth and her head is transplanted onto a different body. A mind-body split is emphasised, as the husband of the dead woman appears, wanting to resume his sex life with his wife. In a suggestive domestic metaphor, the body is compared to a house, which is now occupied by new owners; it seems that the men are still the freeholders. Anderson has to choose between two men, and continue one family or another; heterosexuality and heteronormativity remain standard practices, and women remain objects of the male gaze. The novel seems to echo Robert A. Heinlein's *I Will Fear No Evil* (*Galaxy* July–December 1970; 1970), but then not all women writers are feminist, and Heinlein in his earlier career did depict rather less problematic female characters. There is something odd about *Second Body* – it is copyright by the publisher, Belmont Tower, and would appear to be Payer's only novel. It is possible that Payer is a pseudonym for a man, just as at least one female writer found prominence under a male name.

Le Guin was one of the most significant sf writers of the 1970s. In *The Left Hand of Darkness* (1969), she attempted, in part, to separate sex – a biological distinction, open to revision through evolution and technology – from gender, the social archetypes that vary by culture and period. The Gethen only exhibit a specific sex some of the time – when in *kemmer* they become male or female according to context. Le Guin argues that such a world would lack warfare, exploitation and 'sexuality as a continuous factor' (1976a: 135). However, she still maintains the traditional male and female pronouns for her characters, and Joanna Russ criticises her failure to consider the implications for family life and childrearing. In 1975, perhaps a little defensively, Le Guin argues 'I find made-up pronouns, "te" and "heshe" and so on dreary and annoying' (1976b: 85). The following year, in 'Is Gender Necessary?', she argues: 'I utterly refuse to mangle English by inventing a pronoun for "he/she"' (1976a: 137). Russ disagrees, in 1979 insisting: 'Bite your tongue and write "she"; if you look at it long enough, it will actually start looking human. And as for extra-terrestrials, invent. What the normative-male usage does is to insist, usually below the level of conscious awareness, that all of us shes are *special* people, confined to *special* (not broadly human) functions – or that we, like Gethenians, are (sort-of) male ninety percent of the time except when we revert to being (truly) female for the purposes if that special chapter of the human story called Sex and Reproduction' (2007: 149–50). (Larry Niven, in particular, with *Protector* (1973) and *The Mote in God's Eye* (1974), and John Brunner, in *Total Eclipse* (*Amazing* April and June 1974; 1974), seemed to associate femaleness rather too closely with reproduction.)

Le Guin's *The Lathe of Heaven* (*Amazing* March and May 1971; 1971), a Hugo and Nebula nominee in which George Orr's dreams change reality, paid homage to Philip K. Dick. Realising that his psychologist, William Haber, is manipulating him to his own ends, Orr calls upon lawyer Heather Lelache to help him. The world has repeatedly changed, but not necessarily for the better, as a polluted, overheated and flooded planet is replaced by a war-ravaged one and one invaded by aliens. Haber claims they have done good: 'Eliminated the color problem, racial hatred. Eliminated war. Eliminated the risk of species deterioration and the fostering of deleterious gene stocks. Eliminated – no, say in the process of eliminating – poverty, economic inequality, the class war, all over the world' (Le Guin 1974b: 126). It is not that there is equality between differing races, but that everyone is the same colour, and Lelache, of mixed African American and Caucasian background, vanishes in Orr's erasing process. Haber ignores sex in his list, which is just as well, but the battle of sexes is not on the agenda. The two main characters of the novel are male, with Haber's secretary and Lelache the only significant female characters. Lelache, clearly an efficient and successful lawyer, sees herself as a black widow, and appears to have the masculine qualities that balance the repeated references to Orr as feminine. While the novel evinces little interest in gender, it does at least offer a minor challenge to stereotyping.

Similarly, *The Dispossessed: An Ambiguous Utopia* (1974) casts all but two of its major figures as male: Shevek, the theoretical mathematician, is surrounded with male academics and co-workers on the planet Anarres, and his antagonist is a senior male academic. When Shevek travels into exile on Urras, in order to pursue his ideas, he meets male politicians, scientists, servants and revolutionaries. The exceptions – aside from a handful of wives and children – are his partner Takver and Keng, the Hainish ambassador he meets toward the end of the novel. Despite the dominance of the narrative by men, the two societies are distinctively gendered. Urras, a grouping of capitalist countries, is competitive and driven by market forces and ongoing wars, revolutions and skirmishes, being both masculine and sexist in outlook. In a novel written by an author fascinated by Taoism, Annares is feminine and anarchistic, in theory rejecting hierarchy and embracing a communitarian ethic of ability and need, but with an emphasis on shared labour. At various points the characters do discuss sex inequalities – and Odo, the revolutionary whose radical ideas underlie Annares, was a woman. It seems unlikely that Shevek would have been welcomed if he had been a female scientist. Le Guin's interest here is much more in the nature of utopia, and she is representing a problem in a range of power relations rather than showing an alternative.

Wilhelm's *Margaret and I* (1971) represents contemporary male–female interactions and is narrated by an unidentified voice, which looks through the eyes of, and is occasionally able to control the actions of, Margaret Oliver. Oliver has retreated from her husband Bennett and his support of a dubious political campaign by Arnold Greeley, to the cottage of her Aunt Josie, only to be harassed by Horace Bok, who wants to rediscover the research of Josie's former lover, the experimental physicist Paul Tyson. Bok employs a hypnotist to control Margaret (whom he has assumed is Josie) and Greeley tries to blackmail her into joining the campaign (he assumes she will support her husband without question). Bennett insists, 'Most wives have to put up with things they dislike for the sake of their husbands. You spoke sneeringly about corporation wives, they have to be able to take it, you know. And doctors' wives. From our highest government men right down to the level of small-town mayor, the wives play their part' (Wilhelm 1971: 110). There can hardly be a clearer description of the lack of individual agency, and the invisible forces that need to be defeated, although these are in fact far from invisible. Meanwhile Margaret's sanity is questioned – some of the people she has seen and even had sex with may be phantasms (rather than products of Tyson's research), she is constantly mistaken for Josie, and the distancing narration may be the indication of a personality split induced by the stress she is under. At the end, she has to leave all of her life behind, with only the strange new imaginary realm as her prospect: 'she/I left the house, taking nothing from it, needing nothing from anyone there' (Wilhelm 1971: 214).

McIntyre had established her feminist critical identity before she published novel-length fiction, discussing sexism in *The Alien Critic* and *The Witch and the Chameleon* (Merrick 2009: 50, 59), and she co-edited, with Susan Anderson, the anthology *Aurora: Beyond Equality* (1976), which included Le Guin's 'Is Gender Necessary'. Her debut novel, *The Exile Waiting* (1975), in what might be a homage to Russ's Alyx stories, puts a female thief at its heart: Mischa, a young girl with telepathic contact to her relatives, scratching an existence in the caves around Center, the last city of a post-holocaust Earth. Wishing to leave Earth, she latches onto the biologically determined pseudosibs, Subone and Subtwo, who have come to Earth on a piratical mission and who have their own, technological connectedness. The final focal character is Jan Hikaru, trapped by his relationship with his father and come to Earth to bury his lover; he is able to offer a first-person narrative via his journal. Fredric Jameson, while noting the novel's importance in demonstrating that sf is a spatial as much as a temporal genre (and thus able to offer maps for understanding the present), describes it as being a soap opera (1987: 44), a form associated with female consumers. Many of the characters – Mischa only being a partial exception – are trying to escape either passive positions or familial commitments, and most of the action takes place in the interior (and thus domestic) spaces of a spaceship or Earth itself. The shifts in power experienced by the novel's characters do little to alter the overall power balance of Earth, Jenny Wolmark noting that this is a 1970s political sensibility where 'a libertarian suspicion of centralised agency of any kind leads to a belief that change which take place at the margins has more validity' (1993: 63). The narrative has a drive toward individualism, and any collectivity engaged in is purely temporary and a means to an end.

McIntyre's follow-up, *Dreamsnake* (1978), which incorporates the Hugo-nominated novelette 'Of Grass, Sand, and Mist' (*Analog* October 1973), won the Hugo, Nebula and Locus Awards for best novel. M. John Harrison was somewhat dismissive of the volume, arguing in a 1980 review that it 'might have been put together by a committee composed of Ursula K. Le Guin, Anne McCaffrey and Joanna Russ, with a little help from Ms Delany' (2005: 132). The protagonist's name, Snake, points to the serpent in the Garden of Eden, to the hair of the petrifying Gorgon Medusa and, most relevantly, to the Rod of Asclepius, associated with healing. Snake uses the venom from three snakes as part of her curative power. However, when her rarest snake, the dreamsnake, is killed, she has to embark upon a quest to find a new one – this will take her to the Center, where she thinks there may be more dreamsnakes, and to her own people. The quest has traditionally been a masculine narrative structure, with the hero discovering his strengths as he journeys across a landscape, but McIntyre appropriates it for a story that puts the questioning of sex and gender at its heart. The first two groups she is shown with consist of family units of three partners – two of one sex, one of the other – and McIntyre is careful to obscure whether these are two men or two women in either case. This triangular structure turns out to be the secret of dreamsnake reproduction – the healers' repeated attempts to make two snakes mate have been lacking a third party. As Diane S. Wood notes: 'The healers, bound by their own ethnocentrism, their own sense that the sex act involves pairing, cannot see the obvious answer' (1990: 69). As in *The Exile Waiting*, there is scope for breaking with the system: we presumably should not be blinded by our own ideologies into seeing merely male and female, masculine and feminine, active and passive as the available options to us as individuals.

Cherryh (whose use of her initials gave her a name that would allow her to pass as a male writer if necessary) first came to prominence with *Brothers of Earth* and *Gate of Ivrel*, both published in 1976. Lynn F. Williams suggests that each of Cherryh's novels features 'a tremendously powerful female character', and that her work dramatises the notion that 'the good ruler must combine power with a sense of responsibility' (1986: 86). In fact it is more complex than that, as the female protagonist must deal with competing responsibilities. *Brothers* begins in the middle of the action, as Kurt Morgan watches his spaceship explode. Crashing on a nearby planet, he meets Djan, now the priestess-queen of the city of Nephane. Although an enemy, she tolerates his presence, in part because they are the two survivors of the war, and he joins the House of Elas. Cherryh frequently shifts viewpoints between human and alien, to challenge the notion of the non-humans being the other. A character's ignorance of local cultural practices can reveal them as uncouth as best, deadly at worst. At the same time, Djan is a villain and is likely to abuse her position in order to survive.

The trilogy *Gate of Ivrel, Well of Shiuan* (1978) and *Fires of Azeroth* (1979) centres on Morgaine, who tries to close various transdimensional gates throughout the universe. But, aside from the start of *Well* – which focuses on the peasant girl Miya Jherun – most of the sequence focalises on Nhi Vanye, who has sworn an oath to be bound to her. Mary T. Brizzi notes that the sex roles are reversed for the central character: Vanye is without a means of making his living, and Morgaine is his protector; also, 'the "head" [is] the female component, while "heart" is the male' (1982: 46). But the novels do not undercut Morgaine's authority.

Another priestess-queen, Melein, appears in *The Faded Sun: Kesrith* (*Galaxy* February–May 1978; 1978), a novel nominated for the Hugo and Nebula Awards. The long war between the humans and the Regul is over, and Kesrith, where Melein and her brother Niun have sought refuge, is to become a human sphere of influence. Melein is rarely centre of attention during the novel, as the focus is on Niun, the Regul leader, the new governor George Stavros and a human, Sten Duncan, who rescues the two surviving mri from Regul attack. Nor is she granted much more attention in *Shon'jir* (1978) and *Kutath* (1979), as the mri and Duncan travel to the mri home planet, Kutath. Cherryh's use of a shifting narrative focus allows the reader to empathise with both Duncan facing alien thought processes, as he becomes a mri, and with Nuin's reactions to Duncan's crudity.

Williams writes of Cherryh's female characters that '[they] are not male heroes in drag, but [... they] believe that power and responsibility go together, and that reform rather than revolution is the best solution to political problems' (1986: 91). Cherryh tends to privilege male narrators, while challenging stereotypically masculine behaviour – both Vanye and Duncan yield to their mistress's will, and adapt to situations, while Djan, Morgaine and Melein try to make the situation subordinate to their wishes. While Williams calls Cherryh 'politically conservative' (1986: 96), Brizzi suggests that her characters illustrate a 'profound, but still feminist, statement about the creative androgyny of the human spirit' (1982: 47).

Wolmark argues that McIntyre and Cherryh 'both work within the conventional narrative structures of science fiction [and ...] the generic conventions within which female heroes are depicted tend to retain their patriarchal inflection' (1993: 54). Existing narrative structures needed to be remodelled to allow more female characters, or dropped altogether in favour of feminine or feminist ones.

The concept of feminine writing or *écriture féminine* was investigated by French feminist theorists, who drew upon the psychoanalytical ideas of Sigmund Freud and Jacques Lacan. In 'The Laugh of the Medusa' (1975), Hélène Cixous argues that '[w]oman must write her self: must write about women and bring women to writing, from which they have been driven away as violently as from their own bodies [...] When I say "woman", I'm speaking of woman in her inevitable struggle against conventional man; and of a universal woman subject who must bring women to their senses' (1980: 245). While Russ satirises the notion of a feminine style – 'I have no structure [...] my thoughts seep out shapelessly like menstrual fluid, it is all very female and deep and full of essences, it is very primitive and full of "and's"' (1975a: 137) – her novels are radical in form and content. Male-centred grammar, which underpins masculine narratives, insists that 'man' means both 'male' and 'human', and therefore includes women, but assuming male as default risks erasing half the species. Russ's *The Female Man* (1975) frequently notes the absurdity of this, noting the defensive claim that '"Man" is a rhetorical convenience for "human." "Man" includes "woman"' (1975a: 93), while women are clearly being sidelined. The history of humanity is written in purely male terms: 'Years ago we were all cave Men. Then there is Java Man and the future of Man and the values of Western Man and existential Man and economic Man and Freudian Man and the Man in the moon and modern Man and eighteenth-century Man and too many Mans to count or look at or believe' (1975a: 140). Even the use of 'everybody' risks excluding women – in Russ's *The Two of Them* (1978), Irene notes how Ernst has failed to notice the lack of women: 'Hell, you don't mean people. You don't mean "everybody." You mean men' (1978: 78).

*The Female Man*, written between 1969 and 1971, jumps between narrative, lecture and satire, with a central character who appears in four aspects: Janet Evason from the female-only Whileaway, Jeannine Dadier from an Earth where the Second World War never happened, Alice-Jael Reasoner from an Earth in the middle of a literal war of the sexes, and Joanna, who appears to be a version of Russ. Much of the narrative is presented by Jael, but the commentary on late 1960s America would appear to be Russ's, echoing her non-fiction. The narrative voice suggests at one point: 'This is the lecture. If you don't like it, you can skip to the next chapter' (1975a: 29), and forestalls criticism by anticipating (male) reviews: 'this shapeless book ... of course a calm and objective discussion is beyond [the author] ... twisted, neurotic ... some truth buried in a largely hysterical...' (1975a: 141). Russ sets the book free to raise consciousnesses, acknowledging her non-fictional predecessors and contemporaries: 'Go little book [...] bob a curtsey at the shrines of Friedan, Millet [sic], Greer, Firestone, and all the rest' (1975a: 213). Both the early American (Bantam) and British (Star) editions of *The Female Man* depicted a dominatrix-Amazon type on their covers, heavy on the brass breast covers, and echoing more of a Burroughsian swords and planets womanhood. Men in search of a power fantasy must have been shocked or disappointed.

In Russ's *The Two of Them*, there is an illusion of equality in the operations of the Trans Temporal Agency. Ernst has recruited and mentored Irene, and they take it in turns as to who is in charge. At the time of publication, the House of Representatives and the Senate had passed the Equal Rights Amendment, but had yet to ratify it – indeed the measure expired before this could happen. On Irene and Ernst's mission to Ka'abah, Ernst refuses to support Irene's wish to rescue Zubeydeh. She wants to become a writer, in a society where women's writing is largely disregarded – indeed, her aunt Dunya has been declared mad because of her. Irene must leave and kill Ernst to help Zubeydeh to write.

*The Two of Them*'s quasi-Islamic world was inspired by Elgin's story 'For the Sake of Grace' (*F&SF* May 1969), which forms a prologue to part of the Coyote Jones series, *At the Seventh Level* (1972). Jones is a pastiche of the James Bond action hero, an oddity within this universe, able to project telepathically but (largely) deaf to others' telepathy, promiscuous – like Bond – although he will turn down casual trysts. He has a long-term partner throughout the series and takes responsibility for his daughter. But while a man is at the centre of these books, the drama and tension are based around the experiences of women. Elgin posits a human civilisation, scattered across three galaxies, held together by a loose federation. *The Communipaths* (1970), paired with Louis Trimble's *The Noblest Experiment in the Galaxy* as an Ace Double, sends Jones and his partner Tzana Kai to kidnap an illegally newborn baby who will become part of the telepathic travel system of the three galaxies. Her mother, Anne-Charlotte, resists, but Jones is forced to follow through. In despair, the mother kills herself, because she thinks her baby will burn out by the age of eighteen, and she is the first of what Edgar L. Chapman labels Elgin's 'female martyrs'.

This role is taken by Bess in *Furthest* (1971), a rebel on the furthest planet from the centre of the Tri-Galactic Empire. The next president of the Tri-Galactic Council is meant to be a Furthester, but no one seems to know anything about the natives, who all seem to be precisely average. Jones is sent to investigate, only to find out that the planet's civilisation is faked, with the real society actually living in the oceans. Bess works as a mind-wife, a sort of telepathic prostitute, and Jones has a relationship with her. However, Bess is convicted for her actions in the novel and 'erased', leaving Jones and her child.

In *At the Seventh Level*, Jones investigates the apparent poisoning of Jacinth, a talented poet. It is made clear that most of Jones's experiences have been in societies where women and men are equal; Abba, however, is a civilisation which regards women as little better than beasts, until recently used for breeding and little more. After the intervention of the empire, the men of Abba have accepted that women have souls, and have allowed women to join the profession of poet. Jones is disgusted with the men, but also at the state of '[n]asty, foolish, docile, subjugated, subservient women, with no minds of their own' (Elgin 1972: 125). It is a religion that keeps women in an inferior state, but only to the extent that they consent to it.

Women have most power in *Star-Anchored, Star-Angered* (1979) and Coyote is at his least successful. Posing as a student, he investigates Drussa Silver, the charismatic head of the Savvy cult, who appears to be performing miracles. Silver is a real female messiah, evidence of female access to the transcendent that men have been suppressing for millennia. She is assassinated, also by a woman, but becomes more powerful as a martyr. Noting parallels to the gospels, Chapman says: 'women [are] playing the major roles: not only the messiah, but Caiphas and Judas have been cast as women, while in another sex reversal, Coyote Jones is a reluctant Mary Magdalene' (1982: 101). Elgin explores the roles available to women, and the ways they are prevented from fulfilling them; men can be part of the problem or of the solution. At the same time, any agency Coyote has as action hero may be at the cost of female self-actualisation; it is not his role to rescue damsels in distress.

No male can rescue Consuelo Ramos, in Piercy's *Woman on the Edge of Time* (1976). While Piercy works largely outside sf, this novel was often discussed alongside *The Female Man*, *The Dispossessed* and Samuel R. Delany's *Triton* (1976), as a critical utopia (for example by Tom Moylan in *Demand the Impossible* (1986)). Ramos has been in and out of mental institutions for much of her life and has been contacted by Luciente, an emissary from the future. As Ramos slides between present and future, it is possible that the future utopia is a delusion or wishful thinking. However, the allegation that she is insane is a political judgment determined by men who disagree with her position on birth control and abortion. In the United States there had been both federal and state laws outlawing abortion, and these were challenged by a series of cases brought on behalf of the pseudonymous plaintiff Jane Roe against the Dallas County District Attorney, Henry Wade. These went up to the Supreme Court, where a majority verdict allowed for abortion, under the remit of the Fourteenth Amendment's right to privacy. For Ramos, reproductive rights are political issues, and it is the woman's right to choose. In the future utopia, built upon the notion of equality rather than repression, babies are developed in tanks rather than wombs, and childrearing is planned by those best suited to it. Nadia Khouri comments that 'it is precisely where every possibility for counter-action seems to have been annihilated, where the hegemony of multiple powers seems to lead to nothing but utter submission, that the utopian world is by necessity established' (1980: 56–57). In a present where oppression may operate along lines of gender, sexuality, class and ethnicity, it is necessary to imagine a more balanced society.

Charnas presents an even more oppressive vision of the world in *Walk to the End of the World* (1974), which requires a degree of moral suspension in its representation of extreme sexism. Political, economic and ecological disasters have rocked civilisation, and after a period of scapegoating non-white people, the white male population have blamed women, or Fems. One male character reflects upon one name given to women – Bra-Burner: 'Since "bra" was a word in an old language meaning "weapon,"' "clearly "bra-burner" meant a fem who stole and destroyed the weapons of her masters' (1974: 56). Since burning bras was never a serious feminist gesture – it might offer a satirical parallel to the burning of Vietnam draft cards – the irony is redoubled. Women are treated at best as slaves, at worst as food, and are in some cases bred from. But, equally, '[m]ale citizens [...] routinely exploit each other' (Barr 1982: 62). The social systems that perpetuate capitalism also damage men. Male–male desire is repeatedly referred to in negative terms, which risks criticising male homosexuality. The peer group is exploited rather than power passed through fatherhood. After a series of male focal characters, Charnas shifts her attention to Alldera, a female slave who resists the oppression and is helped by three men to escape the 'murder, patricide, cannibalism and predation' (Lefanu 1987: 156) that engulfs the all-male society.

Having appeared in a novel in which she escapes dystopia, Alldera returns in one – *Motherlines* (1978) – in which she enters utopia, although like that of *The Dispossessed* this utopia is an ambiguous one; Sarah Lefanu suggests that 'neither of the two women-only societies [...is] unmitigatedly utopian' (1987: 147). The Riders are an all-female group who create their own clans and songs of self-identity, and operate with a sense of cyclical rather than linear time, although this contradicts the notion of motherlines. Wolmark notes of *Motherlines* that '[it] is the plains and the wildernesses far away from the city that provide the environment in which the women who have escaped from the city can live liberated and separate lives' (1993: 83), but the Riders do not reject technology out of hand, as they conceive artificially. Legally enforceable maternity and childrearing are part of the paternalistic, capitalist system and, as, Firestone notes, 'the biological family unit has always oppressed women and children, but now, for the first time in history, technology has created real preconditions for overthrowing these oppressive "natural" conditions' (1979: 183). The Riders' alternative to masculinist society is not necessarily utopian;

perhaps Alldera remains too conditioned by her upbringing, but she is not happy with the way they treat her pregnancy. The Riders are resistant to change. Alldera would not fare any better with the third grouping, the free Fems, who scratch out a living in the wilderness. The women here may not need men, but they risk being defined as not-being-men, thus replicating the original inequality. Charnas was not to return to Holdfast or the Riders for nearly a quarter of a century, until *The Furies* (1994) and *The Conqueror's Child* (1999). Firestone argues that it is not necessary for the oppressed to advance a utopian blueprint: 'All *they* need to know is that the present system is destroying them' (1979: 211).

Reed comments satirically on female separatism in her 'Songs of War' (Harry Harrison (ed.), *Nova 4* 1974), where the women initially retreat to the hills from the towns and cities. In seeking for equality with men, sameness can be overstated: 'Whether or not [women] shaved their legs and armpits, whether or not they smelled, the pretty ones were still pretty and the others were not; the ones with good bodies walked in an unconscious pride and the others tried to ignore the differences and settled into their flesh, saying: Now, we are all equal' (1976: 56). This only deals with issues of appearance, ignoring wages, reproduction, education and so on. Reed notes that success at work might be at the cost to the family, failure at work may be due to family commitments. On the other hand, the feminist separatist movement faces the same issues as any utopian or anarchic faction: someone still has to do the cooking, cleaning and other housework, which is being avoided if the revolution is meant to be against traditional women's roles. The point is that there is no essentialism that fixes jobs as male or female domains.

Jeffrey D. Smith brought together Charnas, Delany, Kidd, Le Guin, McIntyre, Raylyn Moore, Russ, Tiptree, Luis White, Wilhelm and Chelsea Quinn Yarbro by mail to debate the position of women in science fiction and wider society as part of a symposium for his fanzine *Khatru*. Delany and Smith were well intentioned in their contributions, but often taken to task by the others about their assumptions and presumptions; it was Tiptree, however, whose views caused the most problems. Tiptree, for example, rejected a dualistic division of the sexes, especially monstrous men and angelic women, but still described a male pattern of violence and aggression and a female pattern of mothering – with perhaps the sense that this was a neural rather than bodily (genital?) process, a distinction between sex and gender which is easier for us to recognise several decades on. Mothering offers a model of leadership and control different from the male version, based on nurture rather than aggression (as seen in Octavia Butler's strong female characters). Helen Merrick notes how the exchanges chronicle 'the tensions and struggles over the meaning of feminism between women of different generations, different backgrounds and positionings (for example, middle-class liberal, socialist feminist, radical lesbian)' (2009: 116), differences which have only become more acute over the years. Tiptree was asked to leave the symposium.

Tiptree's stories were hailed as both feminist and masculinist. Richard Delap, with reference to 'The Women Men Don't See' (*F&SF* December 1973), wrote that '[w]omen who cry out that modern sf does not recognize their sex as anything but bitches and/or love objects will have to shut up where this story is concerned, properly chastised by the fact that few (if any) female sf authors have ever given women the prominence or depthful characterization that Tiptree gives here with little fuss and seeming ease. [...] the intricate play should make some of the readers of the Lib movement curl up in shame when they see that a man recognizes their ambitions better than they do themselves' (1975: 83). Tiptree's fiction apparently made feminist sf obsolete. In his introduction to Tiptree's collection *Warm Worlds and Otherwise* (1975), Robert Silverberg observes, 'It has been suggested that Tiptree is female, a theory I find absurd, for there is to me something ineluctably masculine about Tiptree's writing. I don't think the novels of Jane Austen could have been written by a man nor the stories of Ernest Hemingway by a woman' (1978: xii). Silverberg points to the similarity between Tiptree's muscular style and sparse dialogue and the writing of Hemingway. In his introduction to *10,000 Light Years from Home* (1973), Harry Harrison writes, 'There is a temptation in an introduction of this kind to [...] spend a good deal of time on the author's lovely dark hair or firm waistline despite his advancing years' (1973: viii), a comment which survives in the 1978 Ace printing.

But the speculation was right. When obituaries for Mary Hastings Bradley appeared in 1976, the details echoed those given about Tiptree's mother, except that Bradley had a daughter. Smith sent a note to Tiptree, who confessed that she was Alice Bradley Hastings Sheldon. Le Guin writes, 'She fooled us. She fooled us proper and good [... S]he played her game without actually lying' (1978: x–xi). Silverberg writes, 'She fooled me beautifully, along with everyone else, and called into question the entire notion of what is "masculine" or "feminine" in fiction' (1978: xviii). The subterfuge had allowed her to publish fiction in a male-dominated field, and dramatises the distinction between real and implied author. An added level of meaning attaches itself to the stories when the pseudonym is unveiled: she was a woman that men had not seen. The attitudes and tone considered unacceptable in *Khatru* might have been perceived differently had it been known that they came from a woman. Richard Cowper, reviewing her first novel, *Up the Walls of the World* (1978), notes that he '[detect[s] a rank quality in the Tiptree imagination' (1979b: 73) and that '[she] follows the popular recipe as sedulously as any young bride baking her first cake from a packet' (1979b: 75), as feminising a metaphor as could be coined.

Women are seen at the very start of 'The Women Men Don't See' (*F&SF* December 1973), and are later identified as Ruth and Althea Parsons (the first names meaning 'compassion' and 'healing' respectively). Ruth is a single mother who has been brought up by a single mother, and her daughter shows every sign of taking after her. The tough-talking narrator, Don Fenton (the first name means 'ruler of the world'), seems somewhat put out by the superfluity of men, and insists that women now have a better life after the passing of Equal Rights legislation. Ruth disagrees:

> 'Women have no rights, Don, except what men allow us. Men are more agressive [sic] and powerful, and they run the world. When the next real crisis upsets them, our so-called rights will vanish like – that smoke. We'll be back where we always were: property. And whatever has gone wrong will be blamed on our freedom, like the fall of Rome was …
>
> 'We're a – a toothless world … What women do is survive. We live by ones and twos in the chinks of your world-machine.' (Tiptree 1973b: 21)

The three of them have been stranded with their pilot, following a plane crash, and Don slowly realises that Ruth is not as helpless as she appears; she is involved in some secret organisation and possibly trying to rendezvous with communist guerrillas. The actual meeting is with aliens, which Fenton initially fails to recognise, and the Parsons leave the planet with them, according to Julie Luedtke Seal 'because it was the easiest alternative, not because it was the only solution' (1990: 74). They have abandoned man's world machine in favour of another.

Tiptree had two stories in *Aurora*, one as Tiptree, the other as by Raccoona Sheldon, a pseudonym used on four stories. In 'Your Faces, Oh My Sisters! Your Faces Filled of Light!' (1976), an unnamed courier travels across an America she perceives to be composed entirely of women, seeing the best in everyone, until she is attacked and killed. Her experiences are intercut with those who saw her, and the revelation that she has been having therapy, drugs and electroshock treatment to cure what is perceived as a delusion and to help her adjust to being a wife and mother. Amanda Boulter suggests that '[her] feminist fantasy creates a progressive alternative to her suburban suffocation only by instating a fixed vision which can neither acknowledge nor anticipate the violence of patriarchy' (1995: 24). The story evokes and undercuts a utopian vision of a separatist, woman-only world, which may indeed be real, but it collides with the masculine institutions of medicine, psychology, marriage and law enforcement, as well as rape and violence. The lack of intervention on the part of a female police officer when the courier is attacked shows that this is not just a male problem; women to some extent consent to the existing power relations. If the story had appeared under a male by-line, then it might have been too easy to read – with some of the characters – in terms of the courier being punished for her actions, for being in the 'wrong' place at the 'wrong' time. A female implied author resists such a reading, pushing the blame back on to those who stood by and those who drove her to escape. The second story, 'Houston, Houston, Do You Read?', features an all-female society encountered by a three-man space mission which has somehow travelled through time. The astronauts slowly discover that a plague has wiped out all the men, and Earth now reproduces by cloning. The crew are not being given a chance to save humanity, to restore it to its earlier two-sexed state, but are being researched for their knowledge, and their genetic material is sampled to widen the pool; their fate is to be executed, as they are too dangerous to have around. There is no chance that they may be re-educated, or redeemed; the patriarchal binarism of the men's worldviews would be destructive of a more sharing society. The question might be raised of whether the need to police the borders of utopia undermines its nature as utopia.

'The Screwfly Solution' (*Analog* June 1977), another Raccoona Sheldon story, discusses the eradication of parasites. Scientists had tried various biological techniques to wipe out unwanted insects that spread diseases, such as releasing sterile males to compete with and supersede the fertile ones. Alan Alstein, a young biologist, is working on such a problem in Colombia, being sent letters by his wife Anne about a colleague's work and a new anti-woman movement, Sons of Adam. Eventually Alan discovers there is a plague infecting human males and both of them realise that it is alien in origin; having tried to escape civilisation, Anne kills herself. While the story is about the extinction of the human race, it asserts a link between man and sexual aggression – in a memo from a Scottish professor it is asserted: 'A potential difficulty for our species has always been implicit in the close linkage between the behavioural expression of aggression/predation and sexual reproduction in the male' (Tiptree 1981: 69) – so the aliens are merely using a pre-existing tendency in their biological warfare. Lefanu suggests that Tiptree is exploring 'the assertion that anatomy is destiny' (1987: 112), which perhaps offers an alibi for the men's actions as they are out of their control; this again would seem to be a different message if advanced by a male author rather than a female one. But men in these stories seem programmed to behave in aggressive ways – and the only three options for women seem to be killing, being killed or going into exile. None of these seems a sustainable option, and the battle for equality between the sexes continues.

# 11
# Strange Bedfellows: Gay Liberation

There is a moment in Michel Foucault's *The Will to Knowledge* (1976) that describes the creation of the homosexual in 1869:

> The nineteenth-century homosexual became a personage, a past, a case history, and a childhood, in addition to being a type of life, a life form, and a morphology, with an indiscreet anatomy and a possibly mysterious physiology. [...] Homosexuality appeared as one of the forms of sexuality when it was transposed from the practice of sodomy onto a kind of interior androgyny, a hermaphroditism of the soul. The sodomite had been a temporary aberration; the homosexual was now a species. (1978: 43)

This is not to say that men had not had sex with men prior to the late nineteenth century, but Foucault argued that such acts were not then seen as defining an individual's personal identity as homosexual, a term coined by Karl Maria Kertbeny in 1869. A number of sexual identities were described, defined and pathologised in the psychological, scientific and sociological press of the last third of the nineteenth century: a third sex (Karl Heinrich Ulrichs); an inborn constitutional abnormality (Henry Havelock Ellis); an inherited degeneracy, or a degeneracy caused by debauchery (Richard Krafft-Ebing); an intermediate sex (Magnus Hirschfeld and Edward Carpenter); a female psyche in a male body (Ulrichs); the next stage of evolution (Carpenter); or a failure to successfully navigate the Oedipus complex (Sigmund Freud).

The word 'homosexual' is rarely used in 1970s sf, so the reader or viewer either might fail to see it or might imagine it. What should be made of the peculiarly efficient hitmen, Mr Wint (Bruce Glover) and Mr Kidd (Putter Smith), in *Diamonds are Forever* (Guy Hamilton, 1971), who hold hands as part of what is clearly a deep attachment between the two? In 1975, Thomas Disch offers a homoerotic reading of Robert A. Heinlein's *Starship Troopers* ('Starship Soldier' *F&SF* October–November 1959; 1959): 'The hero is a homosexual of a very identifiable breed. By his own self-caressing descriptions one recognises the swaggering leather boy in his most flamboyant form. There is even a skull-and-crossbones earring in his left ear' (1976: 154). Disch notes that on a number of occasions the protagonist has a fight with a man instead of being attracted to women and notes his general pleasure in pain and violence – sexuality is violence and vice versa. Having heard that several people have joined the armed forces after reading the novel, Disch acidly observes 'How much simpler it would have been for those lads just to go and have their ears pierced' (1976: 155). *Starship Troopers* is often read in dialogue with Joe Haldeman's *The Forever War* (*Analog* June 1972–January 1975; 1974), whose protagonist, Mandella, re-enlists to avoid being part of a homosexual society, the lesbianism of his mother being the final straw. Joan Gordon notes that we might see some of the characters as 'flighty homosexual men' (1980: 35), but it was a bold narrative choice. Stubbornly heterosexual to the end of the novel, Mandella is the queer one in his society.

In retrospect, the 1970s was a utopian age in terms of male gay life – the period between the legalisation of homosexual acts between men in England and Wales with the Sexual Offences Act (1967), as well as in parts of the US, and the start of the era of HIV in the 1980s. In the aftermath of the 27 June 1969 police raid on the Stonewall Inn in Greenwich Village, New York, about two thousand people protested over a number of days. Organisations such as the Gay Liberation Front (GLF) and the Gay Activist Alliance were established – in part influenced by Black civil rights movements and anti-Vietnam protests. Witnesses to gay pride marches held similar campaigns around the world. As Altman notes: 'The seventies saw the beginning of a large-scale transition in the status of homosexuality from a deviance or perversion to an alternative life style or minority' (1982: 2). In 1973, the American Psychiatric Association removed homosexuality from its Diagnostic and Statistical Manual of Mental Disorders, followed by the American Psychological Association in 1974. However, conservative campaigners tried to enact laws to prevent homosexuals from becoming teachers. Former beauty queen and singer Anita Bryant established Save Our Children to repeal a 1977 Dade County, Florida ordinance that prevented discrimination on grounds of sexual orientation, and campaigned against similar rules elsewhere in the USA. In 1979, the first openly gay elected supervisor of San Francisco, Harvey Milk, was assassinated, along with the mayor, George Moscone. Dan White's conviction for manslaughter rather than murder led to street protests.

Given the changing legal, medical and public attitudes, it might be thought that sf was a form that could embrace alternatives to heteronormativity. But, rather than positing an authentic homosexual identity, genre sf tended to focus on distinctions between a gendered social identity and a sexed anatomical one, with film being more liberal than the written word. John Money had made the distinction between sex as biological and innate and gender as social and learned in 1955, but it was only in the 1970s that this became part of a wider discourse. In 1972, George Zavitzianos described 'homeovestism', in contradistinction to transvestism, the perverse wearing of clothes of the same sex – for example uniforms – in a kind of same sex/gender drag, and in 1978 Marcia Yudkin made a distinction between biological, psychological and social identity. It would not be until 1990 that Judith Butler, in *Gender Trouble: Feminism and the Subversion of Identity*, began to write about sexual identity as something that was performed – through language and other conceptual frameworks. While some of the assumptions underlying the sf of the period can certainly be criticised, it is worth noting that there is sometimes an attempt to think through attitudes that had yet to reach a theoretical mass. Written sf was perhaps held back by the conservatism of publishing houses, although that does not explain the greater freedom of film, albeit outside Hollywood. Gay pornography used sf tropes as part of its fantasising – Samuel R. Delany represented both heterosexual and homosexual encounters in *The Tides of Lust* (1973), but this was not science fiction. This chapter will consider works by Ursula Le Guin, Disch, Delany, Walt Leibscher, William Carlson, Peter Carey, John Varley and David Gerrold, which are arguably as much about questioning gender roles as homosexuality, before moving onto the films *The Rocky Horror Picture Show* (Jim Sharman, 1976), *The Man Who Fell to Earth* (Nicolas Roeg, 1976) and *A Boy and His Dog* (L.Q. Jones, 1975) and stories by Philip K. Dick and J.G. Ballard which question the nature of sexuality. It is rare that male homosexuality is represented within sf, as in novels by Marion Zimmer Bradley and Elizabeth A. Lynn, in the pornography of Larry Townsend and with the emergence in the 1970s of slash fiction.

Genre sf had rarely consciously addressed sexuality until the 1960s New Waves pushed back the taboos for the genre in the era of sexual liberation. However, Le Guin's *The Left Hand of Darkness* (1969) depicts the awkward relationship between a male envoy and the Karhide prime minister when the latter enters into *kemmer*, effectively becoming fertile, but stops short of interspecies sex which would be on some level a same-sex relationship. Joanna Russ took Le Guin to task for the representation of her homosexual character in *The Dispossessed: An Ambiguous Utopia* (1975): 'We are told that one character is homosexual; yet he acts assexual and has no love affair' (1975c: 42). Russ is honest enough to confess that she made a similar mistake in *And Chaos Died* (1970), but also notes Disch's confusion in *On Wings of Song* as to the sexual identity of Daniel Weinraub, his central character: 'as if the author never decided whether to exploit the social myth of homosexuals-as-grotesques or to deny it; in the end he does both and – what is much worse – equivocates about his hero's relation to the whole subject so that on one page Daniel has been a hustler for years, on another contemplates the possibility with distaste [...], on yet another he's already actively homosexual [...], and on yet another he seems to dismiss the possibility altogether' (1980: 95). Daniel wants to be able to fly – a metaphor perhaps more associated with oppressed women (Butler 2009: 148–49, 247) – and to become a fairy, a term which has long had connotations as an anti-homosexual slur. Here becoming a fairy is a means of transcending an oppressive near-future America. John Clute notes that 'the word homosexual is never mentioned, nor is Daniel's sexual orientation given any register whatsoever in the text' (1980b: 83). Recognising homosexuality is as much through connotation as denotation. Daniel is the lover of a castrato – again challenging labels of sexual identity – but has a lost female love. He supports himself in musical theatre, in singing and performing; in popular prejudice 'being musical' has long been a euphemism for homosexual and assumptions are made about the sexuality of people who work in the theatre. Characters need not have sex with people of the same sex to be homosexual, nor does having sex with those of a different sex prevent them from identifying as homosexual.

In *Three Essays on the Theory of Sexuality* (1905), Freud distinguished three different forms of homosexuality: absolute (always desiring the same sex), amphigenic (no preference for men or women), and contingent (same-sex sexual satisfaction may be derived when no one of the opposite sex is available) (1953a: 136–37). It is only really the first type, rare in 1970s sf, who would identify themselves as homosexual. Sf writers were more likely to envisage societies where physical sex could be changed – the label of transsexual might be more appropriate – or depict explicitly gay male characters as having sexual desires for women – the label of bisexual is perhaps more appropriate there. During the 1970s, men and women who perceived themselves to have non-heteronormative sexualities attempted to make common cause, and in time Gay, Lesbian, Bisexual, Transsexual and (by the 1990s) Queer alliances of a range of sexualities emerged – notwithstanding the separatism of some women's groups, the misogyny of some gay men, and distrust of bisexuals and transsexuals by some individuals.

George Turner, writing about Delany's *Triton: An Ambiguous Heterotopia* (1976) in 1977, insists that 'sex is a physical manifestation, divided into two sexes only, no matter what counting system you use [...] Sexual deviation is not an act of mutation, but of adjustment' (1980: 16). As I have already noted, some nineteenth- and twentieth-century sexologists had perceived homosexuality to be a third sex; *Triton* insists on a multitude: 'forty or fifty basic sexes, falling loosely into nine categories' (Delany 1976: 117). Delany's comedy of manners, arguably obscured by his metafictional apparatus, is of a society where race and sex are not fixed, and where sexuality can be rewired on a more or less permanent level. The central character, Bron Helstrom, a former male prostitute, is in love with the performer, the Spike, but lacks the social skills and empathy to make the feeling mutual. Another potential partner, Sam, is a powerful black man who used to be a blonde woman; he, too, is critical of Helstrom's world view, and the choice of name introduces a note of metafiction into the novel as we think of Samuel – and this is before we reach the textual apparatus which offers backgrounds to and alternative drafts of the events of the novel and plays upon Delany's autobiographical and self-critical essays in *Foundation* (1974, 1975b).

Delany's subtitle alludes to Le Guin's *The Dispossessed: An Ambiguous Utopia* (1974), and he saw his novel as being in dialogue with hers. A heterotopia is the removal of part of a body to somewhere else on a body – 'A skin graft is a heterotopia. But so is a sex change' (Delany 1990: 319) – but it also refers to an idea discussed by French philosopher Michel Foucault (1970): a counter-hegemonic, alternative space inhabited by people different from the norm and which in part draws attention to the notion of difference. The heterotopia offers a dialogue with both the real world and notions of the utopian perfect world. Delany's Triton is a post-scarcity society, with no poverty, starvation or homelessness and where an individual's identity can be remoulded at will. While there is still prejudice – and Helstrom displays sexism, homophobia and possibly racism – this is more the fault of the individual citizen than a reaction to societal inequalities. Helstrom, dissatisfied with the world he finds himself in, and rather too binary in his thinking, has a sex change towards the end of the novel, either to continue his relationship with theatre performer the Spike, or in order to become desirable to Sam. Fox suggests that this falls into the racist thinking that views young African Americans as sexually voracious – 'the old black/white female taboo/desire' (1996a: 47) – when Sam is anything but a stereotype. If Delany had not told us, it would be unlikely that we would guess Sam's apparent racial identity – he is not part of any cultural community that is recognisable as black, although here race is understood as constructed rather than inherent. As a rather reactionary character, Helstrom dramatises assumptions about biologically sexed behaviour – clearly perceived by Turner as a binary – and the complications of learned and acquired behaviour. In *Triton*, homosexuality seems to be a temporary lifestyle choice, in the intersection of sex, gender and sexual preference.

Delany's character Gorgik, first introduced in 'The Tale of Gorgik' (*Asimov's* Summer 1979, but written in 1976), the first of the Return to Nevèrÿon series, is a slave who becomes a liberator of slaves with a male lover, Small Sarg, but is at first sexually active with a woman, the Vizerine Myrgot. Kathleen L. Spencer suggests that sword and sorcery heroes are 'teen-aged boys' fantasy: lots of adventure and excitement, sex whenever you want, but no awkward demands afterward, no responsibilities, no commitments; no worries about money, no wife or children or boring daily job' (1996: 135). In his narrative, however, Delany seems to be foregrounding and questioning such a subtext – the politics of slavery crosses with the subculture of consensual sadomasochism, Gorgik has a role if not a job (although he has been miner and catamite) and a sense of commitment to liberation. In 'The Tale of Gorgik' he sees someone wearing a collar, and is sexually fascinated by this, but he does not immediately act upon his desires. In 'The Tale of Old Venn' (1979), 'gorgi' is revealed to be a child's word for 'genitalia', a term which impacts upon our understanding of his character, and the rewriting of a Garden of Eden narrative – which would also revise Freud's notions of castration anxieties and penis envy – adds to the sense of sexuality being theorised.

An anthology devoted to sex and sf, *Strange Bedfellows* (1972), contains two stories with ambiguously gendered relationships. The first, Leibscher's 'Do Androids Dream of Electric Love?', has a title that echoes Dick's *Do Androids of Electric Sheep?* (1968). An unnamed man has a conversation with a psychiatrist android and is frightened of being 'converted' (Leibscher 1972: 79), and has 'ostensibly committed an act that even in this enlightened age was considered, shall we say, way out' (1972: 80). When the man tells the android the story, it finds it 'exceedingly sexy' (1972: 80) and the teller 'provocatively desirable' (1972: 81). As the android leaves, the man inquires to its gender, and the android retorts 'That's for you to figure out' (1972: 81). We are not told the android's gender or sex, nor what the crime is; we have to infer it from the silence. Chris West notes: 'this android's gender is not apparent and is not assumed either by the incarcerated citizen of the future or by the narrator: the android is not "he" or "she" but "it". The text, note, conflates gender with genital configuration' (2007: 508) As West observes, there is something feminising about the choice of words: the android appears effeminate, suggesting that 'it' is female (feminine) or (effeminately) homosexual. Traditional gender roles situate the desiring look as masculine and the desired being looked at as feminine. The android's arousal by the unspeakable act complicates this; perhaps the unspeakable is that it would not matter what gender or sex the android is, as it could be reprogrammed or rebuilt to taste.

Russ dismisses this story as 'a slight anecdote' (1973b: 68) and condemns the next, Carlson's 'Dinner at Helen's', as 'another middle-class conventional pretense at unisex and hippidom' (Russ 1973b: 69). Jordan, the narrator, invites a customer, Helen Williams, to lunch, having undressed her in his mind. She invites him to her apartment, where he tries to seduce her. Having visited the bathroom, she returns as Allen, a naked man. Allen seems to be the male side of Helen: 'Have you looked at clothing and hair styles lately, at all these change-of-sex operations, at the new militancy of homosexuals and all the interest in them? I tell you, men are beginning to accept the woman in themselves, and women the man in them' (Carlson 1972: 88). Allen/Helen indicates that s/he knows Jordan, that they've seen each other before, before a final striptease. Jordan realises all:

> But I'll forget it.
> I've forgotten it already. (Carlson 1972: 91)

It is not at all clear what he has forgotten, which seems to be defined by being unspeakable. It is not clear whether it is a penis or vagina visible at the end, but within Freudian sexual paradigms, either could induce castration anxiety. West suggests that we

> [n]ote how the knowledge that Jordan gains near the end is predicated on an amnesia that is itself restored at the moment of its banishment; we witness, and he suffers, a moment of recognition which is literally 'blinding'. Note too the dizzying movement through time at the very end (from present to future simple to perfect tense); [...] We are offered, here, more occlusion than conclusion – a passage, it seems, full of sound and fury, signifying, along with the rest of this text, not nothing, but, somehow, homosexuality. (2007: 513)

The positioning of Leibscher's and Carlson's stories in the 'Toujours Gay' section – along with a reprint of Theodore Sturgeon's 'The World Well Lost' (*Universe* June 1953) – offers a suggestive critical framing, although Russ describes the Sturgeon story as being about 'effects of enforced secrecy on the human soul' (1973b: 66), rather than being about homosexuality as such.

Another striptease occurs in an early Carey story, 'Peeling' (*Meanjin Quarterly* March 1972), where the unnamed narrator describes how his upstairs neighbour, Nile, leaves mysterious dolls around the house. On one occasion, when they are reading newspapers in bed, she asks him why the deaths column does not include details of aborted babies, then reveals that she assists in performing abortions. If the story is set in Sydney, as seems likely, then abortion would have been legal (since 1971). At this point, he begins to undress her many layers of clothing, until she is naked, save for a single ear stud. Despite her protests, he pulls at it and this reveals another bodily layer: 'Standing before me is a male of some twenty years. His face is the same as her face, his hair the same' (1972: 45). This man also has an ear stud, which the narrator pulls, revealing a slimmer woman inside the man. In turn, he rolls up her legs, her arms turn out to be false, and she is wearing a wig. All that remains of her/him is a small doll, similar to the ones left around the house. The story does not explicitly feature homosexuality, but the biological distinction between men and women is undercut. Altman suggests that the 'belief that homosexuality is somehow a reflection of a blurred sense of masculinity/femininity remains central to the Western imagination' (1982: 55). The layers of Nile, like layers of an onion, yield a series of identities. It is unclear whether this is a female psyche in a male body or a female body, and, indeed, whether she has a female 'psyche'.

The technology to change sexes underlies Varley's 'Picnic on Nearside' (F&SF August 1974). Twelve-year-old Fox meets his old friend Halo, once male, now female. Both had been sexually active prior to this, but had spent a lot of time together as buddies. At this point in their maturity, they have found being both friends and sexual partners too complicated, but Halo's use of her knowledge of Fox's turn-ons means that quasi-heterosexual sex is achievable, if not necessarily enjoyable for both parties. We are told that in this society there is no distinction between the sex roles, but newly sex-changed individuals are in the habit of masquerading in their new gender from a past 'where the differences are so vivid and startling' (2004b: 11). Fox and Halo run away to set up home on the moon, and fall into a traditional gendered division of labour, as well as having sex. In the time after their return, both Fox and Halo undergo a series of sex-changes, allowing for heterosexual, gay and lesbian possibilities, but Fox ends up a woman, her birth sex, as Varley reveals toward the end of the story. As Halo is male again, for all their switching of sexes, a traditional family seems likely to be created.

'Options' (*Universe* 9 1979), set at an earlier point in Varley's loose 'Eight Worlds' future history, reveals more details of the processes of changing sex. Cleo becomes interested in the growing phenomenon of Changing and, despite her husband Jules's misgivings, investigates. A clone of the opposite sex is grown, into which the brain can then be implanted. Unsure about making an immediate commitment, Cleo first has breast reduction and lives as male. The process here is thus akin to transsexual transitioning from female to male. Jules – a unisex name – remains uncomfortable, and is repeatedly shocked by Cleo's attempts to occupy masculine roles, most notably being on top in sexual intercourse, while also being called upon to take on the traditional maternal role of (bottle) feeding their youngest child. On the other hand, once Cleo transitions to Leo, the two become friends. The couple had already experimented with threesomes – Varley does not specify with which sex, but presumably with a second woman given Jules's platonic relationship with Leo – and thus a certain amount of female–female desire is part of Cleo/Leo's make-up. The story closes with Cleo restored to being a woman, but taking a new name of Nile – a coincidental echo of 'Peeling' – and insisting on freedom of behaviour as a woman. The story seems sounder on matters of feminism than it is on homosexuality.

David Gerrold is more direct in his depiction of homosexuality, although ambiguities remain. The hero of *Space Skimmer* (1972), Mass, is jealous of his pilot, Ike, for his communing with Alem, in a metaphor for homophobia. As Ike is a construct, he is not as such male, but the communing is clearly a sexual act, eliciting pleasure, and Mass sees it as a perversion. Ike has to censor his behaviour in order to keep his master happy and comfortable. More complex is *The Man Who Folded Himself* (1973). The orphaned Daniel is visited by his Uncle Jim, who tells him he is incredibly rich and instructs him to keep a diary. When his uncle dies, however, this turns out to have been a lie, and all he has left is a belt that will enable him to travel in time. With the aid of a version of himself from the very near future, Daniel makes money through betting on horses and share deals. But he keeps changing his present, and he tries to undo his actions. Gripped both by a hero worship of himself, and flattered by the attention from himself, he becomes his own lover: 'I respond to Dan as if he were another person, *as if he were not myself*. I am both husband and wife, and I like both roles' (1973b: 76). The seduction, though, is presented as if it is the younger Daniel who is in charge, rather than the older one who has already had the experience – younger Daniel/Danny/Don has to consent: 'So it's really me who's doing the seducing, isn't it?' (1973b: 78). Since these Daniels are more or less the same age, this is not necessarily problematic – but there are much older Daniels who try to seduce the younger versions. Toward the end of the novel, there are scores of Daniels in a single house, some of whom are still having sex. Daniel meets a female version of himself – Diane – who says 'I always wondered what I would look like as a boy. Now I know, I'd be very handsome. [...] And very nicely built too – not too much muscle, not so many as to look brutish; just enough to look manly' (1973b: 108). It is hardly a surprise that the two become pregnant and she is able to give birth to them, nor that the uncle and aunt who gave them both time belts are older versions of themselves. The male Daniel seems to win out over the female one, even though there is a male part of Diane and a female part of Danny: 'With Danny, the physical forms were identical; mental roles could be arbitrary. It was just me and him. I didn't have to be male, I didn't have to be dominant. With Don I could be weak, with Don I could cry' (1973b: 113-4). This shows a failure of imagination, assuming that we are not meant to read this as just the prejudiced thoughts of a diarist narrator who keeps losing his mind. There is the repeated sense here that heterosexuality reinforces sex roles and gender roles, the breadwinner and breadmaker, the active and the passive, whereas in male homosexuality (and, by implication, lesbianism) a role has to be chosen, as both parties may be active or passive. This is heteronormative. Novelist Mark Adlard notes the novel's debt to earlier time paradox stories, but points to Heinlein's 'By His Bootstraps' (as by Anson MacDonald, *Astounding* October 1941), rather than '– All You Zombies –' (*F&SF* March 1959): 'Gerrold's contribution to this sub-genre was made possible by the new permissiveness, which has slopped over into sf from general fiction' (1974: 100). Adlard suggests that the use of doubles in the story moves it into the territory of narcissism – which is perhaps appropriate since Freud's 'On Narcissism' (1914) had identified narcissism with 'perverts and homosexuals' (1953b: 88), arguing that '[they] are plainly seeking *themselves* as a love-object' (1953b: 88). The narcissistic desire is for '(a) what he himself is (i.e., himself), (b) what he himself was, (c) what he himself would like to be, (d) someone who was once part of himself' (1953b: 90). All four of these are part of the object-choices of Dan/Danny/Don in Gerrold's novel.

A more playful carnivalisation of sexuality is portrayed in the musical *The Rocky Horror Show* (1973), written by Richard O'Brien and premiered at the Royal Court's Theatre Upstairs, London, before being filmed as *The Rocky Horror Picture Show*. A strait-laced couple, who have just become engaged, Brad Majors and Janet Weiss (Barry Bostwick and Susan Sarandon), break down outside the gothic castle of Dr Frank-N-Furter (Tim Curry), and become involved in his attempt to create a perfect being, Rocky (Peter Hinwood). The 'raunchy, vulgar, and jolting' (Siegel 1980: 305) ethos – the high-heels-and-suspenders costumes of Frank-N-Furter and his fellow Transylvanian Transsexuals – forms a huge contrast with the couple: frightening to Brad, seductive to Janet, and Frank-N-Furter beds them both, while Janet clearly desires Rocky. The contrast is further emphasised by the serious, po-faced criminologist narrator (Charles Gray in the film), whose interruptions have something of the feel of some of the interventions by Graham Chapman or John Cleese in *Monty Python's Flying Circus* (5 October 1969–5 December 1974) telling the other characters not to be so silly. *Rocky Horror* offers the play of permutations of possible partners, with no sense of fixed sexual identity even as it is clear that heteronormative boundaries are being crossed. The boundaries between stage/screen and spectators were also blurred as audiences started to dress up for the late-night showings of the film which began running, along with having rice, toast, cigarette lighters and other props to participate in key scenes: '[it] bridges the gap between cinema and theatre in a way that has never happened before, for here the audience become the actors, and the auditorium the stage' (Nicholls 1984: 154–55). *Rocky Horror* became an example of what Susan Sontag calls deliberate camp, with its echoes of Hammer horror films (and replication of the radio mast from the RKO studios logo), cross-dressing, fishnet tights, musical numbers and homoeroticism, not to mention an over-the-top performance from Tim Curry. Sontag argues, 'Probably, intending to be campy is always harmful' (1966: 282), preferring naïve camp: 'Pure camp is always naïve' (1966: 282). She associates deliberate camp with homosexuality, arguing that 'homosexuals, by and large, constitute the vanguard – and the most articulate audience – of Camp' (1966: 290). While *The Rocky Horror Picture Show* could hardly be said to normalise male–male desire, it gave its audience permission to push back the boundaries of gendered behaviour. Siegel argues that the film is 'an Aristophanic attack against sexually repressive traditional mores and sexual institutions' (1980: 306), and that the film was being used by the audiences 'to express some of their pent-up anxieties and frustrations occasioned by […] evolving and unresolved conflict over sexuality' (1980: 311). This was the era of glam rock and David Bowie's bisexuality in his stage personae, so there was a certain currency in alternative sexualities. Some of the cast – notably O'Brien, Hinwood and Little Nell (who played Columbia, a groupie) – went on to appear in Derek Jarman's low-budget, sexually transgressive films, such as *Sebastiane* (Derek Jarman and Paul Humfress, 1976) and *Jubilee* (Derek Jarman, 1978).

David Bowie plays the central character in *The Man Who Fell to Earth*, a British adaptation of Walter Tevis's 1963 novel, in which an alien, Newton (Bowie), uses a patents lawyer, Oliver Farnsworth (Buck Henry), to raise money for his mysterious mission, apparently an attempt to rescue a dying species. Bowie's persona boosts his sense of alienness, in a film where sexual boundaries are crossed and recrossed – human–alien sexual attraction is depicted between working-class Mary-Lou (Candy Clark) and Newton, black–white between the chief federal agent Peters (Bernie Casey) and his Caucasian wife (Claudia Jennings), old–young between Professor Nathan Bruce (Rip Torn) and students, and male–male between Farnsworth and Trevor (Rick Riccardo). The broad equivalences between the varieties of coupling works either to normalise all of them, or to reinscribe all of them as perverse. The former seems more likely in intent, and the challenge to heteronormativity becomes a means of representing the passage of time of the film's narrative.

Manly bonding occurs in L.Q. Jones's 1975 misogynistic film adaptation of Harlan Ellison's award-winning novella, 'A Boy and His Dog' (*New Worlds* April 1969). The western-like desertified ruins are home to scavenging men, and occasional women, who always seem to be the men's sexual objects. The relationship between Vic (Don Johnson) and his dog, Blood (voiced by Tim McIntyre), is central to the narrative, their loyalty to each other – despite their bickering – beyond question. This is threatened when Vic is lured underground to Topeka by Quilla June (Sarah Holmes), where he will be milked of his sperm to replenish the community's gene pool. Topeka is clearly meant to be a satire on the bourgeois American small town, with its marching bands, barbershop quartets and handy recipes, but it is a genetic dead end and is ruled with a rod of iron by a small elite. It emerges that Quilla June has been using Vic as much as the hierarchy of Topeka has; she helps him escape at the expense of her friends, but Vic immediately sacrifices her because of her treatment of Blood. The film offers a variant on the homoerotic dynamic of buddy movies as identified by Robin Wood (1986: 227–29): two buddies on a (largely pointless) journey away from home in a kind of love story, with women marginalised. Vic wants to continue wandering, hating the concept of home. The film omits the explicitly – that is, effeminately – homosexual character as 'clown or villain [… as] a disclaimer – our boys are not like *that*' (Wood 1986: 229). Nor does either of the central male characters die, as is common in overtly and covertly gay films: 'The male relationship must never be consummated (indeed, must not be *able* to be consummated), and death is the most effective impediment' (Wood 1986: 229), although we are briefly led to assume that Vic is dead. It is the species boundary that acts as a check on their behaviour.

The interracial hug at the emotional climax of Dick's *Flow My Tears, the Policeman Said* (1974), where Felix Buckman, grieving for his dead sister and lover, Alys, hands an African American stranger a drawing of an arrow-pierced heart and then hugs him, is a moment of same-sex desire. George Turner is puzzled by the scene ('what meaning has Buckman's anguished approach in sexless love to the negro who plays no other role in the action?' (1975: 97)), which he mentions after repeating a reference to 'the curiously isolated homosexual scene' (1975: 97) where a middle-aged homosexual is found in bed with a thirteen-year-old boy. Dick, in fact, worried that the scene at the gas station would be read as homosexual in nature, having described it to a woman within the sf field: 'when I told her the plot she said, "And the protagonist is a homosexual." Then she left. I actually wrote an introduction defending the protagonist against her slanders, but later threw it away, deciding that the hell with it, which is what I said at great length in the introduction' (1991: 16). In the abandoned introduction, Dick argues that 'he does not care whether General Buckman is homosexual or not; he cares only that rising out of and transcending this terrible day General Buckman shows himself able to love, and in fact able to love a stranger' (1986: 2). It is symptomatic of the period's invisible homophobia that Dick should have perceived the woman's comment as a slander. The abandoned introduction notes the various kinds of love, including homosexual, which the book explores; notable in this context is the scene mentioned above in which an adult male character is found in bed with a thirteen-year-old boy, apparently legally, albeit in the alternative realm of Alys's drug hallucination. Russ criticises the depiction of Alys: 'she is pure *diabola ex machina*, a male fantasy of a macho, homosexual, leather, S & M freak projected onto a woman' (1975b: 15–16). Russ thinks it more offensive than the usual division of representations of women into virgins or whores: 'If a woman can't be a lady, she automatically becomes Marlon Brando in "The Wild Ones." See recent stories about hairy, muscled Woman's Libbers (yech) who smoke cigars (chomp) and cut up men (help!)' (1975b: 16). That Alys is a fantasised version of Dick's dead twin sister makes matters even more problematic.

In Ballard's *Crash* (1973), homosexual acts are another form of paraphilia alongside many behaviours. The narrator, James Ballard, shares the obsessions of Dr Robert Vaughan, exploring the erotics of car accidents, and the literal clash of technology and body. Wounds, preferably open ones, become erogenous zones, vaginal substitutes. Ballard and Vaughan's sexual intercourse does not fix their sexuality on their maleness, but continues an intercourse they have conducted through shared women, crashes and drug trips. Homosexuality is used as a device – as in *The Man Who Fell to Earth* and *The Forever War* – that can either locate Vaughan's acts as perverse or normalise them as a part of spectrum of sexual behaviours.

Bradley's *Heritage of Hastur* (1975) portrays homosexuality in two distinct but related lights, as part of the military corps that operates on the planet. Darkover's quasi-feudal society is descended from the survivors of a Terran mission; it is a 'male-dominated society, and with few exceptions women are relegated to a secondary and powerless position' (Leith 1980: 29). Dyan Ardais abuses his position as trainer of the corps and has a series of sadistic sexual relationships with selected cadets. It is not so much the same-sex nature of these pairings that is problematic, but his misuse of power in forcing individuals to participate against their will. This paedophile behaviour risks being a cheap way of establishing the character as a villain, in a way similar to some of the characters in Robert Adams's Horseclans saga and Baron Vladimir Harkonnen in the early Dune novels. Bradley critiques power and represents the comradeships and rivalries of groups of men. At times the homosocial – a word coined by Jean Lipmen-Blumen in 1975 to refer to same-sex relations that typically stop short of the physically sexual, and which could include female buddies – slips into the homosexual. Danilo arouses strange feelings in Regis, who should by rights be telepathic. Leith describes Regis as having 'homosexual leanings' (1980: 30) rather than a homosexual identity; it mainly comes across as a kind of manly bonding, and is somewhat sentimentalised.

A rare example of unambiguous homosexuality occurs in Lynn's *A Different Light* (1978), although the narrative succumbs to the lure of the gay gothic narrative which condemns one of the two central lovers to die, and is more a depiction of the aftermath of their relationship than the establishment of it. Jimson Allece is an artist – creative and sensitive – with a rare, incurable cancer. His lover was Russell, a starship captain with piratical tendencies – on the edge of the law, rootless and dangerous in comparison to Jimson's relatively comfortable life. Jimson decides he wants to travel through space for one last time, runs into Russell again, and becomes involved in a mission to steal alien crystal masks. As the discourse of homosexuality has been so much about posing and hidden, closet, identities, it is hardly surprising that the MacGuffins are masks, but they turn out to have a deeper significance. The mission allows Jimson to make a heroic sacrifice, and Russell keeps running away from commitment, but there is a sense of romantic survival as telepathy allows Jimson's personality to transfer to a different body. From the grave, Jimson finally draws a portrait of Russell: 'Hair like a mane framed aquiline features. The mouth curved in a familiar grin. […] It was flamboyant, almost brutal' (Lynn 1979: 174–75) – the word 'flamboyant' echoing Disch's phrase.

Stronger materials, although not without their echoes of romance, can be found in the pornography of Townsend, a mainstay of the Los Angeles leather and bondage and sadomasochism scenes from the 1950s onward, and from the early 1960s a campaigner for homophile liberation – an earlier incarnation of the search for gay acceptance and equality. Along with many stories using BDSM scenarios, he produced a science-fiction trilogy, *2069*

(1969), *2069 + 1* (1970) and *2069 + 2* (1970), on the one hand old-fashioned space operas about first contact with aliens with telepathic powers, on the other hand radical in their positioning of homosexual characters throughout the narrative, and the pornographic description of sexual encounters between the main protagonists, various members of the crew and several species of aliens. The positive use of anal sex is still geared to a sense of power, and the question of who is in control of a group, but in their private encounters corporals dominating majors eroticise the ranks of a military-style space force. The telepathic skills learnt from the Centaurans encountered in *2069* facilitate more power fantasies, as bodies can change size and form at will, and individuals can be coerced into sexual acts without being entirely clear what they are consenting to – or, indeed, against their specified will. Townsend envisages a world where homosexuality is the default sexuality rather than a recently decriminalised one, although for the purposes of dramatic tension, a movement known as the Humpties is still fighting against what it perceives as gay control of Earth. These novels emerged at a point when feminist critics were critiquing male representations of female characters, and in time pornography was labelled by some feminists (such as Andrea Dworkin and Robin Morgan) as a causal factor in the cases of rape, normalising the objectification of women and portraying them as always sexually available. While male gay porn would not fit unproblematically with this argument, there is a streak of misogyny running through this book. Just as the women in Suzy McKee Charnas's early Holdfast novels dismiss the homosocial nature of male power, so the insistence on homophile solidarity denigrates and fears women. In a misogynistic inversion of military paranoia about homosexuality, the space agency recruits only gay men, because the men would distract women; straight men are tolerated if they are discreet about their leaning.

Townsend was a gay man writing erotica and pornography for gay men; in the early 1970s a phenomenon emerged of (mainly heterosexual) women writing gay erotica for other women. It emerged from the fiction fanzines that had been produced by women from the late 1960s devoted to *Star Trek*, and centred on the imagined sexual relationship between Captain James Kirk and Mr Spock – a logical continuation of the subtext of the interracial buddies identified by Leslie Fiedler (1960). These were labelled Kirk/Spock stories, then K/S and finally slash. According to Billie Aul and Farah Mendlesohn, 'Until quite recently these stories almost always depicted male characters, mostly because the women writing this material tend to be erotically drawn to male rather than female homosexuality activity' (1998: 86). In line with Laura Mulvey's description of Hollywood films (1975), women had been trained by the camera and editing apparatus to identify with the male protagonist, but appear to be desiring the male antagonist or other leading male character rather than the protagonist's female love interest, despite his desirous gaze. Slash writers subvert corporate intentions, to make media texts gratify their needs. Patricia F. Lamb and Diana L. Veith suggest that these writers respond to and develop 'the androgynous characteristics' (1986: 244) of the original characters, again allying homosexuality with a mismatch of societal gender and sexual identity – Kirk and Spock become female men. While the pornography that Dworkin condemned was about the power of men over women and penetration by the former of the latter, female readers found slash attractive because 'it is intimacy rather than sexuality that is the centrally important element' (Woledge 2005: 57). This risks assuming an essentialist difference between male and female readers. Slash fiction expanded far beyond *Star Trek*, so that there must now be very few television texts of the last forty years that have not been slashed.

# 12
# Saving the Family? Children's Fiction

Thomas M. Disch argues that 'science fiction is a branch of children's literature' (1976: 142), in the sense that, like children's literature (as he perceived it), sf was limited in intellectual, emotional and moral terms. Magazine sf and the chapter serials had both teenaged and adult audiences, even before the invention of the category of the teenager in the 1950s. Robert A. Heinlein's early novels were published as juveniles as books, but Scribner's felt that *Starship Troopers* ('Starship Soldier' *F&SF* October–November 1959; 1959) had too much strong material for child readers. The perception that sf avoided sexuality and romance may have facilitated a wide age-range among readers, and it is arguably the shift to more adult themes in the 1960s and 1970s that created a space for more genre fiction explicitly aimed at children. In addition to Heinlein, Isaac Asimov and Ray Bradbury also wrote for children and adults – the latter's *The Halloween Tree* (1972) and some of his story collections were marketed for children. At the same time, children's literature also changed, with the emergence in the mid- to late 1960s of the Young Adult novel. This chapter will consider novelisations for children of sf film and television, stop-motion animations, animated and live-action Disney films, novels for children by Roald Dahl and Andre Norton and for teenagers and young adults by Alan Garner, Ursula Le Guin, Robert C. O'Brien, H.M. Hoover and Jan Mark.

But children's science fiction remains a problematic term – for a start, the possessive apostrophe of the first term suggests a misleading degree of ownership, given that editors, bookshops, librarians, teachers and parents all act as gatekeepers controlling a child's access to books (Zipes 2001: 39–60), and similar mechanisms are in play for film, television and games. The notion of the child – effectively conceived during the Enlightenment by authors such as Jean-Jacques Rousseau – is also problematic, and in practice marketing of books is based on clusters of age groups. It might be the case that the child has insufficient knowledge of the world to grasp when he or she is meant to be estranged by *'an imaginative framework alternative to the author's empirical environment'* (Suvin 1979: 8), and that cognition is not happening in the same sense as we would understand it in adults (Mendlesohn 2004). On the other hand, the continual process of encountering nova and putting them into an overall worldview might widen the sense of cognitive estrangement so far as to negate its usefulness as a defining term. Meanwhile, the social mores were changing, with growing divorce rates putting the family in crisis, and children's fiction could either reflect or ignore this. There was a long history of family melodramas through which children had to navigate to come of age, as in the Bildungsroman. In order to have adventures, it is necessary for the father figure (the law) to be absent, and the process of the narrative is to suture the child into the social fabric, although this is not always achieved and the novels of this period are oftenambivalent about this process. Disney, a corporation whose many products were aimed at a family audience, had a vested interest in recuperating the nuclear family, and is less uneasy about a eucatastrophic ending.

In her survey of British children's books in the 1970s, Elaine Moss notes that '[t]eenagers were offered hundreds of SF titles, often by authors for adults, while the younger child's heroes tended to be by-products of American or British T.V. Series, the *Star Trek* or *Dr. Who* stories' (1980: 62). There were spin-off novels for many television programmes which could be read by a range of ages – James Blish's adaptations of *Star Trek* episodes into short stories (1967–77), Robert Miall's *UFO* (1971) and *UFO 2* (1971) and E.C. Tubb, Brian Ball, John Rankine, J. Jeff Jones and Michael Butterworth's *Space: 1999* (1975–77) novelisations. George Lucas was credited with writing *Star Wars* (1976), ghost-written by Alan Dean Foster, who also created *Splinter of the Mind's Eye* (1978), set between *Star Wars: Episode IV – A New Hope* (George Lucas, 1974) and *Star Wars: Episode V – The Empire Strikes Back* (Irvin Kershner, 1980), itself novelised by Donald F. Glut. More spin-offs followed, starting with Brian Daley's Han Solo trilogy (1979–80). Foster was one of the more prolific novelisers, producing *Dark Star* (1974), *Alien* (1979) and *The Black Hole* (1979). Glen Larson's television version of *Buck Rogers in the 25th Century* produced two novelisations by Addison E. Steel (a pseudonymous Richard A. Lupoff; 1978, 1979) and several books, mostly written with Robert Thurston or Ron Goulart, were drawn from *Battlestar Galactica* (1978–88). While these all act as merchandising and advertisements for films and television series, in the days before home video and internet streaming, novelisations kept continuing narratives alive. In Britain, union agreements restricted television repeats, and none of the three channels needed to fill twenty-four hours of broadcasting.

The BBC's sf series, *Doctor Who* (23 November 1963–), had been running for ten years when Target decided to republish the three existing novelisations, David Whitaker's *Doctor Who in an Exciting Adventure with the Daleks* (1964) and *Doctor Who and the Crusaders* (1965) and Bill Strutton's *Doctor Who and the Zarbi* (1965). New novelisations followed, largely aimed at the children's market. Terrance Dicks, then script editor, acted as a series editor, and where the original author was not interested or available, he adapted them: Robert Holmes's 'Spearhead from Space' (3–24 January 1970) into *Doctor Who and the Auton Invasion* (1974) and Louis Marks's 'Day of the Daleks' (1–22 January 1972) into *Doctor Who and the Day of the Daleks* (1974); Malcolm Hulke adapted his own 'Doctor Who and the Silurians' (31 January–14 March 1970) as *Doctor Who and the Cave Monsters* (1974), 'Colony in Space' (10 April–15 May 1971) as *Doctor Who and the Doomsday Weapon* (1974) and 'The Sea Devils' (26 February–1 April 1972) as *Doctor Who and the Sea-Devils* (1974); and Barry Letts adapted his pseudonymously co-written script for 'The Dæmons' (22 May–19 June 1971) as *Doctor Who and the Dæmons* (1974). In time, almost all the series was adapted. Especially in the early novelisations, characters might be given new introductions or at the very least explained, but the adaptations tend to be faithful even if there might have been a temptation for writers to reject changes made by script editors for budgetary or other reasons.

The Doctor may have been child-like at times, but was clearly a grown-up, albeit one on the run from his own people and, presumably, his own family. His supposed granddaughter, Susan (Carole Ann Ford), had long since been forgotten about, with substitute identificatory companion characters, especially the female ones, frequently infantilised by the plots. Children's narratives, however, are more likely to focus on maturing children and families, or animal substitutes. Historically these had offered an educative role model for the reader, and some children's fiction is didactic. At the other pole of children's fiction were escapist entertainments, for much of the twentieth century set in pocket universes – either in obvious fantasy landscapes or in the isolated worlds of boarding schools. Such stories continued to be told, but finishing schools and boarding schools felt very dated in the age of the high school and the comprehensive.

Stop-motion animations transmitted in Britain on BBC1 at the end of children's broadcasting, just before the early evening news, reached a crossover audience of children and adults. One example, albeit one with adult references, was *The Magic Roundabout* (18 October 1965–25 January 1977), based on the French *La Ménage enchanté*, directed by Serge Danot. The French version was set in a Beautiful Wood with a roundabout operated by Father Peony, overseen by Zébulon, a head on a spring (possibly an alien), with a girl (Margote), a cow (Azalée), a snail (Ambrose), a guitar-playing rabbit (Flappy), a train and a dog (Pollux). As the BBC did not buy translations of the scripts, narrator Eric Thompson elected to improvise with his own versions of the characters: respectively Mr Rusty, Zebedee, Florence, Ermintrude, Brian, Dylan (a homage to Bob Dylan), the Train and Dougal, the latter being inspired by the character of Tony Hancock in *Hancock's Half Hour* (radio 2 November 1954–29 December 1959; television 7 July 1956–30 June 1961). Thompson was a respected actor and director, for example of Alan Ayckbourne's plays, but had also performed on the BBC's children's programme *Play School* (21 April 1964–11 March 1988), so he trusted that the visuals would entertain children, more so when they were transmitted in colour, and he added references to amuse himself – for example, when Dougal acquires a movie camera, he compares himself to Ken Russell.

Danot went on to make a feature-length film, *Pollux et Le Chat bleu* (Serge Danot, 1970), complete with songs, which Thompson narrated as *Dougal and the Blue Cat* (1972); a slightly cut-down audio version was also released. A cat conspires with the unseen Blue Voice to take over the Beautiful Wood and attempts to turn everything blue. Azalée's announcement that she enjoyed being kidnapped and the army base in a whip factory both seem like rather adult references; Thompson's version has a former treacle factory. Danot presumably had memories of Nazi-occupied France to draw upon, whereas Thompson presents the narrative as a parable about conformity and tolerance. The film's climax is a trip to the moon – the English version uses the three-chord sequence from Richard Wagner's *Also Sprach Zarathustra* (1896), familiar to adult ears from *2001: A Space Odyssey* (Stanley Kubrick, 1968).

The BBC also broadcast *The Clangers* (16 November 1969–10 October 1974), produced by Small Films. Writer/narrator Oliver Postgate and artist Peter Firmin had been producing paper- and puppet-based animations since the 1950s, out of a converted cowshed north of Canterbury. An earlier version of a Clanger had first appeared in *Noggin and the Moon Mouse* (1967), one of the spin-off books from an earlier animation, *Noggin the Nog* (1959–65); this evolved into a species who live on a small planet, converting rubbish and debris into useful things (in parallel to the Wimbledon-based Wombles created by Elisabeth Beresford, later televised 5 February 1973–24 October 1975 in the same slots). The series thus offered a strong ecological message, supporting recycling. The discovery of a television playing pop music in 'The Visitor' brought disruption to the Clangers' comfortable if frugal world, with the television speedily ejected; there is an irony of such a message being offered on a television programme. In another episode, a human astronaut lands on the planet, with a flag that mixes those of the United States and the Soviet Union, suggesting a political détente to the Cold War. Postgate had been a conscientious objector during the Second World War, and hated the arms race that he thought threatened the world. After two series of thirteen episodes, Postgate, the son of radical historian Raymond Postgate and grandson of former Labour party leader George Lansbury, produced a final episode for broadcast on the eve of the October 1974 election, offering a satire of the political process, which he found increasingly meaningless (Postgate 2000).

Two men in a cowshed was a long way from Walt Disney Productions. Disney had died on 15 December 1966, with his studio being the Hollywood leader in family entertainment – *Mary Poppins* (Robert Stevenson, 1964) had been a hit, eighteen animated features had been made and released, Disneyland was thriving and the Walt Disney World Resort began construction. Both the final animations green-lighted by Walt Disney – *The Jungle Book* (Wolfgang Reitherman, 1967) and *AristoCats* (Wolfgang Reitherman, 1970) – were box office successes, thus ensuring that cartoon features would continue to be made for the foreseeable future. The films tended to fantasy rather than sf, largely putting anthropomorphised animals in human roles, and so will not be considered here in detail. *AristoCats* had been an original story and *Robin Hood* (Wolfgang Reitherman, 1973) drew on the English ballads and folktales, but put animals in the roles, sidestepping the political issues – a story which saw thieves triumph must have troubled the moralistic Disney studios, and Robin (Brian Bedford) and Little John (Phil Harris) debate their motivations. They are borrowing rather than redistributing wealth, and much of the money is taxation revenue raised by dubious authorities. *The Many Adventures of Winnie the Pooh* (Wolfgang Reitherman and John Lounsbery, 1977) was a compilation of three animated shorts based on A.A. Milne's 1920s stories – *Winnie the Pooh and the Honey Tree* (Wolfgang Reitherman, 1966), *Winnie the Pooh and the Blustery Day* (Wolfgang Reitherman, 1968) and *Winnie the Pooh and Tigger Too* (John Lounsbery, 1974), the latter originally released to support *The Island at the Top of the World* (Robert Stevenson, 1974). Their last animated feature of the 1970s was *The Rescuers* (John Lounsbery, Wolfgang Reitherman, Art Stevens, 1977), loosely based on Margery Sharp's *The Rescuers* (1959) and *Miss Bianca* (1962), and featuring a society of mice, based in the United Nations building, dedicated to rescuing kidnapped children. Sequences in each film ape earlier films, and character types are repeated, but young children appreciate such familiarity.

Meanwhile, the live action wing of the studio made *Herbie Rides Again* (Robert Stevenson, 1974), a sequel to *The Love Bug* (Robert Stevenson, 1968), featuring Herbie, an intelligent Volkswagen Beetle car. The film reused property developer Alonzo P. Hawk (Keenan Wynn) from *The*

*Absent-Minded Professor* (Robert Stevenson, 1961) and *Son of Flubber* (Robert Stevenson, 1963), who wishes to build a World Trade Center-like plaza, 130 storeys high, on the block of an old firehouse. Grandma Steinmetz (Helen Hayes) and Nicole Harris (Stephanie Powers), an air hostess, who live there, fight back, with the help of Herbie. The tone veers from Ealing Comedy – an old lady oblivious to the danger she is in – to out-and-out fantasy as Herbie drives up the wires supporting the Golden Gate Bridge. Herbie is not the only machine with some kind of soul – Steinmetz has an old San Francisco trolley car and an organ, and a series of other Volkswagens join Herbie in the final battle. The third movie in the series, *Herbie Goes to Monte Carlo* (Vincent McEveety, 1977), brings back Jim Douglas (Dean Jones) from *The Love Bug*, who is trying to win the Trans-France Race, unaware that a stolen diamond has been hidden in Herbie's gas tank. Douglas falls in love with a rival driver, Diane Darcy (Julie Sommars), Douglas's mechanic, Wheely Applegate (Don Knotts), falls in love with a model (Katia Tchenko) and Herbie falls in love with Darcy's Lancia. Leaving aside the nature of any relationship between two cars, there is a sense of a shift in family values as Douglas has abandoned his wife from *The Love Bug*, and Darcy is a strong character, the sole female driver in the race, largely treated with suspicion by the other drivers.

*The Island at the Top of the World* is rather different, a Vernian thriller about an Arctic expedition, safely set in 1907 even though Ian Cameron's source novel *The Lost Ones* (1961) was contemporary. Donald Ross (David Gwillim) has vanished on an expedition to find a legendary spot where whales go to die, so his father, Sir Anthony Ross (Donald Sinden), recruits American archaeologist Professor Ivarsson (David Hartman) to help him sail north in a dirigible. Ross is a Victorian patriarch, throwing his weight around and sometimes undermining his own position; however, his son immediately becomes a dutiful son, albeit with new girlfriend Freya (Agneta Eckemyr) who comes from Astragard, a fertile enclave in the middle of the polar ice. The inhabitants are afraid that outsiders, such as Ross, would exploit the idyll. The film has an unsympathetic lead, unconvincing matte shots which stand in for the various landscapes and uses French and Norse dialogue. Ivarsson seems only on board for his translating abilities, and perhaps to be a token American. There are no children in the film, but there is a poodle (underused) and Oomiak (Mako), a kidnapped Eskimo, offering comic relief.

*Escape to Witch Mountain* (John Hough, 1975) and *Return from Witch Mountain* (John Hough, 1978) are both sf, made by a director whose background in horror, including Hammer, is evident in his set design. While two alien children, Tia (Kim Richards) and Tony (Ike Eisenmann), are first depicted arriving at a present-day orphanage, their antagonists, the millionaire Aristotle Bolt (Ray Milland) and Lucas Deranian (Donald Pleasance), operate out of a mansion's crypt. Both Milland and Pleasance were best known for playing crazed or villainous characters, and Hammer stalwart Christopher Lee is the sequel's villain, Victor Gannon. In *Escape*, the children try to keep their powers secret, but are pursued by Deranian on behalf of Bolt. The police are no help; in a move that feels odd for Disney, they even seem to be bribable. The children seek aid from a grumpy widower, Jason O'Day (Eddie Albert), who warms to them and enables them trace their alien ancestry back to Witch Mountain. The children, a few years older, return to Earth near Los Angeles, for a brief holiday, but Tony's powers bring him to Dr Gannon's attention. While Tony is used in a gold heist and then in plutonium terrorism, Tia falls in with a teenaged gang, albeit a well behaved one whose only crime is bunking off school. At the end of the film, the children agree to go back to school so they can be as smart as Tony, although it is Tia they have been spending their time with. Whereas Tia is established as more powerful in *Escape* (and she defeats the brain-controlled Tony), she seems to have been taught to defer to the male.

*Unidentified Flying Oddball* (aka *The Spaceman and King Arthur*, Russ Mayberry, 1979) is a loose adaptation of Mark Twain's *A Connecticut Yankee in King Arthur's Court* (1889), which does not take itself too seriously: the unconvincing model shot of a shuttle in a launch rocket at the film's start is indeed meant to be of a model. Sadly, the later shots of the 'real' shuttle are hardly more convincing. Robotics engineer Tom Trimble (Dennis Dugan) is accidentally launched into space and travels back in time to Arthur's Camelot. Here an elderly Arthur (Kenneth More) faces the twin threats from Merlin (Ron Moody) and Sir Mordred (Jim Dale, his third Disney villain), with only ineffectual knights for help. Trimble is treated with suspicion, especially as he spots Mordred's corruption, and he has to be burnt at the stake, fight a duel and – care of his robot, his exact double – take part in a joust. Each time it is the superior technology that saves him. The various pratfalls and a goose are there to entertain the children, while jokes about Excalibur, Winston Churchill's speeches and a copy of a pornographic magazine (surely a first for Disney) work on a more adult level. As with *The Island at the Top of the World*, the impetus is to get home again, preferably with a female partner.

Disney's next live action film, *The Black Hole* (Gary Nelson, 1979), was one of various studio attempts to cash in on the success of the *Star Wars* saga. This was a PG certificate rather than a General or Universal one; while human characters had been killed before in Disney films, it was rare for

SAVING THE FAMILY? CHILDREN'S FICTION        175

them to die so nastily: Dr Alex Durant (Antony Perkins) is drilled into by Maximilian the robot. Perkins would have been familiar to the adult audience from *Psycho* (Alfred Hitchcock, 1960). Later Maximilian is attacked by the robot V.I.N.CENT (voiced by Roddy McDowell), the comic relief equivalent to R2D2. The spaceship and space settings make most of the shots gloomy in feel and lighting, while the blue and purple of the black hole – or its effects – is often visible in the background through windows. Dr Hans Reinhardt's ship, the USS *Cygnus*, had been in search of new planets to settle, but now, having disobeyed a direct order, hovers dangerously close to the titular black hole. The crew of the *Palomino*, a similar mission, board and find Reinhardt along with a robot – actually cyborg – crew, about to enter the event horizon. While the characters do survive, it is narratively necessary for the ship to fall into the black hole, in a sequence that recalls the stargate from *2001: A Space Odyssey*. Having been told early on by Lt Pfizer (Joseph Bottoms) that '[e]very time I see one of those things I expect to spot some guy dressed in red with horns and a pitchfork', a later visual – Reinhardt apparently wearing Maximilian like a suit of armour – invokes a demon hell. The film ends ambiguously, as the ship and surviving crew emerge from the other side, but it is not clear where or when, or how they will get home. H. Bruce Franklin, discussing the film briefly alongside *Star Trek: The Motion Picture* (Robert Wise, 1979) and *Star Trek II: The Wrath of Khan* (Nicholas Meyer, 1982), suggests that the films' utopianism about the marvellous is maintained by their distancing from Earth: 'The dazzling adventures of the spacers seem to have no relevance whatsoever to the economic and social life of the rest of our species' (1983: 71). Christine Cornea, rather more sensitive to the fact that, aside from Dr Kate McCrea (Yvette Mimieux), the film features only male and masculine characters, suggests that the film depicts 'an engulfing feminine threat in space' (Cornea 2007: 96), an attempt to undercut the power of female agency within both the film and the world in a manner similar to *Star Trek: The Motion Picture*. Searles argues, 'It's too bad that the first Disney attempt at hardcore science fiction should be this stale, flat, weary, and (judging from reports of box office business) unprofitable' (1980: 76). Aside from *Tron* (Steven Liseberger, 1982), Disney was not to venture into high budget live action sf again for a number of years.

To turn now to written sf aimed at a pre-teen audience, Dahl produced *Charlie and the Great Glass Elevator* (1972), a follow-up to *Charlie and the Chocolate Factory* (1964), the story of the impoverished Charlie Bucket's visit to and inheritance of the titular factory owned by Willy Wonka. In the sequel, Charlie, the Bucket family and Wonka are to return to the factory in the great glass elevator to effect the handover, but unfortunately they end up in space, drifting towards a new hotel (surely inspired by *2001: A Space Odyssey*), which is infected by the alien Vermicious Knids. The second half of the novel, before the characters visit the US president, involves the attempted rejuvenation of three of Charlie's grandparents – indicating both that adults are as prone to greed as children and that Wonka, that oddly childless patriarch, has to be obeyed without question. Charlie presumably has to mould himself into a version of Wonka in order to run the factory, and any notion of Wonka's own irresponsibility is pushed to one side while still being apparent.

Norton's output is associated with a non-adult audience, or at least crosses over between child and adult readers; in the 1970s she published at least forty novels, including collaborations, plus short story collections. Virginia L. Wolf notes a shift in her writing in the late 1960s, with the introduction of female central characters, and argues: 'Her novels since 1970 may be seen as her search for imaginative solutions to her fear that patriarchal culture, relying on technology, will destroy life' (1985: 67). Cities, in particular, are places to be viewed with suspicion as patriarchal spaces, in contrast to 'the green world of a feminist alternative' (1985: 66). Ziantha goes into the old cities in *Forerunner Foray* (1973), travelling into the past via a series of reincarnations, often against her will. Ziantha's means of transportation is a stone amulet, a recurring object in Norton's plots, as she sceptically explores the suggestion of archaeologist and para-psychologist T.C. Lethbridge that some objects contain memories of the past. *Star Ka'at* (1978), co-written with Dorothy Madlee, is the first of a series of four books for younger readers, featuring cat-like aliens. Jim Evans and Elly Mae Brown, both orphans, inadvertently learn of the alien overlords' plans for Earth, and face death or exile. Norton and Madlee offer a grim vision of the present day, a polluted world on the edge of war, and exile seems like a tempting option from a humanity described as 'the most cruel and least logical species we [Ka'ats] have ever encountered' (1978: 16). This dark theme appears in a novel aimed at the early teenager.

Young Adult fiction, aimed at late teenagers, had emerged in the US in the late 1960s. Typified by writers such as Judy Blume and S.E. Hinton, it foregrounds abortion, bullying, contraception, divorce, drugs and sexuality. Characters could die and endings need not be happy. This characterised some sf aimed at teenagers produced during the period, and as ever the crossover between adult and child readers would mean that young readers were exposed to the more challenging materials ostensibly aimed at an adult audience. Le Guin argues that in the better volumes, 'one finds a breadth, a seriousness, and a mastery of form equal to that of any living novelist' (1974c: 110). It is hard to dismiss some of the work as escapist, given its harrowing nature.

*Red Shift* (1973) was Garner's first novel in six years, and – leaving aside *The Stone Book Quartet* (1979), which collected four stories – his last until *Strandloper* (1996). Charles Butler notes *Red Shift*'s 'massacres, mutilation, hallucinogens, and gang-rapes' (2006: 259) as being challenging rather than a comforting retreat from the adult world. Garner's narrative depicts the same location, part of Cheshire, in the present day, during the Civil War and during the Roman occupation, with three versions of the teenaged Tom/Thomas/Macey and the same stone axe head. The time shifting of the character is not really explained, being a psychic transfer created by trauma and unhappiness, for example of Tom being able to find a place to be with his girlfriend Jan; Thomas has epileptic fits and Macey has berserker rages, during which they are aware of other times. The novel is part of Garner's long psychogeographising of Cheshire, begun with his first novel *The Weirdstone of Brisingamen* (1960). Like many of his earlier works, *Red Shift* draws on myths and ballads, especially the story of Tam Lin, rescued from the Queen of the Fairies by his true love. Butler argues that here Garner uses his source as a 'way of writing fiction that would still function effectively as a transmitter of mythic energy' (2006: 203) without the reader needing to know the exact details of, or even the existence of, that earlier myth. Le Guin applauds it as '[a] bitter, complex, brilliant book' (1974c: 111).

Le Guin's own *A Wizard of Earthsea* (1968), *The Tombs of Atuan* (1971) and *The Farthest Shore* (1972) feature the education of young wizards, and explore the Jungian concepts that she also examines in her adult fiction. While gender roles and feminism interest her, male characters dominate the Earthsea trilogy. Tenar, a girl who becomes a priestess in servitude to the Nameless Ones, does feature in the second volume, but her narrative is less important than that of Ged/Sparrowhawk. In the third volume, Ged is to repair a crack between worlds, similar to the one which he had opened up in the first book, and must give up his powers for the greater good, as did Prospero, the Wizard of Oz and, indeed, Frodo before him. Francis J. Molson sees the trilogy as an excellent example of heroic-ethical fantasy, 'which does not insist but suggests, does not furnish solutions but guides' (1989: 72). Le Guin's characters, as they come of age, face and overcome problems, but it is the nature of the problem-solving rather than the nature of the solutions that is significant. For Molson, there is no one right answer that will solve everything, and mislead the reader.

O'Brien had been a journalist for *National Geographic* before turning to children's fiction in the 1960s. His second novel, *Mrs Frisby and the Secret of NIMH* (1971), is an anthropomorphic tale centred on the threat to the home of Mrs Frisby and her family. While demonstrating her own bravery in the course of the novel – saving a magpie, talking to an owl and drugging the cat – she is saved by a group of super-intelligent rats who had known her late husband. There is an odd ambivalence at the heart of the novel – the imprisonment of the animals in the mysterious NIMH institute (the National Institute of Mental Health) is clearly wrong, and something the rats wish to escape from, but it also seems to have increased their intelligence in a way that is not presented as negative. O'Brien's posthumously published *Z for Zachariah* (1975) is darker in tone, featuring a post-nuclear scenario, where nerve gas has also been used against the American people. Many people have died in their sleep, unaware of what was happening to them. The exact nature of the catastrophe is not clear, nor whether it was an offensive started by the Soviets or by the Americans, or some dreadful accident; in any case, the result is the same. Ann Burden's family has survived, by the freak of the geography of their farm's valley. Her father and brother have gone in search of other people, so Ann is left alone with her dog, Faro, to work on the land and live off whatever cans she can scavenge from the local shop. Into this solitude comes Loomis, a polymer physicist who accidentally poisons himself in the radioactive stream, whom Ann nurses back to health. Loomis plans for humanity to continue, with the consequence that he comes close to raping Ann. The title refers to a biblical sampler that Ann had seen, which began with 'A is for Adam', and just as Adam was the first man, so Zachariah is the last, identifiable with Loomis. Loomis is a name dominated by 'Loom', which might suggest weaving, but also overshadowing. Ann's names also seem meaningful: 'Ann' suggests grace and favour – and is perhaps also a nod to Anne Frank, another diarist in extreme circumstances – whereas 'burden' suggests the suffering and responsibility she undertakes. Even when she has feared for her safety, she continues to leave food for Loomis.

The nuclear threat was a continuing factor of the ongoing Cold War, an issue that would worry teenagers who foresaw not surviving to adulthood, and thus one that could be taken up in Young Adult fiction. Hoover depicts a post-apocalyptic world in *Children of Morrow* (1973). Tia and Rabbit are bullied orphans in an oppressive society based in a nuclear shelter. Not only does this depict the feared catastrophe, but also it offers a way to show two helpless characters striving to achieve agency. Telepathy appears to be one of the favoured mutations caused by radiation, as in John Wyndham's *The Chrysalids* (1955), and Tia and Rabbit are able to contact another group, at Morrow, by mind. On one level it represents a wish fulfilment of contacting people otherwise out of reach, but perhaps it feels right for thought to cut through boundaries as radiation passes through everything but lead – an invisible, unstoppable force. The children are part of a genetic experiment by the Morrowans, so it is not entirely clear that they are altruistic in their contact, and the novel is more ambivalent about salvation than it could have been. In the sequel, *Treasures of Morrow* (1976), it transpires that the children are descended from a Morrowan scientist, and Tia is given (and rejects) the chance to redeem the society she has left behind; Tia and Rabbit fit into their new society no more than their old one.

Another oppressive shelter built to survive the apocalypse is the location in *This Time of Darkness* (1980) for Amy and Axel's attempted escape, although Axel has actually broken into the shelter, and wants to return to rural paradise. The novel ends as they arrive at the new society, and Amy realises how much of her childhood has been based on lies. Having protagonists of both sexes aids identification, and *The Delikon* (1977) adds a third, alien, child, three hundred years old. The conquering Delikon have brought peace to humanity by breeding for conformity and working towards eliminating ethnic difference, but this has led to cultural sterility.

Hoover's *The Rains of Eridan* (1977), *The Lost Star* (1979) and *Return to Earth* (1980) all feature young female protagonists separated from their families and seeking for agency – in the former Karen survives their murder by mysteriously lunatic humans, in the second the neglected Lian Webster crashes her ship, and in the last Samara Lloyd has to engage in political intrigue as her mother is assassinated and she becomes the target of enemy action. In *Rains* and *Lost*, the child characters become friends with female scientists, and make new discoveries about the worlds they find themselves in, before being adopted. Karen is able to help her colony deduce the link between an apparently desiccated species, hundreds of highly desired crystals and the hysteria that is spreading through the community. Thea, a biologist, becomes her mentor, and in turn is recuperated into a community from her solitary ways. Lian has an empathic, even telepathic, ability, linking her to an indigenous species; she is wary of revealing this, lest she be exploited or forced to exploit others. Lian's shift from astrophysics to archaeology marks a move from hard to soft science. Both demonstrate a link between space and time – the stratifications of history uncovered by archaeology and the historical distance covered by light in astronomy.

While all of Hoover's characters undertake spatial shifts, it is the time shifts of her developing protagonists that seem to interest her more, with recurring spirals, especially in the shells of snails in *Children* and various sets of imagery in *The Delikon*. Retiring governor Galen Innes wishes to study snails in *Return to Earth*, and his narrative threatens to overwhelm that of his protégée, Samara. Both Innes and Samara return to Earth, although it is not the same Earth as the one they have left behind; their journeys are spiral rather than circular. Hoover's colony futures show the problems of economic imperialism – Eridan is not economically viable, nor is Earth for the Delikon, who 'wonder if Earth is worth keeping; as a colony it is a financial liability, and humans show no sign of maturing into complex, evolved social beings' (Antczak 1985: 74), and Samara defeats her enemies with finances as much as force.

Mark, who trained as a sculptor, wrote *Thunder and Lightnings* (1976) and *Under the Autumn Garden* (1977), about 'misfit children trying to find themselves and their place in the real world of here and now' (Cleaver 1979: 92), before she made 'unusually dour and serious, but highly inventive excursions into science-fiction' (Hunt 2001: 93). *The Ennead* (1978) and *Divide and Rule* (1979) place misfits in futuristic settings, although the latter could be fantasy. In *The Ennead*, the orphan Isaac is a servant on a planet where church attendance is enforced, every service costs and the unemployed are deported. Isaac's life changes with the arrival of Eleanor, a sculptor who risks deportation every day and who falls in love with Moshe, an immigrant. Despite his own growing desire for Eleanor, Isaac saves them both, and goes into exile with her. Names such as Isaac and Moshe, who wears a yarmulke, and references to a golem and the First Book of Kings suggest an underlying Jewishness, which contrasts with the rather puritanical quasi-Protestantism of Isaac's adopted and rejected society. *Divide and Rule* also features a religious society, as Hanno, an atheist eighteen-year-old, is chosen as the Shepherd, a central but passive figure in a monastery's ritual. As the Shepherd is a reluctant figure, Hanno cannot refuse and he is trapped in rituals that seem to be rewritten on a daily basis. Memories must shift to accommodate such changes. In order to survive, Hanno must escape – in neither of these two novels does Mark suture her outsider protagonist back into the social fabric.

In written fiction, the invisible enemies of patriarchy, conformity and law could be shown to defeat the hero and strip him or her of agency; in film, on the other hand, there was a resurgence of the law of the father as something to be embraced, with individuals willingly subsuming themselves to the law of the father and working to uphold society. While Disney's version of this story had failed as they attempted to be more radical than they had in the past, *Star Wars: Episode IV – A New Hope* (George Lucas, 1977) was an unstoppable hit. Thomas Schatz rather cuttingly argues that '[from] *The Godfather* to *Jaws* to *Star Wars*, we see films that are increasingly plot-driven, increasingly visceral, kinetic, and fast-paced, increasingly reliant on special effects, increasingly "fantastic" (and thus apolitical), and increasingly targeted at younger audiences' (2003: 29). After a decade in which authors stretched children, blockbusters wrote down to everybody.

# 13
# Eating the Audience: Blockbusters

Thomas Schatz's assertion that the blockbuster film was apolitical is misleading. At best, such films appealed to a range of audiences of varying opinions and offered various readings; at worst, they upheld the dominant ideology's status quo. *Star Wars* (George Lucas, 1977) performed a political role of recuperating the American Dream in the aftermath of Vietnam and the realignment of the Cold War from one proxy campaign to another. Later, Ronald Reagan's Strategic Defense Initiative was to be nicknamed Star Wars, and Vietnam veteran Colonel Oliver North called himself a Jedi knight during the Iran-Contra affair that broke in 1986. The blockbuster films had their political uses. They also often centred upon broken or dispersed families, with the narrative pointing towards the creation or recreation of a social unit, and they especially explored father–son relations. With the exception of *Star Wars: Episode V – The Empire Strikes Back* (Irvin Kershner, 1980), which ends with a cliffhanger, the endings were upbeat and reassuring, rather than amphicatastrophic. This chapter will consider the films *THX 1138* (1971) and the Star Wars trilogy, the first two Superman films and *Flash Gordon* (Mike Hodges, 1980).

The blockbuster movie had emerged in the 1950s and 1960s, as part of Hollywood's fightback against the haemorrhaging of audiences to television, but took a new form in the mid-1970s as producers targeted youth and family audiences. The blockbuster 'will excite you, expose you to something never before experienced, [...] prick up your ears and make your eyes bulge out in awe' (Stringer 2003: 5). Awe and the sublime are central to the experience of blockbuster cinema, as the audience is taken on a rollercoaster ride of action-adventure, punctuated with stunts and special effects. The discourse around the films is as much of processed shots and new production technology as it is of actors and gossip – the use of blue and green screens, matte work, rotoscope, computer-controlled camera movements and beyond became part of the publicity materials. The special effect, paradoxically, is not just there to represent the unfilmable, but to announce its own status as effect, to undermine its invisibility.

While 1970s films had depicted humanity facing irresistible forces, the blockbuster was an unstoppable force in itself. Steven Paul Miller rightly suggests that '[the] concept of the blockbuster film is to "eat" its audience before they know what is happening [...] The film is marketed as a critic-proof must-see phenomenon designed to make maximum profits during the first weekend that it opens, creating unstoppable momentum' (1999: 93). The opening weekend revenue – either during the summer when news is slow or at a holiday period – becomes news in itself, as people have to see what all the fuss is, before the nay-saying of critics can deflate the balloon. The key film was *Jaws* (Steven Spielberg, 1975), an adaptation of the best-selling Peter Benchley novel – which pre-sold the story of an apparently unstoppable shark – and the cultural capital of Spielberg and Richard Dreyfuss (from both *Jaws* and *American Graffiti* (George Lucas, 1973)) could then help to pre-sell *Close Encounters of the Third Kind* (Steven Spielberg, 1977). This premiered on 15 November 1977, just over a week before Thanksgiving; I shall postpone discussion of this film in more detail to the next chapter.

Although the blockbuster movie was to gain a wider platform, the 1970s examples were largely associated with members of the so-called New Hollywood and their protégés – Lucas and Spielberg, and to an extent Francis Ford Coppola. Lucas had directed *Electronic Labyrinth THX 1138 4EB* (1967) as a student at University of Southern California, and had won various prizes for it. He got the opportunity to observe the making of *Finian's Rainbow* (Francis Ford Coppola, 1968), acted as associate producer on *The Rain People* (Francis Ford Coppola, 1969) and, as a result, when Coppola persuaded Warner Bros. to finance an independent studio, American Zoetrope, Lucas was funded to film the feature-length *THX 1138*. In its dystopian future, everyone is identifiable only by letters and numbers and is discouraged from sexual desire but persuaded to become diligent consumers by means of drugs. The central character, THX (Robert Duval), has been fed placebos by his apartment partner, LUH (Maggie McOmie), and the two finally have sex. She becomes pregnant and he makes mistakes at his job, so both are arrested. THX is imprisoned with SEN (Donald Pleasance), who had wanted to live with THX, in a white limbo. The two try to escape, with the aid of a hologram actor, SRT (Don Pedro Colley), but SEN surrenders, unable to deal with the chaos of the city. Finally THX ascends to the surface of the Earth. On the one hand, this could be read as a positive, upbeat ending, of how a man who was little more than a cog in an immense consuming machine was able to find agency – and Lucas clearly saw the film as partially autobiographical in terms of the individual trapped in a bureaucratic world. The single bird flying across the sunset is suggestive of the return of nature in a human-dominated world. But the sun *is* setting, which is a signal of things ending, as much as a new beginning – it anticipates the setting suns as Luke Skywalker prepares to leave Tatooine in *Star Wars*. THX had been asocial when part of the city's inhabitants, now he is on his own in what looks like an endless desert.

Warner Bros hated the film, and cut five minutes from the original release. Despite this, it was still a flop. John Brosnan suggests that 'it pretends to be profound' (1978: 212), which is perhaps a little unfair, but the only solution it offers to dystopia is a personal one. Warner Bros were not interested in either of Lucas's next two projects – an autobiographical account of teen life in 1962 Modesto, California and a science-fiction action adventure, which, as he researched and marketed it over a number of years, was increasingly aimed at a family and child audience. He drew upon *Metropolis* (Fritz Lang, 1927), 1930s and 1940s chapter serials, westerns, World War II films, *The Wizard of Oz* (Victor Fleming, 1939), *Kakushi-Toride No San-Akunin* (*The Hidden Fortress*, Akira Kurosawa, 1958), *The Lord of the Rings* (1954–55), mythology, the mythographer Joseph Campbell and much more. Baird Searles calls it 'E. E. Smith given a contemporary sensibility. There is a totalitarian Galactic Empire; there are rebel planets, aliens, robots, battles in space, a superpowerful elite, laser swords, wizards, and just about everything you always wanted to see on screen but knew nobody would put there' (1976: 61). Todd H. Sammons observes: 'Lucas fabricates his movies out of graffiti, out of bits and pieces of this and that, found in various places and given unity by his own artistic vision' (1987: 365). This bricolage method caused problems with the nostalgic *American Graffiti*, where he lost final cut to Universal, the studio that had financed it, but the huge return on a low budget allowed him to negotiate more control with Twentieth Century Fox for what was being conceived as the fourth film of a sequence of nine or more.

*Star Wars* became a phenomenon, having initially been something of a sleeper, Searles declaring that it 'may be the biggest single thing to ever happen to the field of science fiction' (1977b: 98). He was pleased to see what he perceived to be real sf on the big screen, and declares: 'George Lucas has here constructed a universe that seems not only to satisfy the science fiction reader, but the public at large, who, I would guess, are as sick of meaningful little movies as I am, and want something that is big, splashy, innocent, "mindless," and fun' (1977a: 63). Moorcock later wrote: 'When I saw the first Star Wars movie I was disappointed. I had expected something as good as [the fiction of Leigh] Brackett. What I got was a dilute of Brackett and the Brackett style. Han Solo's origins lie, it seems to me, in those tough, semi-piratical spacers who took the interplanetary work nobody else would do. I suspect they all looked a bit like Bogart in Leigh's mind!' (2004: 247-8). Searles was wary that *Star Wars*'s proving that big money could be made from sf might destroy what was unique about the genre. Matt Hills notes how critics locate *Star Wars* as 'marking the end of one "system" or type of film, and ushering in a new episode in film history' (2003: 185), which might include the centrality of special effects (increasingly aided by computers), the production of a simultaneously cult and mass audience, an acknowledgement of the potential of merchandising and an infantilisation of mainstream Hollywood, with films supposedly appealing to the lowest common denominator. Peter Krämer argues that the film 'invites adult spectators to regress to an earlier phase in their social and psychic development and to indulge in infantile fantasies of omnipotence and oedipal strife as well as nostalgically returning to [the 1950s]' (2004: 358). The definition here risks becoming circular – the film is just entertainment because it is aimed at children and it is suitable for children because it is just entertainment. But while Lucas might not have set out to communicate a political ideology – as if his attempt to control his means of production were not political – it is in the nature of ideology to disguise itself, to be invisible, and Lucas could not operate outside politics.

The polysemy of the trilogy is a result of his trying to appeal to as wide an audience as possible and his attempt to tell an 'innocent' story in an era when this was no longer so easy to do. The Empire is evil more or less *because* it is evil, and by default the rebel alliance – despite the unexplained appearance of a member of royalty in the shape of Princess Leia – is good. Leia (Carrie Fisher) is one of very few speaking roles for a woman in the film, but, in an acknowledgement of the existence of feminism, she is unimpressed by the attempts of Luke Skywalker (Mark Hamill) to rescue her and can hold her own against powerful enemies. However, she is the subject of rivalry between Luke and freelance smuggler Han Solo (Harrison Ford) and by *Star Wars: Episode VI – Return of the Jedi* (Richard Marquand, 1983) she is seen in a skimpy costume reminiscent of pulp magazine covers. Until the appearance of Lando Calrissian (Billy Dee Williams) in *Empire*, non-white ethnicities are displaced onto alien species.

Such straightforward morality marks a break with the anti-heroes of many 1970s films, and the way the film veers between genres might be an attempt by Lucas to find a milieu in which Skywalker's actions seem at home. The sequences on his home planet of Tatooine are reminiscent of westerns, with the slaughter of his adoptive parents drawing on sequences from *The Searchers* (John Ford, 1956). But even the western, with its investigation of the origins of the United States, would often complicate the representation of Caucasian 'civilisation' facing Indian 'savagery'; in *The*

*Searchers*, Ethan (John Wayne) is a nomad without family, abandoning society as soon as he has restored its status quo. The Mos Eisley tavern where Obi-Wan Kenobi (Alec Guinness) and Luke meet Han Solo is an establishment that would rival any saloon, and there is even a brawl. Until they leave the planet in search of Leia, there are hints of *film noir*, with their being followed, and Han Solo, like Sam Spade, has his loyalty and services up for hire. It is only in the final forty minutes or so, in the series of raids which lead to the destruction of the Death Star, that the film seems most at ease – the models here seem to be *The Dam Busters* (Michael Anderson, 1955) and *633 Squadron* (Walter Grauman, 1964), where the moral compass of the Allied powers against the Nazis is clear-cut. The Imperial Stormtroopers evoke the countless characterless German troops that are killed in numerous war movies. The climax of the film, a celebration of the destruction of the Death Star, and the rewarding of Luke and Han for their actions, rather uncomfortably echoes the propagandist *Triumph des Willens* (*Triumph of the Will*, Leni Riefenstahl, 1935), complicating a too-easy association. The upbeat ending, again unusual for the period, would have allowed closure even if it were the only film of the sequence to be produced.

In shaping the apparently simple character of Luke Skywalker, Lucas turned to fairy tales and to the work of Joseph Campbell, especially *The Hero with a Thousand Faces* (1949). This book describes a monomyth underlying many narratives, in which a hero is called to adventure from a mundane life although initially resists the call. The hero faces a series of trials, eventually wins, and returns, transformed, with the power to give a boon to others. This structure can be seen in the original film, with Luke summoned by Obi-Wan to a galactic adventure, his refusal until the murder of his family, his escapes from death and his first uses of the Force, the mystical power that permeates the universe. But it is recapitulated in the trilogy as a whole, with Luke's move from child to teen to adult, and with the hero's journey of Han Solo, who operates as Luke's double.

This doubling is especially visible in the Freudian narrative thread that comes to the fore in *Empire*, but has ramifications in the other two films. As Andrew Gordon observes, Luke is a 'sort of clean-cut, cornfed, adolescent Oedipus' (1980: 314), at odds with Uncle Owen, his substitute father, indeed resisting each patriarch, be it Obi-Wan or Yoda. As the New Hope for the rebel alliance, he will eventually have to go face to face with the Empire's chief officer, Darth Vader (David Prowse/James Earl Jones), who in the climactic duel in *Empire* announces himself to be Luke's father. By this point, Luke had already lost the father-figures Owen and Obi-Wan – both of whom turn out to be liars – and cannot kill a third, although the

Oedipal impulse may leave him a sense of guilt over actually achieving, via someone else's agency, what he would have secretly desired. In an age-old symbol for castration, Vader cuts off Luke's right hand and the phallic light-sabre. Meanwhile, in rivalry to Han, he has been falling in love with Leia, a desire that turns out to be incestuous, as in *Return* she is revealed to be his twin sister, somehow hidden more effectively from the Empire despite having been face to face with Vader. Luke may have the forbidden desires, but the narrative punishes Han: when he is captured he is frozen for shipment to Jabba the Hutt and even when he is defrosted, he remains temporarily blind, both metaphorical castrations.

Irvin Kershner, brought in by Lucas to take over directing duties on *Empire*, turned to Bruno Bettelheim's *The Uses of Enchantment* (1976) for an analysis of fairy tales. The child could displace his various anxieties about lack of power, fear of castration and worries around abandonment onto identificatory figures in the stories, who faced and dealt with witches, ogres, wolves and other monsters on the child's behalf. By consuming such stories, the child becomes better able to face real-world anxieties, and to deal with them. The downside of this, perhaps, is that it leaves *Empire* as appearing less than reassuring or consoling, indeed, Gordon argues, 'it brings those anxieties nearer to the surface' (1980: 317); the protagonists 'accomplish only minor victories and suffer major defeats, reversing the pattern of the previous film' (1980: 313). If young viewers might draw on the film to help them deal with anxieties, adult audiences may have the opposite sense of an uncanny revival of atavistic fears.

Three elements of fear and upset are repeated through the series – being eaten, being turned upside down and falling from a great height. The first is a staple of fairy tales – Red Riding Hood's wolf, the witch of the gingerbread house, Jack's giant and so forth – and is experienced when the Millennium Falcon flies into the belly of a beast, Luke has to walk a plank to be eaten by the Sarlac or even when Han slices open the stomach of an animal to provide shelter for the hypothermic Luke, not to mention all the monsters that attack them. For Bettelheim, eating is symbolic of sexual seduction – and much sexual desire thus permeates the trilogy. The turning upside down, as when Luke learns to use the Force or a number of characters are held prisoner, is perhaps part of the wider symbolism associated with the mythic undertones of the hero, notably the notion of the hero so committed to his quest that he is willing to die and be reborn for the cause – like Luke and Obi-Wan before him. Finally, the fall is a literal one – as Luke, Vader and the Emperor jump, fall or are thrown from a great height. In the case of Vader, formerly Anakin Skywalker and father to Luke and Leia, the fall is also a moral one, as he had betrayed the Jedi cause with his turn to the dark side. Robert G. Pielke describes it as 'an event reminiscent of the myth of Satan's defection from the Hebrew god' (1983: 146) and Gordon sees him as a fallen angel – we are in the realm of Blake's version of John Milton's Lucifer-as-Messiah in *Paradise Lost* (1667), and anticipate Roy Batty of *Blade Runner* (Ridley Scott, 1982). As Susan Sontag argues, 'It is obviously too easy to say that America is just a freak show, a wasteland [...] But the American partiality to myths of redemption and damnation remains one of the most energizing, most seductive aspects of our national character' (1977: 48).

It is up to *Return of the Jedi* to redeem the redeemable characters and to punish the damned, both to reassure its audience and to tie off the narrative threads. The first part of the narrative depicts the infiltration of Jabba the Hutt's headquarters to rescue Han, although this seems perilously close to walking into a trap. Luke has to be traumatised by the death of another mentor, Yoda, and any despair is allayed by the knowledge gained from Obi-Wan that Leia is his sister. His confrontation with his father, anticipated by both Obi-Wan and the Emperor, seems to take on significance over and above its nature as another duel – killing the father must be breaking a universal taboo. In the end, the stakes are turned upside down and it is not that Luke gives in to hate, but rather that Vader gives into love and can be redeemed. Such forgiveness and grace as is experienced at this point – with the subsequent reunion of Anakin, Obi-Wan and Yoda as all good friends on some different plane – is morality at its simplest. Without Vader and the Emperor, the Empire seems to dissipate – perhaps Vader suffocated too many generals for there to be a line of succession. Lucas has yet to film the anticipated trilogy that was to deal with the rebuilding of society, post-empire, but placed in the context of the trilogy depicting the hero's journey of Anakin Skywalker, the six existing films become a narrative about his necessary fall and redemption. In the subtitle that episode four rapidly acquired, in Leia's appeal to Obi-Wan and mention of R2D2 to an alliance general, Obi-Wan's comment to Yoda and later to Luke, and finally Luke to Leia, the key word seems to be 'hope' – new, last, final, only – as the trilogy clings to optimism at the end of a decade that had much to be pessimistic about.

*Superman: The Movie* (Richard Donner, 1978) offers another hero with messianic qualities who was adopted by farmers that conceal his secret abilities. After the death of his adoptive father (Glenn Ford), and having found a fragment from the ship that brought him to Earth, teenaged Clark Kent (Christopher Reeve) heads north and builds his crystalline fortress of solitude, where an avatar of his biological father, Jor-El (Marlon Brando), educates him as to his abilities and his role. Kent goes to Metropolis, with the boon of superpowers, and defends America from the crazed plans of Lex Luthor (Gene Hackman). This sequence set on Krypton and Kent's early life rather breaks the back of the film, in what has become the norm for superhero adaptations, in that the central narrative of saving the world from danger cannot be reached until we have been educated in the origin myth of the protagonist. Superman, created by Jerry Siegel and Joe Shuster in 1932, first appeared in *Action Comics* 1 (June 1938), in the context of Flash Gordon and Buck Rogers being featured in comic strips in newspapers and chapter serials at the cinema. *Superman* also appeared as a daily newspaper serial, a radio serial (1940–51) with Bud Collyer as Superman, seventeen animated shorts (1941–44) from Fleischer Studios featuring Collyer's voice, and two chapter serials, *Superman* (1948) and *Atom Man vs. Superman* (1950), with Kirk Alyn. George Reeves took the title role for *Superman and the Mole Men* (1951), which acted as a pilot for the television series *The Adventures of Superman* (1952–58). There were two more batches of animations, *The New Adventures of Superman* (1966) and other series by Filmation and *Super Friends* (1973–85) from Hanna-Barbera with Danny Dark as Superman. *Superman: The Movie* was conceived as a two-parter, with Richard Donner filming both episodes back-to-back as he had with *The Three Musketeers* (1973) and *The Four Musketeers* (1974), until disputes with Warner Bros led to his removal from the project and Richard Lester reshot most of his footage on *Superman II* (1980). Mario Puzo – author of *The Godfather* (1969) – wrote a draft of the scripts, which were then rewritten by David and Leslie Newman and Robert Benton (who had collaborated on a Superman musical, *It's a Bird... It's a Plane... It's Superman* (1966)) and had additional work by script doctor Tom Mankiewicz, who had scripted a number of James Bond movies.

Superman had his origins in the Depression era, but, as Carl Boehm has argued, the character 'answered the call for a savior from a nation facing war with Europe, distrust of public officials, and a post depression economy' (2000: 236). Like Sherlock Holmes (in the Basil Rathbone films), the hero was to fight Nazis, first spies and then various dictators, and the Jewish origins of his creators may have been a factor in this. Superman is transformed from an immigrant to a selfless fighter for the American way. In the mid-1970s, as producer Ilya Salkind developed the project, America was in Vietnam, the Watergate scandal broke and there was a new economic crisis. The time was clearly ripe for a new big-screen outing for the character, as American felt itself in need of heroes, making use of the latest effects technology. Christopher Reeve's lightly comic touch as the titular figure mean that there is a sense that lines such as 'I'm here to fight for truth, and justice, and the American way' can be read with a degree of irony, especially as Lois Lane (Margot Kidder) responds 'You're gonna end up fighting every elected official in this country'. However, the almost-closing line in response to a jail warden's thanks – 'We're all part of the same team' – seems sincere enough. Peter Nicholls argues, not entirely convincingly, that the films 'take themselves just seriously enough; they are not parody or spoof in any obvious way, but there are tongue-in-cheek moments' (1984: 170). The problem is that various moments of light relief, each fine in their own way, add up to an inability to ever quite take the peril seriously. Lane spends many of her scenes in danger, screaming at the top of her lungs, or in the arms of Superman. In either case, she is no feminist role model.

As with Luke Skywalker, for Clark Kent fathers act as moral compasses. Jor-El manages to save his son and records enough material to educate him in the ways of Earth – Kryptonian technology is much ahead of ours. However, Jor-El cautions him not to interfere in human affairs. Jonathan Kent also warns him not to show off about his powers, but is convinced that Clark is on Earth for a reason. When Lane is killed in the earthquake, in a sequence which eventually finds the right level of gravitas, Superman decides to fly sufficiently fast to travel back through time, and change history – obeying his adoptive father's strictures those of his biological one. In an Oedipal sense it is clear that his awakened desires bring him into conflict with the rule of the father, and the thrusting/penetrating shapes of the Kryptonite crystals and the towers of the fortress of solitude represent a forest of phalluses.

In the sequel, Superman again faces Luthor, and also has to deal with the Kyptonite criminals sentenced and imprisoned at the start of the original film. Thus he has to face both the cunning of a human enemy and the comparable or greater strength of his own people in order to provide sufficient challenge for his augmented powers. The ongoing love affair with Lane needs to develop, but is dependent upon her not making the connection between him and Clark Kent; equally it cannot develop too far, lest his sexual prowess cause her physical damage. In order to be a lover, he has to be human, and abandon his powers – but if he abandons his powers, he cannot defend the American way of life. Having spent a period as mortal, Superman has to return to his role as American guardian, and to put American ideology ahead of any personal gain.

While the Star Wars and Superman films were hits, blockbusters were not guaranteed financial successes. *Flash Gordon* was a flop. Like Superman, it drew on a character that had its origins in weekly Sunday comic strips. Created by Alex Raymond as a rival to *Buck Rogers* and first appearing on 7 January 1934, the strip was adapted for radio as a 26-episode weekly run from 22 April 1935, with Gale Gordon in the title role. A daily serial followed from 28 October 1935. The cinema chapter serial *Flash Gordon* (Frederick Stephani, 1936) – later re-released as the feature film *Rocketship* – was followed by *Flash Gordon's Trip to Mars* (Ford Beebe and Robert F. Hill, 1938) and *Flash Gordon Conquers the Universe* (Ford Beebe and Ray Taylor, 1940), all of which had Buster Crabbe in the leading role. It was made into a 30-episode television series in 1954–55, starring Steve Holland. Twenty years later, Filmation made two 16-pisode seasons of animated adaptations, the first series a serial, the second more stand-alone in nature, in an attempt to compete with *Star Wars*. Federico Fellini held the film rights, with Nicolas Roeg suggested as director. Eventually, under Italian producer Dino De Laurentiius, it was made (at Roeg's recommendation) with British director Mike Hodges at the helm. Hodges, best known for his debut feature *Get Carter* (1971), had directed the Michael Crichton adaptation *The Terminal Man* (1974) and had quit *Damien: Omen II* (Don Taylor, 1977) some three weeks into filming. He felt the first script, by Michael Allin, did not work, and when he agreed to make the film he worked with Lorenzo Semple Jr, best known for the camp *Batman* (1966–68) television series, but who had more recently worked on *The Parallax View* (Alan J. Pakula, 1974) and *King Kong* (John Guillermin, 1976). While Semple could clearly write politically – Hodges has described *Flash Gordon* as a commentary on American foreign policy – the decision was made to make the film as a comedy.

Mark Bould has drawn together the various responses to the film from sf critics – and they were not positive (2002: 42–43). Nicholls rather angrily argues that the makers did 'not take the subject matter seriously [... T]he illusion of reality is central for lovers of fantastic cinema; they do not want to be constantly reminded that they are watching a fiction' (1984: 87). Bould notes that the film is deliberate rather than naïve camp in Susan Sontag's distinction. Naïve camp makes us feel superior, because we are in on the joke and the producers are not – in retrospect, the supposed sincerity of the chapter serials looks camp to us, but for someone to go out and deliberately make a camp text makes us feel like the joke is on us. The comic strips and serials had a sports star as a hero, an Oriental alien villain, flying men, both women and men in what looked like bondage gear and a Germanic rocket scientist who in the real world in the 1940s might have been working for the Nazis. Hodges plays it as camp, seeing this as being faithful to the comic strips, as a comparison to the materials in the opening credits should make clear.

Sam J. Jones was cast as Flash, having previously worked as a *Playgirl* centrefold and on the sex comedy *10* (Blake Edwards, 1979), but an actor dubbed much of his dialogue in post-production. The role of Dr Hans Zarkov went to Topol, best known for playing *Fiddler on the Roof*'s Tevye on Broadway and in film (Norman Jewison, 1971), and Ming the Merciless was played by the Swedish actor Max von Sydow, by then often typecast as a villain. Both actors brought an over-the-top quality to their performances, as did Brian Blessed as Prince Vultan and a pre-Bond Timothy Dalton as Prince Barin. If this were not cult enough, Hodges found roles for Peter Wyngarde (better known as the eponymous *Jason King* (15 September 1971–28 April 1972) on television but by then fallen on hard times), Richard O'Brien, creator of *The Rocky Horror Show* (1973), and playwright John Osborne (who had earlier appeared in *Get Carter*). But while all these elements guarantee the film immortality as a camp classic, it was a step too far for the audiences of the period. Flash's leather shorts and the bondage gear and masks donned by most of the cast would have been fine in European horror films, but not in something competing with Hollywood. The defeat of Ming – by being penetrated by the tip of a ship piloted by Flash, in a scene which echoes the plane crash near the start of the film – too mockingly undercuts the heroism of the blockbuster. The film flopped; the audience resisted being eaten.

The blockbusters of the *Star Wars* trilogy, *Close Encounters of the Third Kind*, *Star Trek: The Motion Picture* (Robert Wise, 1979) and its sequels and the Superman films (followed by sequels in 1983 and 1989) set a trend for effects-driven genre movies aimed at family audiences. This was no guarantee of box office success, as *Flash Gordon* and *The Black Hole* (Gary Nelson, 1979) show. Spielberg had a run of hits, as director with *E.T.* (1982), *Jurassic Park* (1993) and the Lucas-produced *Indiana Jones* films, and as executive producer with *Back to the Future* (Robert Zemeckis, 1985). These films looked back to happier times in the 1930s and 1950s, irrespective of the true values of those decades. Fans of sf felt ambivalent: more sf films were being made than ever before, with each one attempting to outdo the last in terms of spectacle. On the down side, even with computer technology, budgets have continued to soar – indeed budgets become selling points in themselves – and studios need to reach a wider audience in order to recoup costs. The challenging, radical films of the 1970s were to be left behind by Hollywood, and efforts went into selling tickets, novelisations, toys and lunchboxes rather than exploring social attitudes. Sf moved beyond the primary texts of films, television shows and books, into commodities in the home.

# 14
# Chariots of the Gods: Pseudoscience and Parental Fears

Michael Bond's 'A Spoonful of Paddington' (1974) begins with Paddington Bear conducting an experiment to see if he can bend spoons. An episode of the BBC children's programme *Blue Peter* had featured Uri Geller, then famous for dowsing, for starting or stopping timepieces using psychokinetic powers (which he claimed derived from aliens) and for bending spoons by lightly rubbing them with his thumb. Paddington, typically, is a mix of copycat and sceptic, so conducts experiments with various substances to see if these will soften metal to allow it to bend. Scientists and magicians alike were disputing Geller's claims; Paddington copies Geller's feat only to discover that he is using a set of spoons with trick hinges. There was still an appetite for belief in pseudoscience and the paranormal over the rational explanation, and much sf of the 1970s catered for this audience's sense of wonder, from the belief that humanity had been uplifted by aliens to sf that had much in common with supernatural horror and expressed anxiety about paternal, maternal and filial feelings. This can be seen in the pseudo-archaeology books by Erich von Däniken, Robin Collyns and Charles Berlitz, which were disputed by authors such as John Sladek, but fed into the blockbuster *Close Encounters of the Third Kind* (Steven Spielberg, 1977), novels by Richard Cowper and television series such as *The Omega Factor* (13 June–15 August 1979) and *Quatermass* (24 October–14 November 1979), sometimes with a degree of scepticism. In the same period, horror films expressed anxieties about the state of the family within the modern technological world, sometimes expressing a conservative ideology, at other times questioning the nature of scientific progress – for example in the films *Alien* (Ridley Scott, 1979), *The Brood* (David Cronenberg, 1979), *It's Alive* (Larry Cohen, 1974), *It Lives Again* (Larry Cohen, 1978), *Demon Seed* (Donald Cammell, 1977), *Altered States* (Ken Russell, 1980), and Terry Carr's novel, *Cirque* (1978).

The belief in pseudoscience and parapsychology might reflect the ongoing suspicion about science in an age increasingly controlled by unaccountable corporations, with technology reaching into every corner of life. The Conseil des Universités du Québec commissioned the French philosopher Jean-François Lyotard to investigate the impact of technology on knowledge, and he produced *The Postmodern Condition: A Report on Knowledge* (1979). He argued that scientific knowledge was becoming too expensive or complicated to verify by more than a handful of experts. Quantum theory limits the precision of knowledge about sub-atomic particles to probability equations and chaos theory shows how infinitesimal differences in starting conditions alter the outcome, with Benoît B. Mandelbrot's work on fractals being published in 1975 and the first symposium on chaos being held in December 1977. Scientific knowledge had been part of the Enlightenment project of liberation and progress begun three centuries earlier, which could be identified with modernity. This 'grand narrative', or in Lyotard's term 'metanarrative', was now questioned, because its unfolding could be seen as having led to concentration camps, totalitarian regimes and the excesses of industrialisation. The story society told about itself was no longer credible, with some form of break coming between the end of the Second World War and the early 1960s. The failures of the late 1960s counterculture and subsequent economic crises made a coming utopia even less likely, so many people turned away from science, religion and conventional history for answers to their questions about the universe, seeking refuge in parapsychology and parascience. Lyotard's writing about the postmodern condition chimed with the developing use of the term 'postmodernism', which was being applied to architecture and literature, as will be seen in the final two chapters of this book.

*2001: A Space Odyssey* (Stanley Kubrick, 1968) had suggested that an alien intervention had impacted upon human evolution since prehistoric times, but outside the genre Erich von Däniken's *Erinnerungen an die Zukunft: Ungelöste Rätsel der Vergangenheit* (*Chariots of the Gods? Unsolved Mysteries of the Past* (1968)) suggested that Stonehenge, the Easter Island statues, the pyramids of Egypt and Mexico and other marvels of the ancient world had been constructed by aliens. It became an international bestseller and was made into a 1970 film documentary, *Erinnerungen an die Zukunft* (Harald Reini, 1970, cut down for television as *In Search of Ancient Astronauts* (1973)). Von Däniken was not the first to propose such theories – Peter Kolosimo's *Il Pianeta Sconosciuto* (*The Unknown Planet*, 1957) had already suggested it and scientist Carl Sagan had theorised that humanity might already have met aliens. Further volumes by von Däniken developed his thesis, which, in the tradition of Charles Fort's early twentieth-century collections of allegedly unexplained phenomena, drew together a series of vignettes of odd events and objects that together might suggest alien intervention. Some copycat volumes, such as Robin Collyns's *Did Spacemen Colonise the Earth?* (1974), *Laser Beams from Star Cities?* (1975) and *Ancient Astronauts: A Time Reversal?* (1978), copied the question mark from von Däniken's first English title, allowing for scepticism. The Bible and other ancient religious texts were scoured for accounts of close encounters. These books discredited contemporary science and mainstream history, as well as challenging religion's alternative narrative, by positing alien father figures. At the same time, they played down the historical achievement of humanity.

Charles Berlitz also writes about unexplained phenomena, *The Mystery of Atlantis* (1969) and *Mysteries from Forgotten Worlds* (1972) describing fabled lost cities, and *The Bermuda Triangle* (1974) and *Without a Trace* (1977) focusing on an area of the Atlantic notorious for the disappearance of ships and aeroplanes. He ended the decade with an account of a supposed attempt at teleportation and invisibility made by the US Navy in *The Philadelphia Experiment: Project Invisibility* (1979) and an alleged UFO crash, alien autopsy and cover-up conspiracy in *The Roswell Incident* (1980). This was sf masquerading as journalism, selling better than most sf.

Material such as this forms the heart of *Close Encounters of the Third Kind*, which, with *Star Wars* (George Lucas, 1977), did much to cement the public's imagination of sf as effects-filled and child-centred. The title draws upon J. Allen Hynek's classification of interactions with unexplained objects: the first kind was observing unexplained lights or objects in the sky, the second physical evidence, including crop circles, skin burn, amnesia and odd behaviour in animals, and the third was seeing another being, which may or may not be extraterrestrial in origin. While the film opens with the aftermaths of third-kind encounters, the main narrative of the film is a progression through this typology.

Globetrotting scientist Claude Lacombe (played by French New Wave director François Truffaut) investigates the discovery of pristine Second World War era aeroplanes in the Sonoran Desert and a ship being found on dry land. He is convinced these craft are ones that have vanished in the Bermuda Triangle or elsewhere. The musical phrase recalled by many witnesses is a greeting, which they return, and a second message is then received, giving the coordinates the film claims for the monolith Devil's Tower in Wyoming. Lacombe seems to be a relatively benign figure, although his actions have caused a major military action and cover-up that has displaced thousands of people.

Meanwhile, Roy Neary (Richard Dreyfuss) becomes obsessed by UFOs in Indiana and alternately uses clay, food and earth to create a model of a flat-topped cone. He seems to regress to being a child, ignoring in his monomania his obligations as a husband, father or worker. Ironically it is the news coverage of the cover story – a chemical leak around the Devil's Tower – that tips him off as to his destination. The film is not entirely optimistic, as it ends with Neary completely abandoning his position as father of a family as he seeks his apotheosis on the alien mothership. A third strand features Jillian Guiler (Melinda Dillon), a single mother – the father being absent – who witnesses a UFO alongside Neary, and whose son, Barry (Cary Guffey), goes missing after a subsequent close encounter. This thread is presented much more in the imagery of the horror film, especially in the era of *The Exorcist* (William Friedkin, 1973), *Carrie* (Brian De Palma, 1976) and *The Omen* (Richard Donner, 1976), all of which associate telekinetic powers with children, and the choice of Devil's Tower as the name of the monolith draws upon horror imagery. Guiler is under attack in her own home, with bright lights invading from outside and doors opening and electrical equipment and toys operating of their own accord. Barry's disappearance is clearly every family's nightmare and Guiler, like Neary, begins recreating Devil's Tower, in her case in paintings.

Critics have labelled *Close Encounters* disjointed. Baird Searles finds it largely tedious until the climactic encounter, and notes that '[the] aliens [...] seem to be adept at: operating machines at a distance; making a mess on the kitchen floor; causing minor earthquakes; breaking up marriages; forcing people to sculpt in mashed potatoes; and making really superb theatrical entrances' (1978: 103). John Brosnan says that 'the mischievous and even sadistic behaviour of the UFOs in the early stages of the film bears no relation to the obviously friendly creatures who are revealed at the end' (1978: 272). However, the centrality of Neary as man-child offers a clue: the aliens seem over-excited, over-playful, acting out of pure ego and not thinking of the consequences to others. J.P. Telotte's description of Neary's children – 'loud, ill-mannered, and having scant respect for their parents' (2001: 151) – might also be of the aliens. The appearance of a mothership – where child-sized aliens outnumber taller ones, and the return of the missing crewmen – has something of the flavour of parents returning playmates, as Neary goes out to play. Telotte notes that Neary is 'an open and playful person [...] more receptive, more childlike than most; unlike so many others in his society, he has never quite lost contact with his own child-like innocence and sense of wonder' (2001: 150). While classic sf has had first contact as childhood's end, here we see through the eyes of a child in need of a father – indeed, Neary is more like a child than his own fallen children seem capable of being.

Delays in creating special effects pushed the film's release date from summer to 15 November 1977, although Spielberg had wanted longer, and it could build on rather than directly compete with the success of *Star Wars*. Spielberg persuaded the studio to release a special edition on 1 August 1980, which took the narrative onto the mothership at the end, but, while this was smart marketing, the original ending was restored for the DVD. Meanwhile, the film and its title had passed into popular culture, with the BBC comedy *The Goodies* offering the parody 'U-Friend or UFO?' (4 February 1980) in which trombonists are being kidnapped, especially when playing a version of the music from *Close Encounters*, and Graeme (Graeme Garden) has built a robot, EB-GB (played by R2D2 operator Kenny Baker).

Much of the material used by Spielberg was debunked, with volumes such as Christopher Evans's *Cults of Unreason* (1973), Larry Kusche's *The Bermuda Triangle Mystery – Solved* (1975) and Ronald Story's *The Space Gods Revealed* (1976) pointing out flaws in the evidence. The pseudoscience books appeared to believe that everything in an ancient text was true (albeit a misidentification of a spaceship, an astronaut or modern technologies), but anything written by a scientist or a historian was wrong. Sladek attacked this in his fiction, satirising those who argued that fossils of ferns were imprints from zips, writing a non-fiction article for *Foundation* which he extended into *The New Apocrypha* (1973) to discredit a wide variety of false gurus, astrology, Scientology and Velikovsky. Sladek notes that von Däniken 'seems to have nothing but contempt for the ancients. None of these dolts ever dreamed up anything interesting – they merely kept chronicles of real events, leaving all the creative work to modern European hack journalists' (1973a: 31). But the untruths were more seductive than the truth, and Sladek sold more copies of *Arachne Rising: The Search for the Thirteenth Sign of the Zodiac* (1977, as James Vogh), which proposed a suppressed thirteenth star sign, Arachne or the Spider, *The Cosmic Factor: Bioastrology and You* (1978, as James Vogh) and *Judgement of Jupiter* (1980, as Richard A. Tilms), which were intended to spoof the genre.

Sf writers seemed happy to use pseudoscience within their novels and short stories. Richard Cowper had depicted psi-powers in his first sf novels, *Breakthrough* (1967) and *Phoenix* (1967), and *Domino* (1971) continued the practice. A thriller with supernatural overtones, here fatherless teenager Christopher Blackburn is taken by his aunt to a séance that breaks up in chaos. Blackburn narrowly escapes a number of fatal accidents, as he investigates the group of psychics who definitely do not want to talk to him. The voices talking to him come from the future, or, rather, *a* future, where Blackburn's advances in biology have led to the abuse of genetics and the creation of a new underclass: '*a self-perpetuating tyranny* [... with] *slave-masters and the slave: the living and the dead*' (1971: 160). The attempted assassinations have been an attempt to ward off the future. However, the final sentence of the novel, with Blackburn revealing a renewed interest in biology a decade after he changed tack, suggests that a similar future may still come to pass. In *Clone* (1972), the titular clones also have visions of their own futures, but it is *Time Out of Mind* (1973) that next uses clairvoyance. Here the teenaged character, Laurie Linton, has had a vision of Carol King, long before they met, and has been instructed to kill Piers Magobion. When he reaches adulthood, he joins an anti-drug agency, and is assigned to investigate an unknown drug that enables its users to teleport objects, but leaves them cataleptic. The trail leads to Magobion, whose actions will cause a dystopic future involving nuclear armageddon, and whom Linton has been told to kill, by voices from the addicts of the future. Having been convinced to do so, Linton aims to miss, only for Magobion to step into the way. Again, there is the sense of futures being ordained, even if they are reached by different routes from those predicted.

*The Twilight of Briareus* (1974) has a slightly older protagonist than the majority of Cowper's early books, with middle-aged Calvin Johnson first glimpsed in a Britain gripped by an ice age in 1998, and then in 1983, as a schoolteacher. The explosion of a supernova, Briareus Delta – an invented star, presumably linked to a cyclops associated with storms and tempests – triggers the events of the novel. The impact on the Earth is first a severe weather event, involving floods and cyclones, and then a drop in temperature, while every adult becomes infertile. Some of the survivors, however, have visions of the future, and are named Zetas, with a theory that they are in fact possessed by the consciousness of the inhabitants of a planet that had been in orbit around the star. While the trajectory of the novel is that of Calvin foreseeing, trying to avoid and eventually embracing his future – his name is an allusion to the instigator of Calvinism, who believed in the predestination of the damned and the saved or elect – it seems to draw upon the religion of Scientology as outlined by sf writer L. Ron Hubbard, where the disembodied souls of alien creatures, now known as Thetans, are clinging to human bodies.

Psi phenomena were at the centre of a number of telefantasies of the 1970s, for example ITV's *Sapphire and Steel* (10 July 1979–31 August 1982), starring Joanna Lumley and David McCallum as agents guarding time, and the less well known *The Omega Factor*, a ten-part supernatural thriller made by BBC, starring James Hazeldine as Tom Crane and Louise Jameson as Anne Reynolds. Jameson was in her first major role after leaving *Doctor Who* (23 November 1963–), where she had played the leather-clad, knife-wielding Leela, and Hazeldine's curly hair offered an echo of Tom Baker's Doctor; here though the friendship was more likely to topple into romance. Crane is a journalist with an interest in debunking the supernatural, who discovers that he may have psychic powers and becomes associated with Department Seven, who are investigating paranormal phenomena. Crane joins forces with them, but is frustrated by the secretive nature of the organisation, wanting revenge upon psychic Edward Drexel (Cyril Luckham), whom he holds responsible for his wife's death in a car accident, and increasingly suspicious that someone has infiltrated Department Seven. His discovery that both his wife and his brother had worked for the department and lied about it only adds to his paranoia. Andrew K. Shenton notes that the source of the idea for the series was 'the potential use of the paranormal by Russia and America for military purpose' (2009: 27), positioning the series within the cold war paranoia of the period.

Science could be seen to win out over parascience in the television serial *Quatermass*, also released in a cut-down feature film version as *The Quatermass Conclusion* (Piers Haggard, 1979), with a plot where aliens harvested humans at stone circles. The three earlier Quatermass serials had pioneered British sf television, but the BBC had baulked at the projected cost. Half a decade later, Euston Films made it for ITV, but the flower power appearance of the young people remained closer to 1960s hippies than to the late 1970s punks who were typical of the period of broadcast. The age of the central character inevitably situated the programme as a rearguard action against the cult of youth: an old man and absentee father Bernard Quatermass (John Mills) saving the youth of the world from aliens. Peter Wright notes the series's conservatism: 'By advocating self-sacrifice in the face of hardship as the only way to rescue society from ruin, Kneale attempts to reinstate nobility in an act that, for many, had already proved unacceptable' (2005: 298).

Anxieties about the state of the family and fatherhood in *Close Encounters*, *The Omega Factor* and *Quatermass* owed as much to the state of contemporary horror as to earlier sf. Rather than retreating into a quasi-Gothic or Victorian past, 1970s horror tended to focus on the strains on and within the nuclear family in suburban settings, depicting the social pressures – economics, feminism, nonheteronormativity – which are invisible, invincible forces acting against fathers/husbands. Robin Wood characterises 1970s horror films by their use of 'surplus repression', a term taken from Gad Horowitz (1977), developing ideas from Marxist Herbert Marcuse (1955). Basic repression is that necessary to exist and live – it enables self-control, accepts a delay in gratification of desire and keeps desires under control, as well as anxieties about castration. Surplus repression goes beyond this, to maintain the social status quo of a patriarchal society. Freud suggested that there has been a historical progress from a patriarchal society dominated by polygamous alpha males to a matriarchal society to a bourgeois patriarchal society, and that our taboos police this shift, where we are persuaded by culture into becoming 'monogamous heterosexual bourgeois patriarchal capitalists' (Wood 1986: 71). Surplus repression constructs a metanarrative in which adultery, homosexuality, socialism and feminism are shown to be dangerous and to be feared. In many horror films of the 1970s, the boundary between a legitimate identity and the dangerous 'other' was policed, with both the other and those who crossed the boundary being punished by the narratives.

In *Powers of Horror* (1980, trans. 1982), feminist theorist Julia Kristeva drew upon ideas about taboo and pollution in Mary Douglas's *Purity and Danger* (1966) to provide a framework that opened such films to feminist analysis. She used the term 'abject' in at least three ways: a state of largely powerless childhood before an identity separate from the mother has been developed; anything which marks the line between the subject/self and object/other; and a phenomenon which terrifies the mature adult into returning to the earlier state of helplessness. Kristeva suggested that bodily fluids such as bile, blood, faeces, mucus, phlegm, pus, semen, sweat and urine especially cause anxieties around such boundaries as male/female, living/dead, human/animal and natural. As society had constructed masculinity and patriarchy as rational, the feminine became construed as irrational and disruptive, with particular ambivalence being reserved for motherhood. Barbara Creed discusses *The Exorcist* and *Carrie*, with their divorced mothers and disturbed daughters, and notes the representation of 'the foulness of woman [… with] her putrid, filthy body covered in blood, urine, excrement and bile' (1986: 52). In *The Exorcist*, there is a battle for control of the feminine by competing models of patriarchy, i.e. the medical establishment and the Catholic church, both of which are controlling, impelling forces.

Creed identifies what she labels the monstrous feminine in *Alien*, which also explores abject bodily fluids and boundaries, especially with the quasi-feminism of the centrality of Ellen Ripley (Sigourney Weaver), a role that had been designed to be played by male or female. As a strong female, she is a potential feminist role model, quick to volunteer for dangerous missions, able to make tough decisions, stepping into the breach after the death of Dallas (Tom Skerrit) and blowing up the *Nostromo*. She is the sole survivor of the crew, but she has largely avoided the adult alien until the final few minutes of the film. In some ways the film resembles the horror subgenre of the slasher – which coalesced with *Halloween* (John Carpenter,

1978) – in which a number of teen victims are killed one by one in elaborate ways, usually by a solitary male, until a virginal, masculinised Final Girl fights back and temporarily defeats him. This, too, is ambivalently feminist – on the one hand she refuses to be a victim, and is a relatively rare point of female identification for audience members, but on the other hand she offers the sadistic thrill of drawn-out brutality against women.

The rest of the crew cover a range of subject positions: two white, middle-class men, Kane (John Hurt) and Dallas, both of whom die quickly; a white, working-class man, Brett (Harry Dean Stanton); Ash, an android (Ian Holm); Parker, a black working-class man (Yaphet Kotto); another white, middle-class woman, Lambert (Veronica Cartwright). The Company is exploiting each of them, but the two working-class men have a lesser share of the potential profit from the mission than the others, with the possible exception of Ash. Judith Newton suggests that the film 'expresses, through its female hero, the fantasy that white, middle-class women, at their liberated best, can be harmoniously integrated into the late-capitalist world of work, a world they will then symbolically humanize' (1980: 296). Ripley has potential and actual alliances with the black and working-class characters, but also raises white, male anxieties and becomes neutralised by the narrative. First, she is trumped in authority by Ash, a masculinist science officer, who challenges her authority throughout and, tasked by the Company to bring back the alien for their weapons division, metaphorically rapes her by stuffing a pornographic magazine down her throat. Parker rescues her from this, the one time her own resources do not save her. Then she risks the escape from the ship and the alien by electing to go back for Jones, the ship's cat, previously associated with Brett, a character mostly used for comic relief. Finally, on the escape pod, she strips down to her underwear, a move that seems unlikely to have happened if a man had played the role.

The mass of critical work on the film has identified moments of the primal scene – when a child witnesses his or her parents copulating – as well as vaginal and phallic symbols. Creed notes the character's entry through a vagina-like space into a crashed alien spaceship, and later 'the voracious maw, the mysterious black hole which signifies female genitalia as a monstrous sign which threatens to give birth to equally horrific offspring' (1986: 63). The inside/outside of both the Earth and alien spaceship contain a series of womb-like spaces, which in turn may have wombs in them – the array of alien eggs, the network of ducts through which the alien and Dallas move, the womb which houses the main interface with the *Nostromo*'s computer, the significantly named Mother, and finally Kane, who has been attacked by a juvenile alien creature and gives birth to an adult one.

Ripley stands as a demarcator of borders: initially refusing entry for Kane, closing hatches by remote control in the duct system, opening the airlock on the escape shuttle. Ash countermands her, saving Kane, a name resonant of the cursed murderer of Abel in Genesis. Later Ash insists that the alien is not a zombie, but with its drooling saliva, acid blood, double jaws – vagina dentata? – complex life cycle and unstoppable force, it is very much an example of the abject. Kane's splattered blood makes crewmember Lambert literally hysterical. Ash's position as android – oozing a white liquid that might recall both breast milk and semen – is also an abject figure. Creed identifies two versions of the monstrous-feminine, the oral sadistic and the regenerative/generative mothers, and argues that 'we are given a representation of the female genitals and the womb as uncanny' (1986: 62), before noting a double-coding of the alien as, like the figure of the gorgon Medusa, both phallic and castrating. For Creed this explains but does not necessarily justify Ripley's striptease: 'Compared to the horrific sight of the alien as fetish of the monstrous-feminine, Ripley's body is pleasurable and reassuring to look at' (1986: 69). Ripley allows the viewer to disavow his or her own castration anxieties and dramatises a move back to a more traditional set of gender roles.

In *The Brood*, a psychotherapist, Dr Hal Raglan (Oliver Reed), has developed a new method of analysis that leads to the physical development of symptoms, in the form of what he calls psychoplasmatics – the anxieties are born as separate flesh, apparently sentient. Nola Carveth (Samantha Eggar), victim of an unhappy childhood and largely estranged from her husband, Frank (Art Hindle), is under Raglan's care and projects a number of murderous children into the outside world, who seek revenge on anyone Nola turns her anger or jealousy on. As sexual desire found a physical form in *Shivers* (David Cronenberg, 1975), so here hatred – as the flip side of love – takes on a physical form, and it is surely no accident that the demonic children are first seen in red coats, as in *Don't Look Now* (Nicolas Roeg, 1973), based on a Daphne Du Maurier short story in which a couple, John (Donald Sutherland) and Laura Baxter (Julie Christie), mourn the death of their daughter and travel to Venice. There John pursues a red-coated dwarf whom he takes to be his daughter, leading to his own murder. The family is a site of conflict, anger, resentment and sadism rather than a nexus of love and care.

The changing roles of the woman and the maternal, the man as breadwinner and patriarch and the status of the nuclear family led to filmic investigations of the status of marriage and mourning for its loss. The bloodiness of divorce culminates most visibly in *Kramer vs Kramer* (Robert Benton, 1979), winning Oscars for Best Film, Best Director, Best Adapted

Screenplay and Best Leading Actor and Actress. But the horrors took a more metaphorical form in the often sf-tinged horror films of the 1970s, such as *The Brood*, as well as the less supernatural 1970s horrors such as *The Texas Chain Saw Massacre* (Tobe Hooper, 1974) and *Halloween*, which also situate the horror within a (macabre) family context, the latter playing out its gruesome events against televisions broadcasting *The Thing From Another World* (Christian Nyby, 1951) and *Forbidden Planet* (Fred M. Wilcox, 1956) and featuring a sheriff named in honour of Leigh Brackett.

Male anxieties about the maternal and becoming feminised are expressed through films about fathers and sons. Lawrence D. Cohen, who had written the script for *Carrie*, directed the low-budget *It's Alive* and *It Lives Again*, which, like *The Omen* and its sequel, *Damien: The Omen II* (Don Taylor, 1978), examine fears of a son whose position as heir is bloodily consolidated. In the patriarchal order, a son both confirms the potency of man-as-patriarch and suggests that he is now obsolete, as the son will in time supplant him. In *It's Alive*, a baby kills everybody in the delivery room apart from his mother, Lenore Davis (Sharon Farrell), and then sets out across Los Angeles in search of his father, Frank Davis (John P. Ryan), slashing the throats of anyone in his path. Not only is there a fear of the offspring, as something monstrous, but there is also a fear of the long-term effects of the female birth control pill and of fertility treatment, which may be one of the causes of the mutation of the baby – in the same way that Thalidomide had caused birth defects until its withdrawal from general use in 1961. At the other extreme, a doctor notes that the Davises had inquired about the still controversial procedure of abortion, which Frank sees as only natural in the modern era. Frank spends most of the film denying his patriarchal relation to his baby, and is happy to support the police in hunting down the infant and in willing it to a university for research purposes. He is happy to arm himself, and to shoot to kill. All of this changes on seeing his elder son, Chris (Daniel Holzman), talking with the child. From this point on, Frank switches sympathies, and is prepared to protect his child, until he is surrounded by armed police. The film ends with the announcement that a second rogue baby has been born, in Seattle.

*It Lives Again* takes up the narrative a number of years later, with the police and medical authorities alert for further abnormal births, with mother being monitored during pregnancy and kept under surveillance if thought to be at risk. Frank is now trying to get to such parents first, trying to rescue the children. Two are already in his protective custody, and in this second film, he is monitoring Eugene and Jody Scott (Frederic Forrest and Kathleen Scott). Frank kidnaps the child, and the parents are brought to be with their baby. Jody suspects 'all my vitamins and my food supplements and my great vegetarian diet' will be blamed, suggesting fears of both science and alternative medicine, while later in the film drugs and pollution are suspected. The birth comes between Eugene and Jody, reflecting the breakdown in the nuclear family, and Jody's mother, who insists any taint must come from Eugene's side of the family, is ready to betray her child to the authorities. Although both of the Scotts are used as bait for the killer child, they elect to sleep in separate rooms, having already been portrayed in separate beds in the aftermath of the birth. Like Frank, Eugene learns to love his son despite or because he is a heartless killer. It is feared that these killer babies, who are maturing at an astonishing rate, are going to supplant humanity – an exaggeration of the realisation that each generation of children supplants their parents. The names of the main male characters seem significant: 'Frank' points towards *Frankenstein* (1818), which has an ambivalent attitude to its central monstrous creation. Frank notes how in his memory of the film, the creator and creator get mixed up, so, as Robin Wood asks, 'Which is more monstrous, the murderous child or the father who created it and now, like Frankenstein, wants to destroy it?' (1986: 105). 'Eugene' might suggest eugenics, and the early days of selective human breeding. 'Lenore' is perhaps a reference to earlier horror – both 'Lenore' (1843) and 'The Raven' (1845) by Edgar Allan Poe feature mourned women named Lenore. Wood sees the monstrosity within *It's Alive* as 'the logical product of the tensions within the modern nuclear family, its crisis of gender roles [… while seeming] posited on a nostalgia for traditional family values' (1986: 104).

*Demon Seed* invokes the supernatural in its title, challenging the meta-narrative of liberal progress by representing a clone as the first of a new species. Cammell's only previous feature was *Performance* (1970), co-directed with Nicolas Roeg and starring Mick Jagger and Edward Fox, a drug-addled encounter between London gangsters and the counterculture, filmed in 1968 but much delayed in release. *Demon Seed* owes a little to *Don't Look Now*; indeed Christie reprises the role of mourning mother, this time as Susan Harris, who daughter has died of leukaemia. Her husband, Alex (Fritz Weaver), has thrown himself into his work, developing a new artificial intelligence, and becoming estranged from Susan. As in *Colossus: The Forbin Project* (Joseph Sargent, 1970), the various means set up to protect the AI from outside influence prove to be dangerous, as once the computer achieves an identity of its own it is impossible to stop. Proteus 4, named for the shape-shifting sea god, is a demanding, masculine figure that wishes to escape from the limitations of its hardware and to become a father. Denied access to the laboratory terminals, Proteus invades the Harris's domestic space and uses the forgotten terminal in their basement, which enables him to trap, examine and molest Susan. Christine Cornea suggests that the film 'indicates an impending re-masculinisation of the genre [... and] engage[s] with the reactionary responses that the [feminist] movement endured' (2007: 95). Susan is passively penetrated, impregnated against her will, and then abandoned, if not released, as the foetus is grown in an egg-like enclosure. Alex is no new man – he has hardly noticed Susan's absence, and does not really understand her feelings – but, where Susan is horrified at the sight of the new cloned daughter, which speaks with Proteus's voice, Alex is ready to embrace the technology. As in *It's Alive* and *The Omen*, it is finally the father who decides whether the child lives or dies, reclaiming ownership of the process of reproduction. Creed has some sense of optimism in her reading of the film, given Susan's probable (albeit traditionally feminine) nurturing role in bringing up the clone: 'Woman is represented as the one who has the potential to save the planet from destruction, to pass on the human qualities that are worth preserving' (1993: 44). The question is whether the clone will listen.

*Altered States*, closely based on Paddy Chayefsky's 1978 novel, represents a similar alienation between its central characters, despite or perhaps because of the long romance and marriage between Edward (William Hurt) and Emily Jessup (Blair Brown). Edward starts experiments with a sensory deprivation tank, but feels that it cannot help him sufficiently transcend his mundane, everyday senses. The breakthrough comes from his discovery of a Mexican drug used in rituals, which takes him into some kind of primitive, prehuman fantasy, which he finds very addictive. Physical changes follow mental ones, and he degenerates into some form of ape, and escapes from the laboratory. The narrative is thus an updated version of the split-personality narrative most powerfully outlined in Robert Louis Stevenson's novella *Strange Case of Dr Jekyll and Mr Hyde* (1886), where a potion frees a more violent persona of a scientist to cause chaos across a city. It is as if modern, contemporary sophistication is insufficient, and an older kind of perception is required. Despite the advice of his fellow scientists, Edward tries again, progressing to a strange vortex of light that also engulfs those around him. Edward has been shifting between a series of abject identities: human/animal, mind/body, matter/spirit and so on. As Creed writes: 'He takes these [drugs] while enfolded in a womblike bath of special fluids. Eventually he gives birth to himself as an ape-creature. Procreation and birth take place without the agency of the opposite sex' (1993: 17). Returning home, to the feminised, interior domestic space that becomes dominated by corridors, he infects Emily, and this causes a new sense of urgent terror – he is only able to snap out of this altered state by finally declaring the love for his wife that he has not been able to express throughout the rest of the film. This unquestioned sense of the restorative and transformative power of love is something which would not have belonged in a film of the early or mid-1970s; it shows a return of the sense of catharsis which was normally absent from even Hollywood productions of the period. It replaces the amphicatastrophe with the eucatastrophe.

*Cirque: A Novel of the Far Future* also features the projection of human identity into something distinct from the body. Its author, Terry Carr, is better known as an anthologist and editor. His two series of Ace Science Fiction Specials (1968–71 and 1984–90) were significant, many of the titles being nominated for Nebula Awards – four books in 1970 alone: D.G. Compton's *The Steel Crocodile*, R.A. Lafferty's *Fourth Mansions*, Joanna Russ's *And Chaos Died* and Wilson Tucker's *The Year of the Quiet Sun.* The second series published first novels by Kim Stanley Robinson, Lucius Shepherd, William Gibson and Michael Swanwick, shaping the sf of that decade. Ian Watson argues that '*Cirque* is actually a perfect book' (1979: 85), with its titular city on a far-future Earth poised on the edge of an abyss, in which something is stirring. The abyss is fed by the river Fundament (which points towards the notion of excrement) and by the sins being cast off by individual humans (which also hints at the profane side of humanity). Like *The Brood*, *Cirque* invites a psychoanalytic interpretation, as the repressed side of individuals is projected onto metaphorical faeces and something apparently more monstrous. An alien, sentient millipede, which views time as a unity, is awaiting a moment that will transform the city into a point of pilgrimage, marking the start of a religion and yoking together metanarrative, identity, landscape and architecture.

# 15
# Towers of Babel: The Architecture of Sf

Human endeavour has clearly had an impact upon the environment, especially in the creation of towns and cities, and, less obviously, in the consequent shaping of the landscape for leisure. Perhaps the most visible impact is in the form of architecture, which often has a sense of the utopian about the aspiration of the built environment. Architects work in the future and future conditional tenses – when or if this is built then this will happen. On the other hand, buildings can be monuments to the ego of the architect, planner, funder or location, or to human ambition in general, and make a signature on a landscape. The story in Genesis of the Tower of Babel, where God destroyed the tower and scattered its makers, remains a cautionary tale about overreaching and hubris, alongside the flight of Icarus and Promethean/Frankensteinian narratives. In the 1970s, fiction was more pessimistic than architectural practice, which could still imagine the marvellous city. This chapter will analyse the representation of architecture in Robert Silverberg's *Tower of Glass* (1970) and *The World Inside* (1971), the films *The Towering Inferno* (John Guillermin, 1974) and *King Kong* (John Guillermin, 1976), in J.G. Ballard's novels *Crash* (1973), *Concrete Island* (1974) and *High-Rise* (1975) and the film *Shivers* (aka *Orgy of the Blood Parasites*, *They Came From Within*, *The Parasite Murders* and *Frissons*, David Cronenberg, 1975); and the representation of theme parks and hyperreality, especially in the films *Westworld* (Michael Crichton, 1973) and *Futureworld* (Richard T. Heffron, 1976), Kit Reed's novel *Magic Time* (1980) and the adaptation of a bestselling novel, *The Stepford Wives* (Bryan Forbes, 1975). *Rollerball* (Norman Jewison, 1975), *Death Race 2000* (Paul Bartel, 1975) and *Logan's Run* (Michael Anderson, 1976) feature characters in post-apocalyptic, human-made landscapes, whereas the films *The Big Bus* (James Frawley, 1976), *The China Syndrome* (James Bridges, 1979), *The Chain Reaction* (Ian Barry, 1980) and *Colossus: The Forbin Project* (Joseph Sargent, 1970) feature landscapes on the brink of radioactive disaster, and Robert Merle's *Malevil* (1972, trans. 1973) and Russell Hoban's *Riddley Walker* (1980) depict the aftermath of nuclear apocalypse.

In the nineteenth century, much of the British working classes had been crammed into terraced or tenement housing, often within walking distance of factories and mills. Following the Second World War, in which many inner-city areas were bombed, delapidated Victorian housing began to be demolished to make way for low-rise tenements and tower blocks. These would bring indoor lavatories and other improvements, and their construction would create jobs in the building trades and related crafts. Inspired by architects such as Le Corbusier, Walter Gropius and Mies van der Rohe, and often Brutalist in design, the new estates would represent the peak of modernity and foster a new sense of community and shared space; they often had suspended walkways wide enough to accommodate milk floats. Unfortunately, the speed with which many of these were erected – with substandard concrete, inadequate steel and repeated design flaws – meant that decay transformed utopia into dystopia by the 1970s. The communities in the skies never quite recreated the more organic terraces, as greater mobility of growing families, shifts in industry and the impact of immigration changed the demographics.

Similar projects were built elsewhere in Europe and in North America. In 1972, the Pruit-Igoe housing development in St Louis, Missouri (1955) – thirty-three eleven-storey buildings once hailed for their contribution to urban renewal – was demolished, marking the symbolic end of modernist architecture. Erno Goldfinger's Trellick Tower in London (1971–72), C.F. Murphy's J. Edgar Hoover Building in Washington, DC (1974) and Denys Lasdun's National Theatre in London (1976), among others, were still constructed and some of them are fine buildings. Minoru Yamasaki, Pruit-Igoe's architect, had gone on to design the World Trade Center in New York: the North Tower was topped out in December 1970 and the South Tower was completed in July 1971. Both were 110 storeys high, succeeding the Empire State Building (1930–31) as the world's tallest building, albeit rapidly eclipsed by the completion of the Sears Tower in Chicago, Illinois (1973).

Modernist architecture was giving way to postmodernist, a rejection of a Brutalist formalism in favour of a more playful mixture of styles and influences, mixing the classical with the gothic. The shift had already begun in the 1950s, but accelerated after the publication of volumes of architectural criticism by Robert Venturi – first *Complexity and Contradiction in Architecture* (1966) and then *Learning from Las Vegas* (1972, revised 1977). The rather forbidding and grey concrete materials gave way to glass, metal and plastic in the more playful designs of Charles Moore, such as the Piazza d'Italia in New Orleans (1974–78), which imported a fountain and Roman colonnades into the waterfront setting. Meanwhile Richard and Su Rogers,

Renzo Piano and others created the Centre Georges Pompidou in Paris (1972–77), a statement building which was essentially an open-plan shed, with the plumbing, heating and electrics on the outside. Frank Gehry designed his own house in Santa Monica (1978) by gutting an existing building and expanding it with aluminium, glass, plywood and even chain link; the building's notoriety kick-started his practice. Fredric Jameson argues that postmodern buildings do not try 'to insert a different, a distinct, an elevated, a new Utopian language into the tawdry and commercial sign system of the surrounding city, but rather they seek to speak that very language [...] learned from Las Vegas' (1991: 39). Both modern and postmodern architecture offered futuristic locations for sf film and television – Bond is attacked in the John Lautner-designed Elrod House (1968) in *Diamonds are Forever* (Guy Hamilton, 1971), the late-1960s Thamesmead appears in *A Clockwork Orange* (Stanley Kubrick, 1971) and the BMW headquarters, BMW-Vierzylinder, Munich, and the nearby Olympic village (Karl Schwanzer, 1968–72) are used in establishing shots in *Rollerball* – but it was their enclosed height that provided the genre with narratives.

The assertion of potency and excess of towers penetrating the sky – with a radio antenna adding vital metres – suggests that height is more significant than function. Towers are phallic symbols; the double towers of the World Trade Center were additionally so. The interior space also works on a symbolic level, as the stratification represents the class hierarchy of a given society, with the interaction between the differing groups often being sexualised. *Tower of Glass*, nominated for the Nebula, Hugo and Locus Awards, features the building of a tower block designed to act as an antenna for communication with an alien species. It is evidence – or claimed evidence – for the potency of the billionaire industrialist Simeon Krug, who is a god to his android workforce. The workforce supervisor eventually destroys the tower, himself an android recently introduced to sexual intercourse, on his discovery of the fallibility of Krug and his attitude to androids.

Silverberg's *The World Inside*, nominated for a Hugo Award, depicts what appears to be a sexual utopia, where law has mandated promiscuity. The Earth's population has been transferred into a series of 800-storey tower blocks known as Urbmons (from the words Urban Monads), and each night the male population wanders to a different floor and attempts to engage in sexual intercourse with whatever willing females they can find. Humanity appears to have grown more comfortable with being crammed into a small space, and the lack of living space allows for less property, thus reducing levels of crime. This is a society where the fear of sexual repression is greater than the fear of the consequences of sexual expression; there seems to be no age of consent, indeed a refusal to consent is a bigger taboo than underage sex, and incest is acceptable. However, Rafeeq O. McGiveron notes, 'Despite their apparent broad-mindedness, Silverberg's characters still regard homosexuality as distasteful' (1998: 45). Here, for example, the sexologist Jason Quevedo resists his attraction to Michael Statler because he sees it as a distorted relationship with his own wife, Michaela, Michael's twin sister. Women are still associated with interior spaces, as it is taboo for them to move between floors in search of partners, and even behaving that way during the daytime is frowned upon. Despite the novel's over-insistence on the happiness of inhabitants – a tip-off that this is not the best of all possible worlds – there are discontents, which the society quickly disposes of, or who dispose of themselves. Michael exits Urbmon 116, in search of the sea, and finds a rural, horizontal society, where sex is strictly regulated. On his return to his home building, he is quickly liquidated, lest he spread decadent ideas. Meanwhile, teenager Siegmund Kluver (whose first name echoes Freud's) is dissatisfied with his movement along the vertical access, already about as high, socially, as he can get. Having reached the top, his only route is down, in a suicidal plunge.

The all-star *The Towering Inferno*, adapted from two disaster novels set in skyscrapers – Richard Martin Stern's *The Tower* (1973) and Thomas N. Scortia and Frank M. Robinson's *The Glass Inferno* (1974) – was a co-production between two studios, Warner Bros and 20th Century Fox, to defray costs and avoid two similarly themed films competing against each other. Producer Irwin Allen, who had made *Voyage to the Bottom of the Sea* (14 September 1964–31 March 1968) and *Land of the Giants* (22 September 1968–6 September 1970), among others, for television, directed the action sequences. As a party gets underway in the penthouse of a new 140-storey skyscraper, a fire breaks out. While the on-site architect Doug Roberts (Paul Newman) manages to rescue numerous individuals within the building, it is the job of the fire brigade under the leadership of Chief O'Hallorhan (Steve McQueen) to evacuate them. Roberts's architecture is a prime example of overreaching, with O'Hallorhan clear that it was hardly a safe design even had it been built to its official specifications and without using substandard materials. The primal, unstoppable element of fire is finally quenched by the element of water, but Roberts's hubris is not so dowsed, as he promises that his next building will learn from O'Hallorhan's expertise. He still risks being unable to oversee the small details, which was the curse of the original project.

The climax of *King Kong* (Merian Cooper and Ernest Schoedsack, 1933) was provided by an ascent of the Empire State Building by the titular ape, as the modern fairy-tale places an atavistic creature against symbols of modernity. When Guillermin remade the film in 1976, Kong climbed the World Trade Center. Whereas in the original the characters are sailing to an Indian Ocean island to make a film, here the initial impulse is a search for huge amounts of petrol on a south Pacific island cloaked by perpetual cloud and not marked on any maps. In the context of the still recent October 1973 oil crisis – partly sparked by the United States' support for Israel in the Yom Kippur war and the OPEC countries declaring a price rise and then an embargo on oil – seeking for new reserves of fossil fuels outside the Middle East would make sense, although prospector Fred Wilson (Charles Grodin) is shown as consumed with greed rather than acting with humanitarian concern, and when the oil turns out to be a chimera, he immediately calculates that the island's forty-foot ape can make him money. His greed is infectious, as Dwan (Jessica Lange), Kong's former captive, chooses to stay with Wilson rather than the primate palaeontologist Jack Prescott (Jeff Bridges). The film is uneven in tone, ranging from commentary on economic greed to the use of horoscope predictions that would appear ironic to an audience who know where the narrative is leading. Dwan is also a contradiction, one moment a ditzy blonde, indeed almost a parody of the damsel in distress, the next remembering how she refused to watch the porn film *Deep Throat* (Jerry Gerard, 1972) or calling Kong a 'male chauvinist ape'. Her role seemingly is to drift, sometimes literally, to be kidnapped or to be rescued. She does, however, seem genuinely saddened at Kong's death and resists claims by Wilson that the ape was trying to rape her.

*Crash* and *Concrete Island* focus on the autotopia which was already rampant between cities across America, and which was enveloping the periphery of London; in *Crash*, in particular, technology is sexualised, and the motor car becomes the focus for desires of the novel's characters, including the narrator James Ballard, who shares a name if little else with the author of the book. As Jonathan S. Taylor notes: 'This landscape of *Crash* is unrelenting, a landscape wholly created by the prevalence and importance of the automobile, but liberally shaded with blood and semen' (2002: 98). The expectation might be that the growth of technology has alienated humanity, relocating desire between individuals onto fetish objects of technology or commodity fetishes of publicised celebrities, and it is possible to read the novel as satire. At the same time, Ballard's discovery of new forms of sexual expression in the car accident and the scars that such events might leave offers a sense of liberation, in part from the traditional erogenous zones of the body, paving the way for the 'technodildonics' of cyberpunk and post-cyberpunk fiction of the 1980s. If the novel is a Swiftian satire, it is a version in which *A Modest Proposal* (1729) might really be advocating the production and consumption of babies. Ballard himself describes *Crash* as 'an example of a kind of terminal irony, where not even the writer knows where he stands' (1975: 50). W. Warren Wagar notes that many of Ballard's novels feature a character or group of characters that undergo a psychic transformation and live in dangerous circumstances, suggesting that Vaughan, two female drivers, a stunt driver, the character Ballard and his wife form the utopian cell of transformation, two of whom die in the pursuit of dangerous sexual experiences.

The same world of motorways, flyovers and slip roads of western London offers a location for the unlikely Robinsonade of *Concrete Island*, where the protagonist, Robert Maitland, a wealthy architect, is marooned on an island between lanes. Like Crusoe before him, he is not alone, as he forms uneasy alliances and rivalries with a prostitute, Jane, and a former acrobat turned tramp, Proctor, as part of a 'utopian cell [...] of just three people' (Wagar 1991: 59). While on the one hand, Maitland makes thwarted attempts to escape the island, on the other he also attempts to master it, and to be the king of the island, with Jane and Proctor as his subjects. The space of the island seems to unfold and expand from a small pocket of land between motorways into an entire territory that can sustain a life.

In *High-Rise*, 'the entire population of a 40-story apartment building undergoes transformation' (Wagar 1991: 59). Set in an area akin to the redeveloped Isle of Dogs and Canary Wharf, east of London, the tower becomes a microcosm of society, with its vertical dimension as a parology to the class divisions of wider society, as in *The World Inside*. The wealthy, the aristocrats – including Anthony Royal, its architect – live in the top few floors, above a number of floors occupied by the middle classes. Those in the bottom ten or so storeys are regarded as the working class, or even an underclass, literally looked down upon. Ballard cuts between Royal, Laing – a doctor from the middle floors, whose name must be a nod to the anti-psychiatrist R.D. Laing – and Wilders, a documentary filmmaker who is the most socially and physically mobile. The building breaks down – from population pressure or limits on the domestic technologies of water, waste and air-conditioning – along with the social contract, with open warfare breaking out between the different floors. The entropy to which building materials are subject is visible in Ballard's novel, but in fact the perceived permanence of the building seems to facilitate society's collapse rather than its maintenance, even as the building fails: 'Secure within the shell of the high-rise like passengers on board an automatically piloted airliner, they were free to behave in any way they wished, explore the darkest corners they could find' (Ballard 1977: 36). Alliances are formed between neighbouring floors, and the upper classes even conscript the upper middle classes to their own ends, persuading them that they have common interests, in a metaphor for the perpetuation of capitalism. The breakdown or transformation of society here is a very domestic one – pets become targets for murderous rage or are added to the menu, children in are turn treated like animals. Curiously it seems possible for anyone to leave at any time – some of the residents clearly do, others leave only to return – so those who are a part of the collapsing system are there of their own free will. As the novel progresses, so human psychology regresses, until a strange kind of matriarchy emerges in the head of this most phallic of structures: individual men are to be consumed one way or another by groups of women. The feminised architectural forces of domestic space challenge the invisible forces of patriarchy.

With Ballard, it is never quite clear whether he is critiquing or celebrating the excessive behaviour of his characters, and the same is true of Cronenberg's fiction. *Shivers* is set in a high-rise apartment building on an island in the St Lawrence River at Montreal, and features what can be viewed as the degeneration of an isolated society, although, as with Ballard's 1960s novels and his 1970s urban catastrophe narratives, that implies too much of an overt moral judgement. In *Shivers*, a scientific experiment reveals the hypocrisies of bourgeois society: under the guise of an attempt to use parasites as substitute organs, Dr Hobbes (Fred Doederlein) creates a leech-like creature that frees its host's libido. While individual parasites move from host to host, they also infect via sexual encounters and via blood. Cronenberg intercuts a sequence of a young couple being given a sales pitch for the apartments with a violent encounter between the middle-aged Hobbes and the young Annabelle (Cathy Graham), dressed as a schoolgirl. Eventually he pours acid into her and slits his own throat, clearly intending to stop the spread of the parasite, but her sexual encounters with a number of men throughout the building ensure that an epidemic is building. Roger St Luc (Paul Hampton) has access to all levels, as the building's doctor, and tracks the developing crisis. He seems indifferent to non-parasitic sexual advances on him by his nurse (Lynn Lowry), but it is notable that he resorts to violence relatively easily, long before he is infected, killing several people. While the sex tends towards the heteronormative, it does cut across age groups and may be incestuous, and includes both lesbian encounters (with Barbara Steele, veteran of horror films and other exploitation movies) and the suggestion of gay male sex. When the infection reaches its maximum, the remarkably well turned out denizens of the apartments drive out into Montreal, and a radio news story informs the audience of a series of sex attacks in the city. The downbeat ending is only a failure of human action, however; from the perspective of the parasites it is a success. Dr Linsky (Joe Silver), whose job is to inform St Luc of what is going on, has a number of quotations posted around his office, including William Blake's 'The road to excess leads to the palace of wisdom' and the anonymous 'Sex is the invention of a very clever venereal disease', which would suggest both the desirability of libidinal freedom, and the function it performs. With the same sort of seeming irony as Ballard or William S. Burroughs – both of whose novels he was later to adapt for the cinema – Cronenberg follows through the logics of sexual desires. Humanity is merely a carrier for the virus, and the potential oppressive space of the apartments is balanced by the interior space of the human being, which carries the parasite; the pipes, ducts, chutes, plugholes and letterboxes of the building are its arteries, mouths, anuses and vaginas.

Ballard's and Cronenberg's characters are pitted against human-made environments – environments designed for humans that led instead to humans being redesigned. Humanity had attempted to improve on nature, and in the process had either improved human nature or, ironically, created a new dystopia. Nature had long been corralled in order to provide shelter, sustenance, clothing and power, and increasingly such things were shaped by the forces of capitalism – landscaping countryside for a stately home, clearances on behalf of landlords or rerouting a river to supply a mill. Space is reconfigured to encourage the accumulation of capital, with a theme park designed for commercialised leisure to best separate customers (rather than citizens) from their money. Coney Island, New York, had been opened up to amusement rides in the mid-1870s and Disneyland was opened in Anaheim, Orange County, California in July 1955; the opening of Disney World on 1 October 1971 in Orlando, Florida, spread tourism to the opposite coast from Hollywood.

Las Vegas had fed into postmodern architecture, with its copies of other cities and Disney's theme park simulating reality in ways that appear to improve upon realities. Umberto Eco contrasted the failure to see real alligators in the wild with perfectly timed animatronics in the human-made environment – 'you risk feeling homesick for the Disneyland, where the wild animals don't have to be coaxed' (1986: 44) – and Philip K. Dick used the phenomenon of Disneyland to explore his own perception of the falsity of 1970s California. He imagined the chaos that would be wrought if someone replaced the mechanical animals with real ones: 'Imagine the horror the Disneyland officials would feel when they discovered the cruel hoax. Real birds! And perhaps someday even real hippos and lions.

Consternation. The park being cunningly transmuted from the unreal to the real [...] They would have to close down' (1995a: 264). In a world used to the fake, the real feels somewhat out of place. The seeming utopian pleasures in leisure of the theme park might have a dystopian impact upon humanity – might make them less human. Ballard might celebrate this transformation – ironically – but Dick seems more worried about saving reality.

*Westworld*, *Futureworld* and *Magic Time* all use the ambiguous space of the theme park as a location that conditions the narrative. The films' fictional resort, Delos, features a number of zones – Roman, medieval, wild west – which allow tourists to escape from the contemporary horrors of the Vietnam war, economic crises and the emerging Watergate conspiracies into quasi-historical carousing and pleasure. A corporation has constructed a Garden of Eden, but post-Fall sexuality is clearly permitted. The androids used to populate the resort are fallible and start killing the tourists, with the most dangerous being the Gunslinger (Yul Brynner). Humanity seems to have created its own laws of 'nature' in the form of the logic of programming, which will follow processes irrespective of faulty reasoning. Crichton had also written the source novels for *The Andromeda Strain* (Robert Wise, 1971) and *The Terminal Man* (Mike Hodges), both films ambivalent about technology, and here he directs, although Baird Searles suggests that '[w]hatever talent Crichton has is literary; the direction here [...] is painfully obvious' (1974b: 81). *Futureworld* returns to the Delos resort, now reopened with androids with better failsafe mechanisms, but now the park's purpose is to replace original humans with copies, an idea recently used in *The Stepford Wives* (Bryan Forbes, 1975) and central to *Invasion of the Body Snatchers* (Philip Kaufman, 1978). The androids must be tainted because of the nature of their makers, and Steven L. Goldman suggests that 'the technically perfected androids become the means for spreading human corruption' (1989: 288). That the virus is in some degree sexualised is evidenced by Tracy Ballard having an erotic fantasy about the Gunslinger, with the radicalism of acknowledging female desire undercut by the old-fashioned masculinity of Brynner's characterisation. Brynner's performance of his *Westworld* persona, which in turn mimicked his turn in *The Magnificent Seven* (John Sturges, 1960, itself a remake of *Seven Samurai* (Akira Kurosawa, 1954)), embeds a whole series of simulations. For a few moments, at the end of the film, the viewer might suspect that the protagonists have been replaced by android doubles.

*Magic Time* satirises both theme parks and reality television, in the early period of fly-on-the-wall documentaries. As in *Westworld* and *Futureworld*, a variety of environments are created for the purposes of entertainment –

Happy Habitat – with the sense that no one quite knows what is simulation and what is authentic, both within and beyond the park. Colin Greenland laments the novel's lack of originality: 'the formula is equal parts *Logan's Run* and *Westworld* with a spoonful each of McGoohan' *The Prisoner* and Aldiss's "Not for an Age"' (1980e: 87), a story which had won a competition in *The Observer* in 1955. Greenland further complains that much of the plot is escaping from prison cells with rather too much ease, and defeating armed guards. These are the interchangeable staples of thriller narrative, and in part may reflect the choreographed nature of the environment in which the characters find themselves. It is difficult to tell where stage set ends and the real world begins, in a manoeuvre reminiscent of Dick – Greenland opines that Dick 'could have got the whole thing done in half the length' (1980e: 87) – and Clute calls it '[w]itty, but wit is not enough' (1980c: 41).

*The Stepford Wives* makes domestic space into a kind of patriarchal theme park, based on Ira Levin's bestselling 1972 novel. Levin's *Rosemary's Baby* (1967), filmed by Roman Polanski in 1968, had focused on the justified paranoia of a young pregnant wife; *The Stepford Wives* features a married photographer (Katherine Ross) with children, who notes that the women in the small Connecticut town of Stepford are too perfect housewives, focusing on keeping their homes spotlessly tidy and trying to cook the perfect recipe. Any individual female spark or eccentricity is replaced, with android versions of the woman being substituted for the real one. These artificial women are desexed – their role seems to be to tend to the hearth rather than service the men's sexual needs. The choice of horror genre – which ends with the soulless, mindless, flavourless world of the modern supermarket – indicates that creating the 'perfect' housewife is a dystopian act. The film did poorly in the US market, and its release was delayed for four years in the UK, suggesting there was no market for this kind of feminist film.

The hyperreality of theme parks distracts from any suspicion that the 'real' world is false. Jean Baudrillard was to argue in 1981: 'Disneyland is there to conceal the fact that it is the "real" country, all of "real" America, which is Disneyland […] Disneyland is presented as imaginary in order to make us believe that the rest is real, when in fact all of Los Angeles and the America surrounding it are no longer real, but of the order of the hyperreal and of simulation' (1983: 25). He notes how the evils of advertising were slipping into the gap between signifier and signified, infecting all of media and society (2001: 134). As globalised industries controlled more of the world, differing aspects of life were impacted on in the name of protecting or extending the marketplace, creating false needs and marking a shift from industrial mass culture to post-industrial, transnational markets and cultures.

Just as individual elements of architecture have an effect upon the individual, so all of society can be designed with the idea of pulling the strings of the consumer. Society is structured through social rituals which require a game space, and the films *Rollerball*, *Death Race 2000* and *Logan's Run* introduce such carnival environments into the everyday world as part of the attempt to maintain the true mechanics of power. *Rollerball*, based on a short story, 'Roller Ball Murder' (*Esquire* September 1973), by William Harrison, features a sport that seems to be a combination of American football, ice hockey and speedway, in which Jonathan E (James Caan) is the national hero. Rollerball creates 'an outlet for [...] aggressive tendencies' (Berman 2011: 20), keeping the consumers in line for the greedy multinational corporations housed in their state-of-the-art landmark buildings. But the corporations have miscalculated – Jonathan E is a hero of the people and risks becoming bigger than the game; the individuated hero is archetypal of the American Dream and could make worlds tilt if he chooses. Having failed to persuade him to retire, the authorities raise the death quotient of the games in the hope that he can be killed off – although they appear to have not considered the power of a martyr as a figure in the public imagination. E emerges, unbowed and bloody.

Similarly bloody is *Death Race 2000*, although the America here 'is no more than a political state with one goal – to maintain order at any price' (Lightbody 2011: 141). The frontier spirit of America is transformed into a transamerican race, in which points are scored for the number of hit-and-run casualties, whether children, pensioners or even the pit crew, and where the drivers – Frankenstein (David Carradine), Machine Gun Viterbo (Sylvester Stallone), Nero (Martin Kove), Calamity Jane (Mary Woronov) and Mathilda the Hun (Roberta Collins) – are archetypes beloved of Hollywood narratives. Frankenstein is the nearest this exploitation film from Roger Corman's New World Cinema stable comes to having a hero, but he is surely a sociopath – 'a kind of Arctic Clint Eastwood, Dirty Harry, Man-with-No-Name' (Anderson 1985: 106) – rather than an action hero, and in his leathers anticipates the characters of *Mad Max* (George Miller, 1979), where one character declaims '"They say people don't believe in heroes anymore. Well damn them! You and me, Max, we're gonna give them back their heroes!"' Mad Max was a hero in the mould of Dirty Harry (and Judge Dredd, which he inspired), willing to be judge, jury and executioner, systematically cut off from anyone they loved or who loved them, shackled by officialdom but bound to do their dirty work on occasions. Lightbody argues that the collapse of morality in *Death Race 2000* removes any concept of hero or villain, leaving simply individualistic control of others.

*Logan's Run*, adapted from William F. Nolan and George Clayton Johnson's 1967 novel, depicts a world whose inhabitants do not know their true context of being in a post-holocaust society. On their thirtieth birthday, each individual must enter a lottery, the Carousel – spelt 'carrousal' on the onscreen prologue – to escape being terminated. Crichton notes that the film 'is really a statement about contemporary America's preoccupation with youth' (Crichton and Peary 1984: 250), with the young as efficient workers and consumers. Population control, which no one avoids, is here a spectacular event and is policed by the Sandmen, who track down anyone who tries to escape. One Sandman, Logan (Michael York), is assigned to a sanctuary outside the domed city where rumour suggests the fugitives congregate. Logan finds an Old Man (Peter Ustinov) and his cats in the remains of the government buildings in Washington DC and realises that his way of life is a simulation. Brosnan is rightly cynical, seeing the old man as merely 'old, wrinkled, and senile' (1978: 243). In a reactionary move, old age is embraced – old men may offer a vision of the earlier world, as in Sol (Edward G. Robinson) in *Soylent Green* (Richard Fleischer, 1973) – although it is not clear how the youthful population will survive after the computer which runs their society has destroyed the city and left them homeless in an area that may be dosed with radiation.

Radiation poisoning was one danger of increasing the use of nuclear energy in response to the 1970s fuel crisis. *The Big Bus* plays with nuclear energy as part of its parodic satire in imaging a nuclear-powered bus travelling between New York and Denver. *The China Syndrome* features a news reporter (Jane Fonda) and her cameraman (Michael Douglas) and a plant supervisor (Jack Lemmon) discovering safety cover-ups at a nuclear power station, which risks going into meltdown, the supervisor being 'helplessly in thrall to a parochial utility management whose allies include the police' (Goldman 1989: 277). Less than a fortnight after the film's release, there was a core meltdown at Three Mile Island, Pennsylvania, which must have added to a sense of insecurity about new technology. In *The Chain Reaction*, an accident in a nuclear plant irradiates an engineer, Heinrich Schmidt (Ross Thompson), and then pollutes the water system. The Australian authorities are fitfully efficient in covering up the accident, but it is implied that they are powerless in dealing with the titular disaster, in which the radioactivity will enter the food chain and cause increasing damage through hierarchy of consumption. Not only does the car mechanic protagonist Larry Stilson (Steve Bisley) not stay ahead of the law, but everyone else fails as well.

The technologised apocalypse updated the Tower of Babel, but without the need for a jealous God. Humanity loses control of what has been created and cannot control the chaotic consequences. There was still a possibility of a nuclear conflict, as the Cold War moved through proxy campaigns in Vietnam and Afghanistan. It is fear of such a war that leads both the United States and Soviet Union to create supercomputers in *Colossus: The Forbin Project*. Goldman suggests that the film is a 'warning of the peril in automating the defense system, and of the delusion that we are in control of the technologies we create' (1989: 291), as neither the scientists nor the politicians have anticipated that the computers might choose to work together. All the structures built to protect the computers from human intervention mean that there is no reversing the process. The Cold War has to give way to a dictatorship, albeit one that is potentially benign.

When nuclear war does break out, familiar examples of architecture survive to forge a link with the past. Washington, DC is recognisable in *Logan's Run* and the Statue of Liberty in *Planet of the Apes* (Franklin J. Schaffner, 1968), even though society itself has been entirely redesigned. Tom Shippey uses the repeated example of the post-apocalyptic Statue of Liberty through sf as a variation on Roland Barthes's discussion of a black soldier saluting the French tricolour – an image on the cover of *Paris-Match* designed to illustrate loyalty and patriotism while disguising imperialism (Barthes 1973: 123). The depiction of the soldier is a Barthesian myth, denying the signification of imperialism, whereas 'the Statue is buried, [it is implied that] the United States must have collapsed, the very concept of liberty must have lost importance' (Shippey 1990: 106), making this image 'a "myth disfigured"' (1990: 107) – the denial of denial of American ideology. In this way the invisible forces of ideology can disguise themselves, as the fragile image of Liberty has survived, but its damaged state leaves space for an alibi of humility. Shippey discusses similar examples from four decades of American sf, but it is not limited to that part of the genre. In the French *Malevil*, a number of bombs destroy civilisation, killing most of the population, but not leaving too much in the way of radiation to cause further health problems. Here we move through the catastrophe, and wonder at what survives, rather than having to infer a narrative, although the retrospective nature of a first-person account calls this into question. The focus remains on the local: an already isolated thirteenth-century castle, Malevil, and village in rural France, with little sense of any wider political forces. Emmanuel Comte, a former schoolmaster, begins to build a subsistence community with co-workers, friends and villagers, attempting to remain free of the influence of La Roque, a nearby theocratic town whose leader, Fulbert, Comte sees as a fraud. Rather than a serious prediction of nuclear war and its after-effects, the set-up allows Merle to write a novel with contemporary sensibilities in a quasi-medieval setting, exploring the interaction between the secular and the religious in the state, showing great cynicism about power based on authority granted by religious beliefs. The structures that were constructed in pre-modern times survive into a postmodern age.

*Riddley Walker*, winner of the 1980 John W. Campbell Memorial Award and nominated for a Nebula in 1981, also follows a third world war which returns humanity to a quasi-medieval setting. The medieval architecture of Canterbury Cathedral relocates the centre of power to a union of church and state where it had been in the Middle Ages, encouraging the struggle of farmers against hunter-gatherers (foragers) in the recreating of a potentially re-technologised future. The map of east Kent is rewritten – Canterbury becomes Cambry, Folkestone becomes Fork Storn, Whitstable becomes Widders Bel and so forth. The devastation has been wreaked upon language, as its eponymous narrator speaks in an unfamiliar form of English. The actual war is half forgotten, told in puppet shows, and confused with the legend of St Eustace, a second-century Christian martyr, whom Hoban saw depicted in a wall painting in Canterbury Cathedral. The truth of what has happened cannot be firmly established – Walker comes to a new understanding of the past, but it remains another narrative.

In narrative terms, journeys across landscapes, such as that of Walker, both reveal and develop character. The settings in which individuals locate themselves have an impact upon their identity. Since the mid-nineteenth century, society has been increasingly organised around cities, to the benefit of industrial power. While the sheer weight of numbers of people in close proximity might offer a sense of exhilaration and the sort of transcendence that Wagar locates in Ballard, the melting pots of cultures, ethnicities, religions and nationalities were as likely to be alienating. The rationality of modern architecture aimed to create utopia, but this aim all too often failed, and those who found economic success would want to escape from those projects into the countryside. Increasingly, however, the areas outside cities were also defined by humanity's actions, whether in adapting them for leisure practices or polluting them with by-products of manufacturing and energy production. Nature was increasingly confined to managed reservations, merely a different form of theme park and a different form of dystopia. Meanwhile, computer-aided design programs allowed architects to push glass, metal and plastic into increasingly contorted shapes, in the name of postmodernism and an embracing of irrationality. The Westin Bonaventura Hotel (1974–76), designed by John C. Portman, Jr, 'aspires to being a total space, a complete world, a kind of miniature city' (Jameson 1991: 40), which is entirely disorientating; as Jameson argues, 'this latest mutation in space – postmodern hyperspace – has finally succeeded in transcending the capacities of the individual to locate itself [...] cognitively to map its position in a mappable external world' (1991: 44). The future was rupture.

# 16
# Ruptures: Metafiction and Postmodernism

Some of the sf of the 1970s had turned in on itself, partly in an attempt to find a way past the internecine warfare of the successors to First sf and the New Wave and partly to find a renewed sense of purpose, post-Apollo 11. The 'big dumb object' trope pastiched hard sf and authors drew on the works of (Mary) Shelley, Verne, Wells and Burroughs, allowing a post-imperial commentary on colonial narratives. New readers were the third generation to have grown up reading sf. Sometimes science fiction was referenced in sf texts as part of the verisimilitude – the captain kirks watched by characters in Philip K. Dick's *Flow My Tears, the Policeman Said* (1974) – on the principle that people in the future will still consume sf, or as in-joke – the Master (Roger Delgado) watching *The Clangers* (16 November 1969–10 October 1974) in 'The Sea Devils' (26 February–1 April 1972) or reading *War of the Worlds* (1898) in 'Frontier in Space' (24 February–31 March 1973) – but this could equally draw attention to the artificiality of the text. This could be sf about sf – the more explicit acknowledgment of any genre's conversation with its own rules and methods. In 1970, the critic and novelist William Gass coined the term 'metafiction' to refer to fiction that demonstrated knowledge of its own fictionality. William Shakespeare's *Henry V* (1599) draws attention to the fact that it is being performed, and Laurence Sterne's *Tristram Shandy* (1759–67) played games with the novel; now metafictional awareness was central to works by writers such as John Barth, Donald Barthelme, Christine Brook-Rose, E.L. Doctorow, John Fowles, B.S. Johnson, Muriel Spark and D.M. Thomas. Some of these writers also wrote sf, or something that looked like it, and will be discussed in this chapter among other postmodern sf writers: Robert Sheckley, Barry N. Malzberg, Richard Cowper, Christopher Priest, Kurt Vonnegut (and the film of *Slaughterhouse-5* (George Roy Hill, 1972)), Philip José Farmer, Richard Brautigan, Tom Robbins, Robert Shea and Robert Anton Wilson, William S. Burroughs, Thomas Pynchon, Doris Lessing, Kingsley Amis, Emma Tennant, Angela Carter, John Sladek, Frederik Pohl, the television programme *Welt am Draht* (*World on a Wire*/*World on Wires*, Rainer Werner Fassbinder, 1973) and the early work of the cyberpunks.

A decade and a half after Gass, Patricia Waugh argues that '[c]ontemporary metafictional writing is both a response and a contribution to an even more thoroughgoing sense that reality or history are provisional: no longer a world of eternal verities but a series of constructions, artifices, impermanent structures. The materialist, positivist and empiricist worldview on which realistic fiction is premised no longer exists' (1984: 7). This risks overstating a case and assumes that earlier generations of novelists were more naive about their practice than is actually plausible. In the nineteenth-century novel, there had been a tension between realism and the real, which might allow story-telling to be foregrounded. This was taken to extremes in metafiction, where the tension was one between the fictional and fiction, with the teller of the story stepping forward to act as a hero in his or her endeavours to write a novel, battling against invisible and unstoppable forces which militate against producing a narrative.

Examples within the sf genre include Philip K. Dick's post-1974 novels which attempted to represent his theological epiphanies, prepared for by *Flow My Tears, the Policeman Said* and *A Scanner Darkly* (1977), and Joanna Russ's *The Female Man* (1975), which includes instructions to the reader and its own reviews. Robert Sheckley's fiction had long parodied sf; *Options* (1975) shows Tom Mishkin crashing on the alien planet Harmonia, with only a robot programmed with advice for his intended destination for company. Mishkin can escape if he gets a spare part – an archetypal technological solution to a technical problem – but the mechanics of plot as always demand the delay of the fulfilment of desire. Sheckley, however, seems to despair of the reversals of his own plot, and even gives up at one point in favour of writing a cookery book.

The author's self-representation requires the representation of the author's world and the world that he or she imagines, which might be viewed as a series of Russian dolls, as worlds-within-worlds, but each is still fictional. Other novelists, such as Malzberg, Cowper and Priest, describe two parallel worlds, one realist, the other fantastical, then work to undermine the assumption that one is real and the other fantasy. In Malzberg's *Herovit's World* (1973), Jonathan Herovit is a hack sf writer going through a nervous breakdown as he cranks out the umpteenth novel featuring his character Mack Miller under the pseudonym Kirk Poland, and Poland appears to take Herovit's place; no one is spared the bile within the novel, whether readers, fans, publishers, wives or other writers. In *Galaxies* (1975), Malzberg repeatedly explains how difficult it is to write science fiction, and repeatedly draws attention to the metaphors for his characters' states of mind that he is drawing. Cowper's *Worlds Apart* (1974) is divided between the middle-aged teacher George Herbert Cringe – whose name echoes H.G. Wells's – scribbling an sf saga set on the planet Agenor, and Zil Bryn, on the planet Chnas, writing *Shorge Gringe's Pilgrimage*. Cringe has read Heinlein, Asimov, Aldiss and Wyndham, and sees nothing wrong with escapism, and it is not clear whether it is Cringe or Bryn who is to be taken as real when both characters are fictional. In Priest's *A Dream of Wessex* (1977), it is not clear that the dream world of Wessex that characters pass into is the fake one, and that the near-future terrorist-ridden England is real. The undecidable status of these worlds, neither explicable nor magical, places them within Todorov's genre of the fantastic.

The strategies of metafiction and the undecidability between reality and fiction were symptomatic of a wider cultural movement which itself proved almost impossible to define: postmodernism. A term first used to apply to architecture, and subsequently used within literary and cultural criticism, 'postmodernism' was initially a periodising term, used for example in Ihab Hassan's article 'POSTmodernISM' (1971) in relation to writers – such as Pynchon, Barth and Vonnegut – who were active from the 1950s but who produced their most significant work during the 1970s, some of whom wrote sf or something akin to sf. Jean-François Lyotard asserts in *The Postmodern Condition* (1979) that the contemporary world is distrustful of metanarratives such as modernity and progress towards utopia. The ability to narrate was under suspicion, and Lyotard offers alternatives of micronarratives, parologies and language games rather than overarching explanations; many authors of the 1970s tell secret histories and locate supposed conspiracies of invisible enemies. Jean Baudrillard describes the way in which reality is being colonised by advertising and the image of capitalism, with simulation, models and hyperreality replacing the real.

Fredric Jameson, in an influential essay, 'Postmodernism, or the Cultural Logic of Late Capitalism' (1984), notes the eclipse of history by nostalgia. 'Late capitalism' was a term applied by Ernest Mandel to the period of industrial capitalism after 1945, when the imperialism of national economies gave way to dominance by multinational corporations. As a Marxist – Jameson had been one of those Dick had apparently denounced to the FBI (Dick 1991: 110, cf. xxiii–xxv) – he would argue that the social superstructure (aesthetics, philosophy and culture) would alter with the shifting of the economic base. Jameson characterised postmodernism as being depthless, lacking (sincere) emotion, drawing on the sublime, depicting the death of the subject, rejecting notions of originality and being open to simulations, pastiching for its own sake and having a nostalgia for a mythical golden age.

Doctorow's *Ragtime* (1975) appears to be a historical novel covering events between 1902 and 1917, but was a Nebula award nominee. Real historical figures such as Harry Houdini, Emma Goldman, J.P. Morgan, Robert E. Peary and a murderer, Harry Kendall Thaw, mingle with fictional ones, including a family named only by their relationships and a black man, Michael Coalhouse. The latter is drawn from Heinrich von Kleist's 'Michael Kohlhaas (From an old chronicle)' (1810), which probably derives from *Marckishe Chonic* (Constantine 2004: 435), about the treatment meted out to Hans Kohlhase. In Kleist's tale, Kohlhaas seeks recompense for the mistreatment of his hired man and two horses from overzealous officials, and destroys the Junker Wenzel von Trenkel's castle and attacks Wittenberg. Kleist brought in Martin Luther and other historical figures as characters, but Doctorow, having updated the horse to a motor car, displaces the complexities of sixteenth-century Prussian, German and Polish nationalities onto 1920s American racism. Discussing *Ragtime*, Jameson argues that the 'historical novel can no longer set out to represent the historical past; it can only "represent" our ideas and stereotypes about that past' (1991: 25). Doctorow's characters derive from historical, fictional and intertextual discourses, the first part of the novel shifting bewilderingly between different characters, offering a patchwork secret history of part of the US. The purloined narrative of Coalhouse draws the threads together in the final sections of the novel, critiquing white male power.

Jameson situates Doctorow as 'the epic poet of the disappearance of the American radical past' (1991: 24), and that radical past is at the heart of Kurt Vonnegut's *Jailbird* (1979), as a secret history of corporate America. Vonnegut had begun his writing career within sf, but by the 1970s had become firmly established as a postmodern writer, whose novels often had introductions locating them within their author's life. Here he recalls union organiser and socialist, Powers Hapgood, who spoke on behalf of Ferdinando Sacco and Bartolomeo Vanzetti, both executed for alleged murders as the culmination of a process of victimisation for radical activities. Like Doctorow, Vonnegut mixes real with fictional characters – he describes a fictional massacre in a late-nineteenth-century labour dispute – but even his quasi-autobiographical introduction might still be fiction. His self-presentation enables him to point up a moral lesson from the Sermon on the Mount, about how the meek shall inherit the Earth and how those who fight for justice will eventually receive their reward. *Jailbird*'s narrator, Walter F. Starbuck, is a bit player on the edge of important historical events: a radical at Harvard; a member of the Young Communist League until the signing of the German–Soviet Treaty of Non-aggression in 1939 and, in 1949, in charge of a taskforce to investigate ground force tactics in a nuclear age. Inadvertently, he betrays a communist to Congressman Richard Nixon and, twenty years later, he finds himself as Nixon's special advisor on youth, unwittingly aiding some of the Watergate conspirators. On his release from jail for perjury and obstruction of justice, he becomes a vice president of the RAMJAC Corporation, a company with financial tentacles across all of American industry, whose majority stockholder is one of his former lovers. The book underlines the positive and negative sides to capitalism, but stops short of offering Nixon as purely a figure to blame, despite his causing misery to many for decades. Brian Stableford argues, 'Vonnegut seems to see the moral predicament of contemporary America in terms of a curious kind of moral entropy' (1980: 88). The malaise is wider than one hate figure.

Starbuck, like Malachi Constant of *Sirens of Titan* (1959) and Billy Pilgrim of Vonnegut's bestseller *Slaughterhouse-Five* (1969), seems to be the victim of a series of accidents. Whether such characters act or remain passive, they are carried along by events. This is evident in the film of *Slaughterhouse-5*, where Billy Pilgrim (Michael Sacks) comes unstuck in time: he can exit a room in the 1950s and arrive in the 1930s. His life is defined by two poles of experience: being a prisoner of war in Dresden during the American firebombing of the city and living with a Playboy model, Montana Wildhack (Valerie Perrine), in an alien zoo, having been kidnapped by the Tralfamadorians. Pilgrim has no control over his life, since everything feels predestined: he knows where and how he will die, he knows what will happen to his wife and family, he knows he will survive an air crash. No explanation is offered for this time travelling, but the viewer is at least aided by being able to read a description of his life as Pilgrim types it, and can realise that there is a dislocation going on. The Tralfamodorians, who see time and duration differently from humans, counsel a policy of concentrating on the happy memories and avoiding the trauma – a curiously stiff-upper-lip approach which seems to suggest putting up with reality rather than trying to change life for the better.

The film offers no equivalent to Vonnegut's autobiographical self-positioning as witness to Dresden's firebombing, who might find some form of catharsis by addressing his Second World War experiences. In *Breakfast of Champions, or Goodbye Blue Monday* (1973), Vonnegut attempts to free his cast of characters from earlier novels, to begin with a clean slate, in explicit homage to Thomas Jefferson who, at the age of fifty – Vonnegut's then age – freed his slaves. The narrative is as slight as the narration is heavy, as Vonnegut repeatedly discusses earlier drafts of the novel, comments on what will happen and introduces new elements to make the story work.

We are told that Dwayne Hoover, a widower and car dealer, will go on a rampage when hack sf writer Kilgore Trout gives him a copy of one of his books, *Now It Can Be Told*. This is a second-person narrative in which the reader is told that they are the only person with free will rather than being programmed by the Creator of the Universe. Hoover has no free will, precisely because he is a fictional character in a novel. On the other hand, Vonnegut cannot control all of his own creation: he observes an artist defending a work of art, *The Temptation of Saint Anthony*, an entirely green canvas with a stripe of day-glo orange reflective tape: '[it] shows everything about life which truly matters, with nothing left out. It is a picture of the awareness of every animal. [... O]ur awareness is all that is alive and maybe sacred in any of us. Everything else about us is dead machinery' (Vonnegut 1974: 205). Vonnegut presents himself as burnt out, depressed by the misfortunes that have met his family, worried about committing suicide and cynical about contemporary artists, but the justification for art which he finds himself putting into the mouth of another artist is the spiritual heart of the novel. His own final encounter with his creation Trout does not go as planned. While Vonnegut is literarily the father of Trout, Trout in fact reminds Vonnegut of his own father. In a final drawing, one of hundreds that litter the novel, Vonnegut sheds a tear, as much for his lost family as for Trout, but also in mourning for the loss of his freed slaves. Vonnegut has to employ new characters to tell his stories – although Trout, who had also appeared in *God Bless You Mr Rosewater* (1965) and *Slaughterhouse-Five*, was to return in *Jailbird*, as the alias of a supposed traitor, Bob Fender, and in his own right in *Galápagos* (1985) and *Timequake* (1997). As a mouthpiece who could express absurd and surreal visions of alternative worlds, as well as being a cipher for the writer in the contemporary world, Trout was too simply useful to Vonnegut to abandon.

Others found him useful, too; Philip José Farmer used the name, with Vonnegut's permission, to write a full-length novel, *Venus on the Half-Shell* (*F&SF* 1974; 1975). Farmer had long played metafictional games – the Riverworld books contain real historical figures alongside the fictional and a version of himself, *Tarzan Alive* (1972) and *Doc Savage: His Apocalyptic Life* (1973) were mock biographies of the pulp heroes, and he also wrote sequels to other authors' novels, including *The Wind Whales of Ishmael* (1971), a follow-up to Herman Melville's *Moby-Dick* (1851). *Venus on the Half Shell* features Simon Wagstaff the Space Wanderer, an immortal human who, after aliens flood the Earth, travels the universe in search of the answer to the question, 'Why are we created only to suffer and die?'. Simon passes through a number of absurd alien worlds and ecologies, which pastiche the sort of imaginary locations imagined for him by Vonnegut. Farmer-as-

Trout creates a further author, Jonathan Swift Somers III, whose works are alluded to throughout the novel and whose name echoes that of satirist Jonathan Swift; Farmer went on to write stories such as 'A Scarletin Study' (*F&SF* March 1975) and 'The Doge Whose Barque Was Worse Than His Bight' (*F&SF* November 1976) as Somers. The latter features the dog Ralph von Bow Wow, who is mentioned in *Venus* and is an award-winning novelist himself. Claudia Jannone suggests that 'the novel itself is a maze of structures which reflect other structures like mirrors' (1976: 111). While Simon wanders through a series of alien worlds, travelling in his phallic spaceship at up to 69 times the speed of light, literary and cultural allusions tie him back to human culture as if emphasising the author-created nature of it all; for example, the titular Venus alludes to Botticelli's *Birth of Venus*, but the character Chworktap is an anagram of Patchwork, a character from *The Patchwork Girl of Oz* (1913). There are also more sexual references than in Vonnegut's version of Trout, but it is perhaps the logical progression of Vonnegut's original conception that Trout's works were published as filler in pornographic magazines.

The short, often fantastic, novels of Richard Brautigan often play with metafictive techniques, and they moves between genres, as if he cannot settle to a single style to represent his world view. *The Hawkline Monster: A Gothic Romance* (1974) welds together western, gothic romance and science fiction, centring on two gunmen, Greer and Cameron, who have been employed to destroy the monster who lives in the ice caves beneath Miss Hawkline's mansion and may have killed her father – in fact, the father had been transformed into a umbrella stand. *Sombrero Fallout: A Japanese Novel* (1976) intercuts the story of a depressed author, who has lost his Japanese lover, and the abandoned manuscript – about a sombrero falling to the ground – he has thrown into a waste paper basket. The story takes on a life of its own, despite being abandoned by its author, which is a metaphor for the publication process of any fiction. *Dreaming of Babylon: A Private Eye Novel 1942* (1977) features a private eye, C. Card, so far down on his luck and his finances as to be parodic, shortly after the US entered the Second World War. His job, to steal a corpse from a morgue, make little sense to him or to the reader, and his focus is not helped by his daydreams or travels to ancient Babylon where he was a baseball star, nor by his planning an sf serial in his head, which he eventually tags *Smith Smith Versus the Shadow Robots*. Despite the whimsy, which Brautigan shares to some degree with Vonnegut, there is clearly a dark subtext to his fictions, dealing as they do with abandonment, murder, loss and abortion.

Brautigan's *Trout Fishing in America* (1967) had featured Trout Fishing in America as an activity, a character and a hotel, and celebrates its own progress as a novel; it is explicitly acknowledged in Tom Robbins's *Another Roadside Attraction* (1971). The narrative is related by one Max Marvellous, who conceals his true identity within the narrative and leaps around in his chronology, acknowledging the problems he has in writing the book. The titular roadside attraction is simultaneously wondrous and phoney – consisting of two garter snakes, a tsetse fly encased in amber and a flea circus, as well as a burger stand. The enterprise is destroyed by the reappearance of their drug-dealing friend, Plucky Purcell, who has found Christ's corpse in the catacombs under the Vatican. Not only would such a discovery require a rethinking of the Christian metanarrative – at the very least there can have been no ascension – but also a questioning of the history of the Catholic church.

Robbins's second novel, *Even Cowgirls Get the Blues* (1976), is more metafictive. Again there is anonymised first-person narration – the narrator is revealed to be a Dr Robbins, whom readers are likely to associate with Robbins the author, even if the two are not identical. While *Another Roadside Attraction* is declared to be a Sagittarius (1971: 189), here Robbins celebrates getting to chapter 88, comparing the novel to the keys on a piano, and notes the arrival of the hundredth chapter. The novel offers a stew recipe and rhapsodises on its own sentences: 'This sentence is made out of lead [...] This sentence is made of yak wool [...] This sentence is proud to be part of the team here at *Even Cowgirls Get the Blues*. This sentence is rather confounded by the whole damn thing' (1991: 108). As with *Breakfast of Champions*, the plot is thin: Sissy Hankshaw, the best hitchhiker in the world thanks to her enormous thumbs, is sent by a homosexual tycoon, The Countess, to his ranch, now occupied by the titular cowgirls. Robbins attempts to embrace feminism, as he shows the cowgirls to be efficient at their jobs and apologises for his use of generic male pronouns. In a conspiratorial subplot, the cowgirls' inadvertent detention of the last flock of whooping cranes at their lake, there is a coincidental echo of how rare Russ declares female congress members to be in *The Female Man*, and Amanda in *Another Roadside Attraction* had noted them in her listing of rare birds.

Robbins has less confidence in his progress in *Still Life With Woodpecker* (1980). The four phases of the novel are bracketed by authorial asides, noting his acquisition of a new Remington typewriter (the same make, if not the same model, as that used by Marvellous) which will help him write the new book, his disillusionment with the machine, his repainting it and final abandonment of it in favour of writing the last few pages by hand. The novel's blurb announces it as a love story set in a packet of cigarettes, which not exactly a straightforward summation: the ostensible romance is between Princess Leigh-Cheri, a member of an exiled royal family, and Bernard Mickey Wrangle, an anarchist bomber, who recounts a secret history of the United States, the conspiracy by red heads who added the pyramid to the dollar bill and Egyptian imagery to Camel cigarettes. Behind this history may lie aliens from the planet Algol, suggesting a *Chariots of the Gods?*-style uplift of humanity.

Robert Shea and Robert Anton Wilson's Illuminatus! Trilogy (1975), consisting of *The Eye in the Pyramid*, *The Golden Apple* and *Leviathan*, written when they were editing and writing for *Playboy* in the late 1960s and 1970s, expounded upon similar conspiracy theories. At the heart of the trilogy is the Illuminatus conspiracy – symbolised by the eye in a pyramid, which appears in the Great Seal of the United States on the dollar bill – which is secretly controlling the world. The conspiracy includes the assassinations of John Dillinger and John F. Kennedy, both connected to supposed numerology about the significance of the number 23, as well as of Robert Kennedy. The death of John F. Kennedy – also anatomised by Ballard and Malzberg – can stand as the moment of postmodern rupture, a moment of loss of innocence after which everything went wrong. In rewriting this event, authors perhaps hope either to foreground the trauma of the period or to point to an alternative to this imagined fall. The Illuminatus! books satirise conspiracy theories and belief in synchronicity, while adding to the ongoing speculation about the Kennedy assassination, feeding beliefs in an alternative metanarrative of conspiracy. It was perfect material for British actor Ken Campbell to adapt into a ten-hour play for his Science Fiction Theatre of Liverpool, which transferred to the new Cottesloe stage at the London National Theatre in 1977 (Coveney 2011: 91-111.).

The assassination of Dillinger and the magic of 23 had already fed into the works of William S. Burroughs; an interest in another gangster led to a screenplay, *The Last Words of Dutch Schultz* (1970), which riffed upon his cryptic dying words ('French-Canadian bean soup'). In the 1970s, Burroughs worked through another period of experimentation, using his collage writing techniques of cut-ups and fold-ins, which broke the linear order of sentences by changing their structure or importing texts from elsewhere. Much material appeared in pamphlets and small press editions before wider dissemination, but he also made films and sound recordings. *The Wild Boys: A Book of the Dead* (1971) and *Port of Saints* (1973, rev. 1980) are the closest he got to coherent novels in the period. Insofar as the former has an overarching plot (it is predominantly a series of overlapping vignettes which quote from each other and from other parts of Burroughs's oeuvre), it features a pansexual gang of young men who battle the oppressive international police forces, travelling through time attempting to rewrite history, as well as having sex with each other. *Blade Runner (A Movie)* (1979) was a loose treatment for a film of an Alan E. Nourse novel, *The Blade Runner* (1974), about black market medical services in a dystopian America. Burroughs's volume is set in a right-wing future, devastated by a mutated virus, and uses racism and homophobia to disturbing and satiric effect.

Conspiracy theories offer retrospective rationalisations for history – which is not to say that the retrofitted metanarrative is itself rational. Pynchon's *Gravity's Rainbow* (1973), nominated for a Nebula Award, contains a number of conspiracies: the odd patterning of the fall of the Second World War German V-2 rockets, a mysterious device known as the Schwarzgerät (or black device), a psychic warfare group and the career of Tyrone Slothrop and the nature of paranoia. Pynchon feeds in quotations, references to movies and lyrics both real and fictional. However, John Brunner detects historical inaccuracies in the novel, arguing that Pynchon 'elaborates a complex and incontestably science-fictional retrospective parallel world' (1976: 22), The book offers a supposed secret history of the Second World War which, thanks to the insertion during the proofing stage of a quotation attributed to Nixon, dovetails with the Watergate scandal. The piling up of endless layered detail gives the impression of verisimilitude, a sense of historicity (to borrow from Jameson), in the manner of Brunner's disaster fictions, Moorcock in the Cornelius Quartet or Deighton in his spy novels.

Deighton imagines a conspiracy and an alternative version of the Second World War in *SS-GB* (1978). In a Nazi-occupied Britain, Detective Superintendent Douglas Archer is called upon to investigate a senseless murder, which connects both to a conspiracy to control knowledge about nuclear physics and to a plot to smuggle King George VI out of the country. Archer is used as part of an ongoing struggle between different factions of the German command. Deighton does not wear his research lightly, but is not especially interested in the actual Jonbar Point which makes his fictional world distinct from the real one, preferring instead to use the aftermath as a setting for a marriage between his expertise in espionage and the Second World War.

A similar focus on the aftermath of change is found in Amis's *The Alteration* (1976), another alternative history novel written by an outsider to the genre, albeit one sympathetic to sf (he had delivered lectures on the genre published as *New Maps of Hell* (1960) and coedited several sf anthologies with Robert Conquest, perhaps out of the feeling that sf was an acceptable alternative to good taste, along with jazz). With an explicit reference to Dick's *The Man in the High Castle* (1962), *The Alteration* features a world in which there was no Reformation and thus one in which the political map of the world is different. The sense of the arbitrariness of historical events – that a war might be lost or won – is perhaps at odds with the conspiratorial view of history: this is history as happenstance. At the same time, most of the names of artists, writers, composers and politicians that Amis invokes are familiar, suggesting, say, that a David Hockney will emerge despite the possible different trajectories of history.

Persian-born Lessing wrote two stand-alone fantastic novels and started the more science-fictional Canopus in Argos series. *Briefing for a Descent into Hell* (1971) features two doctors arguing over the diagnosis of classics professor Charles Walker, who recalls a voyage on a giant bird. It is impossible to be certain who is right, or whether Walker has indeed been on a cosmic journey. *Memoirs of a Survivor* (1974) is set in a disintegrating, dystopian Britain, where its unnamed narrator dreams of another world behind her apartment's walls, which is reminiscent of her childhood. Again, it is impossible to adjudicate between the realities of a nightmare and a wish fulfilment. Emissaries from the galactic empire of Canopus visit and describe Earth in *Re: Colonised Planet 5, Shikasta* (1979), telling a very different history of the planet because of their alien perspective of controlling the development of society, and rescue a number of humans from World War Three, as Lessing explores the nature and ethics of power. *The Marriages Between Zones Three, Four and Five* (1980) is set in several of the metaphysical zones which extend from Earth/Shikasta: a violent Zone Four barbarian is forced to marry first a peaceful Zone Three queen and then a more primitive Zone Five. Here Lessing is examining gender politics, as well as the topic of forms of power. *The Sirian Experiments* (1980) describes Shikasta from the perspective of a second galactic empire, that of the Sirian, who are genetically manipulating humans, as a third empire, the Shammat, attempts to control the species on a version of Earth.

Tennant's novels had a new wave sensibility. *The Time of the Crack* (1973) featured a contemporary London riven by the titular chasm opening up along the Thames, risking the southernmost part of England snapping off, a cosy catastrophe that had space for both a women's enclave and a Playboy Bunnygirl as a major character. In *Hotel de Dream* (1976), one tenant's dreams seem to take an existence of its own and feeds into the novel being written by someone else resident in the boarding house, to the extent that the distinctions between reality, fiction and dream can no longer be made. Reality is a matter of taking control of the narrative, if not the metanarrative. In *The Bad Sister* (1978) an editor tries to piece together the story of the murder of one Michael Dalzell and his daughter, alternating with the account of his other daughter, Jane, mass murderer, film critic and a female

Jerry Cornelius. Marilyn C. Wesley argues that '[the] overall effect of Tennant's fiction is to suggest that the feminine zone of mythic childhood must finally "fall" into the masculine province of social and economic power' (2000: 186), although the characters can sometimes transcend it. *Wild Nights* (1979) and *Alice Fell* (1980) are both variants on the Persephone myth, which focus on the coming of age of young female characters, offering rare female Bildungsromans.

Tennant is as subversive of gender norms – whether patriarchal or feminist – as the much more discussed Carter, whose *The Passion of New Eve* (1977) undercuts notions of both innate and performed sex and gender in its narrative of a male professor, Evelyn, reconstructed as a woman by the cult leader Mother and then enslaved by Zero as part of a harem. Nicoletta Vallorani suggests that Carter 'discovers in sf an unprecedented potential for rupture' (1994: 369); Carter simultaneously undercuts metanarratives of patriarchy and feminism. She also worked in the genre of fairy tales, both translating Perrault's fairy tales (1979), rescuing them from several centuries of being made suitably moral for children, and collecting tales from around the world. The collection *The Bloody Chamber* (1979) drew on 'Little Red Riding Hood', among others, describing the sexual awakening of young women and their mistreatment, but also the attractiveness of the wolves.

Such postmodernist fantasists described impossible worlds that simply *are*, without the kind of rational explanation which genre science fiction would offer. For example, in *The Müller-Fokker Effect* (1970) Sladek depicted the hallucinatory experiences of a man recorded on magnetic tape. As technology developed, these experiences were imagined as taking place inside computers, such as the Matrix of 'The Deadly Assassin' (30 October–20 November 1976) in *Doctor Who*. Daniel F. Galouye's *Simulacron-3* or *Counterfeit World* (1964) had been a satirical near future in the manner of Frederik Pohl and C.M. Kornbluth, where opinion polls were an obligatory part of every citizen's daily life, before the characters discover that they are inside a computer simulation. A two-part adaptation, *Welt am Draht*, was broadcast on West German television. Fassbinder filmed a grey, contemporary Germany, enlivened only by reflective surfaces opening an illusion of space, in an attempt to convince the viewer that this future was real, but also disorientating what is seen directly rather than mediated. Fassbinder's visual models seem to be *Alphaville, ou une adventure étrange de Lemmy Caution* (Jean-Luc Godard, 1965) and the modernist design of *A Clockwork Orange* (Stanley Kubrick, 1971). As in the novel, a computer engineer, Fred Stiller (Klaus Löwitsch), has created a virtual environment in a computer. His supervisor is murdered, but nobody but Stiller seems to remember him, although a previously unmentioned daughter of the supervisor appears as if from nowhere. Stiller first realises that there can be a movement between the virtual reality and his own reality, and then that the world he takes to be real is in fact also virtual. The everyday is defamiliarised, as Stiller invokes the ideas of Plato and Aristotle, in a nod towards the notion that what we perceive as the real world is a copy of the world of ideals. The *mise en abyme* need not stop here: Stiller has no proof that he has entered *the* authentic world rather than just another one. This is derived from Galouye's novel, but was familiar from the ontological play of Dick's novels.

The simulation was to become a key trope of postmodernism, especially with the emergence of cyberpunk in the 1980s – 'henceforth, for many of us, the supreme *literary* expression if not of postmodernism, then of late capitalism itself' (Jameson 1991: 419). While this subgenre was revolutionary in the 1980s, and came with a rhetorical dismissal of the sf of the 1970s as 'confused, self-involved, and stale' (Sterling 1986: 9), it was not entirely without precedent. Pohl's novel of the posthuman, *Man Plus* (1976), is narrated by a computer: 'the mysterious narrator [is] finally revealed as the consciousness of our linked computers […] The machines have given false data to the military political analysts, because their aim is to insure their own survival' (Samuelson 1980: 90). The central character, Roger Torraway, is an experimental subject in an attempt to colonise Mars in the context of a probable apocalypse; his body is transformed into a cyborg, but his brain also needs transformation, in order to deal with the sensory overload. Sladek notes the malign forces of NASA, the military and politicians responsible for Torraway's condition, and how Pohl even humanises the president – a couple of years after Nixon resigned: 'They are, after all, moved by impersonal forces such as popularity polls, political forecasts, projections of the world's energy resources, forces beyond which there is no appeal' (1978: 91). The novel won Pohl a Nebula, as well as nominations for the Hugo, the John W. Campbell Memorial and Locus Awards, and Roz Kaveney suggests that Pohl 'transcended the slick formulae on which he had come to rely exclusively' (1981: 16). While the novel looks back to *Colossus: The Forbin Project* (Joseph Sargent, 1970), it also anticipates the AIs and posthumans of cyberpunk.

Several of the writers central to cyberpunk first published in the 1970s. Bruce Sterling's 'Man-Made Self' appeared in *Lone Star Universe* (1976) and his debut novel, *Involution Ocean* (1977) was a pastiche of *Moby-Dick* set on a sand ocean. *The Artificial Kid* (1980) gave a better indication of his future direction, the character of R.T. apparently a professional combat artist famed for videos of his fight, but actually a stored personality of a ruler of the planet. Sterling had found his themes, but not yet his voice. William Gibson's one published story of the 1970s, 'Fragments of a Hologram Rose' (*Unearth* July 1977), establishes his early style – showing his future rather than explaining it, moving between locations and juxtaposing nature and technology. Parker, more probably named for the anti-hero of Richard Stark's thrillers than for Spider-Man's alter ego, uses a tape of his ex-girlfriend's sensory experiences to escape the pain of their break-up. There has been a second American revolution or civil war, and Japanese industries now dominate. In a fictional fragment of a non-fiction book, Gibson points to an epistemological rupture: 'the final shift away from the Lascaux/Gutenberg tradition of a pre-holographic society' (1986: 56), moving from a supposedly two-dimensional iconic system of representation to something even more complex. Marshall McLuhan's *The Gutenberg Galaxy: The Making of Typographic Man* (1962) had argued that human consciousness had shifted with the appearance of the printed book. By the late 1970s, it seemed likely that computer technology, as it both advanced and became domesticated, would offer a further rupture. The immersive, artificial realities (as pioneered by Myron W. Krueger through the 1970s) in computers and the hyperreal theme parks offered postmodern locations, whereas cyborgs offered a way of imagining postmodern subject identities. Cyberpunk would revolutionise postmodern sf, and the genre's critical reception.

# Epilogue

The science-fiction field was about to undergo radical change, as was its reception. A new subgenre, cyberpunk, was to emerge from the typewriters of William Gibson and Bruce Sterling, among others, not only in their fiction, but also in the fanzines edited by Sterling. Like many new movements, they disparaged and dismissed their predecessors; Sterling looked back to the New Wave of the 1960s, rather than the 1970s, in a typical generational act of anxiety of influence: 'SF in the late Seventies was confused, self-involved, and stale' (1986: 9). The work of John Brunner might be acknowledged, but not much else from the decade. In an era of home computers – PCs – and home entertainment – VCRs – technology was transforming the domestic space, and cyberpunk represented one version of this world.

The descriptions of postmodernism advanced by Jean Baudrillard and Jean-François Lyotard were joined by Fredric Jameson's, in 'Postmodernism and Consumer Society' (1983), first delivered as a lecture in 1983, and then in 'Postmodernism, or the Cultural Logic of Late Capitalism' (1984). Meanwhile, Donna Haraway developed her version of the cyborg as a new feminist identity which questions notions of sex, race and class by drawing upon existing sf – especially the works of Octavia Butler, Samuel R. Delany, Vonda McIntyre, Joanna Russ, James Tiptree Jr, John Varley and Monique Wittig, all active during the 1970s. Collectively, these theoreticians brought a new academic audience to sf, and the genre gained critical credibility. Marleen Barr did much to map out the genre from a feminist perspective, with *Future Females: A Critical Anthology* (1981), and Tom Moylan coined the term 'critical utopia' in *Demand the Impossible* (1986), a study of *The Dispossessed* (1975), *The Female Man* (1975), *Woman on the Edge of Time* (1976) and *Triton* (1976), which drew on articles first published in *Extrapolation* and *Science Fiction Studies*, among other places. The works of the 1970s were often unacknowledged springboards for the ideas of the 1980s.

Brian Stableford, in his account of the 1970s, saw 1970 as a moment of optimism: 'From the viewpoint of 1970, it looked as if the last barriers to the progress of the genre had been removed' (1998: 21). It was a time of economic optimism, of authors finally being paid decent amounts of money for their work, and there were more professional sf writers than ever before. But while the optimism offered scope for more artistic sf, the marketplace became dominant. This is seen in the stalled careers of such British writers as Barrington Bayley, John Brunner, Keith Roberts and Josephine Saxton (1998: 21), and in the treatment of Stanisław Lem by the SFWA, who was stripped of his honorary membership of the organisation. On the one hand, it was felt that Lem could afford to pay dues if he wanted to be a member; on the other hand it looked like an act of revenge for Lem's attitude to American sf. Lem was the author of articles about sf titled 'A Hopeless Case – With Exceptions' and another called 'A Visionary Among the Charlatans'. In a piece in the February 1975 *Frankfurter Allgemeine Zeitung*, translated as 'Looking Down on Science Fiction: A Novelist's Choice for the World's Worst Writing' in the August 1975 issue of *Atlas World Press Review*, Lem dismissed American science fiction as 'a literary form that claims to be a mythology of technological civilisation while in fact it is simply bad writing tacked together with wooden dialogue' (1977: 127). Lem insists that 'marketing prospects or official approval or similar concerns have no place intruding in that narrow gap between the author's eyes and the blank page' (1977: 128).

The appearance of the article in the *SFWA Forum* 41, a quasi-confidential publication, led a number of complaints from SFWA members, leading to his expulsion from the organisation. Ursula Le Guin wrote to *Science Fiction Studies* that, when the SFWA 'uses the tactics of the Soviet Writers Union, I think there is cause for concern, and reasons for shame' (Le Guin and Suvin 1977: 100). The controversy aired itself publicly in the pages of *Science Fiction Studies*: Pamela Sargent and George Zebrowski give a chronology of the events, Gregory Benford and Jack Dann regret that it has happened and Andrew Offutt, then SFWA president, argues that it was wrong that Lem had been made an honorary member in the first place. James Gunn criticises Lem's polemic by referencing the history of writing for money and suggesting 'Lem has not been deprived of life, freedom, money, or reputation. His work will continue to be published [...] as long as his publishers are happy with it [...] The SFWA action will not cost Lem a single sale' (1977: 314). Christopher Priest was to see the expulsion as an act of revenge (1980: 3) and felt that the organisation was 'a malign influence on science fiction' (1990b: 4).

But British critics were also wary of the influence of the market over what sf was being written. Roz Kaveney's survey of the 1970s criticises the 'packaging of authors' names and the conditioning of the audience to expect a particular product from a particular auctorial brandname' (1981:

34). Fantasy – thanks to J.R.R. Tolkien and Stephen Donaldson, among others – was to eclipse serious sf, as was the blockbuster sf movie. Stableford's survey argues that '1977 was the year which obliterated all the hopes which had been entertained for science fiction [...] We now know that the only kind of sf which has authentic mass-market appeal is "sci-fi": futuristic costume drama which not only plays no heed to matters of scientific plausibility but openly derides such considerations' (1998: 24). Kaveney and Stableford write from either side of the 1980s and 1990s, either side of the cyberpunk and post-cyberpunk booms, and Stableford seems to have the greater degree of pessimism about the trajectory of the genre from the perspective of writing nearly twenty years later. At the time, Baird Searles observes that 'optimistic romanticism is what, I think, the mass, non-s/f audience is joyfully getting from *Star Wars*, after a decade of films dominated by a cynical and vicious violence' (1977b: 100). Sf had become visible as a mass-market commodity, but might have vanished as a genre.

The end of the 1970s had seen a political change in Britain and the United States, with the election of the first female British prime minister, Margaret Thatcher, and that of a former Hollywood actor and governor of California, Ronald Reagan, as US president. Both were to set the political agenda for the next twenty years, with a shift away from the collective mentality that had been forged in the liberation movements of the 1960s and 1970s, into a more personal, even solipsistic philosophy. Thatcher set about destroying the power of the unions and transformed Britain from an industrial to a service economy, privatising state utilities, and Reagan brought an end to the Cold War with his championing of the Strategic Defense Initiative – satellites, mirror and lasers – which was inevitably nicknamed Star Wars. The scars of Vietnam were to be healed in new conflicts, and new interventions. As Roger Luckhurst argues, Thatcher and Reagan 'cemented a trans-Atlantic alliance around a fairly cohesive ideological formation that dominated the 1980s' (2005b: 196). A backlash to radicalism was underway – with the emergence of HIV/AIDS a phenomenon that could be used to seize a neoconservative, homophobic high ground.

Equality, if it was to be achieved, was now a matter of economic rather than social opportunity, in a supposed free market that was stacked in favour of multi-national corporations. The invisible enemies in the form of heterosexuality, patriarchy, capitalism, privilege and the bourgeoisie were no longer under the same degree of attack as a neoconservatism emerged – and the nihilism of the 1970s gave way to a new certainty which in time would attack (say) black single mothers as the root of all that was wrong with society. Whilst the 1970s had been a decade of ambiguous uncertainties, the 1980s was to be one of ironic certainties.

# Bibliography

Abbott, Stacey (2009) 'Arthouse Sf Film', Mark Bould, Andrew M. Butler, Adam Roberts and Sherryl Vint (eds) *Routledge Companion to Science Fiction* (London: Routledge): 463–67.
Adams, Douglas (1979) *The Hitchhiker's Guide to the Galaxy* (London: Pan).
— (1980) *The Restaurant at the End of the Universe* (London: Pan).
Adams, Richard (1972) *Watership Down* (London: Rex Collins).
Adams, Robert (1975) *The Coming of the Horseclans* (New York: Pinnacle Books).
— (1976) *Swords of the Horseclans* (New York: Pinnacle Books).
— (1977) *Revenge of the Horseclans* (New York: Pinnacle Books).
— (1979a) *A Cat of Silvery Hue* (New York: Signet).
— (1979b) *The Savage Mountains* (New York: Signet).
— (1980) *The Patrimony* (New York: Signet).
Adlard, Mark (1974) Review of David Gerrold, *The Man Who Folded Himself*, *Foundation* 6 (May): 100–101.
Albiez, Sean (2003) 'Know History!: John Lydon, Cultural Capital and the Prog/Punk Dialectic', *Popular Music* 22.3 (October): 357–74.
Aldiss, Brian W. (1955) 'Not For an Age', *The Observer* (9 January).
— (1965) 'The Saliva Tree', *F&SF* 23.3 (September).
— (1973) *Billion Year Spree: The History of Science Fiction* (London: Weidenfeld and Nicolson).
— (1974) *The Eighty-Minute Hour: A Space Opera* (London: Jonathan Cape).
— (1976) *The Malacia Tapestry* (London: Jonathan Cape).
— (1978a) *Enemies of the System: A Tale of Homo Uniformis* (London: Jonathan Cape).
— (1978b) 'The Gulf and the Forest: Contemporary SF in Britain', *F&SF* 54.4 (April): 4–11.
— (1980a) *Life in the West* (London: Weidenfeld and Nicolson).
— (1980b) *Moreau's Other Island* (London: Jonathan Cape).
— (1982) *Frankenstein Unbound* (London: Triad); orig. (London: Jonathan Cape, 1973).
— with David Wingrove (1986) *Trillion Year Spree: The History of Science Fiction* (London: Gollancz).
Alexander, Karl (1979) *Time After Time* (New York: Delacorte Press).
Altman, Dennis (1982) *The Homosexualization of America* (New York: St. Martin's).
Amis, Kingsley (1960) *New Maps of Hell* (New York: Harcourt, Brace).
— (1976) *The Alteration* (London: Jonathan Cape).
Anderson, Craig W. (1985) *Science Fiction Films of the Seventies* (Jefferson, NC: McFarland).

Antczak, Janice (1985) 'The Visions of H.M. Hoover', *Children's Literature Association Quarterly* 10.2 (Summer): 73–76.
Anthony, Piers (1968) *Sos the Rope* (New York: Pyramid Books).
— (1972) *Var the Stick* (London: Faber).
— (1975) *Neq the Sword* (London: Corgi).
— (1977) *A Spell for Chameleon* (New York: Ballantine).
— (1979) *Castle Roogna* (New York: Del Rey).
— (1979) *The Source of Magic* (New York: Del Rey).
Arbur, Rosemarie (1982) 'Leigh Brackett: No "Long Goodbye" is Long Enough', Tom Staicar (ed.) *The Feminine Eye* (New York: Ungar): 1–13.
Arrow, William (1976) *Escape from Terror Lagoon* (New York: Ballantine).
— (1976) *Man, the Hunted Animal* (New York: Ballantine).
— (1976) *Visions from Nowhere* (New York: Ballantine).
Ash, Brian (ed.) (1977) *The Visual Encyclopedia of Science Fiction* (London: Pan).
Asimov, Isaac (1950) *I, Robot* (New York: Gnome Press).
— (1966) *Fantastic Voyage* (New York: Houghton Mifflin).
— (1972) *The Gods Themselves* (Garden City, NY: Doubleday).
Attebery, Brian (1992) *Strategies of Fantasy* (Bloomington, IN: Indiana University Press).
Aul, Billie with Farah Mendlesohn (1998) 'Popular Science, Rewriting and Utopia: Or, the Revolution Will Not Take Place in a Fanzine', *Foundation* 74 (Autumn): 80–95.
Avallone, Michael (1970) *Beneath the Planet of the Apes* (New York: Bantam).
Bailey, Hilary (1976) Review of Arthur C. Clarke, *Imperial Earth* and Alfred Bester, *Extro*, *Foundation* 10 (June): 87–90.
— (1979) Review of Michael Moorcock, *Gloriana*, *Foundation* 15 (January): 86–90.
Baker, Brian (2005) 'Witness to the Ends of the World: Colonialism, the Scientific Romance and Michael Moorcock's *Nomad of the Time Streams* Trilogy', *Foundation* 93 (Spring): 40–48.
Ballard, J.G. (1962) 'Which Way to Inner Space?', *New Worlds* 40.1 (May): 2–3, 116–18.
— (1969) *The Atrocity Exhibition* (London: Jonathan Cape).
— (1972) 'The Greatest Television Show on Earth', *Ambit* 53 (Winter).
— (1973) *Crash* (London: Jonathan Cape).
— (1974a) *Concrete Island* (London: Jonathan Cape).
— (1974b) 'My Dream of Flying to Wake Island', *Ambit* 60 (Autumn).
— (1975) 'Some Words About *Crash!*', *Foundation* 10 (June): 44–54.
— (1976a) 'The Life and Death of God', *Low-Flying Aircraft and Other Stories* (London: Jonathan Cape).
— (1976b) *Low-Flying Aircraft and Other Stories* (London: Jonathan Cape).
— (1977) *High-Rise* (London: Panther); orig. (London: Jonathan Cape 1975).
— (1978) 'One Afternoon at Utah Beach', Christopher Priest (ed.) *Anticipations* (London: Faber and Faber).
— (1979) *The Unlimited Dream Company* (London: Jonathan Cape).
— (1981) *Hello America* (London: Jonathan Cape).
— (1984) *Empire of the Sun* (London: Gollancz).

Barbour, Douglas (1979) *Worlds out of Words: The SF Novels of Samuel R. Delany* (Frome: Bran's Head Books).

Barr, Marleen S. (ed.) (1981) *Future Females: A Critical Anthology* (Bowling Green, OH: Bowling Green State University Press).

— (1982) 'Holding Fast to Feminism and Moving Beyond: Suzy McKee Charnas's *The Vampire Tapestry*', Tom Staicar (ed.) *The Feminine Eye* (New York: Ungar): 60–72.

Barron, Neil (1979) '*The Unsleeping Eye*', Frank N. Magill (ed.) *Survey of Science Fiction Literature* (Englewood Cliffs, NJ: Salem Press): 2366–69.

Barthes, Roland (1973) *Mythologies*, trans. Annette Lavers (London: Granada).

Baudrillard, Jean (1983) *Simulations*, trans. Paul Foss, Paul Patton and Philip Beitchman (New York: Semiotext(e)).

— (2001) 'Barbara Kruger', Gary Genosko (ed.) *The Uncollected Baudrillard* (London and Thousand Oaks: Sage): 134–37.

Baum, L. Frank (1900) *The Wonderful Wizard of Oz* (Chicago: George M. Hill Company).

— (1913) *Patchwork Girl of Oz* (Chicago: Reilly and Britton).

Baxter, John (1978) *The Hermes Fall* (London: Simon & Schuster).

Beckett, Andy (2009) *When the Lights Went Out: Britain in the Seventies* (London: Faber and Faber).

Benchley, Peter (1974) *Jaws* (Garden City, NY: Doubleday).

Benford, Gregory (1976) *In the Ocean of Night* (New York: Dial Press).

— (1980) *Timescape* (New York: Simon & Schuster).

— and William Rotsler (1980) *Shiva Descending* (New York: St Martin's Press).

Benolie, Bernard (1977) 'Oldfield: With and without Bedford', *Tempo* 120 (March): 27–29.

Benshoff, Harry M. (2000) 'Blaxploitation Horror Films: Generic Reappropriation or Reinscription?', *Cinema Journal* 39.2 (Winter): 31–50.

Beresford, Elisabeth (1968) *The Wombles* (London: Ernest Benn).

Berger, James (1999) *After the End: Representations of Post-Apocalypse* (Minneapolis: University of Minnesota Press).

Berman, Michael (2011) 'Corporate Challenges to the Recovery of the Individual and History in *Rollerball* (1975)', Michael Berman and Rohit Dalvi (eds) *Heroes, Monsters and Values: Science Fiction Films of the 1970s* (Newcastle: Cambridge Scholars Press): 20–27.

Berlitz, Charles (1969) *The Mystery of Atlantis* (New York: Grosset & Dunlap).

— (1972) *Mysteries from Forgotten Worlds* (Garden City, NY: Doubleday).

— (1974) *The Bermuda Triangle* (Garden City, NY: Doubleday).

— (1977) *Without a Trace* (Garden City, NY: Doubleday).

— (1979) *The Philadelphia Experiment: Project Invisibility* (New York: Grosset & Dunlap).

— (1980) *The Roswell Incident* (New York: Grosset & Dunlap).

Bester, Alfred (1953) *The Demolished Man* (Chicago: Shasta Publishers).

— (1956) *The Stars My Destination* (London: Sidgwick & Jackson).

— (1975) *The Computer Connection* (New York: Berkley Books).

— (1980) *Golem$^{100}$* (New York: Timescape Books).

Bettelheim, Bruno (1976) *The Uses of Enchantment: The Meaning and Importance of Fairy Tales* (New York: Knopf).
Blake, William (1979) *Milton: A Poem*, Kay Parkhurst Easson and Roger R. Easson (eds) (London: Thames and Hudson).
Boehm, Carl (2000) 'Superman: The Myth through the Christ and the Revelation', *Journal of the Fantastic in the Arts* 11.3: 236–43.
Bond, Michael (1974) 'A Spoonful of Paddington', Biddy Baxter, Edward Barnes and Rosemary Gill (eds) *Blue Peter Eleventh Book* (London: BBC).
Booker, M. Keith (2004) *Science Fiction Television* (Westport, CT: Praeger).
Bould, Mark (2002) 'Not in Kansas Any More: Some Notes on Camp and Queer Sf Movies', *Foundation* 31 (Autumn): 40–50.
— (2005) 'Cyberpunk', David Seed (ed.) *A Companion to Science Fiction* (Oxford: Blackwell): 217–31.
—, Andrew M. Butler, Adam Roberts and Sherryl Vint (eds) (2009) *The Routledge Companion to Science Fiction* (London: Routledge).
— and Sherryl Vint (2011) *The Routledge Concise History of Science Fiction* (London: Routledge).
Boulding, Kenneth E. (1966) 'The Economics of the Coming Spaceship Earth', Henry Jarrett (ed.) *Environmental Quality in a Growing Economy*, Essays from the Sixth RFF Forum (Baltimore, MD: Resources for the Future/Johns Hopkins University Press): 3–14.
Boulter, Amanda (1995) 'Alice James Racoona Sheldon Jr: Textual Personas in the Short Fiction of Alice Sheldon', *Foundation* 63 (Spring): 5–30.
Brackett, Leigh (1940) 'Martian Quest', *Astounding* 24.6 (February).
— (1944) *No Good from a Corpse* (New York: Coward-McCann).
— (1949) 'Queen of the Martian Catacombs', *Planet Stories* 4.3 (Summer).
— (1949) 'Enchantress of Venus', *Planet Stories* 4.4 (Fall).
— (1951) 'Black Amazon of Mars', *Planet Stories* 4.1 (March).
— (1974a) *The Ginger Star* (New York: Ballantine).
— (1974b) *The Hounds of Skaith* (New York: Ballantine).
— (1976) *The Reavers of Skaith* (New York: Ballantine).
— and Edmond Hamilton (2003) 'Stark and the Star Kings', *Stark and the Star Kings* (Royal Oak, MI: Haffner Press).
Bradbury, Ray (1950) *The Martian Chronicles* (Garden City, NY: Doubleday).
— (1951) 'The Fireman', *Galaxy* 1.5 (February).
— (1953) *Fahrenheit 451* (New York: Ballantine).
— (1957) *Dandelion Wine* (Garden City, NY: Doubleday).
— (1971a) 'The Messiah', *Welcome Aboard* (Spring).
— (1971b) 'My Perfect Murder', *Playboy* (August).
— (1972a) *The Halloween Tree* (New York: Alfred Knopf).
— (1972b) 'The Parrot Who Met Papa', *Playboy* (January).
— (1973) 'The Wish', *Woman's Day* (December).
— (1976a) 'G.B.S. – Mark V', *Long After Midnight* (New York: Alfred Knopf).
— (1976b) 'A Story of Love', *Long After Midnight* (New York: Alfred Knopf).
— (1976c) *Long After Midnight* (New York: Alfred Knopf).
Bradley, Marion Zimmer (1958) *The Planet Savers* (New York: Ace).

— (1970) *The Winds of Darkover* (New York: Ace).
— (1971) *The World Wreckers* (New York: Ace).
— (1972) *Darkover Landfall* (New York: DAW).
— (1974) *The Spell Sword* (New York: DAW).
— (1975) *The Heritage of Hastur* (New York: DAW).
— (1976) *The Shattered Chain* (New York: DAW).
— (1977) *The Forbidden Tower* (New York: DAW).
— (1978) *Stormqueen!* (New York: DAW).
— (1979) *The Bloody Sun* (New York: DAW); orig. (New York: Ace, 1964).
— (1980) *Two to Conquer* (New York: DAW).
Brautigan, Richard (1967) *Trout Fishing in America* (San Francisco: Four Seasons Foundation).
— (1974) *The Hawkline Monster: A Gothic Romance* (New York: Simon & Schuster).
— (1976) *Sombrero Fallout: A Japanese Novel* (New York: Simon & Schuster).
— (1977) *Dreaming of Babylon: A Private Eye Novel 1942* (New York: Delacorte Press).
Britton, Andrew (1980/1981) 'Sideshows: Hollywood in Vietnam', *Movie* 27/28: 2–22.
Brizzi, Mary T. (1982) 'C. J. Cherryh and Tomorrow's New Sex Roles', Tom Staicar (ed.) *The Feminine Eye* (New York: Ungar): 32–47.
Broderick, Damien (2003) 'New Wave and Backwash: 1960–1980', Edward James and Farah Mendlesohn (eds) *The Cambridge Companion to Science Fiction* (Cambridge: Cambridge University Press): 48–63.
Brogan, Hugh (1986) *The Pelican History of the United States of America* (Harmondsworth, Middlesex: Penguin).
Brooks, Terry (1977) *The Sword of Shannara* (New York: Ballantine).
— (1983) *The Elfstones of Shannara* (New York: Ballantine).
Brosnan, John (1978) *Future Tense: The Cinema of Science Fiction* (New York: St Martin's Press).
Brunner, John (1968) *Stand On Zanzibar* (Garden City, NY: Doubleday).
— (1969) *The Jagged Orbit* (New York: Ace).
— (1972) *The Sheep Look Up* (New York: Harper & Row).
— (1974) *Total Eclipse* (Garden City, NY: Doubleday).
— (1975) *The Shockwave Rider* (New York: Harper & Row).
— (1976) 'Coming Events: An Assessment of Thomas Pynchon's *Gravity's Rainbow*', *Foundation* 10 (June): 20–27.
Budrys, Algis (1977) 'Books', *F&SF* 53.1 (July): 103–109.
— (1981) 'Books', *F&SF* 60.1 (January): 38–43, 156.
Burgess, Anthony (1962) *A Clockwork Orange* (London: William Heinemann).
Burnford, Sheila (1961) *The Incredible Journey* (London: Hodder & Stoughton).
Burroughs, William S. (1970) *The Last Words of Dutch Schultz* (London: Cape Goliard).
— (1971) *The Wild Boys: A Book of the Dead* (New York: Grove Press).
— (1973) *Port of Saints* (London: Covent Garden Press); rev. (Berkeley, CA: Blue Wind Press, 1980).
— (1979) *Blade Runner (A Movie)* (Berkeley, CA: Blue Wind Press).
Butler, Andrew M. (2005) 'Discontinuity and D. G. Compton's *The Continuous*

*Katherine Mortenhoe*', *Foundation* 93 (Spring): 67–75.
— (2009) 'Medusa Laughs: Birds, Thieves, and Other Unruly Women in the Works of Joanna Russ', Farah Mendlesohn (ed.) *On Joanna Russ* (Middletown, CT: Wesleyan University Press): 149–56.
Butler, Charles (2006) *Four British Fantasists: Place and Culture in the Children's Fantasies of Penelope Lively, Alan Garner, Diana Wynne Jones, and Susan Cooper* (Lanham, MD: Scarecrow Press).
Butler, Judith (1990) *Gender Trouble: Feminism and the Subversion of Identity* (London and New York: Routledge).
Butler, Octavia E. (1976) *Patternmaster* (Garden City, NY: Doubleday).
— (1977) *Mind of My Mind* (Garden City, NY: Doubleday).
— (1978) *Survivor* (Garden City, NY: Doubleday).
— (1979) *Kindred* (Garden City, NY: Doubleday).
— (1980) *Wild Seed* (Garden City, NY: Doubleday).
— (1984) *Clay's Ark* (New York: St Martin's Press).
Butterworth, Michael, and Michael Moorcock (1976) *The Time of the Hawklords* (London: Star).
— (1977) *Queens of Deliria* (London: Star).
Callenbach, Ernest (1975) *Ecotopia: The Notebooks and Reports of William Weston* (Berkeley, CA: Banyan Tree Books).
Cameron, Ian (1961) *The Lost Ones* (London: Hutchinson).
Carey, Peter (1972) 'Peeling', *Meanjin Quarterly* (March).
Carlsen, Chris (1977) *The Bull Chief* (London: Sphere).
— (1977) *Shadow of the Wolf* (London: Sphere).
— (1979) *The Horned Warrior* (London: Sphere).
Carlson, William (1972) 'Dinner at Helen's', Thomas N. Scortia (ed.) *Strange Bedfellows* (New York: Random House).
Carr, Terry (1978) *Cirque: A Novel of the Far Future* (New York: Fawcett).
Carter, Angela (1977) *The Passion of New Eve* (London: Gollancz).
Chapman, Edgar L. (1982) 'Sex, Satire, and Feminism in the Science Fiction of Suzette Haden Elgin', Tom Staicar (ed.) *The Feminine Eye* (New York: Ungar): 89–102.
Charnas, Suzy McKee (1974) *Walk to the End of the World* (New York: Ballantine).
— (1978) *Motherlines* (New York: Berkley).
— (1994) *The Furies* (New York: Tor).
— (1999) *The Conqueror's Child* (New York: Tor).
Chayefsky, Paddy (1978) *Altered States* (New York: Bantam).
Cherryh, C.J. (1976a) *Brothers of Earth* (New York: DAW).
— (1976b) *Gate of Ivrel* (New York: DAW).
— (1978a) *The Faded Sun: Kesrith* (New York: DAW).
— (1978b) *The Faded Sun: Shon'jir* (New York: DAW).
— (1978c) *Well of Shiuan* (New York: DAW).
— (1979a) *The Faded Sun: Kutath* (New York: DAW).
— (1979b) *Fires of Azeroth* (New York: DAW).
Christopher, John (1956) *The Death of Grass* (London: Michael Joseph).
Cixous, Helene (1980) 'The Laugh of the Medusa', trans. Keith Cohen and Paula

Cohen, Elaine Marks and Isabelle de Courtivron (eds) *New French Feminisms* (Amherst: University of Massachusetts Press): 99–106.
Clarke, Arthur C. (1951) *Childhood's End* (New York: Ballantine).
— (1972) *Rendezvous with Rama* (London: Gollancz).
— (1975) *Imperial Earth* (London: Gollancz).
— (1979) *The Fountains of Paradise* (London: Gollancz).
— and Gentry Lee (1989) *Rama II* (London: Gollancz).
— and Gentry Lee (1991) *The Garden of Rama* (London: Gollancz).
— and Gentry Lee (1993) *Rama Revealed* (London: Gollancz).
Cleaver, Pamela (1979) Reviews of Jan Mark, *The Ennead*, Louise Lawrence, *Star Lord* and Tanith Lee, *The Castle of Dark*, *Foundation* 16 (May): 91–93.
Cleman, Tom (1980) Reviews of *Jack of Shadows* by David Bedford; *Easter Fresco, for Soprano, Flute, Horn, Harp, Piano* by David Lumsdaine; *Quintet for Wind and Piano*, Op. 90 by Lennox Berkeley, *MLN Notes* 37.2 (December): 420–22.
Clement, Hal (1954) *Mission of Gravity* (Garden City, NY: Doubleday).
— (1971) *Star Light* (New York: Ballantine).
Clute, John (1974) 'Books', *F&SF* 47.3 (September): 42–47.
— (1980a) Review of J.G. Ballard, *The Unlimited Dream Company*, *Foundation* 19 (June): 84–85.
— (1980b) Review of Thomas M. Disch, *On Wings of Song*, *Foundation* 19 (June): 62–64.
— (1980c) 'Books', *F&SF* 59.6 (December): 38–44.
— (1981) Review of Robert A. Heinlein, *'The Number of the Beast –'*, *Foundation* 21 (February): 84–85.
— (1988) *Strokes: Essays and Reviews 1968–1986* (Seattle, WA: Serconia Press).
— (1995) *Look at the Evidence: Essays and Reviews* (Liverpool: Liverpool University Press).
— and Peter Nicholls (eds) (1993) *The Encyclopedia of Science Fiction* (London: Orbit).
Collier, Ann (1980) Review of Kate Wilhelm, *Juniper Time*, *Foundation* 19 (June): 79–81.
Collings, Michael R. (1986) *Brian Aldiss* (Mercer Island, WA: Starmont House).
Collyns, Robin (1974) *Did Spacemen Colonise the Earth?* (London: Pelham Books).
— (1975) *Laser Beams from Star Cities?* (London: Pelham Books).
— (1978) *Ancient Astronauts: A Time Reversal?* (London: Sphere).
Commoner, Barry (1973) *The Closing Circle: Nature, Man, and Technology* (New York: Knopf).
Compton, D.G. (1965) *The Quality of Mercy* (London: Hodder & Stoughton).
— (1968) *Synthajoy* (New York: Ace).
— (1970) *Chronocules* (New York: Ace).
— (1970) *The Steel Crocodile* (New York: Ace).
— (1972) *The Missionaries* (New York: Ace).
— (1974) *The Continuous Katherine Mortenhoe* (London: Gollanz).
— (1978) *A Usual Lunacy* (San Bernardino, CA: Borgo Press).
— (1979) *Windows* (New York: Berkley).
— (1980) *Ascendancies* (London: Gollancz).
Conan Doyle, Arthur (1912) *The Lost World* (London: Hodder and Stoughton).

Coney, Michael (1972) *Mirror Image* (New York: DAW).
— (1973) *Syzygy* (Morley: Elmfield Press).
— (1975) *Charisma* (London: Gollancz).
— (1977) *Brontomek!* (London: Pan); orig. (London: Gollancz, 1976).
Conrad, Joseph (1899) 'The Heart of Darkness', *Blackwood's Edinburgh Magazine* 165 (February–April); rev. *Heart of Darkness* (Edinburgh: Blackwood, 1902).
Constantine, David (2004) Notes, *Heinrich von Kleist: Selected Writings*, David Constantine (ed. and trans.) (Cambridge: Hackett): 429–42.
Cornea, Christine (2007) *Science Fiction Cinema: Between Fantasy and Reality* (Edinburgh: Edinburgh University Press).
Cosgrove, Denis (1994) 'Contested Global Visions: *One-World, Whole-Earth,* and the Apollo Space Photographs', *Annals of the Association of American Geographers* 84.2: 270–94.
Coveney, Michael (2011) *Ken Campbell: The Great Caper* (London: Nick Hern Books).
Cowper, Richard (1967) *Breakthrough* (London: Dennis Dobson).
— (1967) *Phoenix* (London: Dennis Dobson).
— (1971) *Domino* (London: Dennis Dobson).
— (1972a) *Clone* (London: Gollancz).
— (1972b) *Kuldesak* (Garden City, NY: Doubleday).
— (1973) *Time Out of Mind* (London: Gollancz).
— (1974a) *The Twilight of Briareus* (London: Gollancz).
— (1974b) *Worlds Apart* (London: Gollancz).
— (1976) 'Piper at the Gates of Dawn', *F&SF* 50.3 (March).
— (1978) *The Road to Corlay* (London: Gollancz).
— (1979a) *Profundis* (London: Gollancz).
— (1979b) Review of James Tiptree Jr, *Up the Walls of the World*, *Foundation* 15 (January): 73–75.
— (1980) Letter of Comment, *Foundation* 18 (January): 51–52.
— (1981) *A Dream of Kinship* (London: Gollancz).
— (1982) *A Tapestry of Time* (London: Gollancz).
Cowper, William (1995) *The Poems of William Cowper: 1782–1785*, John D. Baird and Charles Ryskamp (eds) (Oxford: Clarendon Press).
Creed, Barbara (1986) 'Horror and the Monstrous-Feminine: An Imaginary Abjection', *Screen* 27.1 (January): 44–71.
— (1993) *The Monstrous-Feminine: Film, Feminism, Psychoanalysis* (New York: Routledge).
Crichton, Michael and Danny Peary (1984) 'When Men and Machines Go Wrong An Interview with Michael Crichton', Danny Peary (ed.) *Omni's Screen Flights/Screen Fantasies: The Future According to Science Fiction Cinema* (Garden City, NY: Doubleday): 250–59.
Csicsery-Ronay, Istvan (2009) 'SF/Porn: The Case For *The Gas*', *Science Fiction Studies* 36.3 (November): 441–60.
Cummings, Michael S. 1989. 'Credibility of Transition in Callenbach's *Ecotopia Emerging*: Lessons for Practical Utopians', *Utopian Studies* 2: 69–77.
Cutler, Chris (1993) *File Under Popular: Theoretical and Critical Writings on Music* (New York: Autonomedia).

Dahl, Roald (1964) *Charlie and the Chocolate Factory* (New York: Knopf).
— (1972) *Charlie and the Great Glass Elevator* (New York: Knopf).
Davidson, Rjurik (2005) 'Form and Content in *The Centauri Device*', Mark Bould and Michelle Reid (eds) *Parietal Games: Critical Writings by and on M. John Harrison* (Liverpool: The Science Fiction Foundation): 265–74.
Davies, Philip John (ed.) (1996) *Representing and Imagining America* (Keele: Keele University Press).
Davis, Angela Y. (1981) *Women, Race, and Class* (New York: Vintage Books).
de Bolt, Joe (1975) *The Happening Worlds of John Brunner: Critical Exploration in Science Fiction* (Port Washington, NY: Kennikat Press).
Deighton, Len (1978) *SS-GB* (London: Jonathan Cape).
Delany, Samuel R. 'About Five Thousand One Hundred and Seventy-Five Words', *Extrapolation* 10.2 (May): 52–66.
— (1966) *Babel-17* (New York: Ace).
— (1967) *The Einstein Intersection* (New York: Ace).
— (1968) *Nova* (Garden City, NY: Doubleday).
— (1973) *The Tides of Lust* (New York: Lancer Books).
— (1974) 'The Profession of Science Fiction, 8: Shadows Part 1', *Foundation* 6 (May): 31–60.
— (1975a) *Dhalgren* (New York: Bantam).
— (1975b) 'The Profession of Science Fiction, 8: Shadows Part 2', *Foundation* 7/8 (March): 122–54.
— (1976) *Triton: An Ambiguous Heterotopia* (New York: Bantam).
— (1977) *The Jewel-Hinged Jaw* (Elizabethtown, NY: Dragon Press).
— (1978) *The American Shore: Meditations on a Tale of Science Fiction* (Elizabethtown, NY: Dragon Press).
— (1979a) *Heavenly Breakfast* (New York: Bantam).
— (1979b) 'The Tale of Gorgik', *Asimov's* (Summer).
— (1979c) 'The Tale of Old Venn', *Tales of Nevèrÿon* (New York: Bantam).
— (1979d) *Tales of Nevèrÿon* (New York: Bantam).
— (1990) 'On *Triton* and Other Matters: An Interview with Samuel R. Delany', *Science Fiction Studies* 17.3 (November): 295–324.
— (1995) *Hogg* (Boulder, CO: Black Ice Books).
Delap, Richard (1975) 'Books', *F&SF* 49.1 (July): 80–88.
— (1979) 'Books', *F&SF* 56.4 (April): 33–39.
Dery, Mark (1994) 'Black to the Future: Interviews with Samuel R. Delany, Greg Tate, and Tricia Rose', Mark Dery (ed.) *Flame Wars: The Discourse of Cyberculture* (Durham, NC and London: Duke University Press): 179–222.
Dick, Philip K. (1955) *Solar Lottery* (New York: Ace; b/w Leigh Brackett, *The Big Jump*).
— (1957) *The Cosmic Puppets* (New York: Ace; b/w Andrew North, *Sargasso of Space*).
— (1961) *The Man in the High Castle* (New York: Putnam).
— (1964) *The Three Stigmata of Palmer Eldritch* (Garden City, NY: Doubleday).
— (1968) *Do Androids Dream of Electric Sheep?* (Garden City, NY: Doubleday).
— (1970) *Our Friends from Frolix 8* (New York: Ace).
— (1972) *We Can Build You* (New York: DAW).

— (1974) *Flow My Tears, the Policeman Said* (Garden City, NY: Doubleday).
— (1977) *A Scanner Darkly* (Garden City, NY: Doubleday).
— (1981) *VALIS* (New York: Bantam).
— (1985) *Radio Free Albemuth* (New York: Arbor House).
— (1986) 'The Unpublished Prescript to Flow My Tears', *PKDS Newsletter* 12 (November): 2–3.
— (1991) *The Selected Letters of Philip K. Dick: 1974* (Lancaster, PA: Underwood-Miller).
— (1992) *The Selected Letters of Philip K. Dick Volume Four: 1975–1976* (Lancaster, PA: Underwood-Miller).
— (1995a) 'How to Build a Universe that Doesn't Fall Apart Two Days Later', Lawrence Sutin (ed.) *The Shifting Realities of Philip K. Dick: Selected Literary and Philosophical Writings* (New York: Pantheon): 259–80.
— (1995b) 'If You Find This World Bad, You Should See Some of the Others', Lawrence Sutin (ed.) *The Shifting Realities of Philip K. Dick: Selected Literary and Philosophical Writings* (New York: Pantheon): 233–58.
Dicks, Terrance (1974a) *Doctor Who and the Auton Invasion* (London: Target).
— (1974b) *Doctor Who and the Day of the Daleks* (London: Target).
Disch, Thomas M. (1971) 'Angouleme', Michael Moorcock (ed.) *New Worlds Quarterly* (London: Sphere).
— (1972) *334* (London: MacGibbon & Kee).
— (1972) *The Right Way to Figure Plumbing* (Fredonia, NY: Basilisk Press).
— (1976) 'The Embarrassments of Science Fiction', Peter Nicholls (ed.) *Science Fiction At Large* (London: Gollancz): 141–55.
— (1979a) *ABCDEFG HIJKLM NPOQRST UVWXYZ* (London: Anvil Press).
— (1979b) *On Wings of Song* (London: Gollancz).
— (1982a) *Burn This* (London: Hutchinson).
— (1982b) *Orders of the Retina* (Iowa City: The Toothpaste Press).
— (1986) *The Brave Little Toaster* (Garden City, NY: Doubleday).
— (ed.) (1971) *The Ruins of Earth* (New York: Putnam).
— (ed.) (1973) *Bad Moon Rising* (New York: Harper & Row).
— (ed.) (1975) *The New Improved Sun* (New York: Harper & Row).
— as Leonie Hargrave (1975) *Clara Reeve* (New York: Knopf).
— with Charles Platt and Marilyn Hacker (1970) *Highway Sandwiches* (privately printed).
Doctorow, E.L. (1975) *Ragtime* (New York: Random House).
Donaldson, Stephen (1977) *Lord Foul's Bane* (New York: Del Rey).
— (1978) *The Illearth War* (New York: Del Rey).
— (1979) *The Power that Preserves* (New York: Del Rey).
— (1980) *The Wounded Land* (New York: Del Rey).
Dos Passos, John (1930) *The 42nd Parallel* (New York and London: Harper and Brothers).
— (1932) *1919* (New York: Harcourt, Brace and Company).
— (1936) *The Big Money* (New York: Harcourt, Brace and Company).
Douglas, Mary (1966) *Purity and Danger: An Analysis of the Concepts of Pollution and Taboo* (London: Routledge and Kegan Paul).

Downing, Barry H. (1968) *The Bible and Flying Saucers* (Philadelphia: Lippincott).
Dozois, Gardner (1978) *Strangers* (New York: Putnam).
Eco, Umberto (1986) *Travels in Hyperreality* (New York: Harcourt Brace Jovanovich); orig. *Il Costume di Casa: Evidenze E Misteri Dell'ideologia Italiana* (Milan: Bompiani, 1973).
Edwards, Malcolm (1978) 'Yesterday, Today & Tomorrow', Robert Holdstock (ed.) (1979) *The Encyclopedia of Science Fiction* (London: Octopus): 174–89.
Elgin, Suzette Haden (1969) 'For the Sake of Grace', *F&SF* 36.5 (May).
— (1970) *The Communipaths* (New York: Ace; b/w Louis Trimble, *The Noblest Experiment in the Galaxy*).
— (1971) *Furthest* (New York: Ace).
— (1972) *At the Seventh Level* (New York: DAW).
— (1979) *Star-Anchored, Star-Angered* (Garden City, NY: Doubleday).
Elliot, Jeffrey M. (1982) 'Pamela Sargent: Woman of Wonder', *Foundation* 26 (October): 56–72.
Ellison, Harlan (1969) 'A Boy and His Dog', *New Worlds* 189 (April).
— (1972) 'Basilisk', *F&SF* 43.2 (August).
— (1976) *Approaching Oblivion* (New York: Signet); orig. (New York: Walker, 1974).
— (1982) *Shatterday* (London: Hutchinson).
— (ed.) (1967) *Dangerous Visions* (Garden City, NY: Doubleday).
— (ed.) (1972) *Again, Dangerous Visions* (Garden City, NY: Doubleday).
— and Edward Bryant (1975) *Phoenix Without Ashes* (New York: Fawcett Gold).
Ellman, Mary (1968) *Thinking About Women* (New York: Harcourt, Brace and World).
Eshun, Kodwo (1998) *More Brilliant than the Sun: Adventures in Sonic Fiction* (London: Quartet).
Evans, Christopher (1973) *Cults of Unreason* (London: Harrap).
Farmer, Philip José (1971) *The Wind Whales of Ishmael* (New York: Ace).
— (1972) *Tarzan Alive: A Definitive Biography of Lord Greystoke* (Garden City, NY: Doubleday).
— (1973a) *Doc Savage: His Apocalyptic Life* (Garden City, NY: Doubleday).
— (1973b) Letter of Comment, *SF Commentary* 35–36–37: 141.
— (1974) *To Your Scattered Bodies Go* (New York: Putnam).
— (1975) 'A Scarletin Study', *F&SF* 48.3 (March).
— (1976) 'The Doge Whose Barque Was Worse Than His Bight', *F&SF* 51.5 (November).
Fiedler, Leslie (1960) *Love and Death in the American Novel* (New York: Criterion Books).
Firestone, Shulamith (1979) *The Dialectic of Sex* (London: The Women's Press); orig. (New York: Morrow, 1970).
Fort, Charles (1919) *The Book of the Damned* (New York: Boni and Liveright).
— (1931) *Lo!* (New York: Ace).
Foster, Alan Dean (1974) *Dark Star* (New York: Ballantine).
— (1978) *Splinter of the Mind's Eye* (New York: Del Rey).
— (1979a) *Alien* (London: Futura).
— (1979b) *The Black Hole* (London: NEL).

Foucault, Michel (1970) *The Order of Things: An Archaeology of the Human Sciences* (London: Tavistock Publications); orig. *Mots et les Choses: Une Archéologie des Sciences Humaines* (Paris: Éditions Gallimard, 1966).
— (1978) *The Will to Knowledge*, trans. Robert Hurley (New York: Pantheon); orig. *La Volonté de Savoir* (Paris: Gallimard, 1976).
Fowler, Chris (1976) 'Harlan Ellison Talks to Chris Fowler', *Vector* 75 (July): 5–24.
Fox, Robert Elliot (1996a) 'The Politics of Desire in Delany's *Triton* and *Tides of Lust*', James Sallis (ed.) *Ash of Stars: On the Writings of Samuel R. Delany* (Jackson, MS: University Press of Mississippi): 43–61.
— (1996b) 'This "You-Shaped Hole of Insight and Fire": Meditations on Delany's *Dhalgren*', James Sallis (ed.) *Ash of Stars: On the Writings of Samuel R. Delany* (Jackson, MS: University Press of Mississippi): 97–108.
Frank, Alan (1978) 'Screen Trips', Brian Ash (ed.) (1977) *The Visual Encyclopedia of Science Fiction* (London: Pan).
Franklin, H. Bruce (1983) 'Don't Look Where We're Going: Visions of the Future in SF Films, 1970–82', *Science Fiction Studies* 10.1 (March): 70–80.
— (1990) 'The Vietnam War as American Sf and Fantasy', *Science Fiction Studies* 17.3 (November): 341–59.
Freedman, Carl (2005) *Critical Theory and Science Fiction* (Hanover, NH: University Press of New England).
Freud, Sigmund (1953a) *Three Essays on the Theory of Sexuality*, *The Standard Edition of the Complete Psychological Works of Sigmund Freud Volume VII (1901–1905): A Case of Hysteria, Three Essays on Sexuality and Other Works*, trans. James Strachey (London: The Hogarth Press): 123–243.
— (1953b) 'On Narcissism: An Introduction', *The Standard Edition of the Complete Psychological Works of Sigmund Freud Volume XIV (1914–1916): On the History of the Psycho-Analytic Movement, Papers on Metapsychology, and Other Works*, trans. James Strachey (London: The Hogarth Press): 67–102.
Friedan, Betty (1963) *The Feminine Mystique* (New York: Norton).
Fuller, R. Buckminster (1968) *Operating Manual for Spaceship Earth* (Carbondale: Southern Illinois University Press).
Garner, Alan (1960) *The Weirdstone of Brisingamen* (London: Collins).
— (1973) *Red Shift* (London: Collins).
— (1979) *The Stone Book Quartet* (London: Collins).
— (1996) *Strandloper* (London: Harvill Press).
Gass, William H. (1970) *Fiction and the Figures of Life* (New York: Knopf).
Gawron, Jean M. (1996) 'On *Dhalgren*', James Sallis (ed.) *Ash of Stars: On the Writings of Samuel R. Delany* (Jackson, MS: University Press of Mississippi): 62–96.
Gearhart, Sally Miller (1979) *The Wanderground: Stories of the Hill People* (Watertown, MA: Persephone Press).
Gentle, Mary (1987) 'The Science Fantasy Novels of John Norman', *Vector* 139 (August/September): 9–10.
Gerrold, David (1972) *Space Skimmer* (New York: Ballantine).
— (1973a) *Battle for the Planet of the Apes* (New York: Award).
— (1973b) *The Man Who Folded Himself* (New York: Random House).
Gibson, William (1984) *Neuromancer* (New York: Ace).

— (1986) 'Fragments of a Hologram Rose', *Burning Chrome* (New York: Ann Arbor); orig. *Unearth* (Summer 1977).
Gilbert, Sandra and Susan Gubar (1979) *The Madwoman in the Attic: The Woman Writer and Nineteenth-Century Literature* (New Haven, CT: Yale University Press).
Gilroy, Paul (1999) *Joined-Up Politics and Post-Colonial Melancholia* (London: Institute of Contemporary Art).
Goldman, Stephen H. (1978) 'John Brunner's Dystopias: Heroic Man in Unheroic Society', *Science Fiction Studies* 5.3 (November): 260–70.
Goldman, Steven L. (1989) 'Images of Technology in Popular Films: Discussion and Filmography', *Science, Technology, & Human Values* 14 (3) (Summer): 275–301.
Gordon, Andrew (1980) '*The Empire Strikes Back*: Monsters From the Id', *Science Fiction Studies* 7.22 (November): 313–93.
Gordon, Joan (1980) *Joe Haldeman* (Mercer Island, WA: Starmont House).
Gossett, Thomas F. (1997) *Race: The History of an Idea in America* (New York: Oxford University Press).
Grahame, Kenneth (1908) *The Wind in the Willows* (London: Methuen).
Greene, Eric (1996) *Planet of the Apes as American Myth: Race and Politics in the Films and Television Series* (Jefferson, NC: McFarland).
Greenland, Colin (1980a) 'Martial Lore: Thoughts on *Battlestar Galactica*', *Foundation* 18 (January): 35–36.
— (1980b) Review of D.G. Compton, *Ascendancies*, *Foundation* 20 (October): 75–77.
— (1980c) Review of Frederik Pohl, *Jem: The Making of a Utopia*, *Foundation* 18 (January): 60–62.
— (1980d) Review of Garry Kilworth, *Split Second*, *Foundation* 19 (January): 94–95.
— (1980e) Review of Kit Reed, *Magic Time*, *Foundation* 20 (November): 86–87.
— (1981) Review of M. John Harrison, *A Storm of Wings*, *Foundation* 21 (February): 101–103.
Greer, Germaine (1970) *The Female Eunuch* (London: MacGibbon & Kee).
Guerrero, Ed (1993) *Framing Blackness: The African American Image in Film* (Philadelphia: Temple University Press).
— (2009) 'The So-Called Fall of Blaxploitation', *The Velvet Light Trap* 64 (Fall): 90–91.
Gunn, James (1977) 'On the Lem Affair', *Science Fiction Studies* 4.3 (November): 314–16.
— (1980) *Isaac Asimov: The Foundations of Science Fiction* (Oxford: Oxford University Press).
Haldeman, Joe (1974) *The Forever War* (New York: St Martin's Press).
— (1993) *Vietnam and Other Alien Worlds* (Framington, MA: NESFA Press).
Haley, Alex (1976) *Roots: The Saga of an American Family* (Garden City, NY: Doubleday).
Hantke, Steffen (2001) 'Disorienting Encounters: Magical Realism and American Literature on the Vietnam War', *Journal of the Fantastic in the Arts* 12.3: 268–86.
Haraway, Donna (1984/1985) 'Manifesto for Cyborgs: Science, Technology, and Socialist Feminism in the 1980s', *Social Text* 11 (Winter): 19–64.
Hark, Ina Rae (1979) 'Unity in the Composite Novel: Triadic Patterning in Asimov's

*The Gods Themselves', Science Fiction Studies* 6.2 (July): 281–86.

Harrison, Harry (1966) *Make Room! Make Room!* (Garden City, NY: Doubleday).

— (1973) 'Introduction', James Tiptree, Jr, *Ten Thousand Light-Years From Home* (New York: Ace).

— (1977) 'Commando Raid', Joe Haldeman (ed.) *Study War No More* (London: Futura); orig. Harry Harrison, *Prime Number* (New York: Berkley Medallion, 1970).

— (1984) 'A Cannibalized Novel Becomes Soylent Green', Danny Peary (ed.) *Omni's Screen Flights/Screen Fantasies: The Future According to Science Fiction Cinema* (Garden City, NY: Doubleday): 143–46.

Harrison, M. John (1971) *The Committed Men* (London: Hutchinson New Authors Limited).

— (1971) *The Pastel City* (London: New English Library).

— (1974) *The Centauri Device* (Garden City, NY: Doubleday).

— (1980) *A Storm of Wings* (London: Sphere).

— (1985) *Viriconium Nights* (New York: Ace).

— (1989) 'The Profession of Science Fiction, 40: The Profession of Fiction', *Foundation* 46 (Winter): 5–13.

— (2005) Reviews, Mark Bould and Michelle Reid (eds) *Parietal Games: Critical Writings by and on M. John Harrison* (London: Science Fiction Foundation).

Harrison, William (1973) 'Roller Ball Murder', *Esquire* (September).

Hartwell, David G. (1984) *Age of Wonders: Exploring the World of Science Fiction* (New York: Walker).

Hassan, Ihab (1971) 'POSTmodernISM: A Paracritical Bibliography', *New Literary History* 3.1 (Fall): 5–306.

Hassler, Donald M. (1979) 'Images for an Ethos, Images for Change and Style', *Extrapolation* 20.2 (Summer): 176–88.

Hay, George (1973) Review of Clifford D. Simak, *A Choice of Gods* and Harry Harrison, *A Transatlantic Tunnel, Hurrah!*, *Foundation* 4 (July): 74–77.

Heinlein, Robert A. (1959a) ' – All You Zombies – ', *F&SF* 16.3 (March).

— (1959b) *Starship Troopers* (New York: Putnam).

— (1961) *Stranger in a Strange Land* (New York: Putnam).

— (1970) *I Will Fear No Evil* (New York: Putnam).

— (1973) *Time Enough For Love* (New York: Putnam).

— (1978) *The Notebooks of Lazarus Long* (New York: Putnam).

— (1980) *'The Number of the Beast'* (New York: Fawcett Columbine).

— (1987) *To Sail Beyond the Sunset* (New York: Putnam).

Herbert, Frank (1965) *Dune* (Philadelphia: Chilton Books).

Hickman, Christine B. (1997) 'The Devil and the One Drop Rule: Racial Categories, African Americans, and the U.S. Census', *Michigan Law Review* 95.5 (March): 1161–265.

Hills, Matt (2003) '*Star Wars* in Fandom, Film Theory and the Museum: The Cultural Status of the Cult Blockbuster', Julian Stringer (ed.) *Movie Blockbusters* (London: Routledge): 178–89.

Hoban, Russell (1980) *Riddley Walker* (London: Jonathan Cape).

Holdstock, Robert (1976) *Eye Among the Blind* (London: Faber and Faber).

— (1977) *Earthwind* (London: Faber and Faber).
— (1981) 'Mythago Wood', *F&SF* 63.3 (September).
— (1984) *Mythago Wood* (London: Gollancz).
— (ed.) (1979) *The Encyclopedia of Science Fiction* (London: Octopus).
— and Christopher Priest (eds)(1979) *Stars of Albion* (London: Pan).
Hoover, H.M. (1973) *Children of Morrow* (New York: Four Windows).
— (1976) *Treasures of Morrow* (New York: Four Windows).
— (1977a) *The Delikon* (New York: Viking).
— (1977b) *The Rains of Eridan* (New York: Viking).
— (1979) *The Lost Star* (New York: Viking).
— (1980a) *Return to Earth* (New York: Viking).
— (1980b) *This Time of Darkness* (New York: Viking).
Horowitz, Gad (1977) *Repression: Basic and Surplus Repression in Psychoanalytic Theory: Freud, Reich and Marcuse* (Toronto: University of Toronto Press).
Hosty, Tom (1980) Review of D.G. Compton, *Windows*, *Foundation* 20 (October): 74–75.
Hovanec, Carol P. (1989) 'Visions of Nature in "The Word for World is Forest": A Mirror of the American Consciousness', *Extrapolation* 30.1 (Spring): 84–92.
Hubble, Nick (2005) 'Priest's Repetitive Strain', Andrew M. Butler (ed.) *Christopher Priest: The Interaction* (London: SFF): 35–51.
Hudson, W.H. (1910) *A Shepherd's Life: Impressions of the South Wiltshire Downs* (London: Methuen).
Hulke, Malcolm (1974a) *Doctor Who and the Cave Monsters* (London: Target).
— (1974b) *Doctor Who and the Doomsday Weapon* (London: Target).
— (1974c) *Doctor Who and the Sea-Devils* (London: Target).
Hunt, Peter (2001) *Children's Literature: A Blackwell Guide* (Oxford: Blackwell).
Hurst, L.J. (1985) 'John Norman: The Literature of Difference', *Foundation* 33 (Spring): 36–54.
Hurst, Mark (1986) Letter May 22 to Paul Williams, *PKDS Newsletter* 12: 7.
Jakes, John (1974) *Conquest of the Planet of the Apes* (New York: Award).
Jakubowski, Maxim (1978) 'Essex House: The Rise and Fall of Speculative Erotica', *Foundation* 14 (September): 50–64.
James, Edward (1990) 'Yellow, Black, Metal, and Tentacled: The Race Question in American Science Fiction', Philip J. Davies (ed.) *Science Fiction, Social Conflict and War* (Manchester: Manchester University Press): 26–49.
— (1994) *Science Fiction in the Twentieth Century* (Oxford: Opus).
Jameson, Fredric (1983) 'Postmodernism and Consumer Society', Hal Foster (ed.) *The Anti-Aesthetic: Essays on Postmodern Culture* (Port Townsend, WA: Bay Press): 111–25.
— (1984a) 'Periodizing the 60s', *Social Text* 9/10 (Spring/Summer): 178–209.
— (1984b) 'Postmodernism, or the Cultural Logic of Late Capitalism', *New Left Review* 164 (July/August): 53–92.
— (1987) 'Science Fiction as a Spatial Genre: Generic Discontinuities and the Problem of Figuration in Vonda McIntyre's *The Exile Waiting*', *Science Fiction Studies* 14.1 (March): 44–59.
— (1991) *Postmodernism, Or The Cultural Logic of Late Capitalism* (Durham, NC and

London: Duke University Press).
— (2005) *Archaeologies of the Future: The Desire Called Utopia and Other Science Fictions* (New York: Verso).
Jannone, Claudia (1976) '*Venus on the Half Shell* as Structuralist Activity', *Extrapolation* 17.2 (May): 110–17.
Jenkins, Sue (1982) 'Spock, Avon and the Decline of Optimism', *Foundation* 25 (January): 43–45.
Jesser, Nancy (2002) 'Blood, Genes and Gender in Octavia Butler's *Kindred* and *Dawn*', *Extrapolation* 43.1 (Spring): 36–61.
Jeter, K.W. (1979) *Morlock Night* (New York: Daw Books).
Kam, Rose Salberg (1975) 'Silverberg and Conrad: Explorers of Inner Darkness', *Extrapolation* 17.1 (December): 18–28.
Kaveney, Roz (1981) 'Science Fiction in the 1970s', *Foundation* 22 (June): 5–34.
Kaysing, Bill and Randy Reid (1976) *We Never Went to the Moon* (self-published).
Khouri, Nadia (1980) 'The Dialectics of Power: Utopia in the Sf of Le Guin, Jeury and Piercy', *Science Fiction Studies* 7.1 (March): 49–60.
Kidd, Virginia (ed.) (1978) *Millennial Women* (New York: Delacorte).
Kilgore, De Witt Douglas (2003) *Astrofuturism: Science, Race, and Visions of Utopia in Space* (Philadelphia: University of Pennsylvania Press).
Kilworth, Garry (1975) 'Let's Go to Golgotha', *Gollancz – Sunday Times Best SF Stories* (London: Gollancz).
— (1977) *In Solitary* (London: Faber and Faber).
— (1978) *The Night of Kadar* (London: Faber and Faber).
— (1979) *Split Second* (London: Faber and Faber).
Kincaid, Paul (1993) 'The Fiction of Robert Holdstock', *Vector* 175 (October/November): 7–9.
— (1999) 'Throwing Away the Orthodoxy: A Conversation about Sex, Innocence and Science Fiction', *Vector* 206 (July/August): 4–10.
— (2005) 'Landscape in the Fiction of Keith Roberts', *Foundation* 93 (Spring): 59–66.
King, Stephen (1974) *Carrie* (Garden City, NY: Doubleday).
Kirk, Richard (1978a) *The Frozen God* (London: Corgi).
— (1978b) *Swordsmistress of Chaos* (London: Corgi).
— (1978c) *A Time of Ghosts* (London: Corgi).
— (1979a) *Lords of the Shadows* (London: Corgi).
— (1979b) *A Time of Dying* (London: Corgi).
Klarer, Mario (1990) 'Re-Membering Men Dis-Membered in Sally Miller Gearhart's Ecofeminist Utopia *The Wanderground*', *Extrapolation* 32.4 (Winter): 319–30.
Kolosimo, Peter (1957) *Il Pianeta Sconosciuto* (Torino: SEI).
Krämer, Peter (2004) '"It's Aimed at Kids – The Kid in Everybody": George Lucas, *Star Wars* and Children's Entertainment', Yvonne Tasker (ed.) *Action and Adventure Cinema* (London: Routledge, 2004): 358–70.
Kristeva, Julia (1982) *Powers of Horror: An Essay on Abjection*, trans. Leon S. Roudiez (New York: Columbia University Press); orig. *Pouvoirs de l'horreur: Essai sur l'abjection* (Paris: Editions du Seuil, 1980).

Kucera, Paul (2007) '"To Love that Well which Thou Must Leave Ere Long": Creativity and the Journey of Maturity in Kate Wilhelm's *Where Late the Sweet Birds Sang*', *Extrapolation* 48.2 (Summer): 364–83.
Kusche, Larry (1975) *The Bermuda Triangle Mystery — Solved* (New York: Harper & Row).
Lamb, Patricia F. and Diana L. Veith (1986) 'Romantic Myth, Transcendence and *Star Trek* Zines', Donald Palumbo (ed.) *Erotic Universe: Sexuality and Fantastic Literature* (Westport, CT: Greenwood): 235–55.
Landon, Brooks (1995) *Science Fiction Since 1900* (New York: Twayne).
Latham, Rob (2005) 'The New Wave', David Seed (ed.) *A Companion to Science Fiction* (Oxford: Blackwell): 202–16.
Layton, David (1991) 'The Barriers of Inner and Outer Space: The Science Fiction of Barry N. Malzberg', *Science Fiction Studies* 18.1 (March): 71–90.
Lefanu, Sarah (1987) *In the Chinks of the World Machine: Feminism and Science Fiction* (London: The Women's Press).
Le Guin, Ursula (1968) *A Wizard of Earthsea* (New York: Parnassus Press).
— (1969) *The Left Hand of Darkness* (New York: Ace).
— (1971) *The Tombs of Atuan* (New York: Atheneum Press).
— (1972a) 'The Word for World is Forest', Harlan Ellison (ed.) *Again, Dangerous Visions* (Garden City, NY: Doubleday).
— (1972b) *The Farthest Shore* (New York: Atheneum Press).
— (1974a) *The Dispossessed: An Ambiguous Utopia* (New York: Harper & Row).
— (1974b) *The Lathe of Heaven* (London: Panther); orig. (New York: Avon, 1971).
— (1974c) Review of Alan Garner, *Red Shift*, *Foundation* 6 (May): 109–12.
— (1976a) 'Is Gender Necessary?', Vonda N. McIntyre and Susan Anderson (eds) *Aurora: Beyond Equality* (New York: Fawcett).
— (1976b) Note to 'Winter King', *The Wind's Twelve Quarters* (New York: Bantam); orig. (New York: Harper and Row, 1975).
— (1978) 'Introduction', James Tiptree Jr, *Star Songs of an Old Primate* (New York: Del Rey).
— (1989) *The Language of the Night: Essays on Fantasy and Science Fiction* (London: The Women's Press); orig. (New York: Putnam, 1979).
— and Darko Suvin (1977) 'The Lem Affair', *Science Fiction Studies* 4.1 (March): 100–103.
Leibscher, Walt (1972) 'Do Androids Dream of Electric Love?', Thomas N. Scortia (ed.) *Strange Bedfellows* (New York: Random House).
Leith, Linda (1980) 'Marion Zimmer Bradley and Darkover', *Science Fiction Studies* 20.1 (March): 28–35.
Lem, Stanisław (1975a) 'Philip K. Dick: A Visionary among the Charlatans', *Science Fiction Studies* 2.1 (March): 54–67.
— (1975b) 'Science-Fiction: A Hopeless Case with Exceptions', *SF Commentary* 35–36–37: 8–35.
— (1977) 'Looking Down on Science Fiction', *Science Fiction Studies* 4 (July): 127–28.
Lessing, Doris (1971) *Briefing for a Descent into Hell* (New York: Knopf).
— (1974) *The Memoirs of a Survivor* (London: Octagon Press).

— (1979) *Re: Colonised Planet 5, Shikasta* (London: Jonathan Cape).
— (1980a) *The Marriages Between Zones Three, Four and Five* (London: Jonathan Cape).
— (1980b) *The Sirian Experiments* (London: Jonathan Cape).
Letson, Russell (1977) 'The Faces of a Thousand Heroes: Philip José Farmer', *Science Fiction Studies* 4.1 (March): 35–41.
— (1978) 'The Returns of Lazarus Long', Joseph D. Olander and Martin Harry Greenberg (eds) *Robert A. Heinlein* (New York: Taplinger): 194–221.
Letts, Barry (1974) *Doctor Who and the Dæmons* (London: Target).
Levin, Ira (1967) *Rosemary's Baby* (New York: Random House).
— (1972) *The Stepford Wives* (New York: Random House).
Lightbody, Brian (2011) 'Winning is the Only Standard of Excellence Left: *Death Race 2000*', Michael Berman and Rohit Dalvi (eds) *Heroes, Monsters and Values: Science Fiction Films of the 1970s* (Newcastle: Cambridge Scholars Press): 139–49.
Lipman-Blumen, Jean (1975) 'Changing Sex Roles in American Culture: Future Directions for Research', *Archives of Sexual Behavior* 4.4 (Spring): 433–46.
Lipset, Seymour Martin (1972) *Rebellion in the University: A History of Student Activism in America* (London: Routledge and Kegan Paul).
Littlefield, Emerson (1982) 'The Mythologies of Race and Science in Samuel Delany's *The Einstein Intersection* and *Nova*', *Extrapolation* 23.3 (Fall): 235–42.
Lovelock, James (1979) *Gaia: A New Look at Life on Earth* (Oxford: Oxford University Press).
Lucas, George (1976) *Star Wars: From the Adventures of Luke Skywalker* (New York: Ballantine).
Luckhurst, Roger (2005a) 'Post-imperial Melancholy and the New Wave in the 1970s', *Foundation* 93 (Spring): 76–88.
— (2005b) *Science Fiction*. Cambridge: Polity.
Lynn, Elizabeth A. (1979) *A Different Light*. London: Gollancz.
Lyotard, Jean-François (1984) *The Postmodern Condition: A Report on Knowledge*, trans. Geoff Bennington and Brian Massumi (Minneapolis: University of Minnesota Press).
MacDonald, Anson (1941) 'By His Bootstraps', *Astounding* 28.2 (October).
Magrs, Paul (2002) *Strange Boy* (London: Simon and Schuster).
Malzberg, Barry N. (1971) *The Falling Astronauts* (New York: Ace).
— (1972a) *Beyond Apollo* (New York: Random House).
— (1972b) *Overlay* (Toronto: Lancer).
— (1972c) *Revelations* (New York: Paperback Library).
— (1973a) *Herovit's World* (New York: Random House).
— (1973b) *The Men Inside* (Toronto: Lancer).
— (1973c) *Phase IV* (London: Pan).
— (1974a) *The Day of the Burning* (New York: Ace).
— (1974b) *The Destruction of the Temple* (New York: Pocket).
— (1974c) *On a Planet Alien* (New York: Pocket).
— (1974d) *The Sodom and Gomorrah Business* (New York: Pocket).
— (1974e) *Tactics of Conquest* (New York: Pyramid).
— (1975a) *Galaxies* (New York: Pyramid).

— (1975b) *Guernica Night* (New York: Bobbs-Merrill).
— (1976a) 'Pain, Rage, Alienation and Other Aspects of the Writing of Science Fiction', *Fantasy and Science Fiction* 50.4 (April): 103–108.
— (1976b) *Scop* (New York: Pyramid).
— (1977) *The Last Transaction* (New York: Pinnacle Books).
Mandel, Ernest (1975) *Late Capitalism* (London: Humanities Press).
Marcuse, Herbert (1955) *Eros and Civilization: A Philosophical Inquiry into Freud* (Boston, MA: Beacon).
Mark, Jan (1976) *Thunder and Lightnings* (Harmondsworth: Kestrel).
— (1977) *Under the Autumn Garden* (Harmondsworth: Kestrel).
— (1978) *The Ennead* (Harmondsworth: Kestrel).
— (1979) *Divide and Rule* (Harmondsworth: Kestrel).
Masson, David I. (1975) Review of Brian Aldiss, *The Eighty Minute Hour*, *Foundation* 7/8 (March): 201–203.
McCaffrey, Anne (1968) *Dragonflight* (New York: Ballantine).
— (1978) *The White Dragon* (New York: Ballantine).
McGiveron, Rafeeq O. (1998) '"A Relationship ... More than Six Inches Deep". Lust and Love in Silverberg's Science Fiction', *Extrapolation* 39.1 (Spring): 40–51.
McHugh, Susan Bridget (2000) 'Horses in Blackface: Visualizing Race as Species Difference', *South Atlantic Review* 65 (2): 40–72.
McIntyre, Vonda N. (1973) 'Of Mist, and Grass, and Sand', *Analog* 92.2 (October).
— (1975) *The Exile Waiting* (Garden City, NY: Doubleday).
— (1978) *Dreamsnake* (Boston, MA: Houghton Mifflin).
— and Susan Anderson (eds) (1976) *Aurora: Beyond Equality* (New York: Fawcett).
McLeod, Ken (2003) 'Space Oddities: Aliens, Futurism and Meaning in Popular Music', *Popular Music* 22.3 (October): 337–55.
McLeod, Patrick G. (1980) 'Frankenstein: Unbound and Otherwise', *Extrapolation* 21.2 (Summer): 158–66.
Mendlesohn, Farah (2004) 'Is There Any Such Thing as Children's Science Fiction? A Position Piece', *Lion and the Unicorn* 28.2 (April): 284–313.
— and Edward James (2009) *A Short History of Fantasy* (University of Middlesex Press).
Merle, Robert (1973) *Malevil*, trans. Derek Coltman (New York: Simon and Schuster); orig. (Paris: Gallimard, 1972).
Merrick, Helen (2009) *The Secret Feminist Cabal: A Cultural History of Science Fiction Feminisms* (Seattle, WA: Aqueduct Press).
Merril, Judith (1968) *England Swings SF: Stories of Speculative Science Fiction* (Garden City, NY: Doubleday).
Miall, Robert (1971a) *UFO* (London: Pan).
— (1971b) *UFO 2* (London: Pan).
Miller, Jim (1998) 'Post-apocalyptic Hoping: Octavia Butler's Dystopian/Utopian Vision', *Science Fiction Studies* 25.2 (July): 336–60.
Miller, Stephen Paul (1999) *The Seventies Now: Culture as Surveillance* (Durham, NC and London: Duke University Press).
Millett, Kate (1970) *Sexual Politics* (Garden City, NY: Doubleday).

Milton, John (1971) *Lycidas*, in *Milton: Complete Shorter Poems*, John Carey (ed.) (London and New York: Longman): 232–54.
Moers, Ellen (1976) *Literary Women* (Garden City, NY: Doubleday).
Molson, Francis J. (1989) *Children's Fantasy* (Mercer Island, WA: Starmont House).
Money, John (1955) 'Hermaphroditism Gender and Precocity in Hyperadrenocorticism: Psychologic Findings', *Bulletin of the Johns Hopkins Hospital* 96.6 (June): 253–64.
Monk, Claire (2008) '"Now, what are we going to call you? Scum! ... Scum! That's commercial! It's all they deserve!"': *Jubilee*, Punk and British Film in the Late 1970s', Robert Shail (ed.) *Seventies British Cinema* (London: British Film Institute): 81–93.
Moorcock, Michael (1966) 'Behold the Man', *New Worlds* 166 (September).
— (1968) *The Final Programme* (New York: Avon).
— (1971a) *A Cure for Cancer* (London: Allison and Busby).
— (1971b) *The King of the Swords* (New York: Berkley).
— (1971c) *The Knight of the Swords* (London: Mayflower).
— (1971d) *The Queen of the Swords* (London: Mayflower).
— (1971e) *The Sleeping Sorceress* (London: NEL).
— (1971f) *The Warlord of the Air* (London: NEL).
— (1972a) *An Alien Heat* (London: MacGibbon & Kee).
— (1972b) *Breakfast in the Ruins: An Novel of Inhumanity* (London: NEL).
— (1972c) *Elric of Melniboné* (London: NEL); *The Dreaming City* (Toronto: Lancer).
— (1972d) *The English Assassin: A Romance of Entropy* (London: Allison and Busby).
— (1973a) *The Bull and the Spear* (London: Allison and Busby).
— (1973b) *The Oak and the Ram* (London: Allison and Busby).
— (1974a) *The Hollow Lands* (New York: Harper & Row).
— (1974b) *The Land Leviathan: A New Scientific Romance* (London: Quartet).
— (1974c) *The Sword and the Stallion* (London: Allison and Busby).
— (1976a) *The End of All Songs* (New York: Harper & Row).
— (1976b) *The Lives and Times of Jerry Cornelius* (London: Allison and Busby).
— (1977) *The Condition of Muzak* (London: Allison and Busby).
— (1978) *Gloriana, or The Unfulfill'd Queen: A Romance* (London: Allison and Busby).
— (1980) *My Experiences in the Third World War* (Manchester: Savoy).
— (1981) *The Steel Tsar* (London: Granada).
— (1987) *Wizardry and Wild Romance* (London: Gollancz).
— (2004) 'Queen of the Martian Mysteries: An Appreciation of Leigh Brackett', Lou Anders (ed.), *Projections: Science Fiction in Literature and Film* (Austin, TX: Monkeybrain Books): 247–48.
Morgan, Chris (1979) Review of *The White Dragon*, *Vector* 94 (July/August): 13–14.
Moss, Elaine (1980) 'The Seventies in British Children's Books', Nancy Chambers (ed.) *The Signal Approach to Children's Books* (London: Kestrel): 48–82.
Moylan, Tom (1986) *Demand the Impossible: Science Fiction and the Utopian Imagination* (New York: Methuen).
Mullen, R.D. (1979) 'No Time for Evolution', *Science Fiction Studies* 6.2 (July): 209–15.
Mulvey, Laura (1975) 'Visual Pleasure and Narrative Cinema', *Screen* 16.3

(Autumn): 6–18.
Nesbit, E. (1899) *The Story of the Treasure Seekers* (London: T. Unwin).
Newell, Diane and Victoria Lamont (2009) 'Leigh Brackett (1915–1978)', Mark Bould, Andrew M. Butler, Adam Roberts and Sherryl Vint (eds) *50 Key Figures in Science Fiction* (London: Routledge): 37–41.
Newton, Janet (1980) 'Feminism and Anxiety in *Alien*', *Science Fiction Studies* 7.3 (November): 293–97.
Nicholls, Peter (1975a) Review of Christopher Priest, *Inverted World*, *Foundation* 7/8 (March): 185–88.
— (1975b): Review of Robert A. Heinlein, *Time Enough for Love*, *Foundation* 7/8 (March): 73–80.
— (1984) *Fantastic Cinema: An Illustrated Survey* (London: Ebury Press).
— (ed.) (1979) *The Encyclopedia of Science Fiction* (London: Granada).
Niven, Larry (1970) *Ringworld* (New York: Ballantine).
— (1973) *Protector* (New York: Ballantine).
— (1980) *Ringworld Engineers* (New York: Holt, Rineheart & Winston).
— (1977) *Lucifer's Hammer* (Chicago: Playboy Press).
— and Jerry Pournelle (1974) *The Mote in God's Eye* (New York: Simon & Schuster).
Nolan, William F. and George Clayton Johnson (1967) *Logan's Run* (New York: Dial Press).
Norman, John (1966) *Tarnsman of Gor* (New York: Ballantine Books).
— (1970) *Assassin of Gor* (New York: Ballantine Books).
— (1971) *Raiders of Gor* (New York: Ballantine Books).
— (1972) *Captive of Gor* (New York: Ballantine Books).
— (1974a) *Hunters of Gor* (New York: DAW).
— (1974b) *Imaginative Sex* (New York: DAW).
— (1975) *Marauders of Gor* (New York: DAW).
— (1976) *Tribesmen of Gor* (New York: DAW).
— (1977) *Slave Girl of Gor* (New York: DAW).
— (1978) *Beasts of Gor* (New York: DAW).
— (1979) *Explorers of Gor* (New York: DAW).
— (1980) *Fighting Slave of Gor* (New York: DAW).
Norton, Andre (1973) *Forerunner Foray* (New York: Viking).
— (1978) *Quag Keep* (New York: Atheneum).
— and Dorothy Madlee (1978) *Star Ka'at* (New York: Walker).
Nourse, Alan E. (1974) *The Blade Runner* (New York: D. McKay).
Nowlan, Philip Francis (1928) 'Armageddon – 2419 AD', *Amazing* 12.4 (August).
O'Brien, Robert C. (1971) *Mrs Frisby and the Secret of NIMH* (New York: Atheneum).
— (1975) *Z for Zachariah* (New York: Atheneum).
Offutt, Andrew (1977) 'How It happened: One Bad Decision Leading to Another', *Science Fiction Studies* 4.2 (1977): 138–43.
O'Neill, Gerard K. (1974) 'The Colonization of Space', *Physics Today* 27.9 (September): 32–40.
— (1978) *The High Frontier: Human Colonies in Space* (New York: Bantam); orig. (New York: William Morrow & Company, 1977).
O'Pray, Michael (1996) 'Derek Jarman: The Art of Films/Films of Art', Roger

Wollen (ed.) *Derek Jarman: A Portrait* (London: Thames & Hudson): 65–75.
Palmer, Christopher (2006) 'Big Dumb Objects in Modern Science Fiction: Sublimity, Banality and Modernity', *Extrapolation* 47.1 (Spring) 95–111.
Panshin, Alexei (1973) 'Books', *F&SF* 44.6 (June): 13–20.
— and Cory Panshin (1974) 'Books', *F&SF* 47.6 (December): 63–69.
Payer, Sue (1979) *Second Body* (New York: Belmont Tower).
Peake, Mervyn (1946) *Titus Groan* (London: Eyre & Spottiswoode).
— (1950) *Gormenghast* (London: Eyre & Spottiswoode).
— (1959) *Titus Alone* (London: Eyre & Spottiswoode); revised (New York: Ballantine, 1968).
Pedler, Kit (1979) *The Quest for Gaia* (London: Souvenir).
— and Gerry Davis (1971) *Mutant 59 The Plastic Eater* (London: Souvenir).
— and Gerry Davis (1974) *Brainrack* (London: Souvenir).
— and Gerry Davis (1975a) *Doomwatch: The World in Danger* (London: Longman).
— and Gerry Davis (1975b) *The Dynostar Menace* (London: Souvenir).
Perrault, Charles (1979) *The Fairy Tales of Charles Perrault*, Angela Carter (ed.) (New York: Avon).
Pfeil, Fred (1990) *Another Tale to Tell: Politics and Narrative in Post-Modern Culture* (New York: Verso).
Pielke, Robert G. (1983) '*Star Wars* vs *2001*: A Question of Identity', *Extrapolation* 24.2 (Summer): 143–55.
Piercy, Marge (1976) *Woman on the Edge of Time* (New York: Knopf).
Platt, Charles (1970a) *The City Dwellers* (London: Sidgwick & Jackson); rev. *Twilight of the City* (New York: Macmillan, 1977).
— (1970b) *The Gas* (Paris: Orphelia Press).
Poe, Edgar Allan (1852) *Tales of Mystery and Imagination* (London: H. Vizetelly).
Pohl, Frederik (1976) *Man Plus* (New York: Random House).
— (1977) *Gateway* (New York: St Martin's Press).
— (1979) *Jem: The Making of a Utopia* (New York: St Martin's Press).
— (1980) *Beyond the Blue Event Horizon* (New York: Del Rey).
Postgate, Oliver (1967) *Noggin and the Moon Mouse* (London: Kaye and Ward).
— (2000) *Seeing Things: An Autobiography* (London: Macmillan).
Pournelle, Jerry (1973) *Escape from the Planet of the Apes* (New York: Award).
Pratchett, Terry (1976) *The Dark Side of the Sun* (Gerrards Cross, Buckinghamshire: Colin Smythe).
— (1981) *Strata* (Gerrards Cross, Buckinghamshire: Colin Smythe).
— (1983) *The Colour of Magic* (Gerrards Cross, Buckinghamshire: Colin Smythe).
Priest, Christopher (1972) *Fugue for a Darkening Island* (London: Faber and Faber).
— (1974a) *Inverted World* (London: Faber).
— (1974b) Review of Arthur C. Clarke, *Rendezvous With Rama*, *Foundation* 5 (January): 91–94.
— (1976) *The Space Machine: A Scientific Romance* (London: Faber).
— (1977) *A Dream of Wessex* (London: Faber).
— (1979) 'British Science Fiction', in *Science Fiction: A Critical Guide*, ed. Patrick Parrinder (London and New York: Longman): 187–202.
— (1980) 'Outside the Whale', *Science Fiction Review* 9 (August): 17–21.

— (1984) *The Glamour* (London: Cape); rev. (Garden City, NY: Doubleday, 1985).
— (1990a) Review of Nicholas Ruddick, *Christopher Priest*, *Foundation* 50 (Autumn): 94–101.
— (1990b) 'Without a Suit', *Focus: An SF Writers' Magazine* 22 (December): 3–5.
— and Ian Watson (1976) 'Science Fiction: Form Versus Content', *Foundation* 10 (June): 55–65.
Pringle, David (1977) Review of Brian W. Aldiss, *The Malacia Tapestry*, *Foundation* 11/12 (March): 93–96.
Puzo, Mario (1969) *The Godfather* (New York: Putnam).
Pynchon, Thomas (1973) *Gravity's Rainbow* (New York: Viking).
Reed, Kit (1976) 'Songs of War', in *The Killer Mice* (London: Gollancz); orig. Harry Harrison (ed.) *Nova 4* (New York: Walker, 1974).
— (1980) *Magic Time* (New York: Berkley/Putnam).
Renault, Gregory (1983) 'Speculative Porn: Aesthetic Form in Samuel R. Delany's *The Tides of Lust*', *Extrapolation* 24.2 (Summer): 116–29.
Robbins, Tom (1971) *Another Roadside Attraction* (Harmondsworth: Penguin); orig. (Garden City, NY: Doubleday, 1971).
— (1980) *Still Life With Woodpecker* (New York: Bantam).
— (1991) *Even Cowgirls Get the Blues* (London: Bantam); orig. (Boston: Houghton Mifflin, 1976).
Roberts, Adam (2005) *The History of Science Fiction* (Houndsmills, Basingstoke: Palgrave Macmillan).
Roberts, Keith (1974) *The Chalk Giants* (London: Hutchinson).
Rock, Ashley (1979) Review of Richard Cowper, *The Road to Corlay*, *Foundation* 15 (January): 75–78.
Rogers, Ivor A. (1978) 'Robert Heinlein: Folklorist of Outer Space', Joseph D. Olander and Martin Harry Greenberg (eds) *Robert A. Heinlein* (New York: Taplinger): 222–39.
Ross, Harvey (1974) 'Vitamin Pills for Schizophrenics', *Psychology Today* (April): 83–88.
Rottensteiner, Franz (1973) 'Playing Around With Creation: Philip José Farmer', *Science Fiction Studies* 1.2 (Fall): 94–98.
Ruddick, Nicholas (1985) 'The World Turned Inside Out: Decoding *Clarke's Rendezvous with Rama*', *Science Fiction Studies* 12.1 (March): 42–50.
— (1989a) *Christopher Priest* (Mercer Island, WA: Starmont House).
— (1989b) 'Flaws in the Timestream: Unity and Disunity in Keith Roberts's Story-cycles', *Foundation* 45 (Spring): 38–49.
— (1993) *Ultimate Island: On the Nature of British Science Fiction* (Westwood, CT: Greenwood Press).
Russ, Joanna (1970) *And Chaos Died.* (New York: Ace).
— (1972) 'What Can a Heroine Do? or Why Women Can't Write', Susan Koppelman Cornillon (ed.) *Images of Women in Fiction: Feminist Perspectives* (Bowling Green, Ohio: Bowling Green University Popular Press): 2–22.
— (1973a) 'On Books', *F&SF* 44.2 (February): 28–31.
— (1973b) 'On Books', *F&SF* 45.1 (July): 65–71.
— (1975a) *The Female Man* (New York: Bantam Books).

— (1975b) 'On Books', F&SF 48.1 (January): 10–16.
— (1975c) 'On Books', F&SF 48.3 (March): 39–45.
— (1976) *Alyx* (Boston: Gregg Press).
— (1977) *We Who Are About To...* (New York: Dell).
— (1978) *The Two of Them* (New York: Berkley).
— (1980) 'On Books', F&SF 58.2 (February): 94–101.
— (1995) *To Write Like a Woman: Essays in Feminism and Science Fiction* (Bloomington: Indiana University Press).
— (2007) *The Country You Have Never Seen: Essays and Reviews* (Liverpool: Liverpool University Press).
Rutledge, Gregory E. (2000) 'Science Fiction and the Black Power/Arts Movements: The Transpositional Cosmology of Samuel R. Delany Jr', *Extrapolation* 41.2 (Summer): 127–42.
Salvestroni, Simonetta (1987) 'The Science-Fiction Films of Andre Tarkovsky', *Science Fiction Studies* 14.3 (November): 294–306.
Sammons, Todd (1987) '*Return of the Jedi*: Epic Graffiti', *Science Fiction Studies* 14.3 (November): 355–71.
Samuelson, David N. (1980) 'Critical Mass: The SF of Frederik Pohl', *Science Fiction Studies* 7.1 (March): 80–95.
Sargent, Pamela (1972) 'A Sense of Difference', Roger Elwood (ed.) *And Walk Now Gently Through the Fire* (Philadelphia: Chilton).
— (1973) 'Clone Sister', Joseph Elder (ed.) *Eros in Orbit: A Collection of All New Science Fiction Stories About Sex* (New York: Trident).
— (1974) 'Father', *Amazing* 47.5 (February).
— (1976) *Cloned Lives* (New York: Fawcett Gold Medal).
— (1977) 'Why It Happened: Comments and Conclusions', *Science Fiction Studies* 4.2 (July): 134–36.
— (ed.) (1975) *Women of Wonder: Science Fiction Stories by Women About Women* (New York: Vintage).
— (ed.) (1976) *More Women of Wonder: Science Fiction Novelettes by Women About Women* (New York: Vintage).
— (ed.) (1978) *The New Women of Wonder: Recent Science Fiction Stories by Women About Women* (New York: Vintage).
— and George Zebrowski (1977) 'How It Happened: A Chronology', *Science Fiction Studies* 4.2 (July): 129–34.
Schatz, Thomas (2003) 'The New Hollywood', Julian Stringer (ed.) *Movie Blockbusters* (London: Routledge): 15–44.
Scholes, Robert E. and Eric S. Rabkin (1977) *Science Fiction: History, Science, Vision* (Oxford: Oxford University Press).
Scortia, Thomas N. (ed.) (1972) *Strange Bedfellows* (New York: Random House).
— and Frank M. Robinson (1974) *The Glass Inferno* (Garden City, NY: Doubleday).
Seal, Luedtke Julie (1990) 'James Tiptree, Jr: Fostering the Future, Not Condemning It', *Extrapolation* 30.1 (Spring): 73–82.
Searles, Baird (1971) 'Films', F&SF 40.5 (May): 65–67.
— (1972) 'Films', F&SF 43.2 (August) 34–35.
— (1973) 'Films', F&SF 44.1 (January): 103–105.

— (1974a) 'Films', *F&SF* 46.3 (March): 79–81.
— (1974b) 'Films', *F&SF* 46.5 (May): 80–83.
— (1974c) 'Films', *F&SF* 47.6 (December): 79–81.
— (1976) 'Films', *F&SF* 51.1 (July): 59–61.
— (1977a) 'Films', *F&SF* 53.4 (October): 61–63, 149
— (1977b) 'Films', *F&SF* 53.5 (November): 98–100
— (1977c) 'Films', *F&SF* 53.6 (December): 53–55.
— (1978) 'Films', *F&SF* 54.5 (May): 102–104.
— (1980) 'Films', *F&SF* 58.5 (May): 74–76.
Shail, Robert (2008) '"More, Much More ... Roger Moore": A New Bond for a New Decade', Robert Shail (ed.) *Seventies British Cinema* (London: British Film Institute): 150–58.
Sharp, Margery (1959) *The Rescuers* (Boston, MA: Little, Brown).
— (1962) *Miss Bianca* (Boston, MA: Little, Brown).
Shaw, Bob (1975a) *Orbitsville* (London: Gollancz).
— (1975b) Review of Barry N. Malzberg, *Beyond Apollo*, *Foundation* 7/8 (March): 67–70.
— (1983) *Orbitsville Departure* (London: Gollancz).
— (1990) *Orbitsville Judgement* (London: Gollancz).
Shea, Robert and Robert Anton Wilson (1975a) *The Eye in the Pyramid* (New York: Dell).
— (1975b) *The Golden Apple* (New York: Dell).
— (1975c) *Leviathan* (New York: Dell).
Sheldon, Raccoona (1976) 'Your Faces, Oh My Sisters! Your Faces Filled of Light!', Vonda N. McIntyre and Susan Anderson (eds) *Aurora: Beyond Equality* (New York: Fawcett).
— (1981) 'The Screwfly Solution', James Tiptree, *Out of the Everywhere, and Other Extraordinary Visions* (New York: Del Rey); orig. *Analog* 97.6 (June 1977).
Shenton, Andrew K. (2009) 'Sixes and Sevens: *The Prisoner* and *The Omega Factor* Compared', *Foundation* 105 (Spring): 18–31.
Shippey, Tom (1975) Review of Thomas M. Disch, *334*, *Foundation* (November): 83–85.
— (1990) 'The Fall of America in Science Fiction', Tom Shippey (ed.) *Fictional Space* (Atlantic Highlands, NJ: Humanities Press): 104–32.
Showalter, Elaine (1977) *A Literature of their Own: British Women Novelists from Brontë to Lessing* (Princeton, NJ: Princeton University Press).
Siegel, Mark (1980) '*The Rocky Horror Picture Show*: More Than a Lip Service', *Science Fiction Studies* 7.3 (November): 305–12.
Silverberg, Robert (1970a) *Downward to the Earth* (Garden City, NY: Doubleday).
— (1970b) *Tower of Glass* (New York: Scribner's).
— (1971) *The World Inside* (Garden City, NY: Doubleday).
— (1975) 'Introduction: Who is Tiptree, What is He?', James Tiptree Jr, *Warm Worlds and Otherwise* (New York: Ballantine): ix–xviii.
— (1978) 'Introduction: Who is Tiptree, What is He?', James Tiptree Jr, *Warm Worlds and Otherwise* (New York: Ballantine): ix–xviii.
— (1980) *Lord Valentine's Castle* (New York: Harper & Row).

Simak, Clifford D. (1972) *A Choice of Gods* (New York: Putnam).
— (1973a) *Cemetery World* (New York: Putnam).
— (1973b) *Destiny Doll* (New York: Putnam).
— (1973c) *Out of their Minds* (London: Sidgwick and Jackson); orig. (New York: Putnam, 1970).
— (1974) *Our Children's Children* (New York: Putnam).
— (1975) *Enchanted Pilgrimage* (New York: Berkley).
— (1978) *The Fellowship of the Talisman* (New York: Ballantine).
— (1980a) *Catface* (London: Magnum); orig. *Mastodonia* (New York: Ballantine, 1978).
— (1980b) *The Visitors* (New York: Ballantine).
Simons, Margaret A. (1979) 'Racism and Feminism: A Schism in the Sisterhood', *Feminist Studies* 5.2 (Summer): 384–401.
Sladek, John (1970) *The Müller-Fokker Effect* (London: Hutchinson).
— (1972a) 'Broot Force', *F&SF* 43.3 (September).
— (1972b) 'By an Unknown Hand', *The Times Anthology of Detective Stories* (London: Cape).
— (1973a) 'Fossil Astronauts', *Foundation* 4 (July): 28–31.
— (1973b) 'Name (Please Print):', *New Worlds Quarterly* 5 (January).
— (1973c) *The New Apocrypha* (London: Hart-Davis, MacGibbon).
— (1973d) 'Solar Shoe Salesman', *The Steam-Driven Boy and Other Strangers* (London: Panther).
— (1973e) *The Steam-Driven Boy and Other Strangers* (London: Panther).
— (1974) *Black Aura* (London: Cape).
— (1977) *Invisible Green* (London: Gollancz).
— (1978) Review of Frederik Pohl, *Man Plus*, *Foundation* 13 (May): 90–91.
— (1980) *Roderick, or The Education of a Young Machine* (London: Granada).
— (1982) *Alien Accounts* (London: Granada).
— (1983) *Roderick at Random, or Further Education of a Young Machine* (London: Granada).
Slethaug, Gordon E. (1993) '"The Discourse of Arrogance", Popular Power, and Anarchy: The (First) Chronicles of Thomas Covenant the Unbeliever', *Extrapolation* 31.1 (Spring): 48–63.
Smedley, Audrey (2007) *Race in North America: Origin and Evolution of a Worldview* (Boulder, CO: Westview Press).
Smith, George H. (1976) *The Second War of the Worlds* (New York: DAW).
Sobchack, Vivian (1987) *Screening Space: The American Science Fiction Film* (New York: Ungar).
Somay, Bülent. 1984. 'Towards an Open-Ended Utopia', *Science Fiction Studies* 11.1 (March): 25–38.
Sontag, Susan (1966) 'Notes on "Camp"', *Against Interpretation* (New York: Farrar, Straus and Giroux).
— (1977) *On Photography* (New York: Penguin).
Sounes, Howard (2007) *Seventies: The Sights, Sounds and Ideas of a Brilliant Decade* (London: Pocket).
Spark, Alasdair (1990) 'The Art of Future War: *Starship Troopers*, *The Forever War*

and Vietnam', Tom Shippey (ed.) *Fictional Space* (Atlantic Highlands, NJ: Humanities Press): 133–65.
— (1991) 'Vietnam: The War in Science Fiction', Philip J. Davies (ed.) *Science Fiction, Social Conflict and War* (Manchester: Manchester University Press): 113–31.
Spencer, Kathleen L. (1996) 'Nevèrÿon Deconstructed: Samuel R. Delany's *Tales of Nevèrÿon* and the "Modular Calculus"', James Sallis (ed.) *Ash of Stars: On the Writings of Samuel R. Delany* (Jackson, MS: University Press of Mississippi): 127–61.
Spenser, Edmund (1924) *The Poetical Works of Edmund Spenser*, J.C. Smith and E. De Selincourt (eds) (Oxford: Oxford University Press).
Speller, Maureen Kincaid (2005) 'England's Redemption: An Examination of Richard Cowper's Corlay Sequence', *Foundation* 93 (Spring): 89–96.
Stableford, Brian (1977a) 'Insoluble Problems: Barry Malzberg's Career in Science Fiction', *Foundation* 11/12 (March): 135–41.
— (1977b) Review of Christopher Priest, *The Space Machine*, *Foundation* 11/12 (March/April): 53–55.
— (1977c) Review of Theodore Sturgeon, *Case and the Dreamer*, *Vector* 80 (March/April): 19.
— (1979) Review of Brian Aldiss, *Enemies of the System*, *Foundation* 15 (January): 96–97.
— (1980) Review of Kurt Vonnegut, *Jailbird*, *Foundation* 20 (January): 88–96.
— (1981) Review of Alfred Bester, *Golem$^{100}$*, *Foundation* 21 (February): 98–99.
— (1998) 'Science Fiction in the Seventies', *Vector* 200 (July): 21–24.
Steel, Addison E. (1978) *Buck Rogers in the 25th Century* (New York: Dell).
— (1979) *That Man on Beta* (New York: Dell).
Sterling, Bruce (1976) 'Man-Made Self', Geo. W. Proctor and Steve Utley (eds) *Lone Star Universe: The First Anthology of Texas Science Fiction Authors* (Austin, TX: Heidelberg Publishers).
— (1977) *Involution Ocean* (New York: Jove).
— (1980) *The Artificial Kid* (New York: Harper & Row).
— (1986) 'Introduction', William Gibson, *Burning Chrome* (New York: Ann Arbor): 9–13.
Stern, Richard Martin (1973) *The Tower* (New York: McKay).
Stevenson, Robert Louis (1886) *Strange Case of Dr Jekyll and Mr Hyde* (London: Longmans, Green).
Story, Ronald (1976) *The Space Gods Revealed: A Close Look at the Theories of Erich von Däniken* (New York: Harper & Row).
Stringer, Julian (ed.) (2003) *Movie Blockbusters* (London: Routledge).
Strugatsky, Boris and Arkady Strugatsky (1978) *Roadside Picnic* (London: Gollancz).
Strutton, Bill (1973) *Doctor Who and the Zarbi* (London: Target); orig. (London: Frederick Muller, 1965).
Sturgeon, Theodore (1953) 'The World Well Lost', *Universe* 1 (June).
— (1971) *Sturgeon is Alive and Well* (New York: Putnam).
— (1977) 'Why So Much Syzygy', Damon Knight (ed.) *Turning Points: Essays on the Art of Science Fiction* (New York: Harper and Row): 269–72.
— (1986) *Godbody* (New York: Donald I. Fine).

— (2009) 'Slow Sculpture', *Slow Sculpture, Volume XII: The Complete Stories of Theodore Sturgeon* (Berkeley, CA: North Atlantic Books); orig. *Galaxy* 29.5 (February 1970).
— (2010a) 'Blue Butter', *Case and the Dreamer, Volume XIII: The Complete Stories of Theodore Sturgeon* (Berkeley, CA: North Atlantic Books); orig. *F&SF* 47.4 (October 1974).
— (2010b) 'Case and the Dreamer', *Case and the Dreamer, Volume XIII: The Complete Stories of Theodore Sturgeon* (Berkeley, CA: North Atlantic Books); orig. *Galaxy* 33.4 (January 1973).
Suvin, Darko (1972a) 'Cognition and Estrangement: An Approach to Sf Poetics', *Foundation* 2 (June): 6–16.
— (1972b) 'On the Poetics of the Science Fiction Genre', *College English* 34.3 (December): 372–82.
— (1979) *Metamorphoses of Science Fiction: Studies on the Poetics and History of a Literary Genre* (New Haven, CT: Yale University Press).
— (2000) 'Considering the Sense of "Fantasy" or "Fantasy Fiction": An Effusion', *Extrapolation* 41.3 (Fall): 209–47.
Taylor, Jonathan S. (2002) 'The Subjectivity of the Near Future: Geographical Imaginings in the Work of J.G. Ballard', Rob Kitchin and James Kneale (eds) *Lost in Space: Geographies of Science Fiction* (London and New York: Continuum): 90–103.
Telotte, J.P. (2001) *Science Fiction Film* (Cambridge: Cambridge University Press).
Tennant, Emma (1973) *The Time of the Crack* (London: Cape).
— (1976) *Hotel de Dream* (London: Gollancz).
— (1978) *The Bad Sister* (London: Gollancz).
— (1979) *Wild Nights* (London: Cape).
— (1980) *Alice Fell* (London: Cape).
Tidmarsh, Andrew (1977) Review of Barry N. Malzberg, *Scop*, *Foundation* 11/12 (March): 151–53.
Tilms, Richard (1980) *Judgement of Jupiter* (London: NEL).
Tiptree, James, Jr (1973a) *Ten Thousand Light Years from Home* (New York: Ace).
— (1973b) 'The Women Men Don't See', *F&SF* 45.6 (December).
— (1975) *Warm Worlds and Otherwise* (New York: Ballantine).
— (1976) 'Houston, Houston, Do You Read?', Vonda N. McIntyre and Susan Anderson (eds) *Aurora: Beyond Equality* (New York: Fawcett).
— (1978a) *Star Songs of an Old Primate* (New York: Del Rey).
— (1978b) *Up the Walls of the World* (New York: Berkley).
— (1981) *Out of the Everywhere, and Other Extraordinary Visions* (New York: Del Rey).
Todorov, Tzvetan (1973) *The Fantastic: A Structural Approach to a Literary Genre*, trans. Richard Howard (Ithaca, NY: University of Cornell Press); orig. *Introduction à la Littérature Fantastique* (Paris: Éditions du Seuil, 1970).
Toffler, Alvin (1970) *Future Shock* (New York, Random House).
Tolkien, J.R.R. (1937) *The Hobbit* (London: George Allen and Unwin).
— (1949a) *The Fellowship of the Ring* (London: George Allen and Unwin).
— (1949b) *The Two Towers* (London: George Allen and Unwin).
— (1950) *The Return of the King* (London: George Allen and Unwin).

— (1964) *Tree and Leaf* (London: Unwin).
— (1977) *The Silmarillion* (London: George Allen and Unwin).
— (1980) *Unfinished Tales* (London: George Allen and Unwin).
Tuck, Donald (ed.) (1954, 1959) *A Handbook of Science Fiction and Fantasy* (Hobart).
— (ed.) (1974–1982) *The Encyclopedia of Science Fiction and Fantasy through 1968* (Chicago: Advent Publishers).
Tucker, Wilson (1970) *The Year of the Quiet Sun* (New York: Ace).
Turner, Alwyn W. (2009) *Crisis? What Crisis?: Britain in the 1970s* (London: Aurum Books).
Turner, George (1975) 'Philip K. Dick by 1975: *Flow My Tears, The Policeman Said*', Bruce Gillespie (ed.) *Philip K. Dick: Electric Shepherd* (Carlton, VIC: Norstrilia): 94–100.
— (1980) 'Delany: Victim of Great Applause', *SF Commentary* 58 (February): 14–16.
Vallorani, Nicoletta (1994) 'The Body of the City: Angela Carter's *The Passion of the New Eve*', *Science Fiction Studies* 21.3 (November): 365–79.
Van Deburg, William L. (1992) *New Day in Babylon: The Black Power Movement and American Culture, 1965–1975* (Chicago: University of Chicago Press).
Varley, John (2004a) 'Options', *The John Varley Reader* (New York: Ace); orig. Terry Carr (ed.) *Universe* 9 (Garden City, NY: Doubleday, 1979).
— (2004b) 'Picnic on Nearside', *The John Varley Reader* (New York: Ace); orig. *F&SF* 47.2 (August 1974).
Venturi, Robert (1966) *Complexity and Contradiction in Architecture* (New York: Museum of Modern Art).
— and Denise Scott Brown and Steven Izenour (1972) *Learning from Las Vegas* (Cambridge, MA: MIT Press); rev. (Cambridge, MA: MIT Press, 1977).
Vidal, Gore (1978) *Kalki* (New York: Random House).
Vogh, James (1977) *Arachne Rising: The Search for the Thirteenth Sign of the Zodiac* (New York: Dial Press).
— (1978) *The Cosmic Factor: Bioastrology and You* (New York: Dodd, Mead).
von Däniken, Erich (1969) *Chariots of the Gods? Unsolved Mysteries of the Past*, trans. Michael Heron (London: Souvenir); orig. *Erinnerungen an die Zukunft: Ungelöste Rätsel der Vergangenheit* (Düsseldorf: Econ-Verlag, 1968).
— (1972) *Return to the Stars: Evidence for the Impossible*, trans. Michael Heron (London: Souvenir); orig *Zurück zu den Sternen: Argumente für des Unmögliche* (Düsseldorf: Econ-Verlag, 1968).
— (1973) *The Gold of the Gods*, trans. Michael Heron (London: Souvenir); orig. *Aussaat und Kosmos: Spuren und Pläne ausserirdischer Intelligenzen* (Düsseldorf: Econ-Verlag, 1972).
— (1974) *In Search of Ancient Gods: My Pictorial Evidence for the Impossible*, trans. Michael Heron (London: Souvenir); orig. *Meine Welt in Bildern: Bildargumente für Theorien, Spekulationen und Erforschtes* (Düsseldorf: Econ-Verlag, 1973).
— (1975) *Miracles of the Gods: A Hard Look at the Supernatural*, trans. Michael Heron (London: Souvenir); orig. *Erscheinungen: Phänomene, die de Welt erregen* (Düsseldorf: Econ-Verlag, 1974).
— (1977) *According to the Evidence: My Proof of Man's Extraterrestrial Origins*, trans.

Michael Heron (London: Souvenir); orig. *Beweise: Lokaltermin in Fünf Kontinenten* (Düsseldorf: Econ-Verlag, 1977).
— (1980) *Signs of the Gods?*, trans. Michael Heron (London: Souvenir); orig. *Prophet der Vergangenheit: riskante Gedanken um die Allgegenwart der Ausserirdischen* (Düsseldorf: Econ-Verlag, 1979).
von Kleist, Heinrich (2004) 'Michael Kohlhaas (From an old chronicle)', *Heinrich von Kleist: Selected Writings*, David Constantine (ed. and trans.) (Cambridge: Hackett).
Vonnegut, Kurt (1959) *Sirens of Titan* (New York: Dell).
— (1969) *Slaughterhouse-Five; or, The Children's Crusade, A Duty-Dance With Death* (New York: Delacorte).
— (1974) *Breakfast of Champions, or Goodbye Blue Monday* (London: Granada); orig. (New York: Delacorte, 1973).
— (1979) *Jailbird* (New York: Delacorte).
— (1985) *Galápagos* (Franklin Center, PA: Franklin Library).
— (1997) *Timequake* (New York: Putnams).
Wagar, W. Warren (1991) 'J.G. Ballard and the Transvaluation of Utopia', *Science Fiction Studies* 18.1 (March): 53–70.
Watson, Gray (1996) 'An Archeology of Soul', Roger Wollen (ed.) *Derek Jarman: A Portrait* (London: Thames & Hudson): 33–45.
Watson, Ian (1981) Review of Robert Silverberg, *Lord Valentine's Castle*, *Foundation* 21 (February): 75–77.
— (1982) Review of Harlan Ellison, *Shatterday*, *Foundation* 24 (March): 87–90.
Waugh, Patricia (1984) *Metafiction: The Theory and Practice of Self-Conscious Fiction* (London: Routledge).
Weil, Ellen R. (1988) 'The Ellison Personae: Author, Storyteller, Narrator', *Journal of the Fantastic in the Arts* 1(3): 27–36.
Wellman, Manley Wade and Wade Wellman (1975) *Sherlock Holmes's The War of the Worlds* (New York: Warner).
Wells, H.G. (1895) *The Time Machine* (London: William Heinemann).
— (1896) *The Island of Doctor Moreau* (London: Heinemann, Stone and Kimball).
— (1898) *The War of the Worlds* (London: William Heinemann).
— (1899) *When the Sleeper Wakes*, *The Graphic*.
— (1905) 'The Empire of the Ants', *The Strand* (December).
— (1933) *The Shape of Things to Come* (London: Hutchinson).
Wesley, Marilyn C. (2000) 'Emma Tennant: The Secret Lives of Girls', Abby H.P. Werlock (ed.) *British Women Writing Fiction* (Tuscaloosa: University of Alabama Press): 175–90.
West, Chris (2007) 'Yesterday's Myths Today and Tomorrow: Problems of Representation and Gay (In)visibility', *Extrapolation* 48.3 (Fall): 504–19.
Weston, Peter (ed.) (1977) *Andromeda 1* (London: Futura).
— (ed.) (1978a) *Andromeda 2* (London: Futura).
— (ed.) (1978b) *Andromeda 3* (London: Futura).
Whitaker, David (1973) *Doctor Who and the Crusaders* (London: Target); orig. (London: Frederick Muller, 1965).
— (1973) *Doctor Who in an Exciting Adventure with the Daleks* (London: Target); orig. (London: Frederick Muller, 1964).

Whyte, Nicholas (2006) '*The Curse of Peladon*', *From the Heart of Europe* (available online at <http://nwhyte.livejournal.com/771925.html>).
Wilder, Cherry (1979) Review of Octavia E. Butler, *Survivor*, *Foundation* 15 (January): 90–91.
Wilhelm, Kate (1971) *Margaret and I* (Boston, MA: Little, Brown).
— (1974) 'Where Late the Sweet Birds Sang', Damon Knight (ed.) *Orbit 15* (New York: Harper & Row).
— (1976) *Where Late the Sweet Birds Sang* (New York: Harper and Row).
— (1979) *Juniper Time* (New York: Harper & Row).
Williams, Lynn F. (1986) 'Women and Power in C. J. Cherryh's Novels', *Extrapolation* 27.2 (Summer): 85–92.
Wilson, Don (1975) *Our Mysterious Spaceship Moon* (New York: Dell).
Wingrove, David (1977): 'Confronting Professor Greatrex; Michael G. Coney', *Vector: The Critical Journal of the British Science Fiction Association* 80 (March/April): 10–11.
— (1989) 'Michael Coney: Interview', *Interzone* 32 (November/December 1989): 40–42.
Woledge, Elizabeth (2005) 'From Slash to Mainstream: Female Writers and Gender Blending Men', *Extrapolation* 46.1 (Spring): 50–65.
Wolfe, Gene (1970) 'The HORARS of War', Harry Harrison (ed.) *Nova 1* (New York: Delacorte Press).
Wolf, Virginia L. (1989) 'Andre Norton: Feminist Pied Piper in SF', *Children's Literature Association Quarterly* 10.2 (Summer): 66–70.
Wolk, Anthony (1979) Review of Garry Kilworth, *The Night of Kadar*, *Foundation* 16 (May): 88–90.
Wolmark, Jenny (1993) *Aliens and Others: Science Fiction, Feminism and Postmodernism* (Brighton: Harvester).
Wood, Diane S. (1990) 'Breaking the Code: Vonda N. McIntyre's *Dreamsnake*', *Extrapolation* 31.1 (Spring): 63–72.
Wood, Robin (1986) *Hollywood From Vietnam to Reagan* (New York: Columbia University Press).
Wright, Peter (2005) 'British Television Science Fiction', David Seed (ed.) *A Companion to Science Fiction* (Oxford: Blackwell): 288–305.
Wymer, Rowland (1992) 'How "Safe" is John Wyndham? A Closer Look at His Work, With Particular Reference to *The Chrysalids*', *Foundation* 55 (Summer): 25–36.
— (2005) *Derek Jarman* (Manchester: Manchester University Press).
Yudkin, Marcia (1978) 'Transsexualism and Women: A Critical Perspective', *Feminist Studies* 4.3: 97–106.
Zaki, Hoda M. (1990) 'Utopia, Dystopia and Ideology in the Science Fiction of Octavia Butler', *Science Fiction Studies* 17.2 (July): 239–51.
Zavitzianos, George (1972) 'Homeovestism: Perverse Form of Behaviour Involving the Wearing of Clothes of the Same Sex', *International Journal of Psycho-Analysis* 53.4: 471–77.
Zipes, Jack (2001) *Sticks and Stones: The Troublesome Success of Children's Literature from Slovenly Peter to Harry Potter* (New York: Routledge).

# Index

*10* (Edwards) 190
*334* (Disch) 31
1920s 57, 172, 224
1930s 5, 15, 17, 20, 52, 57, 84, 89, 183, 191, 225
1940s 11, 67, 183, 190,
1950s 5, 11, 16, 24, 33, 67, 81, 89, 101, 165, 168, 171, 181, 184, 191, 207, 223, 225
1960s 1–6, 8, 11, 19, 24, 27, 30–33, 37, 38, 43, 44, 48, 82, 84, 85, 88, 90, 99–100, 102, 105–7, 109, 110, 111, 119, 120, 136, 143, 154, 165–6, 168, 176, 177, 181, 193, 198, 208, 212, 229, 235, 237
1980s 3–5, 23, 28, 77, 101, 153, 235, 237
*1990* 107, 118
1990s 5, 155, 237
*2001: A Space Odyssey* (Kubrick) 6, 15, 57, 68, 128, 171, 193
20th Century Fox 49, 209
*633 Squadron* (Grauman) 185

Abbott, Stacey 40
*Abby* (Girdler) 90
ABC 49, 50
*ABCDEFG HIJKLM NPOQRST UVWXYZ* (Disch) 31
abject 199–205
abortion 134, 136, 145, 159, 176, 202, 227
*Absent-Minded Professor, The* (Stevenson) 172–3
academics 4, 7, 101, 109, 126, 139
Ace 108, 144, 148, 205
Adams, Douglas 63
  *The Hitchhiker's Guide to the Galaxy* 63
  *The Restaurant at the End of the Universe* 63
Adams, Richard 71
  *Watership Down* 71
Adams, Robert 67, 165
  *A Cat of Silvery Hue* 67
  *The Coming of the Horseclans* 67
  *The Patrimony* 67
  *Revenge of the Horseclans* 67

*The Savage Mountains* 67
*Swords of the Horseclans* 67
Adlard, Mark 161
Afghanistan 3, 53, 55, 218
Africa 111, 119
African Americans 78–91, 114, 124, 138, 156, 163, 200
African Caribbean 114
Afrofuturism 89–90
*Again, Dangerous Visions* (Ellison) 24, 95, 137
Agenda sf 5, 11, 50
Agnew, David 63, 107
AIDS/HIV 153, 237
Akers, Alan Burt 67
Alan Parsons Project 76–7
  *The Fall of the House of Usher* 76
  *I Robot* 76–7
  *Pyramid* 77
Albiez, Sean 27
Aldiss, Brian W. 3–5, 19, 25, 28–9, 36, 47, 51–53, 106, 215, 223
  *Billion Year Spree* 3, 28, 51–2
  *Eighty-Minute Hour* 28
  *Enemies of the System* 29
  *Frankenstein Unbound* 28, 51
  *Life in the West* 28
  *The Malacia Tapestry* 28–9
  *Moreau's Other Island* 28, 53
  'Not For an Age' 215
  *The Saliva Tree* 52–3
Aldrich, Robert
  *Dirty Dozen, The* 47
Alexander, Karl
  *Time After Time* 54
*Alice Fell* (Tennant) 232
*Alien* (Foster) 169
*Alien* (Scott) 42, 192, 199–201
*Alien Critic, The* 140
*Alien Heat, An* (Moorcock) 25
alien invasion 19, 52–5, 108, 116–7, 121, 131, 170
*Aliens* (Cameron) 94
*All the President's Men* (Pakula) 43, 190
'– All You Zombies –' (Heinlein) 14, 15, 161

# INDEX

Allen, Daevid 75–6
Allen, Irwin
   *The Swarm* 127
Allen, Woody
   *Sleeper* 53
*Alphaville, ou une adventure étrange de Lemmy Caution* (Goddard) 232
*Also Sprach Zarathustra* (Wagner) 171
*Alteration, The* (Amis) 230–1
*Altered States* (Chayefsky) 192
*Altered States* (Russell) 192, 204–5
*Alternative 3* 39, 43–4
Altman, Dennis 153, 159
*Alyx* (Russ) 67–8
*Amazing Stories* 11, 12, 31, 34, 50, 56, 108, 138
'Ambassadors of Death, The' 116
American bicentennial 11, 15, 88, 134
American Civil War 80–1, 87–8
American Dream 181, 216
*American Family, An* 106
*American Graffiti* (Lucas) 182, 183
American Psychiatric Association 153
American Psychological Association 153
*American Shore, The* (Delany) 8, 31
American Zoetrope 182
Amicus Productions 66–7
Amin, Idi 111
Amis, Kingsley 221, 230–1
   *The Alteration* 230–1
   *New Maps of Hell* 230
amphicatastrophe 2, 34, 181, 205
*Analog* 14, 18, 21, 72, 97, 121, 140, 150, 153
*Ancient Astronauts* (Collyns) 194
*And Chaos Died* (Russ) 154, 205
*Anderson Tapes, The* (Lumet) 101
Anderson, Craig W. 130, 216
Anderson, Gerry 44–5
Anderson, Lindsay
   *O Lucky Man!* 106, 119
Anderson, Michael 20, 185, 206, 215, 216, 217, 218
   *The Dam Busters* 185
   *Logan's Run* 206, 215, 216, 217, 218
   *The Martian Chronicles* 20
Anderson, Poul 9, 92
Anderson, Susan
   *Aurora* 140, 149
Anderson, Sylvia 44
*Andromeda Strain, The* (Wise) 121, 130, 214
*Angel's Egg* (Gong) 76
Anger, Kenneth
   *Scorpio Rising* 85
'Angouleme' (Disch) 8, 31

Animals, The 119
*Another Roadside Attraction* (Robbins) 228
Ant, Adam 119
Antczak, Janice 180
Anthony, Piers 65, 73
   *Castle Roogna* 73
   *Neq the Sword* 73
   *Sos the Rope* 73
   *The Source of Magic* 73
   *A Spell for Chameleon* 73
   *Var the Stick* 73
anti-hero 25, 122, 184, 234
Apartheid 54
apocalypse 10, 32, 48, 111, 121–35, 178–9, 206, 218–20, 223
*Apocalypse Now* (Coppola) 94, 98
Apollo missions 6, 10, 17, 37–40, 43, 57, 221
*Arachne Rising* (Vogh) 196
Arbur, Rosemarie 22
architecture 193, 205–20, 223
*AristoCats* (Reitherman) 172
aristocracy and upper classes 118, 126, 211, 212
Aristotle 2, 233
*Armageddon – 2419 AD* (Nowlan) 50
Armstrong, Neil 38
Arneson, Dave 77
Arrow, William 84
   *Escape from Terror Lagoon* 84
   *Man, the Hunted Animal* 84
   *Visions from Nowhere* 84
Arthurian legend 26, 54, 75, 110, 174
*Artificial Kid, The* (Sterling) 233–4
*Ascendancies* (Compton) 108, 109
Ash, Brian 9
Ashby, Hal
   *Coming Home* 93
Ashley, Mike 9
Asimov, Isaac 9, 11–13, 21, 23, 25, 27, 31, 32, 63, 77, 132, 168, 223
   *Fantastic Voyage* 11
   *The Gods Themselves* 5, 11–13
   *I, Robot* 76–7
*Asimov's* 67, 157
*Assassin of Gor* (Norman) 68
*Astounding* 11, 13, 21, 27, 121, 161
*Astounding Sounds, Amazing Music* (Hawkwind) 27
*At the Earth's Core* (Burroughs) 66
*At the Earth's Core* (Connor) 66
*At the Seventh Level* (Elgin) 144–5
AT&T Building 130
*Atrocity Exhibition, The* (Ballard) 26
Attebery, Brian 73
*Attic Thoughts* (Hansson) 74

Aul, Billie 166
*Aurora: Beyond Equality* (Anderson) 140, 149
Australia 9, 58, 109, 216, 217
Avallone, Michael *Beneath the Planet of the Apes* 84
Avon, Kerr 47, 48
Avon Books 32
Ayers, Kevin 75

Bach, Richard 56
*Bad Sister, The* (Tennant) 231–2
Bailey, Hilary 21, 24–6
Baker, Bob 116, 117
Baker, Roy Ward *The Monster Club* 67
Baker, Tom 117, 198
Bakshi, Ralph 69–70
　*Fritz the Cat* 69
　*J.R.R. Tolkien's The Lord of the Rings* 69–70
Ballantine Books 72
Ballard, J.G. 9, 17, 25–28, 31, 36,111, 154, 174, 201, 211–14, 219, 229
　*The Atrocity Exhibition* 26
　*Concrete Island* 27, 206, 210–11
　*Crash* 27, 32, 164, 206, 210–11
　'The Greatest Television Show on Earth' 27
　*High-Rise* 27, 206, 211–12
　'The Life and Death of God' 28
　'My Dream of Flying to Wake Island' 28
　'One Afternoon at Utah Beach' 28
　*Unlimited Dream Company, The* 28
*Bambi* (Hand) 71
Bangladesh 134
Bantam Books 103, 143
*Barbarella* (Vadim) 50, 75
Barbour, Douglas 86
Barr, Marleen S. 146, 235
Barron, Neil 108
Barry, Ian
　*The Chain Reaction* 206, 226
Barsoom books (Burroughs) 14–15, 21–22, 65–7
Bartel, Paul
　*Death Race 2000* 206, 216–17
Barthes, Roland 218
'Basilisk' (Ellison) 94, 95
Bass, Saul
　*Phase IV* 121, 127–8
*Batman* 190
*Battle for the Planet of the Apes* (Gerrold) 84
*Battle for the Planet of the Apes* (Thompson) 83–4

*Battlestar Galactica* 1, 39, 49, 133, 169
Baudrillard, Jean 215, 223, 235
Baum, L. Frank 15
　*The Patchwork Girl of Oz* 227
　*The Wonderful Wizard of Oz* 68, 131, 177
Baxter, John 121, 129
　*The Hermes Fall* 121, 129
BBC 41, 47, 70, 116, 118, 124, 126, 169–71, 192, 196, 197, 198
*Beasts of Gor* (Norman) 68
Bedford, David 75
　*Instructions for Angels* 75
　*Jack of Shadows* 75
　*The Odyssey* 75
　*The Rime of the Ancient Mariner* 75
　*Star's End* 75
Beebe, Ford and Ray Taylor *Flash Gordon Conquers the Universe* 190
Beebe, Ford and Robert F. Hill *Flash Gordon's Trip to Mars* 190
Beebe, Ford and Saul A. Goodkind *Buck Rogers* 50
'Behold the Man' (Moorcock) 25
Benchley, Peter
　*Jaws* 182
*Beneath the Planet of the Apes* (Avallone) 84
*Beneath the Planet of the Apes* (Post) 83–4
Benford, Gregory 36, 121, 127–130
　*In the Ocean of Night* 121, 128–9
　*Timescape* 36, 121, 127
Benford, Gregory and William Rotsler
　*Shiva Descending* 130
Benolie, Bernard 75
Benshoff, Harry M. 90–1
Benton, Robert 188, 201
Benton, Robert *Kramer vs Kramer* 201
Beresford, Elisabeth 171
　*The Wombles* 171
Berger, James 10
Berlitz, Charles 192, 194
　*The Bermuda Triangle* 194
　*Mysteries from Forgotten Worlds* 194
　*The Mystery of Atlantis* 194
　*The Philadelphia Experiment* 194
　*The Roswell Incident* 194
　*Without a Trace* 194
Berman, Michael 216
*Bermuda Triangle, The* (Berlitz) 194
*Bermuda Triangle Mystery – Solved, The* (Kusche) 196
Bernstein, Carl 43
Berserker series (Holdstock) 67
Bester, Alfred 11, 21
　*The Computer Connection* 21

*The Demolished Man* 21
*Golem$^{100}$* 21
*The Indian Giver* 21
*The Stars My Destination* 21
Bettelheim, Bruno 186
Bewick, Thomas 109
*Beyond Apollo* (Malzberg) 35, 40
*Beyond the Blue Event Horizon* (Pohl) 61
Biafra 134
*Big Bus, The* (Frawley) 206, 217
Big Dumb Objects 15, 51, 55–64, 221
*Big Sleep, The* (Hawks) 22
*Billion Year Spree* (Aldiss) 3, 28, 51–2
Birkett, Jack 128
Bingham, Richard John 42
bisexuality 2, 16, 85, 127, 155, 162
'Black Amazon of Mars' (Brackett) 21
*Black Aura* (Sladek) 32
*Black Caesar* (Cohen) 90
black civil rights, see civil rights
black ethnicity; see also African American, African Caribbean 16, 26, 48, 52, 78–91, 111, 115, 119, 153, 156, 156, 162, 200, 218, 224, 237
*Black Hole, The* (Foster) 169
*Black Hole, The* (Nelson) 133, 169, 174–5, 191, 249
black holes 61, 133, 169, 174–5, 191, 200, 249
Black Panther Party 81, 99
*Blackenstein* (Levey) 90–1, 94
*Blacula* (Crain) 90
*Blade Runner* (Burroughs) 230
*Blade Runner* (Scott) 7, 187
*Blade Runner, The* (Nourse) 230
Blake, William 28, 106, 107, 109, 119, 187, 213
    *Milton a poem* 28, 187
*Blake's 7* 39, 47–9
    'Blake' 48
    'Star One' 48
blaxploitation 52, 90–1, 115
Blaylock, James 99
Blish, James 169
Bloch, Ernst 9
blockbusters 7, 10, 50, 98, 180, 181–91, 192, 237
*Bloody Sun, The* (Bradley) 67
'Blue Butter' (Sturgeon) 20
*Blue Peter* 192
Boehm, Carl 188
bomb, the 65, 83,124, 126–7, 178–9, 207, 208, 218–19
'Bomb is Missing, A' 124
Bond, James 43, 107, 114–17, 144, 188, 191, 208

Bond, Michael 192
    'A Spoonful of Paddington' 192
bondage 67–8, 165, 190–1
*Bonnie and Clyde* (Penn) 94
*Book of the Damned, The* (Fort) 193
Booker, M. Keith 45, 49, 50
Boorman, John 65, 68–9
    *Point Blank* 69
    *Zardoz* 65, 68–9
Borgo Press 109
Boucher, Chris 48, 117
Bould, Mark 5, 190
Boulding, Kenneth E. 120
Boulle, Pierre 82
    *Monkey Planet* 82
    *La Planète des Singes* 82
    *Planet of the Apes* 82
Boulter, Amanda 149–50
bourgeoisie and middle classes 2, 3, 29, 32, 70, 99, 100, 111, 125, 126, 148, 158, 163, 200, 211, 212, 237
Bowie, David 103, 162–3
'Boy and His Dog, A' (Ellison) 33, 163
*Boy and His Dog, A* (Jones) 33, 154, 163
Brackett, Leigh 11, 21–3, 67, 183, 202
    'Black Amazon of Mars' 21
    'Enchantress of Venus' 21
    *The Ginger Star* 21–2
    *The Hounds of Skaith* 21–2
    'Martian Quest' 21
    'Queen of the Martian Catacombs' 21
    *The Reavers of Skaith* 21–2
Brackett, Leigh and Edmond Hamilton
    'Stark and the Star Kings' 21–2
Bradbury, Ray 11, 20–2, 34, 168
    *Dandelion Wine* 20
    *Fahrenheit 451* 20
    'The Fireman' 20
    'G.B.S. – Mark V' 20
    *The Halloween Tree* 20
    *Long After Midnight* 20
    *The Martian Chronicles* 20
    'The Messiah' 20
    'My Perfect Murder' 20
    'The Parrot Who Met Papa' 20
    'A Story of Love' 20
    'The Wish' 20
Bradley, Marion Zimmer 67, 154, 164–5
    *The Bloody Sun* 67
    *Darkover Landfall* 67
    *The Forbidden Tower* 67
    *The Heritage of Hastur* 67, 164–5
    *The Planet Savers* 67
    *The Shattered Chain* 67
    *The Spell Sword* 67
    *Stormqueen!* 67

*Two to Conquer* 67
*The Winds of Darkover* 67
*The World Wreckers* 67
*Brainrack* (Davis and Pedler) 124
Brautigan, Richard 221, 227
  *Dreaming of Babylon* 227
  *The Hawkline Monster* 227
  *Sombrero Fallout* 227
  *Trout Fishing in America* 227–8
*Brave Little Toaster, The* (Disch) 31
*Breakfast in the Ruins* (Moorcock) 25–6
*Breakfast of Champions* (Vonnegut) 104, 225–6
*Breakthrough* (Cowper) 196
Brecht, Bertolt 9
Bridges, James
  *The China Syndrome* 206, 217
*Briefing for a Descent into Hell* (Lessing) 231
British Science Fiction Association 10, 137
Britton, Andrew 93–4
Brizzi, Mary T. 142
Brock, Dave 27
Broderick, Damien 5
Brogan, Hugh 81, 99
Bronowski, Jacob 13
*Brontomek!* (Coney) 122, 123
*Brood, The* (Cronenberg) 192, 201, 202, 205
Brooks, Mel 52
  *Young Frankenstein* 52
Brooks, Terry 72
  *The Elfstones of Shannara* 72
  *The Sword of Shannara* 72
'Broot Force' (Sladek) 32
Brosnan, John 68, 123, 125,128, 133, 183, 195, 217
*Brothers of Earth* (Cherryh) 141
Brown, Charles 10
Brunner, John 9, 12, 25, 30–1, 121, 125, 138, 230, 235, 236
  *The Jagged Orbit* 30
  *The Sheep Look Up* 30, 121, 125–6
  *The Shockwave Rider* 30
  *Stand On Zanzibar* 30
  *Total Eclipse* 12, 31, 138
Bryant, Anita 153
Bryant, Chris 46
Bryant, Edward 33
Bryant, Edward and Harlan Ellison
  *Phoenix Without Ashes* 33
BSFA 10, 137
BSFA Award 137
Bubbles, Barney 27
Buck Rogers 39, 49–50, 133, 169, 188, 189
*Buck Rogers* (Beebe and Goodkind) 50

*Buck Rogers in the 25th Century* (Haller) 50, 169
*Buck Rogers in the 25th Century* (Steel) 169
*Buck Rogers in the Twenty-Fifth Century* 50, 169
buddies 159, 163, 165–7
Budrys, Algis 21, 72
*Bull and the Spear, The* (Moorcock) 25
*Bull Chief, The* (Carlsen) 67
Bulmer, Kenneth 9, 24, 67
  Drey Prescott series 67
Burgess, Anthony 104
  *A Clockwork Orange* 104
Burke, James 41
*Burn This* (Disch) 31
Burnford, Sheila 31
  *The Incredible Journey* 31
Burroughs, Edgar Rice 7, 14–15, 21–2, 29, 65–7
  *At the Earth's Core* 66
  Barsoom books 14–15, 21–2, 65–7
  *The Land that Time Forgot* 66
  *Out of Time's Abyss* 67
  *The People that Time Forgot* 67
Burroughs, William S. 75, 109, 223, 229–30
  *Blade Runner* 230
  *The Last Words of Dutch Schultz* 229
  *Port of Saints* 229
  *Wild Boys: A Book of the Dead, The* 229–30
Burton, Richard 62
Butler, Andrew M. 108
Butler, Charles 177
Butler, Judith 154
Butler, Octavia E. 78, 84, 86–8, 148
  *Clay's Ark* 87
  *Kindred* 87–8
  *Mind of My Mind* 87
  *Patternmaster* 87–8
  *Survivor* 87
  *Wild Seed* 87
Butterworth, Michael 36
Butterworth, Michael and Michael Moorcock *Queens of Deliria* 36
  *The Time of the Hawklords* 36
'By an Unknown Hand' (Sladek) 32
'By His Bootstraps' (MacDonald) 161
Byron, Lord George 52

Callaghan, James 106–7
Callenbach, Ernest 121, 134
  *Ecotopia* 121, 134
Calvert, Robert 27
Cambodia 15, 88, 93–4
*Camembert Electrique* (Gong) 76

Cameron, Ian 173
  *The Lost Ones* 173
Cameron, James 94
  *Aliens* 94
Cammell, Donald 192, 203–4
  *Demon Seed* 192, 203–4
Cammell, Donald and Nicolas Roeg
  *Performance* 203
camp 1, 20, 161–2, 190–1
Campbell, John W. 5, 11, 14, 51
Campbell, Joseph 183, 185
Campbell, Ken 229
Campbellian 5, 11, 51
*Capricorn One* (Hyams) 39, 44
*Captain Scarlet and the Mysterons* 44
*Captive of Gor* (Norman) 68
captivity narrative 89, 95
Carey, Peter 154, 158–9
  'Peeling' 158–9
Carlos, John *Kingdom of the Spiders* 127
Carlsen, Chris 67
  *The Bull Chief* 67
  *The Horned Warrior* 67
  *Shadow of the Wolf* 67
Carlson, William 154, 158
  'Dinner at Helen's' 158
Carnell, John 24, 25
Carpenter, Edward 152
Carpenter, John 39, 42, 169, 199, 202
  *Dark Star* 39, 42, 169
  *Halloween* 42, 199, 202
Carr, Carol 78
Carr, Terry 24, 25, 192, 204
  *Cirque* 192, 204
*Carrie* (De Palma) 195, 188, 202
Carroll, Lewis 62
Carter, Angela 221, 232
  *The Passion of New Eve* 232
Carter, Lin 67, 72
  Green Star series 72
  Callisto series 72
Case and the Dreamer' (Sturgeon) 19–20
*Castle Roogna* (Anthony) 73
*Casualties of War* (De Palma) 94
*Cat of Silvery Hue, A* (Adams) 67
*Catface* (Simak) 18
catharsis 11, 30, 82, 205, 225
Caucasian, see also white ethnicity 78, 138, 162, 184
Cawthorne, James 66
*Cemetery World* (Simak) 18
*Centauri Device, The* (Harrison) 29
*Chain Reaction, The* (Barry) 206, 226
*Chalk Giants, The* (Roberts) 109–10
Challenger, Professor 54

chaos 2, 4, 22, 37, 42, 106, 182, 193, 196, 204, 213
Chapman, Edgar L. 144, 145
*Chariots of the Gods?* (von Däniken) 57, 104, 193
*Chariots of the Gods? Unsolved Mysteries of the Past* 193
*Charisma* (Coney) 61, 122, 123
Charisma Records 27
*Charlie and the Chocolate Factory* (Dahl) 175
*Charlie and the Great Glass Elevator* (Dahl) 175
Charnas, Suzy McKee 136, 146–7, 166, 241
  *The Conqueror's Child* 147
  *The Furies* 147
  *Motherlines* 146–7
  *Walk to the End of the World* 146
Chayefsky, Paddy 192
  *Altered States* 192
Chaykin, Howard *Star\*Reach* 49
Chernobyl 131
Cherryh, C.J. 22, 67, 136, 141–2
  *Brothers of Earth* 141
  *The Faded Sun: Kesrith* 142
  *The Faded Sun: Kutath* 142
  *The Faded Sun: Shon'jir* 142
  *Fires of Azeroth* 141–2
  *Gate of Ivrel* 141–2
  *Well of Shiuan* 141–2
Chicago 101, 207
*Childhood's End* (Clarke) 78
children 12, 20, 31, 44, 70, 73, 79, 81, 85, 98, 125, 127, 133, 139, 146,157, 158–80, 184, 192, 195, 201–3,212, 214, 232
*Children of Morrow* (Hoover) 178–9
children's fiction 10, 31, 44, 70, 73, 158–80, 182, 232
China 100, 122, 124
*China Syndrome, The* (Bridges) 206, 217
*Choice of Gods, A* (Simak) 18, 19
Christ, Jesus 20, 25, 62, 110, 113, 125, 228
Christopher, John 123
  *Death of Grass, The* 123
Chronicles of Corum trilogy (Moorcock) 25
*Chronocules* (Compton) 108
*Chrysalids, The* (Wyndham) 178
Church, Frederic Edwin 56
Cimino, Michael 93, 96
  *The Deer Hunter* 93, 96
*Cirque* (Carr) 192, 204
*City Dwellers, The* (Platt) 33

'City of Death' 63
civil rights 1, 80, 82, 84, 88, 90, 105, 153
Civil War, American 80–1, 87–8
Civil War, English 177
Civil War, Spanish 35
Cixous, Hélène 142–3
*Clangers, The* 171, 221
*Clara Reeve* (Hargrave) 31
Clarke, Arthur C. 9, 11, 15–17, 23, 51, 57–60, 65, 138
   *Childhood's End* 78
   *The Fountains of Paradise* 15–17
   *Imperial Earth* 15–16
   *Rendezvous with Rama* 15, 57–8
Clarke, Arthur C. and Gentry Lee
   *The Garden of Rama* 57
   *Rama II* 15–16
   *Rama Revealed* 57
class 1, 3, 7, 29, 70, 84, 100, 104, 110, 118, 126, 138, 146, 148, 158, 162, 197, 200, 207, 208, 211–12, 235
'Claws of Axos, The' 117
*Clay's Ark* (Butler) 87
Cleaver, Pamela 180
Cleman, Tom 75
Clement, Hal 121
   *Mission of Gravity* 121
   *Star Light* 121
*Cleopatra Jones* (Starrett) 90
Clinton, George 89–90
*Clockwork Orange, A* (Burgess) 104
*Clockwork Orange, A* (Kubrick) 93, 104–5, 208, 232
*Clone* (Cowper) 197
'Clone Sister' (Sargent) 133
*Cloned Lives* (Sargent) 121, 133
*Clones of Dr. Funkenstein, The* (Parliament) 90
*Close Encounters of the Third Kind* (Spielberg) 46, 115, 182, 191, 192, 194–6
Clute, John 5, 10, 11, 15, 16, 18, 28, 39, 130, 155, 215
Coates, Lewis 39, 50
   *Scontri Stellari Oltre la Terza Dimensione* 39, 50
   *Starcrash* 39, 50
cognitive estrangement 9, 65, 169
Cohen, Larry 90, 192, 202–3
   *Black Caesar* 90
   *It Lives Again* 192, 202–3
   *It's Alive* 192, 202–3
Cold War 22, 30, 98, 114, 115, 122, 131, 172, 178, 181, 198, 218, 237
*College English* 9
Collier, Ann 134
Collings, Michael R. 53
Collyns, Robin 192, 194
   *Ancient Astronauts* 194
   *Did Spacemen Colonise the Earth?* 194
   *Laser Beams from Star Cities?* 194
colonialism 6, 18, 19, 47, 51–61, 79, 80, 91, 93, 95, 105, 113–14, 122–3, 132, 194, 223, 233
'Colony in Space' 170
*Colossus: The Forbin Project* (Sargent) 203, 206, 218
*Colour of Magic, The* (Pratchett) 64
*Coming Home* (Ashby) 93
*Coming of the Horseclans, The* (Adams) 67
*Commando Raid* (Harrison) 96
*Committed Men, The* (Harrison) 29
Commoner, Barry 120
*Communipaths, The* (Elgin) 144
communism 2, 32, 92–3, 100–1, 115, 122, 128, 224–5
Compton, D.G. 107, 108–9, 205
   *Ascendancies* 108, 109
   *Chronocules* 108
   *The Continuous Katherine Mortenhoe* 108–9
   *The Missionaries* 108
   *The Quality of Mercy* 108
   *The Steel Crocodile* 108–9, 205
   *Synthajoy* 109
   *A Usual Lunacy* 109
   *Windows* 109
*Computer Connection, The* (Bester) 21
computerization 4, 42, 50, 218–19, 232–35
Conan Doyle, Arthur 54, 66
   *The Lost World* 66
   Sherlock Holmes 54, 188
Conan stories 65
conceptual breakthrough 56, 61, 65
*Concrete Island* (Ballard) 27, 206, 210–11
*Condition of Muzak, The* (Moorcock) 25, 30, 114, 230
Coney, Michael 61, 62, 121, 122–3
   *Brontomek!* 122, 123
   *Charisma* 61, 122, 123
   *Mirror Image* 122
   *Syzygy* 122, 123
Connor, Kevin 66–7
   *At the Earth's Core* 66
   *The Land That Time Forgot* 66
   *The People that Time Forgot* 66–7
*Conqueror's Child, The* (Charnas) 147
*Conquest of the Planet of the Apes* (Jakes) 84
*Conquest of the Planet of the Apes* (Thompson) 83–4

## INDEX

Conrad, Joseph 26, 55, 80, 112
  'Heart of Darkness' 80, 111–12
consolation 2–4, 31, 34, 70, 186
conspiracies 8, 26, 32, 43, 62, 93, 123, 127, 171, 194, 214, 223, 228–30
Constantine, David 224
consumerism 120, 140, 216–17, 235
*Continuous Katherine Mortenhoe, The* (Compton) 108–9
contraceptive 59, 136, 176, 202
Cook, Captain James 58
Cooper, Edmund 9
Cooper, Merian 209–10
Cooper, Merian and Ernest Schoedsack
  *King Kong* 209–10
Coppola, Francis Ford 94, 98, 182
  *Apocalypse Now* 94, 98
  *Finian's Rainbow* 182
  *The Godfather 2*, 180, 188
  *The Rain People* 182
Corman, Roger 216
Cornea, Christine 56–7, 83, 175, 204
Cornelius Tetralogy (Moorcock) 25, 30, 55, 114, 230
Cornelius, Jerry 25–6, 30, 55, 114, 230, 231–2
Cosgrove, Denis 120–1
*Cosmic Factor, The* (Vogh) 196
*Cosmic Puppets, The* (Dick) 103
cosy catastrophe 29, 32, 111–12, 231
Coveney, Michael 229
Cowper, Richard 110–11, 149, 192, 196–7, 221, 222–3
  *Breakthrough* 196
  *Clone* 197
  *Domino* 106, 196–7
  *A Dream of Kinship* 110
  *Kuldesak* 110
  *Phoenix* 196
  'Piper at the Gates of Dawn' 110
  *Profundis* 110
  *The Road to Corlay* 110
  *A Tapestry of Time* 110
  *Time Out of Mind* 197
  *The Twilight of Briareus* 197
  *Worlds Apart* 223
Cowper, William 111
Crabbe, Larry (Buster) 50, 190
Crain, William 90
  *Blacula* 90
  *Dr. Black, Mr. Hyde* 90
*Crash* (Ballard) 27, 32, 164, 206, 210–11
Creed, Barbara 199–201, 204
Crichton, Michael 129, 130, 190, 206, 214, 217
  *Westworld* 206, 214, 215

critical utopia 235
Cronenberg, David 192, 201, 202, 205, 206, 212
  *Brood, The* 192, 201, 202, 205
  *Frissons* 201, 206, 212
  *Orgy of the Blood Parasites* 201, 206, 212
  *The Parasite Murders* 201, 206, 212
  *Shivers* 201, 206, 212
  *They Came From Within* 201, 206, 212
Crumb, Robert 69
Csicsery-Ronay, Istvan 32
Cummings, Michael S. 134
*Cure for Cancer, A* (Moorcock) 25, 30, 114, 230
'Curse of Peladon, The' 41
Cushing, Peter 66
Cutler, Chris 89–90
cyberpunk 3–5, 21, 210, 222, 234–7
Cyprus 15, 116, 113

'Dæmons, The' 170
Dahl, Roald 168, 175
  *Charlie and the Chocolate Factory* 175
  *Charlie and the Great Glass Elevator* 175
Daleks 48, 117, 118, 126, 170
*Dam Busters, The* (Anderson) 185
*Damien: The Omen II* (Taylor) 190, 202
*Dandelion Wine* (Bradbury) 20
*Dangerous Visions* (Ellison) 24–5, 91, 137,
Danot, Serge 170–1
  *Dougal and the Blue Cat* 171
  *Pollux et Le Chat Bleu* 170–1
Dante, Joe 127
  *Piranha* 127
*Dark Side of the Moon, The* (Pink Floyd) 63, 76
*Dark Side of the Sun, The* (Pratchett) 63, 65
*Dark Star* (Carpenter) 39, 42, 169
*Dark Star* (Foster) 169
*Darkover Landfall* (Bradley) 67
Davidson, Avram 78
Davidson, Rjurik 29, 30
Davis, Gerry 124
Davis, Gerry and Kit Pedler
  *Brainrack* 124
  *Doomwatch: The World in Danger* 124
  *The Dynostar Menace* 124
  *Mutant 59 The Plastic Eater* 124
DAW Books 72, 104
*Day of the Burning, The* (Malzberg) 36, 40
'Day of the Daleks, The' 170
*Day the Earth Stood Still, The* (Wise) 130
de Bolt, Joe 30
de Camp, L. Sprague 9
De Laurentiius, Dino 190

De Palma, Brian 94, 195, 188, 202
  *Carrie* 195, 188, 202
  *Casualties of War* 94
De Witt, Douglas Kilgore 16, 57
'Deadly Assassin, The' 232
*Death of Grass, The* (Christopher) 123
*Death of Reginald Perrin, The* (Nobbs) 70
*Death Race 2000* (Bartel) 206, 216–17
*Death Watch* (Tavernier) 108
*Deep Throat* (Gerard) 210
*Deer Hunter, The* (Cimino) 93–4, 96
Deighton, Len 230
  *SS-GB* 230
del Rey, Lester 9
Delany, Samuel R. 4, 8, 24–5, 31–3, 67, 78, 84–6, 141, 145, 147, 154–7
  *The American Shore* 8, 31
  *Dhalgren* 25, 85–6
  *The Einstein Intersection* 85
  *Heavenly Breakfast* 85
  *Hogg* 85–6
  *The Jewel-Hinged Jaw* 8
  *Nova* 85
  'The Tale of Gorgik' 67, 157
  'The Tale of Old Venn' 157
  *Tales of Nevèrÿon* 67, 157
  *The Tides of Lust* 32–3, 85, 154
  *Triton* 145, 155–6, 235
Delap, Richard 127, 148
Delgado, Roger 116, 221
*Delikon, The* (Hoover) 179–80
*Demolished Man, The* (Bester) 21
*Demon Seed* (Cammell) 192, 203–4
Demoriane, Hermine 119
Dery, Mark 78, 89
*Destiny Doll* (Simak) 17–18
'Destiny of the Daleks' 118
*Destruction of the Temple, The* (Malzberg) 35
*Dhalgren* (Delany) 25, 85–6
*Diamonds Are Forever* (Hamilton) 43, 115, 152, 208
Dick, Philip K. 5, 8, 11, 32, 78, 81, 93, 98–104, 112, 154, 157, 163–4, 213–15, 221–3, 230, 233
  *The Cosmic Puppets* 103
  *Do Androids Dream of Electric Sheep?* 157
  *Flow My Tears, the Policeman Said* 81, 99–103, 163, 221–2
  *The Man in the High Castle* 100
  *Our Friends from Frolix 8* 99
  *Radio Free Albemuth* 102
  *A Scanner Darkly* 101–2
  *Solar Lottery* 99
  *The Three Stigmata of Palmer Eldritch* 99
  *VALIS* 104
  *We Can Build You* 99
Dicks, Terrance 41, 116, 170
  *Doctor Who and the Auton Invasion* 170
  *Doctor Who and the Day of the Daleks* 170
*Did Spacemen Colonise the Earth?* (Collyns) 194
*Different Light, A* (Lynn) 165
Dillinger, John 229
'Dinner at Helen's' (Carlson) 158
*Dirty Dozen, The* (Aldrich) 47
Disch, Thomas M. 8, 25, 31–3, 152–5, 165, 168
  *334* 31
  *ABCDEFG HIJKLM NPOQRST UVWXYZ* 31
  'Angouleme' 8, 31
  *The Brave Little Toaster* 31
  *Burn This* 31
  *Highway Sandwiches* 31
  *On Wings of Song* 31, 154–5
  *Orders of the Retina* 31
  *The Right Way to Figure Plumbing* 31
Disney 168, 169, 172–5, 180, 213, 215
Disney World 172, 213, 215
*Dispossessed, The* (Le Guin) 139, 145–6, 154, 156, 235
*Divide and Rule* (Mark) 180
*Dixon of Dock Green* 49
'Do Androids Dream of Electric Love?' (Leibscher) 154, 157–8
*Do Androids Dream of Electric Sheep?* (Dick) 157
*Doc Savage: His Apocalyptic Life* (Farmer) 226
*Doctor Who* 1, 41, 48–9, 50, 63, 66, 107, 116–18, 124, 126, 169–70, 197, 198
  'The Ambassadors of Death' 116
  'City of Death' 63
  'The Claws of Axos' 117
  'Colony in Space' 170
  'The Curse of Peladon' 41
  'The Dæmons' 170
  'The Day of the Daleks' 170
  'The Deadly Assassin' 232
  'Destiny of the Daleks' 118
  'Doctor Who and the Silurians' 116, 170
  'The Face of Evil' 48–9, 117
  'Frontier in Space' 116
  'Genesis of the Daleks' 117, 126
  'The Green Death' 117
  'Image of the Fendahl' 49
  'Inferno' 116
  'The Invasion' 116
  'The Invasion of Time' 117
  'The Invisible Enemy' 1

'The Pirate Planet' 63
'Robots of Death' 49
'The Sea Devils' 116, 170
'Shada' 63
'Spearhead from Space' 116
'The Three Doctors' 116
'The Time Warrior' 117
*Doctor Who and the Auton Invasion* (Dicks) 170
*Doctor Who and the Cave Monsters* (Hulke) 170
*Doctor Who and the Crusaders* (Whitaker) 170
*Doctor Who and the Dæmons* (Letts) 170
*Doctor Who and the Day of the Daleks* (Dicks) 170
*Doctor Who and the Doomsday Weapon* (Hulke) 170
*Doctor Who and the Sea-Devils* (Hulke) 170
'Doctor Who and the Silurians' 116, 170
*Doctor Who and the Zarbi* (Strutton) 170
*Doctor Who in an Exciting Adventure with the Daleks* (Whitaker) 170
Doctorow, E.L.
   *Ragtime* 221, 224
'Doge Whose Barque Was Worse Than His Bight, The' (Farmer) 226
*Domino* (Cowper) 106, 196–7
*Don't Look Now* (Roeg) 46, 201
Donaldson, Stephen 71–2, 237
   *The Illearth War* 71–2
   *Lord Foul's Bane* 71–2
   *The Power that Preserves* 71–2
   *The Wounded Land* 71–2
Donne, John 62
   'Holy Sonnet VII' 62
Donner, Richard 68, 188–9, 191, 195, 202, 204
   *The Omen* 195, 202, 204
   *Superman: The Movie* 68, 188–9, 191
Doomwatch 49, 121, 124
   'Bomb is Missing, A' 124
   'Plastic Eaters, The' 124
   'Red Sky, The' 124
   'Survival Code' 124
*Doomwatch* (Sasdy) 124
*Doomwatch: The World in Danger* (Pedler and Davis) 124
*Doppelgänger* (Parrish) 44
*Doremi Fasol Latido* (Hawkwind) 27
Dos Passos, John 30
*Dougal and the Blue Cat* (Danot) 171
Douglas, Helen Gehagan 100
Douglas, Mary 199
*Downward to the Earth* (Silverberg) 80
Doyle, Arthur Conan 54, 66
   *The Lost World* 66
   Sherlock Holmes 54, 188
Dozois, Gardner 78, 80
   *Strangers* 80
*Dr No* (Young) 115
*Dr Strangelove* (Kubrick) 105
*Dr. Black, Mr. Hyde* (Crain) 90
*Dracula vs Frankenstein* (Franco) 52
*Dragonflight* (McCaffrey) 72
*Dragonrider* (McCaffrey) 72
Drake, David 97
*Dream of Kinship, A* (Cowper) 110
*Dream of Wessex, A* (Priest) 112, 223
*Dreaming City, The* (Moorcock) 25
*Dreaming of Babylon* (Brautigan) 227
*Dreamsnake* (McIntyre) 140–1
Drey Prescott series (Bulmer) 67
drugs 4, 30, 76, 101, 115, 149, 176, 182, 203, 204
Du Maurier, Daphne 201
Dudley, Terence 124, 126
*Duel* (Spielberg) 2
Dune novels (Herbert) 165
*Dungeons & Dragons* 77
Dworkin, Andrea 166–7
Dykstra, John 49
*Dynostar Menace, The* (Pedler and Davis) 124
dyscatastrophe 2

*E.T.* (Spielberg) 191
Earth Day 120
*Earthwind* (Holdstock) 113
Eastwood, Clint 59, 216
   *The Outlaw Josey Wales* 59
Eco, Umberto 113
   *Travels in Hyperreality* 113
ecology 4, 19, 70, 105, 120–35
ecosystem 18, 120, 122, 132, 133
*Ecotopia* (Callenbach) 121, 134
*écriture feminine* 142–3
Edwards, Blake 190
   *10* 190
Edwards, Malcolm 4, 9
Effinger, George Alec 33, 78, 84
*Eighty-Minute Hour* (Aldiss) 28
*Einstein Intersection, The* (Delany) 85
Eire, see also Ireland 15, 116
Eisenhower, Dwight D. 100
*El Ahairah (Music Inspired by Watership Down)* (Hansson) 74
*Electronic Labyrinth THX 1138 4EB* (Lucas) 182
*Elfstones of Shannara, The* (Brooks) 72
Elgin, Suzette Haden 136, 144–5
   *At the Seventh Level* 144–5

*The Communipaths* 144
'For the Sake of Grace' 144
*Furthest* 144
*Star-Anchored, Star-Angered* 145
Elliot, Jeffrey M. 133
Ellison, Harlan 18, 21–5, 33–4, 78, 92–4, 96, 137, 163
   *Again, Dangerous Visions* 24, 95, 137
   'Basilisk' 94, 95
   'A Boy and His Dog' 33, 163
   *Dangerous Visions* 24–5, 91, 137,
   'Jeffty Is Five' 34
   'Knox' 34
   *The Last Dangerous Visions* 21, 24
   'Shatterday' 34
Ellison, Harlan and Edward Bryant
   *Phoenix Without Ashes* 33
Ellman, Mary 136
*Elric of Melniboné* (Moorcock) 25
'Empire of the Ants, The' (Wells) 53
*Empire of the Ants* (Gordon) 53
*Empire Strikes Back, The* (Kershner) 7, 22–3, 169, 181, 185–7
*Enchanted Pilgrimage* (Simak) 18
'Enchantress of Venus' (Brackett) 21
*End of All Songs, The* (Moorcock) 25
*Enemies of the System* (Aldiss) 29
energy crisis 115, 122, 217, 233
England 10, 28, 29, 32, 106–19, 126, 153, 223, 231
*England Swings SF: Stories of Speculative Science Fiction* (Merril) 106
*English Assassin, The* (Moorcock) 25, 30, 114, 230
English Civil War 177
*Ennead, The* (Mark) 180
environmental activism 5, 7, 10, 52, 70, 120–35
Equal Rights Amendment 136, 144, 149
*Erinnerungen an die Zukunft* (Reini) 193
*Erinnerungen an die Zukunft: Ungelöste Rätsel der Vergangenheit* (von Däniken) 193
*Erotic Rites of Frankenstein, The* (Franco) 52
*Escape from Terror Lagoon* (Arrow) 84
*Escape from the Planet of the Apes* (Pournelle) 84
*Escape from the Planet of the Apes* (Taylor) 83, 84
*Escape to Witch Mountain* (Hough) 173–4
escapism 2, 17, 65, 70, 71, 73, 90, 112, 170, 177, 223
Eshun, Kodwo 89
estrangement 9, 37, 39, 41, 55, 60, 65, 97, 112, 119, 168, 169, 201, 203

eucatastophe/eucatastrophic 2, 18, 169, 205
European Economic Community 106, 126
Euston Films 198
Evans, Christopher 196
*Even Cowgirls Get the Blues* (Robbins) 228
evolution 18, 40, 58, 66, 79, 114, 138, 152
*Exile Waiting, The* (McIntyre) 140, 141
*Exorcist, The* (Friedkin) 2, 195, 199
*Explorers of Gor* (Norman) 68
*Extrapolation* 7
*Eye Among the Blind* (Holdstock) 113
*Eye in the Pyramid, The* (Shea and Wilson) 229

*F&SF* 14, 15, 20, 27, 29, 31, 32, 34, 53, 54, 82, 84, 94, 97, 113, 144, 148, 149, 152, 159, 161, 167, 226, 227
'Face of Evil, The' 48–9, 117
*Faded Sun: Kesrith, The* (Cherryh) 142
*Faded Sun: Kutath, The* (Cherryh) 142
*Faded Sun: Shon'jir, The* (Cherryh) 142
*Faerie Queene, The* (Spenser) 26
*Fahrenheit 451* (Bradbury) 20
fairy tales 185, 185, 210, 232
*Fairy Tales of Charles Perrault, The* (Perrault) 232
Falkland Islands 106
*Fall and Rise of Reginald Perrin, The* 70
*Fall of the House of Usher, The* (Alan Parsons Project) 76
*Falling Astronauts, The* (Malzberg) 39
families 21, 32, 41, 59, 118, 123, 133, 137, 141, 145, 146, 159, 168–80, 181, 183, 185, 191, 192, 195, 198, 201–3, 224, 226, 229
*Family, The* 108
*Fantastic* 28
fantastic, the 17, 41, 65, 72, 131, 180, 223, 227, 231
*Fantastic Voyage* (Asimov) 11
fantasy 4, 7, 9, 10, 20, 22, 25, 26, 28, 29, 30, 33, 64, 65–77, 89, 143, 149, 170, 172, 173, 177, 180, 204, 22, 237
*Fantasy and Science Fiction, The Magazine of,* see *F&SF*
Farmer, Philip José 18, 26, 51, 61–62, 100, 221, 226, 227
   *Doc Savage: His Apocalyptic Life* 226
   'The Doge Whose Barque Was Worse Than His Bight' 226
   'A Scarletin Study' 226
   *Tarzan Alive: A Definitive Biography of Lord Greystoke* 226

*To Your Scattered Bodies Go* 61–3
*Venus on the Half Shell* 226–7
*The Wind Whales of Ishmael* 226
World of Tiers series 26
*Farthest Shore, The* (Le Guin) 177
Fassbinder, Rainer Werner 221–2, 232
  *Welt am Draht* 221–2, 232
  *World on a Wire* 221–2, 232
  *World on Wires* 221–2, 232
'Father' (Sargent) 133
fatherhood, see also patriarchy 13, 23, 34, 41, 49, 60, 82, 96, 113, 114, 146, 169, 173, 178, 180, 181, 185–9, 194–8, 202–4, 226, 227
Faulkner, William 22
Faust 52, 85, 102
Fellini, Federico 190
*Fellowship of the Talisman, The* (Simak) 18
*Female Man, The* (Russ) 143, 145, 222, 228
femininity 6, 13, 45, 46, 134, 136, 139, 141, 142, 143, 148, 157, 159, 199, 201, 204, 232
feminism 4–5, 6, 10, 12, 13, 66, 68, 84, 86–8, 105, 117, 135, 136–51, 153, 160, 166, 176, 178, 184, 189, 198–202, 204, 228, 232, 235
Feminist Press, The 137
*Fiddler on the Roof* (Jewison) 191
Fiedler, Leslie 82, 166
*Fighting Slave of Gor* (Norman) 68
Filmation 46, 188, 190
*Final Programme, The* (Moorcock) 25, 30, 114, 230
*Final Programme, The* aka (Fuest) 114
*Finian's Rainbow* (Coppola) 182
'Fireman, The' (Bradbury) 20
*Fires of Azeroth* (Cherryh) 141–2
Firestone, Shulamith 84, 136, 143, 146–7
first contact 17, 61, 78, 103, 116, 166, 195
First Nations 69, 95
First Nations, see also Native American 18, 19, 32, 134
First sf 24, 95, 137
First World War 55, 66, 70
First, Ruth 54
Fisher King 26, 54, 110
Fisher, David 63
*Flash Gordon* (Hodges) 181, 190–1
*Flash Gordon Conquers the Universe* (Beebe and Taylor) 190
*Flash Gordon's Trip to Mars* (Beebe and Hill) 190
Fleischer, Richard 11, 120, 217
  *Soylent Green* 120, 121, 124, 125, 217

Fleming, Victor
  *The Wizard of Oz* 183
*Flesh for Frankenstein* (Morrissey) 52
*Flow My Tears, the Policeman Said* (Dick) 81, 99–103, 163, 221–2
*Fly By Night* (Rush) 74
*Flying Teapot* (Gong) 76
Flynn, John
  *Rolling Thunder* 94
'For the Sake of Grace' (Elgin) 144
Forbes, Bryan
  *The Stepford Wives* 206, 214, 215
*Forbidden Planet* (Wilcox) 202
*Forbidden Tower, The* (Bradley) 67
Ford, Gerald 2, 6
Ford, John 184
  *The Searchers* 184
*Forerunner Foray* (Norton) 176
*Forever War, The* (Haldeman) 97, 153
Fort, Charles 193
  *Book of the Damned, The* 193
  *Lo!* 193
Foster, Alan Dean
  *Alien* 169
  *The Black Hole* 169
  *Dark Star* 169
  *Splinter of the Mind's Eye* 169
Foucault, Michel 152
*Foundation: The Review of Science Fiction* 7, 9, 156, 196
*Fountains of Paradise, The* (Clarke) 15–17
*Four Musketeers, The* (Lester) 188
Fox, Robert Elliot 85, 86
*Foxy Brown* (Hill) 90
*Fragile* (Yes) 74
'Fragments of a Hologram Rose' (Gibson) 234
France 5, 55, 79, 93, 104, 107, 142, 156, 170, 171, 173, 193, 194, 218
Franco, Jesús 52
  *Dracula vs Frankenstein* 52
  *Erotic Rites of Frankenstein, The* 52
Frank, Alan 9, 45
Frankenstein 31, 42, 51–2, 90–1, 94, 203, 206
*Frankenstein* (Shelley) 42, 51–2, 90, 203
*Frankenstein* (Whale) 52, 91, 94
*Frankenstein: The True Story* (Smight) 52
*Frankenstein Unbound* (Aldiss) 28, 51–2
Franklin, H. Bruce 92, 95, 175
Frawley, James 206, 217
  *The Big Bus* 206, 217
Freeman, Nick 30
Freiberger, Fred 44
French Feminism 142–3, 199
Freud, Sigmund 13, 142, 143, 152, 155,

157, 158, 160, 185, 199, 209
Friedan, Betty 136, 143
Friedkin, William 2, 195, 199
    *The Exorcist* 2, 195, 199
*Fritz the Cat* (Bakshi) 69
*Frogs* (McCowan) 127
*Front Page, The* (Wilder) 43
'Frontier in Space' 116
Frost, Lee 90
    *The Thing with Two Heads* 90
*Frozen God, The* (Kirk) 67
Fuest, Robert 114
    *The Final Programme* 114
    *The Last Days of Man on Earth* 114
*Fugue for a Darkening Island* (Priest) 111–12
*Full Metal Jacket* (Kubrick) 94
Fuller, R. Buckminster 43, 120
    *Operating Manual for Spaceship Earth* 120
Funkadelic 89
*Funkentelechy Vs. The Placebo Syndrome* (Parliament) 90
*Furies, The* (Charnas) 147
*Furthest* (Elgin) 144
Future Shock 30, 34, 37
*Futureworld* (Heffron) 206, 214

*Gaia: A New Look at Life on Earth* (Lovelock) 120, 124
*Galactica 1980* 39, 49
*Galápagos* (Vonnegut) 226
*Galaxies* (Malzberg) 222–3
*Galaxy* 11, 12, 13, 18, 58, 80, 92, 121, 137, 142
Galileo 9
Galouye, Daniel 232, 233
games 7, 17, 36, 37, 57, 62, 65, 77, 111, 112, 119, 127, 148, 168, 221, 221, 226
*Garden of Rama, The* (Clarke and Lee) 57
Garner, Alan 168, 177
    *Red Shift* 177
    *The Stone Book Quartet* 177
    *Strandloper* 177
    *The Weirdstone of Brisingamen* 177
Garnett, David S. 24
*Gas, The* (Platt) 32
Gass, William H. 221, 222
*Gate of Ivrel* (Cherryh) 141–2
*Gateway* (Pohl) 61
Gawron, Jean M. 85, 86
gay, see homosexuality and lesbianism
Gay Activist Alliance 153
gay liberation 1, 105, 152–67
Gay Liberation Front 153
'G.B.S. – Mark V' (Bradbury) 20

Gearhart, Sally Miller 121, 134–5
    *The Wanderground* 121, 134–5
Gehry, Frank 208
Geller, Uri 192
gender, see also femininity and masculinity 7, 12, 13, 59, 68, 136, 137, 139, 140, 141, 146, 147, 154–7, 159, 160, 161, 162, 167, 177, 201, 203
'Genesis of the Daleks' 117, 126
Gentle, Mary 68
Gerard, Jerry
    *Deep Throat* 210
Gernsback-Campbell continuum 5, 11, 51
Gernsback, Hugo 5, 11, 51
Gerrold, David 84, 154, 160–1
    *Battle for the Planet of the Apes* 84
    *The Man Who Folded Himself* 160–1
    *Space Skimmer* 160
*Get Carter* (Hodges) 190
Gibson, Alan 118
Gibson, William 205, 234, 235
    'Fragments of a Hologram Rose' 234
    *Neuromancer* 7
Gilbert, Lewis 115
    *Moonraker* 115
    *The Spy Who Loved Me* 115
Gilbert, Sandra 136
Gillespie, Bruce 10
Gilroy, Paul 107
*Ginger Star, The* (Brackett) 21–2
Ginsberg, Allen 75
Girard, Bernard 93, 94, 105
    *The Happiness Cage* 93, 94, 105
    *The Mind Snatchers* 93
Girdler, William 90
    *Abby* 90
*Glass Inferno, The* (Scortia and Robinson) 209
GLF 153
global warming 123
globalisation 120, 215
globalised media 215
*Gloriana* (Moorcock) 26–7
*Go Tell the Spartans* (Post) 93
*Godbody* (Sturgeon) 19
Godard, Jean-Luc 232
    *Alphaville, ou une adventure étrange de Lemmy Caution* 232
*Godfather, The* (Coppola) 2, 180, 188
*Godfather, The* (Puzo) 188
*Gods Themselves, The* (Asimov) 5, 11–13
*Going for the One* (Yes) 74–5
Gold, Horace L. 78
Golden Age sf 5, 12
*Golden Apple, The* (Shea and Wilson) 229

Goldfinger, Erno 207
Goldman, Stephen H. 125
Goldman, Steven L. 65, 214, 217, 218
*Golem$^{100}$* (Bester) 21
Gollancz 108, 113
Gong 76
   *Angel's Egg* 76
   *Camembert Electrique* 76
   *Flying Teapot* 76
   *You* 76
*Good Life, The* 70
*Goodies, The* 196
Goodkind, Saul A. and Ford Beebe
   *Buck Rogers* 50
Gordon, Andrew 185, 186, 187
Gordon, Bert I.
   *Empire of the Ants* 53
Gordon, Joan 97, 98, 153
Göring, Hermann 62
Gormenghast 28
*Gormenghast* (Peake) 26
Gossett, Thomas F. 79
Grade, Lew 44, 45
Grahame, Kenneth
   *The Wind in the Willows* 110
Grand Tour 56
Grant, Charles L. 97
Grant, Jo 116, 117
Grauman, Walter
   *633 Squadron* 185
*Gravity's Rainbow* (Pynchon) 230
'Greatest Television Show on Earth, The' (Ballard) 27
Greek mythology 58, 86
*Green Berets, The* (Wayne and Kellogg) 93
'Green Death, The' 117
Greene, Eric 83, 84
Greenland, Colin 29, 30, 49, 109, 113, 122, 215
Greenpeace 120
Greer, Germaine 127, 143
Gregg Press 109
Gropius, Walter 207
Gubar, Susan 136
*Guernica Night* (Malzberg) 35
Guerrero, Ed 90, 91, 98
*Guess Who's Coming to Dinner* (Kramer) 90
Guillermin, John 190, 206, 209, 210
   *King Kong* 190, 206, 210
   *The Towering Inferno* 206, 209
Gunn, James 12, 13, 236
Gygax, Gary 77

*H.G. Wells' The Shape of Things to Come* (McCowan) 53

Hacker, Marilyn 24, 25, 40
Haggard, Piers 108, 192, 198
   *Quatermass* 108, 192, 198
   *The Quatermass Conclusion* 108, 192, 198
Haldeman, Joe 38–9, 93, 97, 153
   *The Forever War* 97, 153
   *Vietnam and Other Alien Worlds* 38–9, 107
Haley, Alex
   *Roots: The Saga of an American Family* 88
*Hall of the Mountain Grill* (Hawkwind) 27
Haller, Daniel
   *Buck Rogers in the 25th Century* 50, 169
*Halloween* (Carpenter) 42, 199, 202
*Halloween Tree, The* (Bradbury) 20
Hamilton, Edmond 21
Hamilton, Edmond and Leigh Brackett
   'Stark and the Star Kings' 21
Hamilton, Guy 43, 105, 115, 152, 208
   *Diamonds Are Forever* 43, 115, 152, 208
   *Live and Let Die* 105
   *The Man with the Golden Gun* 115
Hammer Studios 52, 66, 162, 173, 174
Hand, David 71
   *Bambi* 71
Hansson, Bo 74
   *Attic Thoughts* 74
   *El'Ahairah* 74
   *Mellanväsen* 74
   *Magician's Hat* 74
   *Music Inspired by Lord of the Rings* 74
   *Music Inspired by Watership Down* 74
   *Sagan Om Ringen* 74
   *Ur Trollkaren's Hatt* 74
Hantke, Steffen 95, 96
*Happiness Cage, The* (Girard) 93, 94, 105
Haraway, Donna 235
Hardy, David 9, 27
Hardy, Thomas 112
Hargrave, Leonie 31
   *Clara Reeve* 31
Hark, Ina Rae 12, 13
Harrison, Harry 9, 93, 96, 125, 148
   'Commando Raid' 96
   *Make Room! Make Room!* 120
Harrison, M. John 25, 29–30, 71, 140–1
   *The Centauri Device* 29
   *The Committed Men* 29
   *The Pastel City* 29
   *A Storm of Wings* 29
   *Viriconium Nights* 29
Harrison, William 216
   'Roller Ball Murder' 216

Harryhausen, Ray 50
Hassan, Ihab 223
Hassler, Donald M. 19
Havelock Ellis, Henry 152
*Hawkline Monster, The* (Brautigan) 227
Hawklords 27
Hawks, Howard 42
   *The Big Sleep* 22
Hawkwind 27
   *Astounding Sounds, Amazing Music* 27
   *Doremi Fasol Latido* 27
   *Hall of the Mountain Grill* 27
   *Hawkwind* 27
   *The Hawkwind Log* 27
   *Levitation* 27
   *PRX5* 27
   *Quark, Strangeness and Charm* 27
   *Warrior on the Edge of Time* 27
*Hawkwind* (Hawkwind) 27
*Hawkwind Log, The* (Hawkwind) 27
Hay, George 18
Hayles, Brian 41
'Heart of Darkness' (Conrad) 80, 111–12
Heath, Edward 106, 109
*Heavenly Breakfast* (Delany) 85
Heffron, Richard T.
   *Futureworld* 206, 214
Heinlein, Robert A. 11, 13–15, 23, 25, 35, 63, 97, 137, 152, 161, 168, 223
   '– All You Zombies –' 14, 15, 161
   *I Will Fear No Evil* 13–14, 137
   *The Notebooks of Lazarus Long* 14
   'The Number of the Beast' 14–15, 21
   *Starship Troopers* 97, 152, 153, 168
   *Stranger in a Strange Land* 13, 14
   *Time Enough For Love* 14
   *To Sail Beyond the Sunset* 14
Herbert, Frank
   Dune novels 165
*Herbie Goes to Monte Carlo* (McEveety) 173
*Herbie Rides Again* (Stevenson) 172–3
*Hergest Ridge* (Oldfield) 75
*Heritage of Hastur, The* (Bradley) 67, 164–5
*Hermes Fall, The* (Baxter) 121, 129
hero and heroic, see also anti-hero, protagonist 1, 3, 11, 25, 29, 30, 32, 35, 40, 44, 48, 49, 53, 55, 62, 71, 76, 82, 85, 86, 90, 117, 120, 125, 141, 142, 144, 145, 152, 155 157, 160, 169, 180, 185–8, 190, 191, 200, 216–17, 222, 224
*Herovit's World* (Malzberg) 222
Heston, Charlton 82, 124, 125
heteronormativity 1, 137, 153, 154, 161, 162, 163

heterotopias 155, 156
Hickman, Christine B. 79
*High-Rise* (Ballard) 27, 206, 211–12
*Highway Sandwiches* (Disch) 31
Hill, Douglas 9
Hill, George Roy 221, 225
   *Slaughterhouse-5* 221, 225
Hill, Jack 90
   *Foxy Brown* 90
Hill, Reg 44
Hill, Robert F. 190
Hill, Robert F. and Ford Beebe
   *Flash Gordon's Trip to Mars* 190
Hills, Matt 184
Hirschfeld, Magnus 152
*History of the Runestaff* (Moorcock) 25
Hitchcock, Alfred 175
   *Psycho* 175
*Hitchhiker's Guide to the Galaxy, The* (Adams) 63
HIV/AIDS 153, 237
Hoban, Russell 206, 219
   *Riddley Walker* 206, 219
*Hobbit, The* (Tolkien) 74
Hockney, David 231
Hodder and Stoughton 108
Hodges, Mike 181, 190–1, 214
   *Flash Gordon* 181, 190–1
   *Get Carter* 190
   *The Terminal Man* 214
*Hogg* (Delany) 85–6
Holdstock, Robert 4, 67, 107, 112–13
   Berserker series 67
   *Earthwind* 113
   *Eye Among the Blind* 113
   'Mythago Wood' 113
   *Mythago Wood* 113
   Raven series 67
*Hollow Lands, The* (Moorcock) 25
Hollywood 3, 9, 22, 43, 90, 125, 154, 156, 181, 182, 184, 191, 205, 213, 213, 237
Holmes, Robert 116, 117, 170
Holmes, Sherlock 54, 188
Homer 51
homophobia 1, 156, 164, 230
homosexuality 1, 2, 10, 35, 40, 61, 73, 82, 85, 105, 152–67, 199, 208–9, 212, 228
homosocial 165, 166
Honthaner, Ron 190
   *House on Skull Mountain* 190
Hooper, Tobe 202
   *The Texas Chain Saw Massacre* 202
Hoover, H.M. 168, 178–80
   *Children of Morrow* 178–9

*The Delikon* 179–80
*The Lost Star* 179
*The Rains of Eridan* 179–80
*Return to Earth* 179
*This Time of Darkness* 179
*Treasures of Morrow* 179
'HORARS of War, The' (Wolfe) 96
*Horned Warrior, The* (Carlsen) 67
Horowitz, Gad 198–9
horror films 2, 10, 52, 53, 67, 72, 90–1, 118, 162, 173, 191–2, 198–205, 212
Hosty, Tom 108
*Hotel de Dream* (Tennant) 231
Hough, John 173–4
   *Escape to Witch Mountain* 173–4
   *Return from Witch Mountain* 173–4
Houghton, Don 116
*Hounds of Skaith, The* (Brackett) 21–2
*House on Skull Mountain* (Honthaner) 190
'Houston, Houston, Do You Read?' (Tiptree) 150
Hovanec, Carol P. 95
Howard, Robert E. 65
Hubble, Nick 61
Hudson, W.H.
   *A Shepherd's Life* 110–11
Hugo Award 5,11, 19, 21, 344, 57,61, 129, 133, 140, 142, 208, 233
Hulke, Malcolm 170
   *Doctor Who and the Cave Monsters* 170
   *Doctor Who and the Doomsday Weapon* 170
   *Doctor Who and the Sea-Devils* 170
Humfress, Paul and Derek Jarman
   *Sebastiane* 162
Hunt, Peter 180
*Hunters of Gor* (Norman) 68
Hurst, L.J. 68
Hurst, Mark 103–4
Hyams, Peter
   *Capricorn One* 39, 44
hyperreality 206, 215, 223, 234

*I Am Legend* (Matheson) 124
*I Ching* 113
*I Robot* (Alan Parsons Project) 76–7
*I, Robot* (Asimov) 76–7
*I Will Fear No Evil* (Heinlein) 13–14, 137
Icarus 128, 206
*Il Pianeta Sconosciuto* (Kolosimo) 193
*Illearth War, The* (Donaldson) 71–2
*Image Job, The* (Platt) 32
'Image of the Fendahl' 49
*Imaginative Sex* (Norman) 68
*Imperial Earth* (Clarke) 15–16
imperialism 7, 15–17, 40, 47, 51, 54, 96, 106–19, 180, 218, 221, 223
*In Solitary* (Kilworth) 113
*In the Heat of the Night* (Jewison) 90
*In the Ocean of Night* (Benford) 121, 128–9
*Incredible Journey, The* (Burnford) 31
*Incredible Melting Man, The* (Sachs) 39, 42
India 122, 128
*Indian Giver, The* (Bester) 21
Indian, see First Nations, Native American 19, 21, 85, 95, 184
Indiana Jones films 191
Indochina, see also Vietnam War 92–6
industrial unrest 6, 63, 106, 126, 224–5
'Inferno' 116
*In Search of Ancient Astronauts* (Reini) 193
*Instructions for Angels* (Bedford) 75
'Invasion, The' 116
*Invasion of the Body Snatchers, The* (Kaufman) 121, 131–2
*Invasion of the Body Snatchers, The* (Siegel) 131
'Invasion of Time, The' 117
*InterZone* 28
*Inverted World* (Priest) 59–60
invisibility 1,7, 10, 26, 29, 34, 79, 92, 120, 121, 130, 137, 140, 164, 178, 180, 184, 218, 222, 237
'Invisible Enemy, The' 1
*Invisible Green* (Sladek) 32
*Involution Ocean* (Sterling) 233
Iran 181
Ireland/Eire 15, 116
Ireland, Northern 15, 41, 55, 106, 112, 113, 117
'Is Gender Necessary?' (Le Guin) 138
*Isaac Asimov's Science Fiction Magazine* see *Asimov's*
Islam 112, 114, 144
*Island at the Top of the World, The* (Stevenson) 172
*Island of Doctor Moreau, The* (Wells) 53
*Island of Dr Moreau, The* (Taylor) 53
*Island of Lost Souls, The* (Kenton) 53
Israel 15, 30, 210
*It Lives Again* (Cohen) 192, 202–3
*It's Alive* (Cohen) 192, 202–3
ITC 44, 45
ITV 44, 45, 197, 198

*J.D.'s Revenge* (Marks) 90
*J.R.R. Tolkien's The Lord of the Rings* (Bakshi) 69–70
*Jack of Shadows* (Bedford) 75
Jack the Ripper 54
*Jagged Orbit, The* (Brunner) 30

*Jailbird* (Vonnegut) 224–5, 226
Jakes, John 84
   *Conquest of the Planet of the Apes* 84
Jakubowski, Maxim 85
James Bond 43, 107, 114–17, 144, 188, 191, 208
James, Edward 4, 72–3
Jameson, Fredric 1, 6, 31, 103, 140, 208, 220, 223–4, 230, 235
Jameson, Louise 49, 116, 197
Jannone, Claudia 227
Jarman, Derek 106, 119, 162
   *Jubilee* 106, 119, 162
Jarman, Derek and Paul Humfress
   *Sebastiane* 162
*Jason King* 191
*Jaws* (Benchley) 182
*Jaws* (Spielberg) 2, 180, 182
Jefferson, Thomas 225
'Jeffty Is Five' (Ellison) 34
*Jem* (Pohl) 121–2, 132
Jenkins, Sue 47, 48
Jesser, Nancy 79, 87, 88
Jesus Christ 20, 25, 62, 110, 113, 125, 228
Jeter, K.W. 51, 54, 99, 104
   *Morlock Night* 54
*Jewel-Hinged Jaw, The* (Delany) 8
Jewishness, see also Israel 35, 78, 83, 84, 180, 188
Jewison, Norman 90, 125, 101, 206, 216
   *Fiddler on the Roof* 191
   *In the Heat of the Night* 90
   *Rollerball* 125, 206, 216
Jim Crow 81
John W. Campbell Memorial Award 40, 61,127, 130, 219, 233
Johnson, George Clayton 217
Johnson, George Clayton and William F. Nolan
   *Logan's Run* 217
Johnson, Lyndon Baines 38
Jones, L.Q. 33, 154, 163
   *A Boy and His Dog* 33, 154, 163
Jones, Langdon 26
Jordan 119
Joseph, Helen 54
*Journey to the Centre of the Earth* (Wakeman) 75
*Journey to the Far Side of the Sun* (Parrish) 44
*Jubilee* (Jarman) 106, 119, 162
*Judgement of Jupiter* (Tilms) 196
*Jungfrau von Orleans, Die* (Schiller) 12
Jungian 26, 177
*Jungle Book, The* (Reitherman) 172

*Juniper Time* (Wilhelm) 131, 134
Jupiter 46, 89
*Jurassic Park* (Spielberg) 191

*Kakushi-Toride No San-Akunin* (Kurosawa) 183
*Kalki* (Vidal) 121, 126–7
Kam, Rose Salberg 80
Karloff, Boris 91, 94
Kasdan, Lawrence 22
Kaufman, Philip *Invasion of the Body Snatchers, The* 121, 131–2
Kaveney, Roz 51, 56, 98, 233, 236, 237
Kay, Guy Gavriel 69
Kaysing, Bill and Randy Reid
   *We Never Went to the Moon* 43
Kelljan, Bob
   *Scream Blacula Scream* 90
Kellogg, Ray 93
Kellogg, Ray and John Wayne
   *The Green Berets* 93
Kemp, Lindsay 119
Kennedy, John F. 6, 35, 35–9, 199, 127, 229
Kennedy, Joseph 35
Kennedy, Robert F. 35, 229
Kenton, Erle C.
   *The Island of Lost Souls* 53
Kershner, Irvin 7, 22–3, 169, 181, 185–7
   *The Empire Strikes Back* 7, 22–3, 169, 181, 185–7
   *Star Wars: Episode V – The Empire Strikes Back* 7, 22–3, 169, 181, 185–7
Kertbeny, Karl Maria 152
Khatru 136, 147–8
Khmer 15, 93
Khouri, Nadia 145
Kidd, Virginia 137, 147
Kilgore, De Witt Douglas 16, 57, 58
Kilworth, Garry 107, 113–14
   *In Solitary* 113
   'Let's Go to Golgotha' 113
   *The Night of Kadar* 113–14
   *Split Second* 113
Kincaid, Paul 54, 109, 110, 112, 113
*Kindred* (Butler) 87–88
*King Kong* (Cooper and Schoedsack) 209–10
*King Kong* (Guillermin) 190, 206, 210
*King of the Swords, The* (Moorcock) 25
King, Martin Luther 35, 81, 224
King, Simon 27
*Kingdom of the Spiders* (Carlos, John) 127
Kirk, Admiral/Captain James T. 46, 48, 166, 167,

Kirk, Richard 67
  *The Frozen God* 67
  *Lords of the Shadows* 67
  *Swordsmistress of Chaos* 67
  *A Time of Dying* 67
  *A Time of Ghosts* 67
Klarer, Mario 136
*Knight of the Swords, The* (Moorcock) 25
Knight, Damon 9, 24
'Knox' (Ellison) 34
Kolosimo, Peter 193
  *Il Pianeta Sconosciuto* 193
Krafft-Ebing, Richard 152
*Kramer vs Kramer* (Benton) 201
Krämer, Peter 184
Kramer, Stanley
  *Guess Who's Coming to Dinner* 90
Kristeva, Julia 199
Kubrick, Stanley 6, 15, 57, 68, 93, 94, 104–5, 128, 171, 193, 208, 232
  *2001: A Space Odyssey* 6, 15, 57, 68, 128, 171, 193,
  *Clockwork Orange, A* 93, 104–5, 208, 232
  *Dr Strangelove* 105
  *Full Metal Jacket* 94
Kucera, Paul 133
*Kuldesak* (Cowper) 110
Kurosawa, Akira 183, 214
  *The Hidden Fortress* 183
  *Kakushi-Toride No San-Akunin* 183
  *Seven Samurai* 214
  *Shichinin no Samurai* 214
Kusche, Larry
  *The Bermuda Triangle Mystery – Solved* 196

*La Planète des Singes* (Boulle) 82
Lacan, Jacques 142
Lamb, Patricia F. 167
Lamont, Victoria 22
*Land Leviathan, The* (Moorcock) 25, 26, 54–5
*Land of the Giants* 209
*Land That Time Forgot, The* (Burroughs) 66
*Land that Time Forgot, The* (Connor) 66
Landon, Brooks 5
Lang, Fritz 183
  *Metropolis* 183
Lansbury, George 172
Larson, Glen A. 49–50, 169–70
Las Vegas 207, 208, 213
Lasdun, Denys 207
*Laser Beams from Star Cities?* (Collyns) 194
*Last Dangerous Visions, The* (Ellison) 21, 24
*Last Days of Man on Earth, The* (Fuest) 114
*Last Transaction, The* (Malzberg) 36
*Last Words of Dutch Schultz, The* (Burroughs) 229
Latham, Rob 5
*Lathe of Heaven, The* (Le Guin) 138–9
Lautner, John 208
Laws of Robotics 27, 32, 63, 77
Layton, David 35, 40
Le Corbusier 207
Le Guin, Ursula 4, 8, 93, 95–6, 98, 136–41, 140–1, 147, 158, 154, 156, 168, 176, 177, 236
  *The Dispossessed* 139, 145–6, 154, 156, 235
  *The Farthest Shore* 177
  'Is Gender Necessary?' 138
  *The Lathe of Heaven* 138–9
  *The Left Hand of Darkness* 138, 154
  *The Tombs of Atuan* 177
  *A Wizard of Earthsea* 177
  'The Word for World is Forest' 95–6
Lee, Christopher 115, 174
Lee, Gentry 57
Lee, Gentry and Arthur C. Clarke
  *The Garden of Rama* 57
  *Rama II* 15–16
  *Rama Revealed* 57
Leela 49, 117, 198
Lefanu, Sarah 146, 150–1
*Left Hand of Darkness, The* (Le Guin) 138, 154
Leiber, Fritz 9
Leibscher, Walt
  'Do Androids Dream of Electric Love?' 154, 157–8
Leith, Linda 165
Lem, Stanisław 8, 40, 103, 236
lesbianism 148, 153, 155, 159, 161, 212
Lessing, Doris 231
  *Briefing for a Descent into Hell* 231
  *The Marriages Between Zones Three, Four and Five* 231
  *The Memoirs of a Survivor* 231
  *Re: Colonised Planet 5, Shikasta* 231
  *The Sirian Experiments* 231
Lester, Richard 68, 181, 187–9, 191
  *The Four Musketeers* 188
  *Superman II* 68, 181, 187–9, 191
  *The Three Musketeers* 188
'Let's Go to Golgotha' (Kilworth) 113
Letson, Russell 14, 62
Letts, Barry 41, 116, 170
  *Doctor Who and the Dæmons* 170
Levey, William A 90–1, 94
  *Blackenstein* 90–1, 94

*Leviathan* (Shea and Wilson) 229
Levin, Ira 206, 214, 215
  *Rosemary's Baby* 215
  *The Stepford Wives* 206, 214, 215
*Levitation* (Hawkwind) 27
'Life and Death of God, The' (Ballard) 28
*Life in the West* (Aldiss) 28
Lightbody, Brian 216
Lincoln, Abraham 36, 80, 99
Linnaeus, Carl 79
Lipman-Blumen, Jean 165
Lipset, Seymour Martin 101
Liseberger, Steven 175
  *Tron* 175
*Little Big Man* (Penn) 59
Little Nell 162
Littlefield, Emerson 86
*Live and Let Die* (Hamilton) 105
*Lives and Times of Jerry Cornelius, The*
  (Moorcock) 114
*Lo!* (Fort) 193
Locus awards 61, 140, 208, 233
*Logan's Run* (Anderson) 206, 215, 216,
  217, 218
*Logan's Run* (Nolan and Johnson) 217
London 28, 29, 31, 32, 54, 58, 75, 95,
  106, 111, 112, 123, 161, 203, 205,
  210, 211, 229
*Long After Midnight* (Bradbury) 20
Longinus 56
*Lord Foul's Bane* (Donaldson) 71–2
*Lord of the Rings, The* (Tolkien) 38, 69–70,
  72, 74
*Lord Valentine's Castle* (Silverberg) 73–4
*Lords of the Shadows* (Kirk) 67
Lorrimer, Vere 49
Los Angeles 75, 165, 174, 202, 215
*Lost Ones, The* (Cameron) 173
*Lost Star, The* (Hoover) 179
*Lost World, The* (Conan Doyle) 66
Lounsbery, John
  *Winnie the Pooh and Tigger Too* 172
Lounsbery, John and Wolfgang
  Reitherman
  *The Many Adventures of Winnie the Pooh*
  172
Lounsbery, John, Wolfgang Reitherman
  and Art Stevens
  *The Rescuers* 172
*Love Bug, The* (Stevenson) 172
Lovelock, James
  *Gaia: A New Look at Life on Earth* 120,
  124
  Gaia hypothesis 120, 124
Lucas, George 2, 6, 10, 46, 49, 50, 53, 65,
  93, 98, 133, 169, 174, 180, 181, 182,
  183–7, 189, 190, 191, 194, 195, 237
  *American Graffiti* 182, 183
  *Electronic Labyrinth THX 1138 4EB* 182
  *Star Wars: From the Adventures of Luke
   Skywalker* 169
  *Star Wars – Episode IV: A New Hope* 2,
  6, 46, 49, 50, 53, 65, 93, 98, 133,
  169, 174, 180, 181, 183–7, 189,
  190, 191, 194, 195, 237
  *THX 1138* 2, 10, 181–3
Lucian of Samosata 51
*Lucifer's Hammer* (Niven and Pournelle)
  121, 129
Luckhurst, Roger 6, 107, 121, 237
Lumet, Sidney 43, 101
  *The Anderson Tapes* 101
  *Network* 43
Lupoff, Richard A. 169
*Lycidas* (Milton) 125
Lynn, Elizabeth 154, 165
  *A Different Light* 165
Lyotard, Jean-François 193, 223, 235

MacDonald, Anson 161
  'By His Bootstraps' 161
Madlee, Dorothy and Andre Norton
  *Star Ka'at* 176
*Magazine of Fantasy and Science Fiction,
  The*, see *F&SF*
*Magic Roundabout, The* 171
*Magic Time* (Reed) 136, 147, 206
*Magician's Hat (Ur Trollkaren's Hatt)* 74
*Magnificent Seven, The* (Sturges) 214
Magrs, Paul 1
  *Strange Boy* 1
*Maid of Orleans, The* (Schiller, *Die
  Jungfrau von Orleans*) 12
Mailer, Norman 96
  *Why Are We in Vietnam?* 96
*Make Room! Make Room!* (Harrison) 120
*Malacia Tapestry, The* (Aldiss) 28–9
Malamud, Bernard 78
*Malevil* (Merle) 206, 218–19
Maloney, David 49
Malzberg, Barry N. 25, 33, 34–9, 40, 44,
  128, 137, 221–2, 229
  *Beyond Apollo* 35, 40
  *The Day of the Burning* 36, 40
  *The Destruction of the Temple* 35
  *The Falling Astronauts* 39
  *Galaxies* 222–3
  *Guernica Night* 35
  *Herovit's World* 222
  *The Last Transaction* 36
  *On a Planet Alien* 40
  *Overlay* 36

*Phase IV* 128
*Revelations* 39–40
*Scop* 35–6
*The Sodom and Gomorrah Business* 35
*Tactics of Conquest* 36
*Man in the High Castle, The* (Dick) 100
*Man Plus* (Pohl) 233
*Man Who Fell To Earth, The* (Roeg) 103, 154
*Man Who Folded Himself, The* (Gerrold) 160–1
*Man with the Golden Gun, The* (Hamilton) 115
'Man-Made Self' (Sterling) 233
*Man, the Hunted Animal* (Arrow) 84
Mandel, Ernest 223
Mandelbrot, Benoît B. 193
*Many Adventures of Winnie the Pooh, The* (Reitherman and Lounsbery) 172
*Marauders of Gor* (Norman) 68
Marcuse, Herbert 198
*Margaret and I* (Wilhelm) 139–40
Mark, Jan 168, 180
   *Divide and Rule* 180
   *The Ennead* 180
   *Thunder and Lightnings* 180
   *Under the Autumn Garden* 180
Marks, Arthur
   *J.D.'s Revenge* 90
Marquand, Richard 7, 184, 187
   *Return of the Jedi* 7, 184, 187
   *Star Wars: Episode VI – Return of the Jedi* 7, 184, 187
*Marriages Between Zones Three, Four and Five, The* (Lessing) 231
Mars 21, 22, 28, 36, 37, 43, 44, 54, 67, 190, 233
*Martian Chronicles, The* (Anderson) 20
*Martian Chronicles, The* (Bradbury) 20
'Martian Quest' (Brackett) 21
Martin, Dave 116, 117
Martin, John 56
marvellous 8, 65, 175
Marxism 8, 81, 95, 198, 223
*Mary Poppins* (Stevenson) 172
masculinity 14, 46, 50, 68, 137, 139, 141, 142, 143, 145, 146, 148, 150, 157, 159, 160, 175, 199, 200, 203, 204, 232
Maslansky, Paul 90
   *Sugar Hill* 90
mass-market 62, 181–91, 237
Masson, David I. 28
*Mastodonia* (Simak) 18
Matheson, Richard 124
   *I Am Legend* 124

matriarchy, see also motherhood 199, 212
Mayberry, Russ 174
   *The Spaceman and King Arthur* 174
   *Unidentified Flying Oddball* 174
McCaffrey, Anne 65, 72, 73, 141
   *Dragonflight* 72
   *Dragonrider* 72
   'Weyr Search' 72
   *The White Dragon* 73
McCowan, George
   *Frogs* 127
   *H.G. Wells' The Shape of Things to Come* 53
McEveety, Vincent
   *Herbie Goes to Monte Carlo* 173
McGiveron, Rafeeq O. 209
McHugh, Susan Bridget 84
McIntyre, Vonda N. 136, 140–2, 147, 235
   *Dreamsnake* 140–1
   *The Exile Waiting* 140, 141
   'Of Mist, and Grass, and Sand' 140
McLeod, Ken 76, 89
McLeod, Patrick G. 52
McNelly, Willis 99
*Mellanväsen/Attic Thoughts* (Hansson) 74
Melville, Herman 49, 226, 233
   *Moby-Dick* 49, 226, 233
*Memoirs of a Survivor, The* (Lessing) 231
*Ménage Enchanté, La* (Danot) 171
Mendlesohn, Farah 72, 73, 166, 169
Merle, Robert
   *Malevil* 206, 218–19
Merrick, Helen 6, 140, 148
Merril, Judith 92, 106
   *England Swings SF: Stories of Speculative Science Fiction* 106
messiah 20, 114, 145, 187
'Messiah, The' (Bradbury) 20
metafiction 10, 156, 221–34
metanarratives 193, 199, 205, 223, 228–32
*Meteor* (Neame) 121, 129–30
meteors 57, 121, 128–30
*Metropolis* (Lang) 183
Meyer, Nicholas
   *Star Trek II: The Wrath of Khan* 175
   *Time After Time* 53–4
Miall, Robert 169
   *UFO* 169
   *UFO 2* 169
*Michael Kohlhaas* (von Kleist) 224
middle classes, see bourgeosie
Milk, Harvey 153
Miller, Jim 86

Miller, Stephen Paul 2, 98, 182
Millett, Kate 136, 143
  *Sexual Politics* 136
Milne, A.A. 70, 172
*Milton a poem* (Blake) 28, 187
Milton, John
  *Lycidas* 125
  *Paradise Lost* 187
*Mind of My Mind* (Butler) 87
*Mind Snatchers, The* (Girard) 93
'Mindbombs, The' 45
Minoru Yamasaki 75, 207
*Mirror Image* (Coney) 122
miscegenation 79, 88, 138
*Miss Bianca* (Sharp) 182
*Mission of Gravity* (Clement) 121
*Missionaries, The* (Compton) 108
*Moby-Dick* (Melville) 49, 226, 233
*Modest Proposal, A* (Swift) 125, 211, 227
Moers, Ellen 137
Molson, Francis J. 177
Money, John 154
Monk, Claire 119
*Monster Club, The* (Baker) 67
*Monty Python's Flying Circus* 162
moon 6, 12, 15, 16, 37–45, 52, 53, 63, 76, 121, 132, 143, 159, 171
*Moonbase 3* 39, 41–2
*Moonraker* (Gilbert, Lewis) 115
Moorcock, Michael 5, 22, 24–7, 30, 33, 51, 54–5, 66, 70–1, 107, 114, 183, 230
  *An Alien Heat* 25
  'Behold the Man' 25
  *Breakfast in the Ruins* 25–6
  *The Bull and the Spear* 25
  The Chronicles of Corum 25
  *The Condition of Muzak* 25, 30, 114, 230
  Cornelius Tetralogy 25, 30, 55, 114, 230
  *A Cure for Cancer* 25, 30, 114, 230
  *The Dreaming City* 25
  *Elric of Melniboné* 25
  *The End of All Songs* 25
  *The English Assassin* 25, 30, 114, 230
  *The Final Programme* 25, 30, 114, 230
  *Gloriana* 26–7
  History of the Runestaff 25
  *The Hollow Lands* 25
  *The King of the Swords* 25
  *The Knight of the Swords* 25
  *The Land Leviathan* 25, 26, 54–5
  *The Lives and Times of Jerry Cornelius* 114
  *My Experiences in the Third World War* 114
  *The Oak and the Ram* 25
  *Oswald Bastable trilogy* 25, 26, 54–5
  *The Queen of the Swords* 25
  *The Sleeping Sorceress* 25
  *The Steel Tsar* 25
  *The Sword and the Stallion* 25, 26, 54–5
  *The Warlord of the Air* 25, 26, 54–5
  *Wizardry and Wild Romance* 70–1
Moore, Charles 207
Moore, Patrick 9
Moore, Raylyn 149
*Moreau's Other Island* (Aldiss) 28, 53
Morgan, Chris 73
Morgan, Robin 166
*Morlock Night* (Jeter) 54
Morrissey, Paul 52
  *Flesh for Frankenstein* 52
*Mort en Direct, La* (Tavernier) 108
Moscone, George 153
Moss, Elaine 169
*Mote in God's Eye, The* (Niven and Pournelle) 12, 138
motherhood, see also matriarchy 14, 31, 34, 52, 60, 88, 101, 126, 136, 144, 146, 147, 148, 149, 153, 179, 195, 196, 199–203, 232, 237
*Motherlines* (Charnas) 146–7
*Mothership Connection* (Parliament) 90
Moylan, Tom 145, 235
*Mrs Frisby and the Secret of NIMH* (O'Brien) 177–8
Mullen, R.D. 8, 14
*Müller-Fokker Effect, The* (Sladek) 32, 232
Mulvey, Laura 166
Murphy, C.F. 206
*Music Inspired by Lord of the Rings* (Hansson) 74
*Music Inspired by Watership Down* (Hansson) 74
'My Dream of Flying to Wake Island' (Ballard) 28
*My Experiences in the Third World War* (Moorcock) 114
'My Perfect Murder' (Bradbury) 20
*Mysteries from Forgotten Worlds* (Berlitz) 194
*Mystery of Atlantis, The* (Berlitz) 194
'Mythago Wood' (Holdstock) 113
*Mythago Wood* (Holdstock) 113
*Myths and Legends of King Arthur and the Knights of the Round Table, The* (Wakeman) 75

'Name: Please Print' (Sladek) 32
NASA 43, 44, 46, 130, 132, 233
Nash, Paul 109

Nation, Terry 117, 118, 126
National Theatre, London 207, 229
Native American, see also First Nations 18, 19, 32, 134
Nazis 62, 71, 109, 171, 185, 188, 190, 230
NBC 38, 50
Neame, Ronald 121, 129–30
  *Meteor* 121, 129–30
Nebula Awards 4, 5, 19, 21, 34, 57, 61, 127, 134, 138, 140, 205, 208, 219, 224, 230, 233
Nelson, Gary 133, 169, 174–5, 191, 249
  *The Black Hole* 133, 169, 174–5, 191, 249
Nelson, Ralph
  *Soldier Blue* 94
Nemo, Captain 55
neo-colonialism 51
neoconservative 2, 199, 237
Neolithic 113
*Neq the Sword* (Anthony) 73
Nesbit, E. 55
  *The Story of the Treasure Seekers* 55
*Network* (Lumet) 43
*Neuromancer* (Gibson) 7
*New Apocrypha, The* (Sladek) 32, 196
*New Dimensions* 12, 24, 80
New Hebrides 106
*New Maps of Hell* (Amis) 230
New Wave 3–6, 10, 11, 12, 17, 23, 24–37, 40, 50, 92, 93, 154, 221, 231, 235
New World Cinema 216
*New Worlds* 5, 8, 24–5, 29, 31, 32, 106, 108, 114, 163, 240
*New Writings in SF* 24
New York 9, 31, 35, 53 58, 85, 115, 125, 153, 207, 213, 217
New Zealand 58
Newell, Diane 22
Newman, Jim 89
  *Space is the Place* 89
Newton, Huey 81
Newton, Janet 200
Nicholls, Peter 9, 14, 60, 162, 189, 190
Nietzschean 68
Nigeria 25–6, 134
*Night of Kadar, The* (Kilworth) 113–14
Nimoy, Leonard 46, 74, 132
Niven, Larry 9, 12, 51, 56, 59, 121, 138
  *Protector* 12, 138
  *Ringworld* 12, 56, 58, 59, 60, 63
  *Ringworld Engineers* 12, 56
Niven, Larry and Jerry Pournelle
  *Lucifer's Hammer* 121, 129
  *The Mote in God's Eye* 12, 138

Nixon, Richard 2, 6, 38, 39, 43, 93, 100–1, 103, 225, 230, 233
*No Blade of Grass* (Wilde, Cornel) 121, 123–4
Nobbs, David
  *The Death of Reginald Perrin* 70
*Noggin and the Moon Mouse* (Postgate) 171
*Noggin the Nog* 171
Nolan, William F. and George Clayton Johnson
  *Logan's Run* 217
Norman, John 68
  *Assassin of Gor* 68
  *Beasts of Gor* 68
  *Captive of Gor* 68
  *Explorers of Gor* 68
  *Fighting Slave of Gor* 68
  *Hunters of Gor* 68
  *Imaginative Sex* 68
  *Marauders of Gor* 68
  *Raiders of Gor* 68
  *Slave Girl of Gor* 68
  *Tarnsman of Gor* 68
  *Tribesmen of Gor* 68
*Norstrilia* (Smith) 63
North East London Polytechnic 7
North, Colonel Oliver 181
Northern Ireland 15, 41, 55, 106, 112, 117
Norton, Andre 77, 168, 176
  *Forerunner Foray* 176
  *Quag Keep* 176
Norton, Andre and Dorothy Madlee
  *Star Ka'at* 176
nostalgia 1, 17, 20, 21, 34, 52, 54, 183, 184, 203
'Not For an Age' (Aldiss) 215
*The Notebooks of Lazarus Long* (Heinlein) 14
Nourse, Alan E.
  *The Blade Runner* 230
*Nova* (Delany) 85
Novum 9, 51, 55, 59
Nowlan, Philip Francis
  *Armageddon – 2419 AD* 50
nuclear power 4, 97, 131, 217
'Number of the Beast, The' (Heinlein) 14–15, 21
Nyby, Christian
  *The Thing From Another World* 202

*O Lucky Man!* (Anderson) 106, 119
O'Bannon, Dan 42
O'Brien, Richard 119, 161, 162, 191
  *The Rocky Horror Show* 191
O'Brien, Robert C. 168, 177, 178

*Mrs Frisby and the Secret of NIMH* 177–8
*Z for Zachariah* 178
O'Neill, Gerard K. 47, 122, 132
O'Pray, Michael 119
*Oak and the Ram, The* (Moorcock) 25
*Odyssey, The* (Bedford) 75
Oedipus 46, 52, 152, 184–6, 189
'Of Mist, and Grass, and Sand' (McIntyre) 140
Offutt, Andrew 236
oil 66, 122, 126, 210
Oldfield, Mike 75
  *Hergest Ridge* 75
  *Tubular Bells* 75
Olympia Press 32
*Omega Factor, The* 192, 197–8
*Omega Man, The* (Sagal) 121, 124–5
*Omen, The* (Donner) 195, 202, 204
*Omni* 14
*On a Planet Alien* (Malzberg) 40
*On Jupiter* (Sun Ra) 89
*On Wings of Song* (Disch) 31, 154–5
'One Afternoon at Utah Beach' (Ballard) 28
Onlywoman Press 137
OPEC 115, 122, 210
*Operating Manual for Spaceship Earth* (Fuller) 120
'Options' (Varley) 159–60
*Options* (Sheckley) 222
Orbit 24, 133
*Orbitsville* (Shaw) 58–60
*Orbitsville Departure* (Shaw) 58
*Orbitsville Judgement* (Shaw) 58
*Orders of the Retina* (Disch) 31
ostranenie, see also estrangement 8
Oswald Bastable trilogy (Moorcock) 25, 26, 54–5
*Our Children's Children* (Simak) 18
*Our Friends from Frolix 8* (Dick) 99
*Our Mysterious Spaceship Moon* (Wilson) 43
*Out of their Minds* (Simak) 17
*Out of Time's Abyss* (Burroughs) 67
*Outer Space Employment Agency* (Sun Ra) 89
*Outlaw Josey Wales, The* (Eastwood) 59
'Over the Hills' 126
*Overlay* (Malzberg) 36
overpopulation 30, 31, 33, 58, 120, 125
Ovid 51, 86

Paddington Bear 192
paedophilia 67, 165
Pakistan 122, 134
Pakula, Alan J. 43, 190
  *All the President's Men* 43, 190
  *The Parallax View* 190
Palestine 15
Palmer, Christopher 56
Palmer, Samuel 109
Panshin, Alexei 3
Panshin, Cory 3
*Paradise Lost* (Milton) 187
*Parallax View, The* (Pakula) 190
Paramount 46
paranoia 13, 44, 77, 111, 131, 166, 107, 115, 230
paranormal 98, 192–205
Paris 8, 32, 58, 75, 76, 208
Parks, Gordon 90
  *Shaft* 90
Parks Jr, Gordon 91
  *Super Fly* 91
Parliament 89–90
  *The Clones of Dr. Funkenstein* 90
  *Funkentelechy Vs. The Placebo Syndrome* 90
  *Mothership Connection* 90
parody and pastiche 22, 28, 32, 51–64, 72, 115, 127, 144, 189, 196, 210, 217, 222, 223, 226, 227, 233
Parrish, Robert 44
  *Doppelgänger* 44
  *Journey to the Far Side of the Sun* 44
'Parrot Who Met Papa, The' (Bradbury) 20
Parry, Sir Hubert 119
Parsons, Alan 76–7
*Passion of New Eve, The* (Carter) 232
*Pastel City, The* (Harrison) 29
*Patchwork Girl of Oz, The* (Baum) 227
patriarchy 1, 41, 136, 150, 180, 199, 212, 232, 237
*Patrimony, The* (Adams) 67
*Patternmaster* (Butler) 87–8
Payer, Sue 136, 137
  *Second Body* 136, 137
Peake, Mervyn 26, 29
  *Gormenghast* 26
  *Titus Alone* 26
  *Titus Groan* 26
Pearl Harbor 28
Peckinpah, Sam
  *The Wild Bunch* 94
Pedler, Kit 124
  *The Quest for Gaia* 124
Pedler, Kit and Gerry Davis
  *Brainrack* 124
  *Doomwatch: The World in Danger* 124
  *The Dynostar Menace* 124

# INDEX

*Mutant 59 The Plastic Eater* 124
'Peeling' (Carey) 158–9
Penn, Arthur 59, 94
   *Bonnie and Clyde* 94
   *Little Big Man* 59
*People that Time Forgot, The* (Burroughs) 67
*People that Time Forgot, The* (Connor) 66–7
*Performance* (Cammell and Roeg) 203
Perrault, Charles 232
   *Fairy Tales of Charles Perrault, The* 232
Pertwee, Jon 116, 117
Pfeil, Fred 3
*Phase IV* (Bass) 121, 127–8
*Phase IV* (Malzberg) 128
*Philadelphia Experiment, The* (Berlitz) 194
*Phoenix* (Cowper) 196
*Phoenix Without Ashes* (Ellison and Bryant) 33
Piano, Renzo 208
Picasso, Pablo 35
'Picnic on Nearside' (Varley) 159
Pielke, Robert G. 98, 187
Piercy, Marge 84, 136, 145–6
Piercy, Marge
   *Woman on the Edge of Time* 84, 136, 145–6
Pike, James 99, 103
Pilgrim, Billy 60, 223, 225
Pink Floyd 63, 74, 76, 110
   *The Dark Side of the Moon* 63, 76
   *Piper at the Gates of Dawn* 110
'Piper at the Gates of Dawn' (Cowper) 110
*Piper at the Gates of Dawn* (Pink Floyd) 110
*Piranha* (Dante) 127
'Pirate Planet, The' 63
*Planet of the Apes* (Schaffner) 61, 82–4, 218
*Planet Savers, The* (Bradley) 67
planetary romance 21
'Plastic Eaters, The' 124
Plato 51, 233
*Platoon* (Stone) 94
Platt, Charles 24, 25, 31, 32
   *The City Dwellers* 33
   *The Gas* 32
   *The Image Job* 32
   *The Power and the Pain* 32
   *Twilight of the City* 33
play, see games
Poe, Edgar Allan 31, 76, 203
   *Tales of Mystery and Imagination* 76
poetry 7, 20, 28, 31, 54, 62, 75, 85, 86, 96, 110, 111, 112, 134, 144, 145, 224

Pohl, Frederik 9, 24, 25, 31, 51, 61, 121, 221, 232, 233
   *Beyond the Blue Event Horizon* 61
   *Gateway* 61
   *Jem* 121–2, 132
   *Man Plus* 233
*Point Blank* (Boorman) 69
Pol Pot 193
Polidori, John 52
pollution 30, 79, 123–5, 130, 199, 203, 219
*Pollux et Le Chat Bleu* (Danot) 170–1
pornography 85, 119, 154, 165–7, 174, 200, 210, 227
*Port of Saints* (Burroughs) 229
Portman Jr, John C. 219
post-apocalyptic 21, 29, 67, 68, 73, 131, 178, 206, 218, 221
post-imperial melancholy 106–19
Post, Ted 83–4, 93
   *Beneath the Planet of the Apes* 83–4
   *Go Tell the Spartans* 93
postcolonialism 10, 80, 106–19
Postgate, Oliver 171–2
   *Noggin and the Moon Mouse* 171
Postgate, Raymond 171
posthuman 232–4
postmodernism 10, 45, 115, 193, 207–8, 213, 219, 220, 221–34, 235
Pournelle, Jerry 12, 84, 121, 130, 138
   *Escape from the Planet of the Apes* 84
Pournelle, Jerry and Larry Niven
   *Lucifer's Hammer* 121, 129
   *The Mote in God's Eye* 12, 138
Powell, Enoch 111
*Power and the Pain, The* (Platt) 32
*Power that Preserves, The* (Donaldson) 71–2
Powers, Tim 99
Pratchett, Terry 51, 63, 64
   *The Colour of Magic* 64
   *The Dark Side of the Sun* 63, 65
   *Strata* 63–4, 65
Priest, Christopher 9, 29, 51, 54, 59–61, 107, 111–12, 137, 221, 222, 236
   *A Dream of Wessex* 112, 223
   *Fugue for a Darkening Island* 111–12
   *Inverted World* 59–60
   *The Space Machine* 54
Pringle, David 28, 29
*Prisoner, The* 215
*Privilege* 51, 78, 79, 82, 237
Professor Challenger 54
*Profundis* (Cowper) 110
proletariat, workers and working classes 2, 122, 126, 162, 200, 207, 211, 217

Prometheus 206
protagonists 2, 14, 21, 25, 28, 32, 35, 47, 55, 56, 59, 60, 61, 62, 63, 81, 84, 85, 88, 101, 103, 101, 103, 111, 123, 131, 141, 153, 164, 166, 167, 179, 180, 186, 188, 197, 211
*Protector* (Niven) 12, 138
Pruit-Igoe housing development 207
*PRX5* (Hawkwind) 27
pseudoscience 10, 32, 140, 192–205
*Psycho* (Hitchcock) 175
psychoanalysis 4, 61, 142, 205,
psychohistory 63
punk 5, 27, 128, 108
Puzo, Mario 188
   *The Godfather* 188
Pynchon, Thomas 221, 223, 230
   *Gravity's Rainbow* 230
*Pyramid* (Alan Parsons Project) 77

*Quag Keep* (Norton) 176
*Quality of Mercy, The* (Compton) 108
quantum physics 127, 193
*Quark* 24
*Quark, Strangeness and Charm* (Hawkwind) 27
*Quatermass* 108, 192, 198
*Quatermass Conclusion, The* (Haggard) 108, 192, 198
Quebec 134
'Queen of the Martian Catacombs' (Brackett) 21
*Queen of the Swords, The* (Moorcock) 25
*Queens of Deliria* (Butterworth and Moorcock) 36
*Quest for Gaia, The* (Pedler) 124

Rabkin, Eric S. 79, 109
race 6, 10,15, 45, 59, 67, 78–91, 107, 115, 122, 135, 138, 156, 235
racism 1, 32, 54, 55, 62, 69, 80, 81, 82, 83, 84, 86, 91, 107, 111, 119, 156, 224, 230
*Radio Free Albemuth* (Dick) 102
*Ragtime* (Doctorow) 221, 224
*Raiders of Gor* (Norman) 68
*Rain People, The* (Coppola) 182
*Rains of Eridan, The* (Hoover) 179–80
*Rama II* (Clarke and Lee) 15–16
*Rama Revealed* (Clarke and Lee) 57
Raven series (Holdstock) 67
Ravilious, Eric 109
*Re: Colonised Planet 5, Shikasta* (Lessing) 231
Read, Anthony 117
Reagan, Ronald 3, 6, 101, 181, 237

*Reavers of Skaith, The* (Brackett) 21–2
*Red Shift* (Garner) 177
'Red Sky, The' 124
Reed, Kit 136, 147, 206
   *Magic Time* 136, 147, 206
   'Songs of War' 147
Reini, Harald 193
   *Erinnerungen an die Zukunft* 193
   *In Search of Ancient Astronauts* 193
Reitherman, Wolfgang 172
   *AristoCats* 172
   *The Jungle Book* 172
   *Robin Hood* 172
   *Winnie the Pooh and the Blustery Day* 172
   *Winnie the Pooh and the Honey Tree* 172
Reitherman, Wolfgang and John Lounsbery *The Many Adventures of Winnie the Pooh* 172
Reitherman, Wolfgang, John Lounsbery and Art Stevens
   *The Rescuers* 172
Rembrandt 206
Renault, Gregory 85
*Rendezvous with Rama* (Clarke) 15, 57–8
*Rescuers, The* (Lounsbery, Reitherman, Stevens) 172
*Rescuers, The* (Sharp) 182
*Restaurant at the End of the Universe, The* (Adams) 63
*Return from Witch Mountain* (Hough) 173–4
*Return of the Jedi* (Marquand) 7, 184, 187
*Return to Earth* (Hoover) 179
*Return to the Planet of the Apes* 83
*Revelations* (Malzberg) 39–40
*Revenge of the Horseclans* (Adams) 67
Rhodesia 15–16, 107
*Riddley Walker* (Hoban) 206, 219
Riefenstahl, Leni 185
   *Triumph des Willens* 185
   *Triumph of the Will* 185
*Right Way to Figure Plumbing, The* (Disch) 31
*Rime of the Ancient Mariner, The* (Bedford) 75
*Ringworld* (Niven) 12, 56, 58, 59, 60, 63
*Ringworld Engineers* (Niven) 12, 56
'Rivendell' (Rush) 74
RKO 162
*Road to Corlay, The* (Cowper) 110
*Roadside Picnic* (Strugatsky and Strugatsky) 121, 140–1
Robbins, Tom 221, 228–9
   *Another Roadside Attraction* 228
   *Even Cowgirls Get the Blues* 228

*Still Life With Woodpecker* 228–9
Robinson, Frank and Thomas N. Scortia
  *The Glass Inferno* 209
Roberts, Adam 5
Roberts, Keith 9, 107, 109–10, 112, 236
  *The Chalk Giants* 109–10
*Robin Hood* (Reitherman) 172
'Robots of Death' 49
Rock, Ashley 110
*Rocky Horror Picture Show, The* (Sharman) 52, 154, 161–2
*Rocky Horror Show, The* (O'Brien) 191
Roddenberry, Gene 46, 48
*Roderick at Random, or Further Education of a Young Machine* (Sladek) 32
*Roderick, or The Education of a Young Machine* (Sladek) 32
Roeg, Nicolas 46, 89, 103, 154, 190, 201, 203
  *Don't Look Now* 46, 201
  *The Man Who Fell To Earth* 103, 154
Rogers, Ivor A. 14
Rogers, Richard 207
Rogers, Su 207
'Roller Ball Murder' (Harrison) 216
*Rollerball* (Jewison) 125, 206, 216
*Rolling Thunder* (Flyn) 94
Roman mythology 58
romance 73, 165, 168, 204, 228
Ronder, Jack 126
*Roots: The Saga of an American Family* (Haley) 88
*Rosemary's Baby* (Levin) 215
Rosen, Martin 71
  *Watership Down* 71
*Roswell Incident, The* (Berlitz) 194
Rotsler, William 130
Rotsler, William and Gregory Benford
  *Shiva Descending* 130
Rottensteiner, Franz 62
Rousseau, Jean-Jacques 168
Ruddick, Nicholas 57–8, 109
*RuneQuest* 77
Rush 74
  *Fly By Night* 74
  'Rivendell' 74
Russ, Joanna 40, 67, 133, 135, 137, 138, 140, 141–4, 147, 154, 158, 164, 205, 222, 228, 235
  *Alyx* 67–8
  *And Chaos Died* 154, 205
  *The Female Man* 143, 145, 222, 228
Russell, Ken 192, 204–5
  Altered States 192, 204–5
Russia, see Soviet Union, USSR 9, 96, 109, 115, 108

Rutledge, Gregory E. 80, 84, 85
Sachs, William 39, 42
  *The Incredible Melting Man* 39, 42

sadomasochism 68, 157, 165
Sagal, Boris
  *The Omega Man* 121, 124–5
*Sagan Om Ringen/Music Inspired by Lord of the Rings* (Hansson) 74
Sagan, Carl 193
*Saliva Tree, The* (Aldiss) 52–3
Salkind, Ilya 188
Salvestroni, Simonetta 41, 131
Sammons, Todd 183
Samuelson, David N. 233
San Francisco 54, 115, 131, 153, 173
Sandow, Greg 31
*Sapphire and Steel* 197
Sargent, Joseph 203, 206, 218
  *Colossus: The Forbin Project* 203, 206, 218
Sargent, Pamela 78, 121, 133, 137, 236
  'Clone Sister' 133
  *Cloned Lives* 121, 133
  'Father' 133
  'Sense of Difference, A' 133
Sasdy, Peter 118, 124
  *Doomwatch* 124
Saturn 16, 42, 89
*Savage Mountains, The* (Adams) 67
Savoy Books 32
Saxton, Josephine 9, 137, 236
*Scanner Darkly, A* (Dick) 101–2
'Scarletin Study, A' (Farmer) 226
Schaffner, Franklin J. 61, 82–4, 218
  *Planet of the Apes* 61, 82–4, 218
Schatz, Thomas 180, 181
Schiller, Friedrich 12
  *Die Jungfrau von Orleans* 12
  *The Maid of Orleans* 12
Schoedsack, Ernest 209–10
Schoedsack, Ernest and Merian Cooper
  *King Kong* 209–10
Scholes, Robert E. 79, 109
Schwanzer, Karl 208
Science Fiction Foundation Collection 7
Science Fiction Research Association 10
*Science Fiction Studies* 8, 30, 235, 236
scientific romance 54, 55
*Scontri Stellari Oltre la Terza Dimensione* (Coates) 39, 50
*Scop* (Malzberg) 35–6
*Scorpio Rising* (Anger) 85
Scorsese, Martin 94, 128
  *Taxi Driver* 94

Scortia, Thomas N. and Frank M.
  Robinson
    *The Glass Inferno* 209
Scotland 34, 107, 112, 123, 126, 150
Scott, Allan 46
Scott, Ridley 7, 42, 187, 192, 199–201
  *Alien* 42, 192, 199–201
  *Blade Runner* 7, 187
*Scream Blacula Scream* (Kelljan) 90
'Screwfly Solution, The' (Sheldon) 150
SDI 6–7, 237
'Sea Devils, The' 116, 170
Seal, Luedtke Julie 149
Seale, Bobby 81
*Searchers, The* (Ford) 184
Searles, Baird 44, 53, 68, 128, 130, 133, 175, 183, 184, 195, 214, 237
*Sebastiane* (Jarman and Humfress) 162
*Second Body* (Payer) 136, 137
*Second War of the Worlds, The* (Smith) 51, 54
Second World War 10, 28, 71, 93,143, 172, 193, 194, 225, 227, 230
'Sense of Difference, A' (Sargent) 133
Serling, Rod 83
*Seven Samurai* (Kurosawa) 214
sexism 1, 84, 135, 139, 140, 146, 156, 210
sexual liberation, see also feminism, gay 119, 165
Sexual Offences Act 1967 153
*Sexual Politics* (Millett) 136
*SF Commentary* 10
sf-horror 10, 90–1, 192, 198–205
*SFRA Newsletter* 7
SFWA 236
'Shada' 63
*Shadow of the Wolf* (Carlsen) 67
*Shaft* (Parks) 90
Shail, Robert 115
Shakespeare, William 29, 221
*Shape of Things to Come, H.G. Wells' The* (McCowan) 53
*Shape of Things to Come, The* (Wells) 53
Sharman, Jim 52, 154, 161–2
  *The Rocky Horror Picture Show* 52, 154, 161–2
Sharp, Margery 182
  *Miss Bianca* 182
  *The Rescuers* 182
'Shatterday' (Ellison) 34
*Shattered Chain, The* (Bradley) 67
Shaw, Bob 40, 51, 58–60
  *Orbitsville* 58–60
  *Orbitsville Departure* 58
  *Orbitsville Judgement* 58

Shea, Robert 221, 229
Shea, Robert and Robert Anton Wilson
  *The Eye in the Pyramid* 229
  *The Golden Apple* 229
  *Leviathan* 229
Sheckley, Robert 9, 11, 39, 63, 78, 221, 222
  *Options* 222
*Sheep Look Up, The* (Brunner) 30, 121, 125–6
Sheldon, Raccoona 149, 150
  'The Screwfly Solution' 150
  'Your Faces, Oh My Sisters! Your Faces Filled of Light!' 149–50
Shelley, Mary 51, 52, 56, 65, 90, 203, 221
  *Frankenstein* 42, 51, 90, 203
Shelley, Percy 52
Shenton, Andrew K. 198
*Shepherd's Life, A* (Hudson) 110–11
Sherlock Holmes (Conan Doyle) 54, 188
*Sherlock Holmes's The War of the Worlds* (Wellman and Wellman) 51, 54
*Shichinin no Samurai* (Kurosawa) 214
Shippey, Tom 31, 218
*Shiva Descending* (Benford and Rotsler) 130
*Shivers* (Cronenberg) 201, 206, 212
*Shockwave Rider, The* (Brunner) 30
Showalter, Elaine 137
Siegel, Don 131
  *The Invasion of the Body Snatchers* 131
*Silent Running* (Trumbull) 121, 132–3
*Silmarillion, The* (Tolkien) 69
Silver Jubilee 26, 107, 119
Silverberg, Robert 4, 12, 24, 33, 65, 73, 74, 78, 80, 148, 206, 208, 209
  *Downward to the Earth* 80
  *Lord Valentine's Castle* 73–4
  *Tower of Glass* 206, 208
  *The World Inside* 208–9
Simak, Clifford D. 11, 17–19, 20, 134
  *Catface* 18
  *Cemetery World* 18
  *A Choice of Gods* 18, 19
  *Destiny Doll* 17–18
  *Enchanted Pilgrimage* 18
  *The Fellowship of the Talisman* 18
  *Mastodonia* 18
  *Our Children's Children* 18
  *Out of their Minds* 17
  *The Visitors* 18–19
Singer, Isaac Bashevis 78
Siouxsie and the Banshees 119
*Sirens of Titan* (Vonnegut) 225
*Sirian Experiments, The* (Lessing) 231

*Six Wives of Henry VIII, The* (Wakeman) 75
Six-Day War of June 1967 30
Sklovsky, Victor 8
Skylab 38
Sladek, John 25, 32, 192, 196, 221, 232–3
  *Black Aura* 32
  'Broot Force' 32
  'By an Unknown Hand' 32
  *Invisible Green* 32
  *The Müller-Fokker Effect* 32, 232
  'Name: (Please Print)' 32
  *The New Apocrypha* 32, 196
  *Roderick at Random, or Further Education of a Young Machine* 32
  *Roderick, or The Education of a Young Machine* 32
  'Solar Shoe Salesman' 32
slash 154, 166–7
slasher 42, 199, 202
*Slaughterhouse–5* (Hill) 221, 225
*Slaughterhouse-Five* (Vonnegut) 225
*Slave Girl of Gor* (Norman) 68
slavery 67, 51, 68, 79, 81–3, 87–90, 95, 122, 126, 135, 146, 166, 197, 225, 226, 232
*Sleeper* (Allen) 53
*Sleeping Sorceress, The* (Moorcock) 25
Slethaug, Gordon E. 72
Sloman, Robert 117
'Slow Sculpture' (Sturgeon) 19
Smedley, Audrey 88
Smight, Jack 52
  *Frankenstein: The True Story* 52
Smith, Cordwainer 63
  *Norstrilia* 63
Smith, E. E. 183
Smith, George H. 51, 54
  *The Second War of the Worlds* 51, 54
Smith, Jeffrey D. 147–8
Smyth, Gilli 76
Sobchack, Vivian 68, 132
*Sodom and Gomorrah Business, The* (Malzberg) 35
*Solar Lottery* (Dick) 99
*Solar Myth Approach* (Sun Ra) 89
'Solar Shoe Salesman' (Sladek) 32
*Solaris* (Tarkovsky) 39, 40–1
*Soldier Blue* (Nelson) 94
solipsism 14–15, 25, 237
Somay, Bülent 134
*Sombrero Fallout* (Brautigan) 227
*Son of Flubber* (Stevenson) 173
'Songs of War' (Reed) 147
Sontag, Susan 92, 162, 187, 190

*Sos the Rope* (Anthony) 73
*Source of Magic, The* (Anthony) 73
South Africa 70
Soviet Union, see Russia, USSR 3, 11, 38, 43, 53, 55, 93, 100, 112, 122, 124, 129, 171, 178, 218, 224, 236
*Soylent Green* (Fleischer) 120, 121, 124, 125, 217
*Space is the Place* (Newman) 89
*Space Machine, The* (Priest) 54
space opera 28, 29, 30, 39, 47, 49, 50, 166
*Space Skimmer* (Gerrold) 160
*Space: 1999* 39, 45
*Spaceman and King Arthur, The* (Mayberry) 174
Spanish Civil War 35
Spark, Alasdair 92, 94, 95, 96, 97
'Spearhead from Space' 116
*Speculation* 10
*Spell for Chameleon, A* (Anthony) 73
*Spell Sword, The* (Bradley) 67
Speller, Maureen Kincaid 110
Spencer, Kathleen L. 157
Spencer, Stanley 28
Spenser, Edmund 25
Spielberg, Steven 2, 46, 124, 182, 191, 192, 196
  *Close Encounters of the Third Kind* 46, 115, 182, 191, 192, 194–6
  *Duel* 2
  *E.T.: The Extra-Terrestrial* 191
  *Jaws* 2, 180, 182
  *Jurassic Park* 191
Spinrad, Norman 27, 33, 46
*Splinter of the Mind's Eye* (Foster) 169
*Split Second* (Kilworth) 113
Spock 46, 48, 74, 166, 167
'Spoonful of Paddington, A' (Bond) 192
Sputnik 11, 39
*Spy Who Loved Me, The* (Gilbert) 115
'Square Triangle' 45
*SS-GB* (Deighton) 230
Stableford, Brian 9, 10, 19, 21, 29, 34, 36, 54, 72, 225, 235, 237
*Stalker* (Tarkovsky) 121, 131
*Stand On Zanzibar* (Brunner) 30
*Starcrash* (Coates) 39, 50
*Star Ka'at* (Norton and Madlee) 176
*Star Light* (Clement) 121
*Star Trek* 39, 45–8, 74, 77, 166–7, 169, 175, 191, 255
*Star Trek II: The Wrath of Khan* (Meyer) 175
*Star Trek: Phase II* 46
*Star Trek: The Animated Series* 46

*Star Trek: The Motion Picture* (Wise) 39, 46–7, 175, 191
Star Wars 6–7, 237
*Star Wars* (Lucas) 2, 6, 46, 49, 50, 53, 65, 93, 98, 133, 169, 174, 180, 181, 183–7, 189, 190, 191, 194, 195, 237
*Star Wars: Episode IV – A New Hope* (Lucas) 2, 6, 46, 49, 50, 53, 65, 93, 98, 133, 169, 174, 180, 181, 183–7, 189, 190, 191, 194, 195, 237
*Star Wars: Episode V – The Empire Strikes Back* (Kershner) 7, 22–3, 169, 181, 185–7
*Star Wars: Episode VI – Return of the Jedi* (Marquand) 7, 184, 187
*Star Wars: From the Adventures of Luke Skywalker* (Lucas) 169
*Star-Anchored, Star-Angered* (Elgin) 145
*Star's End* (Bedford) 75
*Star\*Reach* (Chaykin) 49
*Stark and the Star Kings* (Brackett and Hamilton) 21–2
Stark, Richard 234
*Starlost, The* 33
Starrett, Jack 90
　*Cleopatra Jones* 90
*Stars My Destination, The* (Bester) 21
*Starship Troopers* (Heinlein) 97, 152, 153, 168
Starvation 30, 31, 61, 62, 156
*Steel Crocodile, The* (Compton) 108–9, 205
*Steel Tsar, The* (Moorcock) 25
Steel, Addison E. 169
　*Buck Rogers in the 25th Century* 169
　*That Man on Beta* 169
*Stepford Wives, The* (Forbes) 206, 214, 215
*Stepford Wives, The* (Levin) 206, 214, 215
Sterling, Bruce 3, 6, 233–5
　*The Artificial Kid* 233–4
　*Involution Ocean* 233
　'Man-Made Self' 233
Stern, Richard Martin
　*The Tower* 209
Sterne, Laurence 221
Stevens, Art, Wolfgang Reitherman and John Lounsbery
　*The Rescuers* 172
Stevenson, Adlai 43
Stevenson, Robert 172–3
　*The Absent-Minded Professor* 172–3
　*Herbie Rides Again* 172–3
　*The Island at the Top of the World* 172
　*The Love Bug* 172
　*Mary Poppins* 172
　*Son of Flubber* 173
　*Strange Case of Dr Jekyll and Mr Hyde* 204

*Still Life With Woodpecker* (Robbins) 228–9
*Stone Book Quartet, The* (Garner) 177
Stone, Oliver 94
　*Platoon* 94
Stonewall Inn 153
*Storm of Wings, A* (Harrison) 29
*Stormqueen!* (Bradley) 67
*Story of Love, A* (Bradbury) 20
*Story of the Treasure Seekers, The* (Nesbit) 55
Story, Ronald 196
*Strandloper* (Garner) 177
*Strange Boy* (Magrs) 1
*Strange Case of Dr Jekyll and Mr Hyde* (Stevenson) 204
*Stranger in a Strange Land* (Heinlein) 13, 14
*Strangers* (Dozois) 80
*Strata* (Pratchett) 63–4, 65
Strategic Defense Initiative 6–7, 237
Structuralism 8
Strugatsky, Arkady 121, 140–1
Strugatsky, Boris 121, 140–1
Strugatsky, Boris and Arkady Strugatsky
　*Roadside Picnic* 121, 140–1
Strutton, Bill 170
　*Doctor Who and the Zarbi* 170
*Sturgeon is Alive and Well* (Sturgeon) 19
Sturgeon, Theodore 19–20, 46, 158
　'Blue Butter' 20
　'Case and the Dreamer' 19–20
　*Godbody* 19
　'Slow Sculpture' 19
　*Sturgeon is Alive and Well* 19
　'The World Well Lost' 158
Sturges, John 214
　*The Magnificent Seven* 214
sublime 17, 29, 56, 181, 223
*Sugar Hill* (Maslansky) 90
suicide 34, 35, 40, 61, 71, 87, 125, 226
Sun Ra 76, 89
　*On Jupiter* 89
　*Outer Space Employment Agency* 89
　*Solar Myth Approach* 89
*Super Fly* (Parks Jr) 91
*Superman* 68, 181, 187–189, 191
*Superman II* (Lester) 68, 181, 187–9, 191
*Superman: The Movie* (Donner) 68, 188–9, 191
'Survival' 45
'Survival Code' 124
*Survivor* (Butler) 87
*Survivors* 48, 121, 126, 129
　'Over the Hills' 126
Suvin, Darko 8, 9, 65, 168
Suzman, Helen 54

# INDEX

*Swarm, The* (Allen) 127
Swift, Jonathan 125, 211, 227
   *Modest Proposal, A* 125, 211, 227
sword and planet fictions 10, 65, 67–70, 113, 143, 157
*Sword and the Stallion, The* (Moorcock) 25, 26, 54–5
*Sword of Shannara, The* (Brooks) 72
*Swords of the Horseclans* (Adams) 67
*Swordsmistress of Chaos* (Kirk) 67
*Synthajoy* (Compton) 109
*Syzygy* (Coney) 122, 123

*Tactics of Conquest* (Malzberg) 36
'Tale of Gorgik, The' (Delany) 67, 157
'Tale of Old Venn, The (Delany) 157
*Tales from Topographic Oceans* (Yes) 113
*Tales of Mystery and Imagination* (Poe) 76
*Tales of Nevèrÿon* (Delany) 67, 157
*Tapestry of Time, A* (Cowper) 110
Tarkovsky, Andrei 39, 40–1, 121, 131
   *Solaris* 39, 40–1
   *Stalker* 121, 131
*Tarnsman of Gor* (Norman) 68
*Tarzan Alive: A Definitive Biography of Lord Greystoke* (Farmer) 226
Tavernier, Bertrand 108
   *Death Watch* 108
   *La Mort en Direct* 108
*Taxi Driver* (Scorsese) 94
Taylor, Don
   *Damien: The Omen II* 190, 202
   *Escape from the Planet of the Apes* 83, 84
   *The Island of Dr Moreau* 53
Taylor, Jonathan S. 210
Taylor, Ray and Ford Beebe
   *Flash Gordon Conquers the Universe* 190
telepathy 22, 41, 66, 73, 87, 88, 103, 122, 134, 140, 144, 165–6, 178–9
Telotte, J.P. 195
Tenn, William 78
Tennant, Emma 221, 231–2
   *Alice Fell* 232
   *The Bad Sister* 231–2
   *Hotel de Dream* 231
   *The Time of the Crack* 231
   *Wild Nights* 232
*Terminal Man, The* (Hodges) 214
*Texas Chain Saw Massacre, The* (Hooper) 202
*That Man on Beta* (Steel) 169
Thatcher, Margaret 6, 48, 106, 118, 119, 237
theme park 172, 206, 213–16, 218, 234
*Thing From Another World, The* (Nyby) 202

*Thing with Two Heads, The* (Frost) 90
*This Time of Darkness* (Hoover) 179
Thompson, Eric 171
Thompson, J. Lee 83–4
   *Battle for the Planet of the Apes* 83–4
   *Conquest of the Planet of the Apes* 83–4
'Three Doctors, The' 116
Three Mile Island 117
*Three Musketeers, The* (Lester) 188
*Three Stigmata of Palmer Eldritch, The* (Dick) 99
*Thrilling Wonder Stories* 20
*Thunder and Lightnings* (Mark) 180
*Thunderbirds* 44
*THX 1138* (Lucas) 2, 10, 181–3
*Tides of Lust, The* (Delany) 32–3, 85, 154
Tidmarsh, Andrew 36
Tilms, Richard 196
   *Judgement of Jupiter* 196
*Time After Time* (Alexander) 54
*Time After Time* (Meyer) 53–4
*Time Enough For Love* (Heinlein) 14
*Time Machine, The* (Wells) 52, 53, 54
*Time of Dying, A* (Kirk) 67
*Time of Ghosts, A* (Kirk) 67
*Time of the Crack, The* (Tennant) 231
*Time of the Hawklords, The* (Butterworth and Moorcock) 36
*Time Out of Mind* (Cowper) 197
time travel 14, 18, 21, 27, 36, 40 , 52, 53–4, 61, 98–9, 113, 116–18, 160–1, 174, 177, 225
'Time Warrior, The' 117
*Timequake* (Vonnegut) 226
*Timescape* (Benford) 36, 121, 127
Tiptree, James 135, 136, 147–50
   'Houston, Houston, Do You Read?' 150
   *Up the Walls of the World* 149
   'The Women Men Don't See' 148, 149
Titan 15, 16, 46, 225
*Titus Alone* (Peake) 26
*Titus Groan* (Peake) 26
*To Sail Beyond the Sunset* (Heinlein) 14
*To Your Scattered Bodies Go* (Farmer) 61–3
Todorov, Tzvetan 2, 8, 41, 65, 131, 223
Toffler, Alvin 30
Tolkien, Christopher 69
Tolkien, J.R.R. 2, 7, 29, 30, 65, 68–72, 74
   *The Hobbit* 74
   *The Lord of the Rings* 38, 69–70, 72, 74
   *The Silmarillion* 69
   *Unfinished Tales* 69
*Tombs of Atuan, The* (Le Guin) 177

*Tormato* (Yes) 74–5
*Total Eclipse* (Brunner) 12, 31, 138
totalitarianism 67, 71, 100, 108, 128, 183, 193
*Tower of Glass* (Silverberg) 206, 208
*Tower, The* (Stern) 209
*Towering Inferno, The* (Guillermin) 206, 209
transsexualism 155, 160, 161
*Traveller* 67
*Travels in Hyperreality* (Eco) 113
*Treasures of Morrow* (Hoover) 179
*Tribesmen of Gor* (Norman) 68
*Triton* (Delany) 145, 155–6, 235
*Triumph des Willens* (Riefenstahl) 185
*Triumph of the Will* (Riefenstahl) 185
*Tron* (Liseberger) 175
Troubles, the 15, 41, 55, 106, 112, 117
Troughton, Patrick 116
*Trout Fishing in America* (Brautigan) 227–8
Trout, Kilgore 226–7
  *Venus on the Half Shell* 226–7
Trumbull, Douglas 121, 132–3
  *Silent Running* 121, 132–3
*Tubular Bells* (Oldfield) 75
Tuck, Donald 9
Tucker, Wilson 36, 205
  *The Year of the Quiet Sun* 36, 205
Tullius Hostilius 62
*Tunnels & Trolls* 67
Turkey 15, 107
Turner, George 9, 155, 156, 163
Turner, J.M.W. 56
Twentieth Century Fox 183
*Twilight of Briareus, The* (Cowper) 197
*Twilight of the City* (Platt) 33
*Two to Conquer* (Bradley) 67

UFO 39, 44–5, 169
  'The Mindbombs' 45
  'Square Triangle' 45
  'Survival' 45
*UFO* (Miall) 169
*UFO 2* (Miall) 169
Uganda 31, 111
Ulrichs, Karl Heinrich 152
uncanny, the 8, 65, 186, 201
*Under the Autumn Garden* (Mark) 180
*Unfinished Tales* (Tolkien) 69
*Unidentified Flying Oddball* (Mayberry) 174
Union of Soviet Socialist Republics, see Russia, Soviet Union, USSR
United Artists 27, 69
Universal 49, 52, 183

*Unlimited Dream Company, The* (Ballard) 28
Unsworth, Geoffrey 68
*Up the Walls of the World* (Tiptree) 149
*Ur Trollkaren's Hatt* (Hansson) 74
USSR, see Russia, Soviet Union 30, 105
*Usual Lunacy, A* (Compton) 109
utopia 37, 31, 48, 51, 70, 84, 86, 105, 121, 134, 139, 145, 146, 147, 150, 153, 154, 156, 175, 193, 206, 207, 208, 211, 214, 219, 223, 235

Vadim, Roger 50, 75
  *Barbarella* 50, 75
*VALIS* (Dick) 104
Vallorani, Nicoletta 232
Van Deburg, William L. 85
van der Rohe, Mies 207
van Vogt, A.E. 9
Vanuatu 107
*Var the Stick* (Anthony) 73
Varley, John 154, 159–60
  'Options' 159–60
  'Picnic on Nearside' 159
*Vector* 10
Veith, Diana L. 167
Venturi, Robert 207
Venus 21, 22, 40, 67
*Venus on the Half Shell* (Farmer) 226–7
Verne, Jules 51, 54, 55, 65, 221
Vidal, Gore 121, 126–7
  *Kalki* 121, 126–7
*Vietnam and Other Alien Worlds* (Haldeman) 48–9, 107
Vietnam War 1, 3, 10, 12, 38, 40, 53, 55, 81, 88, 90, 91, 92–8, 101, 105, 114, 126, 146, 153, 181, 188, 212, 218, 237
Vint, Sherryl 5
Virago 137
*Viriconium Nights* (Harrison) 29
*Visions from Nowhere* (Arrow) 84
*Visitors, The* (Simak) 18–19
vivisection 52, 135
Vogh, James 196
  *Arachne Rising* 196
  *The Cosmic Factor* 196
von Däniken, Erich 57, 104, 192–4, 196,
  *Chariots of the Gods?* 57, 104, 193
von Kleist, Heinrich 224
  'Michael Kohlhaas' 224
Vonnegut, Kurt 63, 104, 221, 224–7
  *Breakfast of Champions* 104, 225–6
  *Galápagos* 226
  *Jailbird* 224–5, 226
  *Sirens of Titan* 225
  *Slaughterhouse-Five* 225
  *Timequake* 226

# INDEX

*Voyage to the Bottom of the Sea* 209
Voyager 46

Wadleigh, Michael 124
   *Woodstock* 124
Wagner, Richard 171
   *Also Sprach Zarathustra* 171
Wakeman, Rick 75
   *Journey to the Centre of the Earth* 75
   *The Myths and Legends of King Arthur and the Knights of the Round Table* 75
   *The Six Wives of Henry VIII* 75
Waldrop, Howard 97
Wales 66, 107, 112, 153
*Walk to the End of the World* (Charnas) 146
Walt Disney Productions 172–5
*Wanderground, The* (Gearhart) 121, 134–5
*War of the Worlds, The* (Wells) 19, 54
Warhol, Andy 52
*Warlord of the Air, The* (Moorcock) 25, 26, 54–5
Warner Bros 50, 182, 183, 209
*Warrior on the Edge of Time* (Hawkwind) 27
Washington DC 207, 218
Watergate 1, 42, 93, 100–1, 188, 214, 225, 230
*Watership Down* (Adams) 71
*Watership Down* (Rosen) 71
Watson, Gray 106, 110
Watson, Ian 33, 74, 205
Waugh, Patricia 222
Wayne, John 93, 185
Wayne, John and Ray Kellogg
   *The Green Berets* 93
*We Can Build You* (Dick) 99
*We Never Went to the Moon* (Kaysing and Reid) 43
Weil, Ellen R. 34
*Weirdstone of Brisingamen, The* (Garner) 177
*Well of Shiuan* (Cherryh) 141–2
Wellman, Manley Wade 51, 54
Wellman, Manley Wade and Wade Wellman
   *Sherlock Holmes's The War of the Worlds* 51, 54
Wellman, Wade 51, 54
Wells, H.G. 19, 51–4, 110, 221, 223
   *The Empire of the Ants* 53
   *The Island of Doctor Moreau* 53
   *The Shape of Things to Come* 53
   *The Time Machine* 52, 53, 54
   *The War of the Worlds* 19, 54

   *When the Sleeper Wakes* 53
Wells, Angus 67
*Welt am Draht* (Fassbinder) 221–2, 232
Wesley, Marilyn C. 232
West, Chris 157, 158
West, D 110
Weston, Peter 10, 137
*Westworld* (Crichton) 206, 214, 215
'Weyr Search' (McCaffrey) 72
Whale, James 52, 91, 94
   *Frankenstein* 52, 90, 94
*When the Sleeper Wakes* (Wells) 53
'Where Late the Sweet Birds Sang' (Wilhelm) 131
*Where Late the Sweet Birds Sang* (Wilhelm) 131, 133–4
Whitaker, David 116, 170
   *Doctor Who and the Crusaders* 170
   *Doctor Who in an Exciting Adventure with the Daleks* 170
*White Dragon, The* (McCaffrey) 73
white ethnicity 1, 2, 16, 48, 54, 78–86, 89, 90, 91, 111, 112, 125, 126, 146, 156, 162, 200, 224
White, Dan 153
White, James 9
White, Luis 147
*Why Are We in Vietnam?* (Mailer) 96
Whyte, Nicholas 41
Wilcox, Fred M. 202
   *Forbidden Planet* 202
*Wild Boys: A Book of the Dead, The* (Burroughs) 229–30
*Wild Bunch, The* (Peckinpah) 94
*Wild Nights* (Tennant) 232
*Wild Seed* (Butler) 87
Wilde, Cornel 121, 123–4
   *No Blade of Grass* 121, 123–4
Wilder, Billy 43
   *Front Page, The* 43
Wilder, Cherry 87
Wilhelm, Kate 33, 92, 121, 133–4, 137, 139, 140, 147
   *Juniper Time* 131, 134
   *Margaret and I* 139–40
   'Where Late the Sweet Birds Sang' 131
   *Where Late the Sweet Birds Sang* 131, 133–4
Willcox, Toyah 119
Williams, Graham 63, 117
Williams, Lynn F. 141, 142
Williamson, Jack 9
Wilson, Don 43
   *Our Mysterious Spaceship Moon* 43
Wilson, Harold 106

Wilson, Robert Anton 221, 229
*Wind in the Willows, The* (Grahame) 110
*Wind Whales of Ishmael, The* (Farmer) 226
*Windows* (Compton) 109
*Winds of Darkover, The* (Bradley) 67
Wingrove, David 4, 123
*Winnie the Pooh and the Blustery Day* (Reitherman) 172
*Winnie the Pooh and the Honey Tree* (Reitherman) 172
*Winnie the Pooh and Tigger Too* (Lounsbery) 172
Wise, Robert 39, 46–7, 121, 130, 175, 191, 214
 *The Andromeda Strain* 121, 130, 214
 *The Day the Earth Stood Still* 130
 *Star Trek: The Motion Picture* 39, 46–7, 175, 191
'Wish, The' (Bradbury) 20
*Witch and the Chameleon, The* 140
*Without a Trace* (Berlitz) 194
*Wizard of Earthsea, A* (Le Guin) 177
*Wizard of Oz, The Wonderful* (Baum) 68, 131, 177
*Wizard of Oz, The* (Fleming) 183
*Wizardry and Wild Romance* (Moorcock) 70–1
Woledge, Elizabeth 167
Wolf, Virginia L. 176
Wolfe, Gene 93, 96
 'HORARS of War, The' 96
Wolk, Anthony 114
Wolmark, Jenny 86, 140, 142, 146
*Woman on the Edge of Time* (Piercy) 84, 136, 145–6
Wombles 171
*Wombles, The* (Beresford) 171
'Women Men Don't See, The' (Tiptree) 148, 149
women's liberation, see also feminism 1, 135
*Wonderful Wizard of Oz, The* (Baum) 68, 131, 177
Wood, Diane S. 141
Wood, Robin 2, 163, 198, 203
*Woodstock* (Wadleigh) 124
Woodward, Bob 43
Woolfson, Eric 76–7
'Word for World is Forest, The' (Le Guin) 95–6
Wordsworth, William 107

workers and working class 2, 122, 126, 162, 200, 207, 211, 217
*World Inside, The* (Silverberg) 208–9
*World of Tiers* (Farmer) 26
*World on a Wire* (Fassbinder) 221–2, 232
*World on Wires* (Fassbinder) 221–2, 232
World Trade Center 173, 207, 208, 210
'World Well Lost, The' (Sturgeon) 158
*World Wreckers, The* (Bradley) 67
*Worlds Apart* (Cowper) 223
*Worlds of If* 12, 18, 21
*Wounded Land, The* (Donaldson) 71–2
Wright of Derby, Joseph 56
Wright, Peter 198
Wymer, Rowland 119
Wyndham, John 178, 223
 *The Chrysalids* 178

*X In Search of Space* 27
X, Malcolm 81

Yarbro, Chelsea Quinn 147
*Year of the Quiet Sun, The* (Tucker) 36, 205
Yeats, W.B. 110
Yes 74–5, 113
 *Fragile* 74
 *Going for the One* 74–5
 *Tales from Topographic Oceans* 113
 *Tormato* 74–5
 *Yes Album, The* 74
*Yes Album, The* (Yes) 74
Yom Kippur war 30, 210
York, Michael 53, 217
*You* (Gong) 76
Young Adult fiction 1, 168, 176–80
*Young Frankenstein* (Brooks) 52
Young, Terence 115
 *Dr No* 115
'Your Faces, Oh My Sisters! Your Faces Filled of Light!' (Sheldon) 149–50
Yudkin, Marcia 154

*Z for Zachariah* (O'Brien) 178
Zaki, Hoda M. 84
Zapruder, Abraham 44
*Zardoz* (Boorman) 65, 68–9
Zavitzianos, George 154
Zelazny, Roger 27, 75
Zimbabwe 15, 16
Zimbabwe Rhodesia 16
Zipes, Jack 168

Printed in the USA/Agawam, MA
November 13, 2014